Music and Tourism

ASPECTS OF TOURISM
Series Editors: Professor Chris Cooper, *University of Queensland, Australia*
Dr C. Michael Hall, *University of Otago, Dunedin, New Zealand*
Dr Dallen Timothy, *Arizona State University, Tempe, USA*

Aspects of Tourism is an innovative, multifaceted series which will comprise authoritative reference handbooks on global tourism regions, research volumes, texts and monographs. It is designed to provide readers with the latest thinking on tourism world-wide and in so doing will push back the frontiers of tourism knowledge. The series will also introduce a new generation of international tourism authors, writing on leading edge topics. The volumes will be readable and user- friendly, providing accessible sources for further research. The list will be underpinned by an annual authoritative tourism research volume. Books in the series will be commissioned that probe the relationship between tourism and cognate subject areas such as strategy, development, retailing, sport and environmental studies. The publisher and series editors welcome proposals from writers with projects on these topics.

Other Books in the Series
Tourism Employment: Analysis and Planning
  Michael Riley, Adele Ladkin and Edith Szivas
Marine Ecotourism: Issues and Experiences
  Brian Garrod and Julie C. Wilson (eds)
Classic Reviews in Tourism
  Chris Cooper (ed.)
Progressing Tourism Research
  Bill Faulkner, edited by Liz Fredline, Leo Jago and Chris Cooper
Managing Educational Tourism
  Brent W. Ritchie
Recreational Tourism: Demand and Impacts
  Chris Ryan
Coastal Mass Tourism: Diversification and Sustainable Development in Southern Europe
  Bill Bramwell (ed.)
Sport Tourism Development
  Thomas Hinch and James Higham
Sport Tourism: Interrelationships, Impact and Issues
  Brent Ritchie and Daryl Adair (eds)
Tourism, Mobility and Second Homes
  C. Michael Hall and Dieter Müller
Strategic Management for Tourism Communities: Bridging the Gaps
  Peter E. Murphy and Ann E. Murphy
Oceania: A Tourism Handbook
  Chris Cooper and C. Michael Hall (eds)
Tourism Marketing: A Collaborative Approach
  Alan Fyall and Brian Garrod
Tourism Development: Issues for a Vulnerable Industry
  Julio Aramberri and Richard Butler (eds)

For more details of these or any other of our publications, please contact:
Channel View Publications, Frankfurt Lodge, Clevedon Hall,
Victoria Road, Clevedon, BS21 7HH, England
http://www.channelviewpublications.com

ASPECTS OF TOURISM 19
Series Editors: Chris Cooper (*University of Queensland, Australia*),
C. Michael Hall (*University of Otago, New Zealand*)
and Dallen Timothy (*Arizona State University, USA*)

Music and Tourism
On the Road Again

Chris Gibson and John Connell

CHANNEL VIEW PUBLICATIONS
Clevedon • Buffalo • Toronto

Library of Congress Cataloging in Publication Data
Gibson, Chris
Music and Tourism: On the Road Again/ by Chris Gibson and John Connell.
Aspects of Tourism: 19.
Includes bibliographical references and index.
1. Music and tourism. 2. Music–Social aspects. 3. Music–Economic aspects.
I. Connell, John. II. Title. III. Series.
ML3795.G49 2004
306.4'842–dc22   2004017133
A catalog record for this book is available from the Library of Congress.

British Library Cataloguing in Publication Data
A catalogue entry for this book is available from the British Library.

ISBN 1-873150-93-8 (hbk)
ISBN 1-873150-92-X (pbk)

Channel View Publications
An imprint of Multilingual Matters Ltd

UK: Frankfurt Lodge, Clevedon Hall, Victoria Road, Clevedon BS21 7HH.
USA: 2250 Military Road, Tonawanda, NY 14150, USA.
Canada: 5201 Dufferin Street, North York, Ontario, Canada M3H 5T8.

Typeset by Florence Production Ltd.
Printed and bound in Great Britain by the Cromwell Press.

Contents

Preface

How much sweeter music sounds at the end of a day of walking, bathing, sunning, sipping, than of a day of working! Music, of course, is a holiday in one crucial sense: a holiday from the mind.

Bernard Levin, 1981: 4

Tourism has boomed in recent decades and a key component has been the rise of cultural tourism. Music tourism is one part of that and one that has hitherto never been documented in comprehensive form. This book seeks to do just that, and provide a global perspective on this rapidly evolving phenomenon across all continents and musical genres. Twenty years ago, such a book might not have been possible; even a decade ago it might only have discussed Graceland, Elvis Presley's mansion in Memphis. In this century, the proliferation of musical events and tourist sites obliges such a book.

The combination of music and tourism is on the whole a pleasant one and tracing that relationship has meant journeys of our own to such places as Graceland, and the tiny Australian country town of Parkes, for the annual Elvis Presley Revival Festival. In between we have visited Liverpool, Vienna, Takarazuka, obscure graveyards and dusty opera houses, the Bob Marley Museum in Jamaica, travelled part of Route 66 and escaped on virtual journeys with Herb Alpert, Ry Cooder and a host of others.

We have not always travelled alone, in any sense, and many people have helped us along the way. These include Ali Wright who was there at the beginning and end of the journeys, provided invaluable assistance in the field, advice on early drafts and support at home; and so many others who provided tea – or something stronger – and sympathy (or envy), data or advice on obscure references and destinations, notably Arun Saldanha, Karen Buchan, David Keeling, Sara Cohen, Maya Kneafsey, Linda Malam, Kelly Atkinson (in Parkes), Kathryn Maiden (at Abbey Road), Neil Flenley (Liverpool), Sachiko Yokota, Sonjah Niaah-Stanley (in

Kingston), Wendy Shaw (in New Orleans), Rob Freestone (in Branson), Natascha Klocker (Salzburg), Daniel Robinson, Deb Davidson and Michelle Bonamy. At various points in the text we have referred to websites which were current at the time of writing. Some of these may now no longer exist.

We are particularly grateful to those who sifted through the text and reminded us that we were ignorant of certain genres and regions, were cavalierly anglophone, needed to get out more and, simultaneously, read more. We should also be thankful to our universities who never really questioned why we needed to go to festivals or wanted petty cash to purchase CDs, but no doubt the bean-counters, who now constitute university administrations, will welcome one more publication to tick off on some government checklist.

We are indebted to Mike Grover for his enthusiasm for this book and for accommodating our ever-changing delivery date. We are particularly grateful, as so often we have been, to Robert Aldrich for his extraordinarily thorough reading of the first draft. The remaining flaws must be ours, but it is hard to believe that he could have missed them!

John Connell and Chris Gibson
November 2003

Chapter 1
Tourism and Music

In one of the more recent transformations of tourism, music – in different genres and guises – has rapidly become a new rationale for travel, and therefore a market for tourists in a rapidly expanding industry. It is a now familiar story that tourism experienced spectacular growth in the second half of the 20th century, initially in more affluent Western nations and more recently in the emerging countries of the developing world, notably in Asia (Hall, 1998; Williams, 1998). As tourist numbers increased, and tourism became a regular phenomenon, the quest for new sites, sights and experiences grew more complex, while travellers sought, at least on occasion, specific forms of tourism that met their personal needs. In part this was a response to, and rejection of, the mass tourism that had transformed areas like the western Mediterranean coast. Niche tourism became increasingly significant. This book seeks to discuss one such niche – music tourism, where people travel, at least in some part, because of music – and the significance of this for culture, economics and identity.

The rise of niche tourism has coincided with, and is part of, the growing significance of culture in the construction of tourism and recreation. The combination of the emerging 'heritage industry' alongside nostalgia, one nurturing the other, has resulted in the increased commodification of culture and attempts to preserve the historical fabric of city centres, archaeological sites and even old industries. Early forms of niche tourism were those that focused on history, whether of buildings or landscapes, and that enabled the survival of many stately homes in Britain or castles on the continent, alongside the expansion of national parks and wilderness areas on an almost global scale. Ecotourism is one niche that has achieved more than mere minority significance.

Over time, niches became less general and more focused. Literary tourism took visitors to places like the Lake District, where Beatrix Potter had produced the tales of Peter Rabbit and where Wordsworth had eulogised on daffodils (Squire, 1988, 1993), to the moors of Haworth in west Yorkshire made famous by the Brontë sisters (Drabble, 1979) or Marcel Proust's Cambray. Somewhat later a number of films and television series

1

attracted tourists to such regions as north Yorkshire, where one part of the county became James Herriot country and another was Heartbeat country (Tooke & Baker, 1996; Mordue, 1999), and in North America where film locations, including *The Bridges of Madison County*, gained new visitors (Riley *et al.*, 1998), or New Zealand where the filming of Tolkien's *Lord of the Rings* brought tourist development to several places. Other niches have followed, including art, crime, religion, sport (Priestley, 1995; Standeven & de Knop, 1999; Hinch & Higham, 2001), food and wine (Charters & Ali-Knight, 2002; Hall *et al.*, 2000; Hjalager & Richards, 2002; Long, 2004; du Pont de Bie, 2004), battlefields (Lloyd, 1998), book towns (Seaton, 1999) and, at least for a handful of individuals, even more esoteric quests, such as Anthony Bourdain's *A Cook's Tour: In Search of the Perfect Meal* (2001) or especially those that were spelled out graphically in Decca Aikenhead's book *The Promised Land: Travels in Search of the Perfect E* (2001) – a global quest for enlightenment through ecstasy. In different ways music has also become a new niche, or a series of niches, within cultural tourism.

Music tourists have often been individuals, from Bernard Levin taking himself on a *Conducted Tour* (1981) through a dozen classical music festivals, to Henry Shukman's *Travels with my Trombone: A Caribbean Journey* (1993) and the American guitarist Banning Eyre's *In Griot Time* (2000), recording his seven months of 'total immersion' in Malian music. Others too have taken their musical instruments on tour. Some have been deliberately journalistic as in Mick Brown's *American Heartbeat* (1993), subtitled *Travels from Woodstock to San Jose by Song Title*, which came with a cassette or a CD. Robert Craft (2000) travelled in search of any manifestation of Stravinsky, while Jason Webster (2002) placed himself within Spanish flamenco. Most have been nostalgic, like Randy McNutt's 'journey to the crossroads of rock 'n' roll' (2002), those small American recording centres that preceded the metropolitan studios of the conglomerates. The Scottish author Duncan McLean's book, subtitled *On the Trail of Bob Wills and his Texas Playboys*, evokes this spirit:

> I'm three thousand miles from home . . . I'm not from these parts. I've come a long way in search of real live western swing. I won't find real live Bob Wills that's for sure: he's been dead twenty years. But his spirit lives on; I know it, I feel it. It lives on . . . somewhere. Not in the battered fiddle case in the museum upstairs [Memphis] . . . . And now I am after something. I don't know exactly what it is, and I don't know exactly where I'm going to find it. But *somewhere* out there, further south and further west – out amongst the country dance halls, the ranch to market roads, the old musicians hunched over tin-tack pianos and tenor banjos – somewhere in the wide, sun-struck wilds of Texas, that's where I'm going to track down the spirit of Bob Wills. That's where I'm going. (McLean, 1997: 3)

Only a handful of such tours, and inevitably the most idiosyncratic, have been transformed into text. More frequently, music tourism has been somewhat prosaic.

Tourism is simultaneously a social, economic, cultural, environmental and political phenomenon. It transfers capital between people and places, influences the social organisation of destinations, enables the revitalisation, preservation and also the destruction of cultural phenomena, and creates new landscapes. It results in the intervention of local and national governments, and private individuals, in each of these contexts, not least in the promotion of particular destinations. Each of these themes, with the partial exception of environmental impact, are as crucial to music tourism as they are to other kinds of tourism, and all will be examined here. Indeed since no other book discusses music tourism, it is intended to be as comprehensive as possible.

This chapter provides a historical background to music tourism, with particular reference to the better-documented European context and to classical traditions. The following chapter looks at the manner in which music created virtual tourism, before recreational travel had become a common activity. Chapter 3 provides an overview of the diverse contexts of music tourism in a range of global locations, and sets the scene for the three following chapters which centre on the economics of this particular niche, the significance of music tourism for personal and place identities and the very different experiences of travel, from hedonism to pilgrimage. The penultimate chapter examines festivals, whose themes encompass all those discussed previously.

From the Grand Tour to Niches

Travel has always existed but tourism is relatively new. Annual mass movements of people from their homes is a recent phenomenon that got underway in the 19th century in relatively industrialised countries. It dramatically burgeoned in the second half of the next century with the simultaneous rise of affluence, the greater provision of leisure time (including paid holidays) and technological changes in transport. Until the Renaissance relatively few travelled for pleasure, despite trade fairs and pilgrimages, and not many travelled far, but in the 17th century the Grand Tour brought the start of tourism to Europe.

The gradual achievement of law and order in Western Europe, and the emergence of an elite group of statesmen, merchants and scholars 'began to legitimize the gallants' jaunts which thus imperceptibly merged into the educative and educational institution known as the Grand Tour' (Fairburn, 1951: 118). By the middle of the 18th century it had become fashionable for such elites, and especially those from Britain, to travel in continental Europe in the search for education and recreation. A few decades later the Tour increasingly focused on the pursuit of pleasure and many inveighed against its supposedly corrupting influence. This was the first of many phases of tourism, perhaps tourist cycles, where the high ideals of the earliest travellers were seen to have degenerated into mere hedonism. An intriguing element of the Grand Tour was its somewhat conventional and regular form – again a precedent for what was much later to follow – where time periods (preferably three years) and particular itineraries (which usually involved a long stay in Paris, almost a year in the major cities of Italy and a return by way of Germany, Switzerland, Belgium and the Netherlands) were prescribed. It was primarily intended to ensure the greatest exposure to the sites of antiquity and the cultural achievements of western continental Europe, which the rest of the world seemingly lacked.

The parallel development of spas, again principally in Western Europe, brought a new phase in tourism, focusing on the physical benefits to be gained from particular forms of escapism. By the end of the 18th century England alone had more than a hundred spas, a measure of the way that 'taking the waters' had attracted growing numbers of the middle classes. By the 19th century they were evident even in such remote colonies as the French Pacific territory of New Caledonia, while the emergence of hill stations virtually throughout the tropics further emphasised the apparent curative properties of tourism and recreation in appropriate places. The health benefits of tourism, first open to the elites, were eventually extended to the working classes, notably following the construction of railways in the 19th century, bringing the growth of seaside resorts throughout the western world. Seaside resorts and sea bathing gradually replaced the spas.

At the core of the Grand Tour had been the notion of high culture: the inculcation of knowledge, partly through self-education, in the centres of civilisation. While the Grand Tour emphasised the literary, archaeological, architectural and artistic culture of Europe, music often played a relatively small part, whether by attending concerts and recitals or the acquiring new musical skills. Instrumental music was not particularly popular, though opera, especially in Italy, was a key part of the Tour (Black, 1992: 252–260). Only in relatively rare cases, such as that of Vincent and Mary Novello, was music the central focus of travel; their journeys, from London to Salzburg in 1829, were very much a precursor of contemporary specialised tours. They left a detailed record in diary form of a series of concerts in theatres, churches and town squares for several parts of Western Europe (Hughes, 1955). Just 12 years after the Novellos' travels, the first Thomas Cook's tour took place, inaugurating a quite different form of tourist experience.

By the time that tourism had incorporated spas, the focus had shifted from education to recreation. Recreation and residence in the spas were often accompanied by music and the seaside resorts, modelled on the spas, were furnished with promenades and rotundas, and supported musical concerts and even lectures (Figure 1.1). The rise of seaside resorts, in England at least, was a result of the Napoleonic wars that had brought the Grand Tour to an end by discouraging overseas travel. Moreover the resultant presence of many military camps on the south coast directly provided music to the nearby resorts as, apparently, their 'brass bands captivated the ladies with stirring martial music' (Robinson, 1976: 11). The larger resorts developed more complex musical cultures. By the late 19th century in Brighton, the beach had become a noisy place:

> There was the town band playing a little west of the Bedford Hotel; there was a French string band off Regency Square and there were other bands of nigger [*sic*] minstrels shouting their wish to be in Dixie .... There is a squealing, squalling, screaming, shouting, singing, bawling, howling, whistling, tin-trumpeting, and every luxury of noise. Two or three bands work away; niggers clatter their bones; a conjuror throws his heels in the air; several harps strum merrily different strains. (Gilbert, 1954: 184–186)

No doubt Brighton also had organ grinders and their monkeys, as on the main streets of the largest cities. The heyday of music in the spas and 'watering places' was between 1880 and 1950, an era captured in one elegant attempt to record in literary form 'some of the echoes of the dead-and-gone music of the spas and seaside places before they finally fade into a harmonic empyrean beyond living memory' (Young, 1968: 12). Music accompanied recreation and tourism in a variety of guises, including the rise of brass bands, the diffusion of organs (and monkeys) and black minstrels, which pointed to the mobility of the performers, between countries and continents.

Figure 1.1 Scarborough bandstand, July 1919

In continental Europe the situation was similar, as music accompanied tourism. Visitors to the great cities during the 19th century sampled theatres, ballets and concerts of various kinds, and military bands entertained passers-by in the gardens of cities such as Vienna. Many cities had opera houses and other venues. As with troubadours in the Middle Ages, travelling players provided the working class with more 'fringe' entertainment. Thus in Italy, bagpipe players from Romagna and the kingdom of Naples entered Rome in companies in the late 19th century, their hymns filling the city, especially at festival times. In Australia, Aboriginal gum-leaf orchestras (where tree leaves are the main instrument, blown across in the style of a flute reed) were formed on mission settlements, touring rural and coastal towns with their cheap, ever-present instruments (Dunbar-Hall & Gibson, 2004). In the cities of Japan, the travelling No dancers were exotic attractions. Throughout the 19th century such entertainments were primarily for the residents, and the musicians rather than the bulk of urban residents were the most mobile.

Only exceptionally was a distinctive form of tourism shaped by music. Thus in Bayreuth, in southern Germany, the birthplace and home of the composer Richard Wagner, performances of the Wagner Ring Cycle of operas, in the theatre built by King Ludwig of Bavaria, brought tourists from great distances. Indeed, since the sacred drama *Parsifal* could only be performed in Bayreuth, those who wished to hear it were forced to travel. A late 19th-century guide described the situation:

> When the festival takes place, admirers of Wagner flock from all parts of Europe to hear it. The festival generally lasts for about a month . . . . During the intervals [in *Parsifal*] the whole audience leaves the theatre . . . those who wish to do so can take tea or dinner in the well-managed restaurants close at hand or walk up and down on the terrace in the woods that surround the theatre, watching the sunset glow on the sweet landscape of the Bavarian hills. Anything more unlike the ordinary surroundings of a theatre can hardly be imagined. The summons to return to the theatre is given by a group of trumpeters. (Loftie, 1890: 117–118)

A handful of other places, such as Vienna and Salzburg, similarly benefited from the fame of their composers, symphony orchestras and opera companies, but they were rare exceptions, primarily meeting the needs of a European elite.

Seaside resorts dominated the tourist landscapes of the Western world until the middle of the 20th century, when a series of changes transformed the structure and content of tourism. The post-war era, after the hiatus of the war itself and the Great Depression, brought longer holidays (often paid for by employers), increasing affluence, a rise in car ownership and, from the 1960s, the possibility of relatively cheap air transport. 'I'm leaving on a jet plane/Don't know when I'll be back again' were not merely the words of a song but the symbol of the emerging tourist industry, and of 'drifter' or backpacker tourism. These changes contributed to larger numbers of people becoming tourists, and tourists taking longer and longer holiday breaks, thus enabling travel to more distant places, and eventually the emergence of 'second holidays' within one year (that might take a different, more specialised form than the first). The rapid expansion of tourism also emphasised the shift from the residual high culture of the Grand Tour, though never entirely to disappear, to the more evident populist recreational forms established in the late 19th century. Meanwhile some popular 19th century destinations, such as the Isle of Man, had long since lost their importance, as tourists sought the greater excitement and warmer climate of more distant places. Before the end of the 20th century, tourism had become the world's largest international industry.

One key effect of the rise of tourist numbers and democratisation of the tourist experience was the emergence of mass-produced holiday accommodation: in England, the Butlin's camps of the post-war decades, and the more global Club Med. The resultant 'package' tourism was characterised by large numbers of people travelling to seemingly mass-produced resorts in a small number of destinations (characterised, to many, by the rise of tourism in the Costa del Sol, Spain, or in Florida). For many people this marked the first experience of overseas travel, as through the 1960s and 1970s the cost of an overseas vacation remained much the same while wages rose. A second effect was greater institutional participation in tourism, from the rise of travel agencies to attempts by governments to regulate, control and boost tourism, as it became a significant economic phenomenon. A third was the massive expansion of tourist literature and especially the explosion of tourism guides that gradually focused on specialist activities, and moved away from an emphasis on the landscape, whether natural or constructed, towards a range of recreational possibilities. These increasingly emphasised means of reducing the costs of travel ('Europe on $10 a Day', 'Asia on a Shoestring' etc.) and became more comprehensive as competition increased.

Greater affluence and time, more frequent holidays (and leisure time generally) and the increased versatility and flexibility provided by cars and planes – alongside a growing reaction against mass tourism – brought the rise of more distinctive forms of tourism, some focused around particular forms of recreation such as mountaineering, golf or even sex and, increasingly, others that focused on various facets of culture, such as architecture, literature, photography or art. Over time such niches also produced institutional interest, with travel agencies organising specific tours and governments seeking to maximise the attractions of particular places, usually through emphasising heritage features, to capture the expanding market. Music became an element of this.

The expansion of leisure interests, and a growing significance of heritage and nostalgia, was accompanied by the rapid expansion in numbers of museums and festivals. Moreover, museums no longer looked towards antiquity, ethnography and 'high' culture for their justification, but happily embraced the very recent past and popular themes. Similarly, festivals, once largely classical, diversified. In Europe the number of museums grew dramatically in the last quarter of the 20th century, as specialist museums (in Amsterdam, from sex to cannabis) were established. Specialist music museums, for particular composers, genres or even instruments, and heritage centres were part of this trend. Festivals grew from mere local to global events, producing acute competition for custom.

As the example of Brighton showed, music was probably ubiquitously a part of the tourist experience but as an adjunct to it rather than a rationale for it. One guide for retired travellers has emphasised this idea:

> We were steadily discovering that there are many agreeable aspects of Saga holidays that we had not expected. One is that these holidays often include an evening of folk music of the area concerned. In Andalucia it had naturally been flamenco. In Portuguese Lagos the entertainment took the form of song and dance by an enthusiastic and well-drilled troupe of juvenile dancers and musicians. (Smith, 1995: 145)

Music was increasingly seen to be a part of travel experiences:

> A must-do in Lisbon is fado, the uniquely Portuguese tradition of putting poetry to music. We chose Parrereinha de Alfama, a small but good fado restaurant in a back street in the Alfama district. The restaurant was full with diners, many of them locals – always a good sign. The food was excellent and the haunting fado singing, to a 12-string pear-shaped guitar, was sometimes soulful, sometimes happy. (Potts, 2003)

But over time travel in search of music, in various guises, became a central component rather than merely an adjunct of travel, however enthusiastically received, at least for an emerging niche group. At the same time, even the most seemingly unpropitious places, such as the small northern English industrial town of Rochdale, have advertised the diverse musical pleasures that are available. In a brochure widely distributed in the North of England in 2002, Rochdale was advertising:

> January provides a further chance to enjoy all the fun of the pantomime season with Cinderella and Middleton's Amateur Operatic and Dramatic Society's annual pantomime. Rochdale plays host to the Symphony Orchestra from Chetham's world famous music school and international artists the Polmar Ambache trio who have performed in over 33 countries.

Elsewhere, the brochure directed possible visitors to afternoon tea dances, sequence ballroom and line dancing, tap and salsa dancing, and the visits of the Bill Bailey Big 6 Jazz Band, the Heritage Singers and the Blue Magnolia Jazz Orchestra (Rochdale Metropolitan Borough Council, 2001). In this array of contemporary possibilities there was no hint however that Rochdale had once been the home of the famous music hall singer Gracie Fields.

Music tourism, whether associated with classical or popular music, or linked to visits to places of performance (such as opera houses), places of musical composition, places enshrined in lyrics (from the Mull of Kintyre to Dixie), places of births and deaths (including such cemeteries as Père Lachaise in Paris) or museums, grew in significance in the last decades of the 20th century. It has shaped distinct patterns of recreation and tourism, transformed some places, become a valuable source of income generation, and reshaped memories and identities of music and musicians.

A Musical Niche?

As Bayreuth illustrates, the first musical tourism was associated with classical music. A few other places associated with classical music were similarly important in the 19th century as part of the legacy of the Grand Tour. New mobility in the 20th century usually increased their prominence, as at Salzburg:

> It started with 'Everyman' and Mozart, and today includes everything from Bach to Richard Strauss. Mozart may have been the original excuse for being festive, but the dynamic forces which Salzburg's Renaissance and baroque tradition still contains made a much bigger and much greater thing of it . . . . What draws the thousands from all parts of the world, half of whom know nothing about music, nothing about Goethe and nothing at all about the traditions of the place? . . . All Salzburg is a stage. (Czernin, 1937: 86)

In nearby Vienna, the same sort of tourism, oriented around occasional festivals and the finest European performers and orchestras, had a similar impact on the city, although the appreciation of music could be combined with other forms of recreation, as Newth found:

> The more select of the Danube-strand baths are above the city . . . but one of the most popular is the Gansehaufel, the municipal bathing beach on an island in the old Danube. This is one of the sights of the city even if you are not anxious to bathe . . . . Great stretches of sand are the background for a kaleidoscopic scene of brilliant bathing costumes and pyjamas, worn by hundreds of bathers of all ages and shapes, who lie in the sun . . . sleeping, talking, reading or playing

the gramophone. After their day in the sun plenty of people seem to have energy enough for the Wurstelprater, for Sunday evening is the busiest time of all in this big funfair at the foot of the great wheel. And if the crowd and din become too tiring they can walk in the great gardens and avenues. (1931: 166)

Despite such possible diversions,

> Music is still the most important thing in life for the true Viennese, as you may see and hear for yourself at any time and anywhere, from the Opera to the Heurigen. The Opera . . . is open all the year round . . . . Equally renowned is the Vienna Philharmonic Orchestra, which plays always to crowded audiences in the two big halls, the Musikverein and the Konzerthaus. And on any summer evening you may sit under the trees of the Burggaten and listen to the Symphony Orchestra playing in the most perfect setting . . . Church music you will hear in the Cathedral and the larger churches. The lighter music for which Vienna is hardly less well-known persists in her characteristic light opera, which is sought more than ever today by London, New York and the other capitals of the world. And Viennese dance music, which for years we thought we could do without, has swept back with an even greater charm . . . it is the Viennese waltz that always fills the floor, danced with the same sweeping, swirling grace as in its imperial heyday. (Newth, 1931: 166–167)

Vienna too was both the birthplace and deathplace of several of the world's greatest composers, and the homes and graves of many, some close together in the Simmering cemetery, were already places for tourists to visit. Outside such few notable places music tourism scarcely existed.

Evident in Newth's account of the musical attractions of Vienna was an implicit hierarchy of musical attractions: one that placed the high culture of opera and symphony above that of 'light music' and dance. Indeed, this corresponded with the structure of tourism, while it remained primarily an elite phenomenon, although Newth was at pains to point out that, at least in Vienna, symphonies in the parks appealed 'not only to those who have come for the concert but to the policemen and waiters and parkkeepers' (1931: 167). Other musical attractions that Vienna might have offered, and there was certainly folk music and jazz, seemed not worth mentioning.

The exclusion and marginalisation of folk music and jazz were evident elsewhere. Even more obviously, risqué venues such as the Moulin Rouge or the Folies Bergères in Paris, although they drew tourists from Europe and America long before the end of the 19th century, were likely to be given short shrift in most guidebooks. But then, as travellers like the English writer Arnold Bennett discovered, their musical attractions were often their secondary role (Bennett, 1913). At much the same time one of the attractions of the opera season in Bayreuth was, for some, its elitism and exclusivity:

> The painted, over-dressed women whose object it apparently is to attract as much attention to themselves as possible, and who frequently talk, even at concerts, all through the performance, are conspicuous by their absence at Bayreuth. Their smartness and their jewels would not be seen in the blessed darkness there . . . the absence of everything that is noisy, irritating, vulgar and disturbing prepares the mind to receive the full impression which the play is capable of producing. (Loftie, 1890: 118)

The opera could not thus be seen as mere recreation and entertainment; it contributed to demarcating society. Other examples of opposition to particular forms of entertainment, and their links to social status, were rarely subtle. After the Second World War the author of one guide to the Western Isles of Scotland, exasperated with 'pretty crude' Gaelic folk singing and 'uncritical, undiscerning' audiences, wrote:

> Performer and audience are fully satisfied with the naive standards of the homely ceilidh . . . . This primitive screeching and caterwauling may be all right round the peatfire of a winter's evening; but one must surely take exception to it being transferred, remuneratively to the cities, there to be accorded professional status.

Indeed, he concluded with evident relief that 'though this institution survives in the remoter parts, it is gradually being superceded in the more accessible, where alternative forms of entertainment are available. The picture house and the dance-hall are now preferred to the ceilidh' (MacGregor, 1949: 211). Similar attitudes to jazz, especially in the interwar years, and, rather later, to pop music were widespread, although rarely found their way into guidebooks. Potential invasions of the 'wrong' sort of music intermittently invoked middle-class moral panics. As guide-books, until the 1970s at least, largely focused on the buildings and landscapes of destinations, rather than their social possibilities, they also focused on the more impressive opera houses and symphony concert halls and rarely mentioned the smaller places where jazz, folk music and other forms of popular music were performed. Tourists were not expected to be interested. High culture was expected to prevail.

Nevertheless, long before different genres of music had stimulated tourism, even if classical music remained dominant, in some part because tourism remained a more middle-class phenomenon. In the mid-19th century brass band competitions in Britain took bands and their supporters, much like contemporary sports teams, to distant places; these supporters were some of the earliest travelling music enthusiasts (see Chapter 6). By the 1920s, Paris hosted numerous clubs and theatres drawing tourists from America and many parts of Europe, and featuring jazz, musicals, dance halls and a variety of cabaret shows; the Charleston dance craze swept through Paris after a post-war explosion of appreciation for African-American music, particularly jazz, to the extent that Parisian nightspots imported African-American musicians, notably Josephine Baker (Levenstein, 1998: 243–244; Simeone, 2000). New York (notably at Harlem's Cotton Club), New Orleans, Berlin and a handful of other great cities echoed such trends. In hundreds of other tourist destinations, such as the British seaside resorts, dancing was an eagerly anticipated summer pleasure, and piers and promenades reverberated to the sounds of orchestras and bands (Walton, 2000: 105–107). Music was no mere middle-class attraction.

Music tourism thus first emerged in terms of classical music, most evidently in the guidebooks that trumpeted the charms of architecture and the classics, but as the legacy of the Grand Tour faded and tourism became more widespread, new forms appeared. For many decades, however, it remained virtual rather than real, in the sense that actual tourism abroad for music was a mere fraction of the imaginary tourism undertaken in private homes when 'exotic' musical styles were imported into the West (Chapter 2). Yet in the last decades of the 20th century the rise of a new phase of popular music, the revival of folk music and the continued importance of classical music, alongside intensified affluence and mobility, and new nostalgia among the 'baby boom' generation, brought the considerable expansion and diversification of music tourism. Most crucially tourism extended from the elite high culture of earlier years to a massive range of opportunities and possibilities. Music tourism no longer filled only one significant niche, but encompassed many genres and forms.

Music and the Construction of Meaning

The rise of music tourism took music from being simply an expected, or occasionally quite unexpected, adjunct of a holiday to a central role. As tourism has become organised around different music genres, the diversity of relationships between place and music became evident. From an initial focus almost entirely on places of performance, as in 19th-century Bayreuth and Vienna, tourism has extended to include cemeteries and birthplaces, places of music creation and production, such as the extraordinary Opera House in Manaus (Brazil) or La Scala (Milan), and places identified in lyrics, such as the restaurant in Rio de Janeiro from which 'The Girl from Ipanema' emerged. Most recently it has involved museums, including that of La Scala (Rossi, 1995: 321–331), the House of Fado in Lisbon, the extraordinary Siegfried's Mechanisches Musikkabinet in Rudesheim, Germany – a collection of over 300 mechanical musical instruments – and the Cité de la Musique in Paris, a myriad of festivals and such constructed places of 'tribute' as Dollywood in Tennessee. In some respects this is remarkable since music is, strictly speaking, invisible, and often ephemeral, and the essence of tourism – the 'tourist gaze' – has only the most tenuous connection with music.

That music remains, and is frequently advertised as, an adjunct of tourism suggests at least that there is also a 'tourist ear', and that certain countries, including Ireland, Iceland and Austria (Chapter 3), and places such as Memphis and Tamworth stress the merits of their own regional music as one reason for tourism. Many tourist brochures and websites advertise musical attractions, from buskers to operas, festivals to bars, and local distinctiveness to the heights of international excellence. In East Asia do-it-yourself music, in the form of karaoke, is an anticipated and advertised component of many holidays. Airlines too have seen a possible role for music in tourism: Air Pacific invariably plays the haunting Fijian song, Isa Lei, on departure from Fiji to remind tourists to return, Qantas has made much of Peter Allen's 'I Still Call Australia Home', while in 2002 the Indian domestic airline Air Sahara, decided to liven up evening domestic flights by featuring post-dinner entertainment in the form of strolling musicians playing violins or guitars.

Music tourism is much more than mere observation and the 'tourist ear', however significant this may be, as it takes on a new diversity of possibilities, involves more people and destinations, and results in new forms of expenditure. Growth has gone alongside with promotion, both privately and publicly, and in particular places, such as Graceland (Memphis), has conserved, but also substantially transformed landscapes.

Like other forms of cultural tourism, such as art tourism and most kinds of heritage tourism, music tourism can be short-lived. Cultural goods are rapidly consumed and smaller cultural centres rarely attract visitors for long. Even festivals last for no more than a few days. However, the proliferation of festivals in recent years is indicative of the promotion of events that may keep visitors in place for more than a day, or at least overnight (see Chapter 7). Nonetheless, although the cultural resources of cities were in many cases perceived as purely local amenities and not part of a wider tourism resource base, the arts are now considered to have a considerable economic importance and even smaller towns, such as Rochdale, have touted their cultural attractions widely because of their potential economic importance, the positive image that this provides, but sometimes also because they have little else to offer. Cultural tourism has enabled the revitalisation of declining city centres or industrial towns, and in many British and other towns, cultural and arts districts have been deliberately planned to stimulate tourism and create more vibrant city centres.

In a number of places the rise of music tourism reveals ways in which localities have attempted to confront structural economic changes, as old industrial hearths decline and service economies take their place, or are engineered to take their place. Music tourism may constitute one component of strategies within local economies to generate new kinds of economic growth. Moreover, music tourism generates questions about how music can actively shape places, both in a discursive sense, through representations and stereotypes of places, and materially, through altering the built infrastructure of cities and towns. The role of music in social constructions of place varies substantially from place to place, from sites that have deep histories of musical expression and production, where tourism strategies build on an existing spatial and cultural discourse (for example, in New Orleans), to others where musical connections are to various extents 'invented' – for example at Tamworth, Australia or Branson, Missouri – as part of wider strategies to reinvigorate local economies or foster local cultural distinctiveness.

Despite the inherent aesthetic musical and contextual differences between, for example, Graceland (Memphis) or Abbey Road studios (London), travellers searching for Jim Morrison's grave in Paris or Jacques Brel's in the Marquesas, and tourists enjoying classical music in Vienna, trying the tango in Buenos Aires or raving in Goa, each of these share certain functions in tourist economies and generate similar (yet still diverse) meanings in cultural spheres.

Music tourism has become a distinct component of the new cultural tourism and has been generally seen as an area of substantial future expansion (Quinn, 1996; Sellars & Wilson-Youlden, 1996). The cultural industries – music, literature, film, art – relate to tourism in various ways, appropriating myths of place, transforming localities materially and discursively, thus supporting tourist development. Music is both a key cultural industry, and a text through which places are known and represented (Smith, 1994; Kong, 1995; Leyshon *et al.*, 1995, 1998; Halfacree & Kitchen, 1996), providing a new source of images and sounds for tourism promotion. Music remains a powerful presence in global mediascapes, in both the images and associations with place captured in lyrics, in connections between artists, bands or whole 'scenes' and certain places (hence the 'Seattle sound', the links between both soul and techno music and Detroit, or between the band REM and Athens, Georgia). Such associations, combined with music's powerful, emotive role in acts of consumption, create patterns of demand that translate into new local cultural economies, as discourses of 'authenticity' and 'distinctiveness' are mobilised across markets at a variety of scales, and become means of transforming places. As with any other form of economic development, music-related tourism involves complex social integrations (and disintegrations), appropriations of cultural resources, political negotiations, and sometimes conflicts with local populations and institutions.

As this book indicates, the diversity of music tourism is considerable, from an examination of the aesthetics of opera house design to youthful dusk to dawn beach parties on tropical islands. Music tourists are similarly varied, although nostalgia is a part of many travels. Vast numbers of studies have examined tourist motivations. Reasons that were once simply summarised as 'wanderlust' and 'sunlust' have become fragmented and diverse to include physical, cultural, social and spiritual motivations, some of which have been combined into social-psychological models of motivation, that link both avoidance (of the humdrum and mundane) and search for the sublime (Hall, 1998: 62–68). Most studies of the rationale for tourism have been at a national or regional level and have less frequently focused on niche tourists. Almost never have such studies been conducted on music tourists. Hall (1998: 269) has argued that 'special-interest tourists' may be characterised by the search for novel, authentic and quality experiences, but this says little more than that niche tourists are perhaps less likely to seek the more obviously hedonistic pleasures of mass tourists. Similarly, Derrett argues that 'special interest tourists demonstrate a desire for authenticity and real experiences that offer them active identification with host communities in a non-exploitative manner' (2001: 3), but that presupposes the existence of a 'host community' that may be absent in some forms of music tourism.

Music tourism, like other elements of cultural tourism, might be thought simply to link nostalgia with some concern for heritage and authenticity. Cultural tourism, of which music is a part, has been perceived as 'the pursuit of a social taste-forming minority elite' undertaken by 'cosmopolitans' who adopt 'an intellectual and aesthetic stance of openness towards divergent experiences from different national cultures' (Urry, 1994: 92). Yet that description, largely oriented at art tourists, privileges the elite status of certain elements of music tourism and ignores its diversity. As festivals have become increasingly significant, music tourists, even in the limited sense of festival goers, are quite varied and have little to do with Urry's definition. Moreover, there may be little, if anything, in common between a visitor to Mozart's grave in Vienna, an audience member in a blues festival in rural Australia and a participant in a month-long drumming course in West Africa, other than a common interest in some kind of music. Music tourism cannot exist apart from other elements of tourism; most tourists seek experiences of landscape, all eat and drink, choose particular modes of transport and accommodation, and shape their experiences and itineraries according to factors – such as financial status and time available – that are apart from the music.

It is thus difficult to define music tourism. As will become obvious throughout this book, there is no typical music tourist. Given the range of experiences and participants, and the ability of individuals to move between them, music tourists cannot easily be defined and classified. Music tourism constitutes a cluster of possible tourists, activities, locations, attractions, workers and events which utilise musical resources for tourist purposes. Music tourism sites exist within a set of networks of transport and tourist infrastructures, social relations, business linkages and cultural practices which support certain activities and economies. It can be seen as a range of practices where sites of music production and expression (whether in past or present 'scenes') become the points of attraction for tourists, and may also become central to strategies employed by the local state, tourist promotion boards and companies to market musical heritage and a musical environment. Crucially, music tourism, in addition to its economic role, is also an act of consumption that involves complex rituals, and suggests the powerful emotive role of music in contemporary societies.

Music tourism is clearly a discretionary activity, and fashion plays a part in every component of cultural tourism – hence music tourism may be a transitory phenomenon as have been other forms of cultural tourism. Ashworth argues that

> The cultural tourist, growing annually in experience and adventur-
> ousness, can exercise an increasingly fanciful, arbitrary and fickle
> choice from a fast expanding array of attractions. The established
> classics of the Western cultural canon whether in music, theatre,
> fine arts or architecture and urban design have been increasingly
> supplemented by an ever-widening range of cultural experiences.
> (1995: 275)

Music tourism both fits this description and adds to it. It is highly likely that the tourism cycle, where consumer choices may change quite rapidly, and lead to the decline in the attraction of a particular destination or phenomenon (Butler, 1980), will calibrate the ever-changing nature of musical fashions.

Notions of elitism and privilege tend to imbue a large part of the discussion of cultural tourism. Many such discussions (e.g. Richards, 1996) exhibit a conspicuous lack of reference to music, and where music is fleetingly mentioned, it is classical music. Similarly, national attempts to promote cultural tourism, as in the United Kingdom (Foley, 1996), exclude pop and rock concerts (and usually also sporting events). This book naturally neither excludes music, but rather sees it as a central component of music tourism, nor engages in attempts to distinguish a 'high' culture of classical music from a 'low' culture of popular music. All forms of music play some part in cultural tourism.

Seemingly central to much of music tourism (other than festivals), as to many other components of cultural tourism, is its retrospective nature – the search for experiences that replicate those of the past or at least provide reminders of them – a form of 'nostalgia consumption' (Dann, 1994). This in turn has stimulated a heritage industry within music tourism that has fed on nostalgia by reifying cultural experiences of the past, either in festivals, museums or other contemporary creations.

Music has gone from an adjunct of tourism, and a pleasant background, albeit often an important one, to a central element of much tourism, at least for a minority. That minority, often seeking both recreation and nostalgia, have produced a largely new series of niches within the tourist industry, that have had substantial cultural and economic significance in a range of places, from Kingston, Jamaica to Reykjavik, Iceland or Tanna, Vanuatu. Music tourism is often about fun and escape, but it also goes beyond the trivial, as this book hopes to illustrate, through connections to complex cultural issues – of authenticity, essentialism and heritage – and economic factors, including investment, employment creation and conditions, and the stimulus to regional and national economies. It is reflective of other forms of cultural tourism (like literature and film tourism), and is unique, not least in its reliance on the aural as well as visual. This book sets out to explore how music tourism is an important, if neglected, component of cultural tourism, and how it is a particular practice in itself, with its own histories, sites, economic trends and social practices. The next chapter discusses the various ways in which musical recordings pre-figured the emergence of tourism, acting as a symbolic field where places and peoples were represented (in sound, and in the iconography of promotional artwork, album covers etc.). Music has enabled 'virtual tourism', which partly informs and explains the emergence of actual music tourism.

Chapter 2
Virtual Tourism

In every era demand for tourism has exceeded supply. Recreation time has rarely been enough for most people, and capital constraints have always hindered travel and tourism. This was particularly true in the 19th century, when leisure time was scarce, paid holidays were rare and the cost of reaching even nearby places was considerable. Few travelled far. Distant places were destinations for a few well-off tourists though they figured in the dreams of many. Over time such distant places became accessible in alternative ways, through photographs, paintings and eventually through music. Such representations were as much reflections of the gaze of European travellers as in any sense accurate depictions of other places. By the mid-19th century audiences in Western Europe were being entertained through presentations of paintings and sketches, accompanied by appropriate music, from particular places: some of the first forms of virtual tourism. This chapter traces some of the ways through which music preceded and eventually accompanied tourism itself.

In the 1860s, the wonders of Ireland were shown in various British cities and towns, through displays of, as the associated booklet described, 'colossal paintings, executed in the highest style of art' and accompanied with 'Vocal and Instrumental Music, introducing the Choicest Irish Melodies, executed by Talented Artists'. Such melodies were mainly sentimental songs such as 'Norah, the Pride of Kildare', 'Coleraine Whiskey' and 'Kathleen Mavourneen'. The booklet touted press opinions of the travelling diorama, including one typical observation that

> There are few entertainments in which the visitor can so profitably spend two hours, in which so much interesting information may be learned, so many pleasurable sensations excited, or old associations revived, than in witnessing the beautiful scenery or listening to the melodies of old Ireland than that which has been provided in the Rotundo. (Corry, 1866)

Such travelling shows took urban populations away, however briefly, to destinations more exotic and colourful than their own homes. They foreshadowed late 20th century commercial slide shows for potential tourists to even more distant places.

Hula Sounds

While there was a history of fascination with distant places in the earliest operas, one of the most exotic of virtual destinations was Hawaii, largely a fabled group of islands to other than a very select few, and where links between music and tourism became evident early on. Moreover, while dioramas such as those that evoked the splendours of Ireland largely used music to create a background and amosphere – indeed a sentimental mood that would capture the interest and nostalgia of the many Irish migrants who had fled rural Ireland during the famine years of the 1840s – in Hawaii the seemingly exotic nature of music and dance was at least as significant in creating an image of a very different tourist landscape. Whereas Ireland was relatively familiar, Hawaii was very much the 'other' to distant Western populations, and dance and music were central to tourism, but especially to virtual tourism.

Within the United States, and beyond, the sounds of Hawaiian music, from steel and slack guitars to ukeleles, alongside Polynesian words and phrasing, gave the music a languid distinctiveness that was relatively easy to link to tourism. Distinctiveness and romanticism were further enhanced through such songs as 'Aloha Oe' (1878) written by the last Hawaiian queen, Liliuokalani. A largely temperate continental United States seemed so different. Tourism began in Hawaii in the 19th century, largely based around its natural landscapes, and linked to writings by Robert Louis Stevenson, Mark Twain and others. Hawaiian performers had appeared in the United States long before the end of the century, and by the 1910s tourism had become linked to music and dance. Hula girls began to appear in advertising and by the 1920s they were commonplace in tourist promotions as Hawaiian culture became 'commodified and enacted through dance shows as a way of authenticating the destination image' (Desmond, 1999: 6). Hawaii thus became an early site of cultural tourism.

Stereoscopic photographs took late 19th century Hawaii to a wider world, a vision further developed by postcards in the next century. One postcard from that era of a bare-breasted young woman in a grass skirt posed in front of Diamond Head was captioned: 'Dancing is one of the favorite amusements of the people, and the hula hula is the national dance. It is a love dance and with it goes a sad and doleful music on gourds, tom-toms, flutes, guitars or ukeleles' (quoted in Desmond, 1999: 42). Dances once banned or frowned on by missionaries as lascivious were being revived for tourist consumption, one of the earliest examples of such revivalism. Music and dance took Hawaii to a wider world and restructured its image towards that of exotic tourist destination.

Distant Places

Outside Hawaii few other places were so cherished in song, although places of outmigration stimulated waves of nostalgic songs, and returning colonists composed and sung songs of distant empires. In certain places particular songs became iconic; Sieczynski's 'Vienna, City of My Dreams' (1914) was a big hit and a symbol of the city, especially at it became central to the repertoire of the Austrian born tenor, Richard Tauber. Kreisler's 'Viennese Caprice' also enhanced the inter-war charms of Vienna. Elsewhere in Europe the songs of Maurice Chevalier captivated global audiences and extolled the pleasures of Paris. In the Depression years, urban delights were still triumphed, including a variety of songs describing New York, and countered the harshness of poverty and unemployment; 'Lullaby of Broadway' and similar songs offered aural escapes at a time when few could even dream of travel.

Just as the Irish dioramas had come at a time when emigration from Ireland was considerable, hence art and music reminded people of the places they had lost, so much of the popular music of the first half of the 20th century, whether folk or blues, was inspired by the places that migrants had left ('way down upon the Swanee river', 'carry me back to old Virginny' or 'in my old Kentucky home') and offered nostalgic images of homelands: places to be encountered in dreams and memories, perhaps one day to be revisited but as tourists rather than returning residents. The arrival of the gramophone in the late 19th century, and the radio in the 1920s, allowed many to listen to music of their choice. Music's role in nostalgia and place construction was already evident.

Ambient Music: Domestic Dreaming

The post-war years brought new versions of virtual tourism. As tourism grew rapidly so too did virtual tourism, and music played a critical role. In the 1930s specialist music programmes, soon to be known as 'muzak', were created with the intent of transmitting music into factories and homes to combat boredom. Rather than be given specific titles, or identified with particular composers, the music was linked to its intended purpose, the spaces where they were intended to be broadcast or with which they were intended to be associated:

> Natural landscapes, the flight of migratory birds, sunsets, rippling shores, orphans running through war-torn streets, a Tokyo massage parlor, cattle roaming through vast fields, lovers ogling on a beach, big city lights, Saturday afternoon at the rodeo, international travel – the infinite tableaux of set designs with their attendant tunes boggle the mind. (Lanza, 1994: 62)

Muzak increasingly invaded open spaces, shopping malls, lifts and tele-
phones to give places and contexts particular identities and, hopefully,
remove mundane cares. Music became an emotional and commercial
tool.

From the 1950s the recorded music industry, which had a distant relationship to muzak and pre-programmed music in general, began to adopt
the rhetoric, if not the format, of these types of music. Whereas a long
standing assumption had not surprisingly been that consumers bought
recordings to actively listen to them, many records were released that
were specifically designed to create particular home environments:
'music as wallpaper' played in the background to add a mood, create a
particular atmosphere, or convey the sounds of exotic, otherworldly
places that consumers might dream of visiting. The liner notes to various
albums indicated the uses to which recorded music could be put (*Music
for Dining, Music for Dancing* . . .). Many albums from the 1960s attempted
to 'capture' the sounds of far away places, vicariously transporting the
armchair listener to idyllic holiday destinations, mysterious Pacific
Islands, Alpine heights and cosmopolitan European streetscapes (Figure
2.1). *In Love in Paris* by the Musette of Renaud and Carlini's *World of
Strings* (both undated), re-created the archetypal romantic French
encounter: 'Montmartre, the Champs Elysee [*sic*], The Seine – all speak
of the romance of Paris. Here is a musical journey to Paris by night
. . . Renaud with the World of Strings is your passport to Paris'. Other
records emphasised the almost symbiotic relationship between music
and tourism; from the 1960s too, the liner notes to Percy Faith and His
Orchestra's *Bon Voyage! Continental Souvenirs* made obvious links:

> Coming home from Europe the American traveler brings a good a
> many things, as much as the weight allowance or the stateroom will
> handle. French perfume, Italian leather, British brushes, Swedish
> glass, Belgian lace, German carvings – all these and many more find
> their way back to the States. And a lot of it winds up in the attic.
> Not so the lovely lively melodies that have lately poured forth from
> the Continent however. These linger on, as good songs do, to become
> unforgettable, and fragrantly evocative souvenirs of the Grand Tour.
> In this enchanting collection, Percy Faith applies his suave touch to
> a dozen continental songs, largely from France and Italy, giving them
> such glowing colors that they take on a nostalgic patina even to
> those who have never been abroad. (Anon., 1959)

Such was the essence of virtual tourism, at a time when travel was
prohibitively expensive for most people (hence, no doubt, the reference
to stateroom here).

Meanwhile, Mantovani's *Continental Encores* (Anon., 1959) took the
format of the 'musical journey' to its extreme. The record's packaging

Figure 2.1 European cities were commonly depicted on LPs released in the 1950s and 1960s as they became desired destinations, principally for Americans (but also for Canadians, Australians and New Zealanders) with newfound capacity to travel. Paris, most often depicted on 'easy listening' records, was usually associated with themes of romance, sophistication and history. Images of Paris in recorded form (and in cover art) served to act as place marketing for actual tourism, while LPs were themselves souvenirs.

included a ten-page photo album of various European locations: a map of Paris, shots of cafés, Spanish churches, Venetian gondolas at sunset, folk dancers and bikini-clad bathers on Mediterranean shores:

> For a long time now entertainers have known about the power of music to evoke atmosphere. The circus and the fairground have always used their own special brands of cheerful melody, which are

as much a part of those entertainments as the exuberant, closely packed type on their posters. With sound track and disc recording far advanced in technique it is possible now to use this power of association over an ever wider range, and moreover to bring it into our own home. To put it another way, it can now be employed to take you out of your home, and lead you gently by the ear to familiar or imagined places. And so with all the tunes in this album Mantovani produces a sort of heightened impression of the places he takes us to in his music ... a musical flip round the continent takes in Italy, France, Switzerland and Germany, each one a natural home of easy, spontaneous melody ... . Coupled with the photographs in this great Mantovani album, this is as vivid and comfortable a journey in sound as anyone could possibly devise. (Anon., 1959)

The liner notes for Martin Denny's *Afrodesia* (1959) observed:

Once again Mr Denny stimulates the jaded palate of everyday civilization with music that is pure escape ... . We become armchair travellers with our magic carpet, our hi-fi (or stereo) equipment and this album. We see and feel the searing veldt ... the moody reaches of the jungle ... a tribal initiation fete and sheer encompassing beauty. (Quoted in Leydon, 1999: 53)

Stanley Black and His Orchestra's *Place Pigalle* emphasised these ideas in a particularly essentialised view of Paris, appealing to an Anglo-American fascination with European cosmopolitanism, and the fears of the outside world that often accompanied overseas travel:

Why go to all the bother of getting a passport, travelling on boats, trains and planes, buying sea-sick tablets, worrying about the customs, bothering your head by complicated sums with francs and pounds involved. Why not just put on this wonderful record and let Stanley Black take you on a conducted musical tour. This most reliable of guides who has already taken us to South America, the tropics, and the South Sea Islands with the utmost safety, will find no difficulty in such a short flip as Paris. Sure enough, the moment you put this record on the turntable you only need to close your eyes and there you are strolling along the banks of the Seine being shocked by the postcards – the price that is, or nibbling at your croissant accompanied by a French coffee at a table on the sidewalk as the sun rises over Paris, dodging the rush of French taxis ... wandering in the Place Pigalle in the lamplight .... (Anon., 1958)

The liner notes to *Place Pigalle* speculated on the reasons why music evokes place:

Even if you have never been nearer to Paris in your life than the stony shores of Folkestone, you can quite easily imagine you have been there simply by listening to the music. There seems to be some extra sense, not yet explained by the scientists, that connects every place in the world with its representative themes. (Anon., 1958)

Evocative song titles, in the music of Martin Denny alone, ranged from general concepts of exotic places ('Exotica', 'Return to Paradise'), specific distant places ('Hong Kong Blues', 'On a Little Street in Singapore', 'Bangkok Cockfight'), fauna and flora ('Lotus Land', 'Bamboo Lullaby'), vague mysticism ('Jungle Drums', 'Vovdoo [sic] Dreams') and islands and seas ('Island of Dreams', 'Beyond the Reef', 'The Enchanted Sea') that linked nature and mystery with exotic perceptions of otherness (Hosokawa, 1999a: 88). At a time when mass tourism was only getting under way, such recordings, some incorporating local bird sounds, became a feature of Western suburban homes, alongside other creature comforts, which were just beginning to include stereo music systems.

Despite the increasing diversity of virtual destinations, Hawaii never lost its prominence. Arthur Lyman was the most prominent of those who brought Hawaiian music into lounge rooms. The cover design and notes to Sam Kailuha and the Islanders' *Destination Honolulu* (Figure 2.2) were typical of a series of albums that were created to advertise new Pan Am airline routes (including those to Rome, Paris, London, Vienna, Berlin and Barcelona) and so emphasised the links between tourism, place and music:

The eight islands of the archipelago now make up the 50th state in the Union, but Hawaii has lost none of its Polynesian charm. Ale-brown hula girls in grass skirts still sway to the strains of 'Sweet Leilani' and the air is forever fragrant with hibiscus and frangipani. The sky is as blue as the sea lapping against the sandy shores of Waikiki and the secluded coves of the outer islands . . . . Out here where the thermometer hugs 70-odd degrees summer and winter there is no peak season. Any day of the week is the occasion for a bit of revelry, and no-one should miss the famous 'luau', traditional feast of Hawaii . . . . Once deserted except for a few grass shacks, Kalakaua is now the swingingest street in the Pacific. Here are the Gold Coast skyscrapers and hotels of Waikiki, gourmet restaurants and shops selling everything from aloha shirts to Oriental art treasures . . . . Getting around Hawaii is a simple affair, as there is a variety of flights to the outer islands. Honolulu is itself less than five hours by Pan Am Jet Clipper from the West Coast of the United States. Just short of taking a trip or a lesson in the hula, nothing captures the sultry beauty of the islands as does the music of Hawaii. Using the steel guitar, ukelele and the drum, Sam Kailuha and the

Figure 2.2 Sam Kailuha's LP, released to promote Pan Am's route to Hawaii, was one of a number in a series dedicated to new destinations opened up by improving air transport. It mobilised images of Hawaii already etched in the global imagination through earlier phases of musical distribution: of beach-side paradises, palm trees and romantic sunsets.

> Islanders carry the listener off to Waikiki, where girls in bikinis do the hula and brawny surfers ride the 'soup'.

What distinguished this record was that it had been sponsored by Pan Am, in a deliberate strategy of releasing albums to coincide with the development of new airline routes, and the marketing of the new destinations. BOAC, Continental Airlines and others followed suit, releasing albums to promote transcontinental routes (Figure 2.3). One Continental Airlines release, celebrating the opening of their Hawaiian route in the 1960s, even came with a full 50-page fold-out travel guide to each of the

Figure 2.3 The British Overseas Airways Corporation (BOAC), later to be amalgamated within British Airways, also produced albums to coincide with the announcement of new airline routes. This EP, released to commemorate the opening of BOAC's Pacific route to Sydney, featured songs with essentialised representations of big city lights, 'exotic' South Sea culture and 'primitive' Australian Aborigines. The link between musical representations and prevailing tourism images is clear.

islands, with descriptions of Hawaii's geography, shopping districts and local history and culture, as well as space for travellers to record their own diary of experiences (Figure 2.4).

Just a few years afterwards a ten-album Readers' Digest/RCA compilation of *Magical Melodies* devoted half of one album to Hawaiian music, introduced with what had become a familiar theme:

> America's newest state furnishes us with one of the oldest recipes for contentment in the world: equal parts of warm breeze, starlit sky, languid waves lapping at a perfect beach, and in the distance the mellow sounds of massed guitars. Of course there are songs of the South Seas being played on those guitars to swaying rhythms that have no equal in the realm of music anywhere. Care fades away, anxiety disappears and in their place come relaxation and content.

Earlier Hawaiian songs were continually reinvented in different formats and genres, as electrification transformed sounds (thus 'Across the Sea' (1919) was revived in 1941 by Ray Kinney 'and his suave, guitar-accented band, the Hawaiian Musical Ambassadors'), and new songs such as 'Hawaiian Sunset' continued themes firmly established before the start of the century. The marketing of Hawaiian music, largely to mainland

Figure 2.4 *Honeymoon in Hawaii* (1969) by the Hilo Hawaiians, was an LP produced and given away to customers on the first Continental Airlines flights from mid-west and western US hubs to Hawaii in 1969. The LP, sponsored also by American Express and Hawiian Airlines (hence including a map of internal Hawaiin flights), featured lavish photographs, fold-out maps, diary spaces for tourists to record their experiences, detailed descriptions of individual islands, tips on 'what to bring' and advertisements for Continental Airlines routes. It is the most exuberant example of music as place promotion and soundtrack to tourism, yet despite its many pages, the actual recording artists are barely mentioned.

Americans, conveniently smoothed over the discontent and dispossession of American colonialism – indigenous sovereignty obscured by idyllic Pacific sounds that both exoticised and celebrated the opening up of a new tourism destination.

Away from the northern hemisphere, in countries more isolated from mass tourism, such as Australia, virtual tourism survived rather longer. As recently as 1974 the sleeve for the International Promenade Orchestra's *The Songs and Moods of a Continental Holiday* suggested:

> Here is a musical passport to romance and reminiscence of a Continental Holiday. Lush strings and intimate accordion – musette, the warmth of mandolins as we take a turntable tour of France and Italy. Then on to the grandeur of the bullfight and soft warm nights in Malaguena – the happy 'brau-haus' oompah of Munich and the sweet nostalgia of Vienna. All yours in this programme of a Continental Holiday. (Anon., 1974)

As real tourism replaced its vicarious form, the specific role of such records largely disappeared, though ironically to be revived as parody and kitsch in the lounge music of the late 20th century. However, producing music to create a sense of space, or to re-create the impression of particular environments, boomed with the advent of ambient music.

Ambient music, designed to encourage relaxation and even sleep, emphasised 'special' places both generic and real, remote from urban centres and physically attractive – with mountains, falling or flowing water (in streams rather than rivers), rainforests, coasts and oceans, occasionally deserts, and more generally 'wilderness'. Such places were imbued with spiritual powers, or associated with particular animals regarded as having special qualities, especially birds, dolphins and whales. The liner notes to Andy Holm's *Blue Mountain Tales* (1996), on Primal Harmony Records, stressed the significance of the World Heritage site – the Blue Mountains National Park – immediately west of Sydney:

> During my frequent travels to the Blue Mountains I have always been inspired to pick up my instruments and play out the feelings that arise within me. This album is the product of the precious moments. Whether I played my flute at the bottom of Wentworth Falls or the didjeridu at Echo Point, the vibration of the surroundings always influenced a strong tribal and spiritual sound, a reflection of my inner self opening up at the Blue Mountains beauty. Although this album is a fairy tale story, it is reflecting on my true emotions brought forward by the ambience of the Blue Mountains. Close your eyes while you are listening, let the narrator be your guide and join me on a magnificent voyage through time, sound and space, and a dimension you will find within yourself listening to this work.

Similarly, the Australian musician Ken Davis, seeking to enter the North American market, released four albums in 2001: *Tai Chi Music*, *Pan Flutes by the Ocean*, *Dolphin Magic* and *Spirit of Sedona*. On the last of these, Sedona was described as 'a spiritual centre one hundred miles north of Phoenix and is world-renowned for its spiritual energy and geological splendour . . . a focus for people seeking a spiritual environment. It is known for its healing spirits'. Some performers actually recorded within the natural landscape, or occasionally in such sites as the Taj Mahal, but more frequently entitled their albums with names of tourist places (such as Uluru (Ayers Rock) and Kakadu, in Australia) with particular natural and spiritual significance.

At the same time that indigenous peoples and places were becoming tourist attractions, ambient music stressed the mystical and 'cosmic' life forces associated with 'traditional peoples', their links to the earth and their musical instruments. In Australia the didjeridu features in much ambient music, especially that of the Aboriginal performer David Hudson, but panpipes and flutes have been common (although not necessarily tied to their geographical origins). Beyond generic indigenous peoples, others claiming particular spiritual powers might also feature: shamans on North American music and monks in Ireland. For David and Steve Gordon's *Sacred Spirit Drums* (Planet Earth Music, 2001) the company website exulted in a: 'Melodic, magical, danceable story about a Shaman who journeys into the Spirit world to find a way to heal the Earth and its people . . . Finally, the copious nature sounds were recorded at various National Monuments and parks'. *Celtic Inspiration: An Irish Soundscape* (Headline, 1995), recorded 'among the cathedrals, churches, monastic cells, forest and lake of Glendalough' deliberately took listeners on a journey there, as on the sixth track where 'Slowly we move round the banks of the tranquil lake. Inevitably gentle rain starts to fall and we take shelter under the trees'. Irish ambient music often incorporated uilleann pipes and Scottish music the bagpipes. Natural sounds (an explicit identification of indigenous peoples as 'natural') contributed to the primitivist fantasies of tranquillity, timelessness and human interaction with nature. Relaxation and spiritual healing were the promised and anticipated consequences.

Ambient music stressed virtual tourism, both in its content and marketing, which centred on tourist venues and airports rather than music stores, and was designed to emphasise and enhance travels that might already have been accomplished. The notes to Ken Davis's *Early Morning in the Rainforest* (1985), which blended bird song and electronic music, enjoined 'Experience the feeling of being in the rainforest while still in the comfort of your own home'. Rather differently, the website of Australian performer, Tony O'Connor, included a 'guestbook' where listeners could record their thoughts on his music, as Clare Power from the Isle of Man registered in 2001:

> Australian friends introduced me to your music some years ago . . . . I introduced the wonderful flowing sounds to the T'ai Chi Chuan Group, for Shibashi practice. Also your *In Touch, Bushland Dreaming, Kakadu* and *Uluru* keep me in touch with my daughter's family and my friends 'down under' . . . . Thank you again, Namaste. (www. tonyoconnor.com, accessed 2001)

Emigrant Australians, such as Robert, an 'Aussie in Denmark', may 'listen to your music when I am homesick'. Ambient music, with links to new age and world music, and its combination of the electronic and the natural, creates a series of generic and particular places, that reflect and induce harmony. The genre has become exceptionally popular, yet remains largely distinct from other forms of music through its tourist orientation and the absence of live performance.

Classical Movements

Classical music, even such obviously national music as *Finlandia*, has only rarely been directly used in ways that were linked to tourism, although just as the music of Percy Faith and others sought to transport listeners beyond humdrum suburban lives, some of the liner notes for classical music, especially the light classics, made similar but more subtle references. Works such as Offenbach's *Gaité Parisienne*, Strauss's 'The Vienna Woods' and 'The Blue Danube', Respighi's 'Fountains of Rome' and Mendelssohn's Italian and Scottish Symphonies (the latter with its Fingal's Cave Overture) often made references to the links between music and place with exactly the same intention. Record covers too used the same images of place. Buildings such as the Eiffel Tower became clichés, and European castles, cathedrals and rustic countrysides were almost synonymous with classical covers.

Tourist links were usually implicit rather than explicit. Beethoven's *'Pastoral' Symphony* was seen to reflect and represent his walks in the woods and fields around Vienna. In the liner notes to the Hollywood Bowl Symphony Orchestra's *Grand Canyon Suite*, from the 1960s, the composer, Ferde Grofe, accredited his inspiration to living in Arizona:

> Roaming the desert and mountain country as an itinerant pianist. This was first hand experience for me and I knew the terrain of the Grand Canyon region, its animal and bird life, and the people and their habits and customs. The richness of the land and the rugged optimism of the people had fired my imagination. I was determined to put it all to music one day.

Here, as in so many other cases, including Vila Lobos's *New York* music and Smetana's *Down the River Volga*, composers sought to conjure up the image of particular places in a way that would evoke those places to distant listeners. Copland's *Appalachian Spring* and Gershwin's *An American in Paris* were said to convey clear and evocative images, and their covers invariably emphasised their physical charms. Although they rarely invited listeners to engage in virtual tourism, as lighter music had done, *An American in Paris* did become the theme music for United Airlines.

Inevitably, however, some did escape, in England, at least, through the music of Holst, Elgar or Vaughan Williams, and thus to largely pastoral landscapes, but there were sometimes more esoteric departures, as for Richard Morrison:

> With the help of Delius's *Song of the High Hills* we can be transported mentally to the Cumbrian fells. The dissonances of Harrison Birtwhistle's *Grimethorpe Aria* can carry us deep into the scarred industrial wastelands of the north. Or, if you prefer your countryside

tamer and prettier, the delightful 18th-century airs of Thomas Linley, the 'English Mozart', could waft us across some elegantly contrived Repton landscape. (Morrison, 2001: 17)

Morrison did indeed walk across the Malvern Fells of Western England, listening on headphones to Elgar's music that precisely evoked that landscape.

Light classical music sometimes involved Spanish guitars and flamenco beats, invariably with essentialist record covers of Spanish scenes, and Rodrigo's *Concierto de Aranjuez* and *Concierto de Andaluz* evoked nostalgia for Spain. Ravel's 'Bolero' had a similar effect. Such music simply emphasised the pleasures of mainly European destinations, in one more variant of vicarious tourism.

Lightness at Large

Where ambient and classical music offered travel dreams through cover designs and direct invocations in liner notes, lyrics could directly stress the virtues of other places. Most early lyrics, from a time when tourism was an elite experience, were nostalgic – songs of lost places – rather than of contemporary pleasures. Others, like the dozens on the US state of Georgia, were onomatopoeic. Occasionally, such themes might be combined. Singers like Brendan O'Dowda created an imaginary Ireland with such favourites as 'The Sun on Connemara', 'The Quiet Land of Erin' and 'Moonlight on the Mournes', just as Kenneth McKellar championed the virtues of Loch Lomond and the Isle of Skye, when contemporary tourism was slight. In time, various sentimental songs contributed to such places becoming immortalised as tourist destinations.

Musicals such as *Showboat, Desert Song, Oklahoma, The King and I* or *West Side Story* made generic or more obvious links to place but rarely in a way that linked distant places to travel, although many conveyed the excitement of places such as New York. The great exception was *The Sound of Music* which, as much as any other single musical work, eventually made the transition from virtual tourism to tourism itself. In time, the sound of music and tourism transformed the hills around Salzburg, a somewhat ironic shift since the film was never translated into German (see Chapter 3).

Some specific types of music were indistinguishable from tourism. The cover of *German Drinking Songs*, from the early 1970s, advised:

How to enjoy this album –
Pour yourself a stein of beer. Put the record on the turntable and turn it on. Sit down in a comfortable chair, take a sip of beer, close your eyes and visualise this scene. A small German village snuggled in a valley, surrounded by high snow-capped mountains – a

large circus tent pitched in the town square, completely encircled by stalls, selling trinkets, games, and variations of German foods, sausages and beer .... For this is the traditional Oktoberfest, the most popular of all German festivals.

From the same time period, the Yugoslavian National Orchestra's *Holiday in the Balkans* (Figure 2.5), and *Music from the Greek Islands* by Tacticos and his Bouzoukis, emphasised parallel but more enduring themes. As the cover notes to the latter observed:

> In recent years more and more travellers have been discovering the beauty of Greece and the delights of the myriad islands which bask around it in the Aegean Sea. Once regarded as the preserve of archae-ologists, it is not realised that Greece combines an incomparable history with all the attractions of idyllic scenery and a Mediterranean climate; but among the memories of ivory temples, dolphins cavorting in blue waves, the tinkling of donkey bells and the dusky-green of the olive groves, none will be cherished more by the returning traveller than the memory of the warmth and friendliness of the Greek people, their natural hospitality, their courageous accep-tance of life's pains, and their unabashed embrace of life's pleasures .... The music of Manos Tacticos and his Bouzoukis evokes the true flavour of the Aegean and the islands of Greece, the whitewashed houses shining in the sun, the gentle waves of Homer's 'wine-dark' sea, and the scintillating notes of the bouzoukis crystallize the spirit of Greece and its people, their friendship, their passions, their open-hearted love of life.

As that cover also noted, images of Greece had been enhanced by films such as *Never on Sunday* and *Zorba the Greek* – for which latter film the music of Tacticos and Mikis Theodorakis had provided the soundtrack. No longer was it necessary merely to imagine and dream to a musical background as film diversified the virtual experience.

A parallel series of books, movies (and musicals often became movies) took up similar themes. Many versions of 'Three Coins in the Fountain' from the romantic 1954 film emphasised Rome's charms. Bob Hope, Bing Crosby and Dorothy Lamour took various roads, including those to Singapore, Morocco, Zanzibar and Bali (although the films had strange images of these locales), and *The King and I* encouraged new romantic images of the Orient. Earlier films had featured the exotic singer, Carmen Miranda, who brought a Hollywood simplicity and distortion to Latin American locations from Rio to Havana. *South Pacific* painted an indelible impression of an exotic Oceania where Bali Hai was 'that one special island' calling 'come to me, come to me' (Toop, 1999; Connell, 2003). Once again, a handful of exotic locations were exercising peculiar charms.

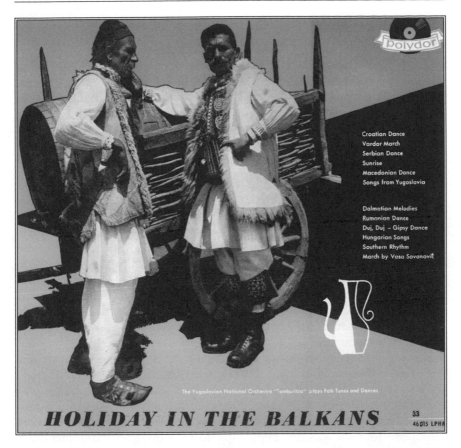

Figure 2.5 Air travel opened up European locations to tourism from Britain, particularly in Greece and Spain. On this LP by the Yugoslavian National Orchestra, 'traditional' music and costumes of the Balkans are celebrated, emphasising a place and time distant from the (then) contemporary concerns of the Cold War.

Travelling the World

No genre of music more obviously sought to transport listeners to other worlds than world music, the end point of a long-established process of incorporating alien sounds into popular music, evident in the 19th century with the fad for 'Ethiopian' music in early British music halls, Palm Court orchestras and eventually the success of performers from other regions. Exhibitions and festivals displayed unusual discoveries from other worlds, while artists such as Gauguin and composers such as Debussy, Bizet and others absorbed influences from Asia, the Pacific and Latin America into the European canon:

> The expositions were models of the shopping mall as well as being the precursors of themed entertainments, trade shows, post-Woodstock rock festivals . . . choice fruits of empire, living proof of conquest and self-aggrandisement in the face of imminent decline. (Toop, 1995: 20–21)

Music played a part in this, as instruments such as banjos were incorporated early into European music, and musical genres similarly spread, often far beyond their apparent origins. By the 1930s, for example, Hawaiian music and the rumba were both well established in Japan, markers of a lifestyle quite different from that of the host nation (Hosokawa, 1994, 1999b). Two decades later, the more successful introductions became occasional exotic entries to the lower reaches of hit parades; the Weavers sang 'in the jungle, the mighty jungle, the lion sleeps tonight, Wimoweh' (1962), which took its place along Israeli songs such as the Spotnicks' 'Hava nagila', and the Cuban 'Guantanamera'. The cute Japanese song 'Sukiyaki' became a global hit, as did the bossa nova song 'The Girl from Ipanema' (1963). More exotic sounds and places gradually became familiar to a wider world.

Harry Belafonte's two major calypsos of the 1950s, 'Kingston Town' (1956) and 'Banana Boat Song' (1957), with obvious African influences, sung of a place 'where the nights were gay' and banana loading was enjoyable (the height of romanticisation of a town viewed quite differently a decade or so later when reggae became Jamaica's largest export). Caribbean tourism was just beginning to take off, and these and other calypsos were the spirit of the times. The construction of romantic tropical destinations was a small part of the establishment of urban modernity. In South Africa the Manhattan Brothers brought themes that offered 'a romanticized, mythological continent, a timeless Africa of animals and jungles and hunting rituals and mystery: the west's exotic other' (Ballantine, 1999: 16). Such appropriations underpinned early easy listening music of the 1960s, from Bert Kaempfert's *A Swinging Safari* (1962) and Martin Denny's *Exotic Love* (1968), to Morton Gould and His Orchestra's *Jungle Drums* (1962) and the Ei'e Band's *Polynesian Playmate* (1962), many of which represented the people (and places) of exotic locations in simplistic gendered terms (Connell & Gibson, 2003: 146–147). Such exotica formed a distinct genre where:

> The elaborate fiction of the tropical paradise functioned as an exoticised complement to American suburbia: a colourful, dangerous, mysterious, heterogeneous Other which contrasted with the safe predictable, homogeneous and sexually repressive environment at home. (Leydon, 1999: 48)

Earl Grant's *Trade Winds* (1964) 'evokes a romantic imagery of tropical isles . . . moonlit sands . . . and soft-serenades. It creates a languor
and stirs a longing for far-off lands . . . a musical magic carpet', that took
listeners to a particularly diverse range of locations, from Ipanema ('our
visa for a vicarious stopover in Brazil') to Manakoora, Venice, Hawaii
and Spain. At much the same time Richard Hayman and His Orchestra's
Come With Me To Far Away Places offered:

> If 'far away places and strange sounding names' are calling but you
> can't get away right now, then sit back and listen as Richard Hayman
> plays you round the world in 12 musical ways on a Grand Tour of
> Europe, Asia, South America and the South Pacific. It's a magical
> holiday in music, designed to evoke rich memories of journeys past
> for confirmed travel-bugs, and satisfy the anticipatory wanderlust
> of those who have yet to leave home.

That tour included such familiar landmarks as Paris, Vienna and Hawaii,
but also Cuba, Madagascar, Persia (and 'the grandeur and glory of the
British Isles reflected in the sweetly sentimental "White Cliffs of Dover" ')
though geography was nevertheless sometimes distorted (as where 'the
veiled enchantment of the mysterious East is echoed by the exotic "In
a Chinese Temple Garden" '). Obviously flamboyant Latin American
dance styles were particularly popular through such albums as Manuel
and his Music of the Mountains' *Shangri-La*, and the enormous numbers
of discs that came from performers such as Edmundo Ros, Sergio Mendes
and Herb Alpert's Tijuana Brass (though Alpert himself was from
California). They were rather more exotic versions of the lounge music
that invoked the charms of Paris and Salzburg, and they put such
places as Tijuana and Rio de Janeiro on the map as exotic spaces and
vicarious destinations.

The music of those performers who became successful in the West, with
distinct new styles (and sometimes distinctive instruments), eventually
became known as 'world music', a category that proved difficult to define
in other than a commercial sense. Nevertheless, a world of much greater
mobility, transience, urbanisation and rapid technological change
was marked by musical diversity, eclecticism and new perspectives on
distant places. Much of world music was hybrid, displaying a 'strategic
inauthenticity' that emphasised natural places and peoples, whereas
performers such as Youssour N'Dour actually sang about themes that
reflected the changes of modernity, including the impacts of tourism and
environmental degradation (Taylor, 1997). World music became increasingly diverse, combining what were marketed as the exotic and pristine
(yet accessible) charms of unknown artists from remote, natural places;
in short it became a form of 'aural tourism' (Cosgrove, 1988), taking
fragments of other cultures for the benefit of jaded Western tastes.

One of the major purveyors of world music was advertising in 1999: 'Travel the World with Creative Vibes', while a year later, Putumayo, a major world music label, urged of a new CD:

> Gardens of Eden is an exquisite selection of acoustic music from some of the Earth's most beautiful places. Since time immemorial, people have been on a quest for remote idyllic hideaways where life approaches perfection. The music of Gardens of Eden has an organic ambient quality that conjures up images of a magical, tropical paradise where humanity's day to day stress disappears ... a musical journey to the world's Shangri-La's. Be transported! (www.putumayo.com)

Putumayo have focused on the notion of travel, specifically in their Odyssey series which includes 'voyages' across continents and regions. Thus, *A Mediterranean Odyssey: Athens to Andalucia* invites listeners to 'take a musical cruise of the Mediteranean'. Other albums have more explicitly focused on the concept of travel. For the compilation *Islands*, the website proclaims:

> It's a word that conjures up images of verdant, sunsplashed hideaways. Maui, Tahiti, Tortola. We think about escape, relaxation, and regeneration on palm-lined, white sandy beaches running into turquoise seas. Islands are stages for love romance and passion. Since you can't always get to them, we're taking you on a sonic world cruise from the more familiar Puerto Rico and Hawaii to the mysterious Cape Verde and Madagascar and ports in between. For what defines a land more than its music – full of local colors, rhythm and language? (www.putumayo.com)

Large numbers of Putumayo, Celestial Harmonies and other albums similarly offered the experience of exotic worlds from the jungles of Africa, and their pygmy music, to the remoteness of Cape Verde, Tibet or Mongolia. Notions of discovery, authenticity, heritage, uniqueness, metaphors of travel and a distinct sense of place were never far from the covers and tracks of world music albums.

Where world music came from quite remote and inaccessible locations, vicarious tourism rarely became reality. Perhaps the greatest exception to this followed Ry Cooder's 'unearthing' of Cuban music and the enormous success of the Buena Vista Social Club that precipitated a wave of tourism, to some extent in search of the pure Latin sounds seemingly kept vibrant within the confines of a shadowy and secretive socialist state (see Chapters 3 and 5). World music soon spread through compilation albums, like those of Putumayo, and festivals, such as WOMAD (World of Music and Dance), where an array of exotic sounds from a diversity of locations was decontextualised and brought together.

Here world music brought together a range of sounds from 'exotic' places, just as those places began to experience the early phases of tourism development.

'We're All Going on a Summer Holiday'

More directly, popular music lyrics have confidently stressed the virtues of travel, holidays and broad notions of escapism. Road music (which largely preceded road movies) emphasised the pleasures of voyage, although there were common notions in blues and country music that escape was from sorrow or poverty and not from an inherent desire to travel. In country music the geographical path was a spiritual one, such that Cecilia Tichi claimed that 'the idea of the voyage in life is entrusted to country music, as it has been entrusted to other arts in American culture' (1994: 193). The 'beat generation' of the 1950s made mobility a philosophical adventure, a search for self and salvation, and rock music transformed the notion that travel was about heartache. The Shangri-Las exulted in the 'Leader of the Pack' (1965) and Steppenwolf's 'Born to be Wild' (1968) became the theme of the movie *Easy Rider* and an anthem for a generation of escapists. Truck-driving songs offered the camaraderie of the truck-stops and the idea of endless movement; the travelling life was life itself.

The epitome of the highway song was 'Route 66', as Nat King Cole, the Rolling Stones and many others suggested that you could 'get your kicks' on Route 66, winding through the heartland of America and climaxing in LA. So famous was the song and the images that it inspired, that Route 66 eventually became a tourist destination (see Chapter 6). Highway songs were American; highways offered open spaces without borders, flatlands for fostering dreams and illusions that escape was possible; indeed, as Leyshon *et al.* (1995: 430) have firmly noted 'the glamour of the transcontinental highway doesn't quite work in Essex' where clear skies, emptiness and distance are absent.

Wilderness and deserts, just as in ambient music, offered similar escapist prospects. In U2's 'In God's Country' and 'Heartland', both recorded as part of the band's quasi-tourist explorations of North America in the late 1980s, the link with open spaces and highways was again clear: 'Mississippi and the cotton wool heat/Sixty-six and the highway speaks/Of deserts dry and cool green valleys/Gold and silver veins – shining cities'. The inner heart of the continent was a place to discover inner truths. Such reflections were often the products of the northern hemisphere, although Kasey Chambers' 'Nullarbor Song' (2000) took up similar themes of emptiness and introspection in Australia.

The Beach Boys provided the quintessential music of summer, surfing and sex; indeed, so powerful was their music in the 1960s that it somehow convinced the world that summer and California were inextricably related. Strings of hits, such as 'Surfin' Safari', 'Surfer Girl' and 'All Summer Long' were linked through others such as 'Little Deuce Coupe' and 'I Get Around' into messages of escape. California became a world where

> Age is suspended at 25 and school is outlawed and Coke flows free from public fountains and the perfect cosmic wave unfurls endlessly at Malibu . . . surf city, two girls for every boy. Drive-ins and muscle beach parties . . . . (Cohn, 1969: 94)

Movies took up the same theme and southern California became one particular kind of perfect tourist destination.

Particular places and regions have been enshrined in lyrics as tourist destinations, none more than the surfing havens of California and islands from the Caribbean to the Pacific. Some like Jimmy Buffett's 'Margaritaville' (Bowen, 1999) were as imaginary as ambient destinations. Islands were always attractive. Hawaii was revitalised in the music of Arthur Lyman (Fitzgerald & Hayward, 1999) and took on a new life as Elvis Presley sang, and appeared in, *Blue Hawaii*; Abba made 'Happy Hawaii' (1977), although far from one of their great hits: 'Hey Honolulu/ We're going to happy Hawaii/I can imagine the beach and the sand/Walking with someone and holding his hand'. More than a decade later the Screeching Weazels sang in 'This Ain't Hawaii': 'In droves they hit the beach in Porsches and Ferraris/The sun has cooked their brains/They're on a surf safari/This isn't Hawaii, this is Illinois'. The Beach Boys actually offered alternatives to California in 'Kokomo' (1988):

> Aruba, Jamaica, ooh I wanna take ya
> Bermuda, Bahama, come on, pretty mama
> Key Largo, Montego, baby why don't we go
> Martinique, that Montserrat mystique
> Port au Prince, I wanna catch a glimpse.

The choices remained largely predictable. Typical Tropical made 'Barbados' a hit in 1975, Black Lace encouraged holidaymakers to dance the 'Agadoo' (1985), but many were content with generic islands that isolated travellers from the world's dull cares. Harry Belafonte sang of his 'Island in the Sun' (1957) and the Springfields triumphed with 'Island of Dreams' (1962). In several cases such seemingly idyllic locations were simultaneously emphasised in films and television series.

Conversely, cities were places from which to escape at summer time, evident in the Lovin' Spoonful's 'Summer in the City' (1966): 'Hot town/Summer in the City/Back of My Neck's Gettin' Dirty and Gritty'. Exceptionally, cities were places for travel and tourism; Scott McKenzie famously sung of San Francisco and the need to wear flowers in your hair in the 'summer of love', and the Flowerpot Men quickly took up the theme in 'Let's go to San Francisco' (1967). Numerous singers left their hearts there. Petula Clark generally noted that 'the lights are much brighter there/forget all your troubles/forget all your cares/and go downtown' (1964). London town and New York offered attractions to many, while Dionne Warwick asked the way to San Jose. Otherwise, summer was a time to travel, explore, escape and perhaps find love; in Britain that was encapsulated in Cliff Richard's big hit 'Summer Holiday' (1963):

> We're all going on a summer holiday,
> No more worries for a week or two
> We're going where the sun shines brightly,
> We're going where the sea is blue,
> We've seen it in the movies,
> Now let's see if it's true.

Its trite simplicity was perfect for the season and the times. Mungo Jerry made 'In the Summer Time' (1970) almost as famous with similar themes. Nat King Cole's 'Those Lazy Hazy Crazy Days of Summer' (1970) and John Travolta and Olivia Newton-John's 'Summer Nights' (1979) from *Grease* further emphasised seasonal hedonism.

Vast numbers of songs by dozens of performers have somehow dreamed of summer, from Marianne Faithfull's 'Summer Nights' (1965), Joni Mitchell's 'The Hissing of Summer Lawns' (1975) and Seals and Croft's 'Summer Breeze' (1972) to Gershwin's 'Summertime' from *Porgy and Bess*. The Drifters got 'Sand in my Shoes' (1964) when 'Under the Boardwalk' (1964) and Horst Jankowski took 'A Walk in the Black Forest' (1965). Getting there was often excitement enough; Peter Paul and Mary were 'Leaving on a Jet Plane' (1960) and Burt Bacharach offered a variety of alternatives in 'Trains and Boats and Planes' (1965), where once there might only have been the Chattanooga Choo-Choo. Martha and the Muffins 'Echo Beach' (1980) spoke of the simple pleasures of escape: '9 to 5 I have to spend my time at work/my job is very boring, I'm an office clerk/the only thing that helps me pass the time away/is knowing I'll be back on Echo Beach one day' (quoted in Jarvis, 1995: 108). Almost all have evoked the pleasures of summer and holidays, although Eddie Cochran got the 'Summertime Blues' (1958) and, in Allan Sherman's comedy hit 'Hello Muddah, Hello Fadduh' (1963), the youthful singer, stuck for a summer in Camp Granada, was utterly miserable until the sun began to shine. Several performers wrote love letters in the sand to absent partners, and Bryan Hyland was inconsolable at the distance and the fears that 'yes, it's gonna be a long lonely summer' in 'Sealed with a Kiss' (1962). Travel and escape could not occur without loss.

Summer songs largely emerged from the northern hemisphere and from places with cold winters, though in Australia Little Pattie had a double-sided hit with 'Stompin' at Maroubra' (a Sydney beach) and 'He's My Blonde-Headed Stompie Wompie Real Gone Surfer Boy' (1963). Until John Denver hinted at mountain idylls in the 1980s, holidays were almost always in warmer climes. The myriad of summer holiday songs came mainly from the 1960s, a period when lyrics were designed to be audible, and were less elusive than in later decades, at a time of accelerated affluence in the Western world. Listeners might reasonably experience what performers sang about. The same decade witnessed a profusion of car songs, spearheaded by Chuck Berry and later the Beach Boys, that triumphed masculinity (Heining, 1998). Mobility, mass travel and tourism were becoming fashionable and so to be celebrated.

Never again was so much popular music as simplistic or escapist, at least not until three decades later when the Venga Boys anticipated 'sex on the beach' for which 'We're going to Ibiza' (2001):

> We're going to Ibiza
> Back to the island
> We're going to Ibiza
> We're going to have a party
> In the Mediterranean Sea.

Islands, seasides and hedonism had never really disappeared; they were simply less likely to be triumphed in song. At least in the west places like Ibiza were now open to all.

Vicarious Pleasures: 'We Gotta Get Out of this Place'

Music in a variety of forms has provided metaphors for being elsewhere, most obviously where lyrics espoused the delights of travel, and less directly in invocations to sit back, relax and dream of distant pleasures. At least briefly, there were opportunities to capture moments of escape to elsewhere. Album sleeves, such as those of Sam Kailuha or Tacticos, were even more evocative of the pleasures of travel than the tourist fliers that were to succeed them. Remarkably, though tourism now encompasses so many once-distant places, the legacy of virtual tourism lives on (Connell & Gibson, 2004a). Petrol Records' city series, subtitled 'the sex, the city and the music', began in 2002 with Istanbul, Tokyo and Paris; the CD sleeve for Tokyo recommended 'enjoy the sense of discovery as we uncover the charming, quirky, fluid, striking and above all exciting sounds of Tokyo'. A similar Petrol series on various countries, subtitled 'the greatest songs ever', exhorted would-be listeners to 'crank up the volume and let the music take you all over the world'; the Cuba CD stressed that 'Cuba explodes into a Latin frenzy, with a sound born from the fusion of Spanish and African influences. It's idea for creating an energetic party atmosphere'. Six Degrees Records launched its travel series at the same time, with records from most continents including Asia, where the CD *Asian Travels* was advertised as 'music as varied as the Asian diaspora itself'. If invocations to travel were more muted, critics sometimes took up these themes enthusiastically, as in one review of *Chill: Brazil 2* (2003) which observed 'You can almost feel the Copacabana breeze, see the bronzed, G-stringed bottoms and taste the caipiroskas' (*Sun-Herald*, 31 August 2003), while the impact of *Music of Madagascar* (2003) was such that 'you will be totally seduced. You will want to pack your bags and head straight for Madagascar knowing that there, indeed, is a society where the music makes you feel happy to be alive' (*Sydney Morning Herald*, 15 July 2003).

Where music (and album covers and their notes), whether classical or popular, have in some way enjoined travel, they have focused on, and celebrated, a very limited number of iconic places, such as Paris, New York, California, the Grand Canyon and the Taj Mahal and, rather later, generic and real 'natural' spaces, such as Ayers Rock/Uluru or the Rocky Mountains. The Orient was popular before the Vietnam War and its becoming Asia, while the charm of Araby faded as it became the Middle East. All such places were seen through the prism of essentialism, reflecting the rose-tinted gaze of Europeans rather than experiences of reality. Music has consequently emphasised the delights of a handful of special places, and created distorted depictions of them. It may have eventually boosted tourism to these destinations (as it certainly did for Route 66), or may simply have encouraged an urge to travel, but most tourism has always been independent of musical invocation. Indeed once mass tourism began to get underway the simplicities of virtual music tourism were largely replaced.

Every society claims some link between people and place, and invariably some means of expressing this, however loosely, through music, while so many places may be remembered through music, whether as tourism or nostalgia. As one tourist writer has suggested:

> Noise is a vital element of travel, with some sounds instantly associated with certain cities or counties. In Shanghai it is bicycle bells; in Muslim countries the call of the muezzin. In Manila the incessant horn-blowing by jeepney drivers provides a mad mobile orchestra. In New Orleans it's the wail of a sly trombone from behind a shuttered window in the French Quarter. In many Asian countries it's the yowl of karaoke from basement dives. In Paris there's always a suggestion of Piaf singing in the shadows. In Vienna it's Strauss – the whole city moves to the tempo of a waltz – while in Salzburg it's Mozart (unless you're on a Sound of Music bus tour, in which case it's Julie Andrews). (Kurosawa, 2000: 47)

Directly, but more importantly metaphorically,

> The best of popular music acts as a tour guide, visiting not only
> significant places but pertinent times from the past. . . . Rhythm is a
> glue that adheres the jagged spaces of memory . . . the familiar is
> validated and the nostalgic promoted. . . . Between the fluidity of
> melody and a fixity of lyric, a place can be located and remembered
> . . . The craving for rhythm feeds a desire for meaning and memory.
> (Brabazon, 2000: 112)

At the very least there are places in music that offer familiarity, nostalgia,
a sense of difference and a place in which to escape and relax. More
obviously, as the following chapters demonstrate, a variety of other ways
and other places have emerged where actual music tourism exists.

Chapter 3
Musical Landscapes, Tourist Sites

Certain places are so strongly and sometimes uniquely identified with music that they have become tourist sites, in response to new affluence, mobility and nostalgia. This is particularly evident with country music and pop/rock styles and artists of the 1950s and 1960s, though music tourism began with classical music and that legacy has remained. This chapter discusses various places that have become known for, and through, music, and have in different ways seen the emergence of tourism economies connected to musical heritage. Many such sites did indeed come to be associated with artists or musical movements that had their genesis in the 1950s and 1960s, though a significant number of other locations – some predictable, some unexpected – have created tourism economies from associations with music. The chapter begins by examining those locations where successful music was made, before discussing other less obvious places and types of music tourism. The aim is to chart a broad typology of places where music has enabled tourism in different ways, from studios to cemeteries, and examine how some of these have been deliberately transformed into tourist destinations. More detailed discussion of the various issues and themes surrounding these places and forms of tourism – from cultural change and the construction of authenticity to the economic impact of festivals – are taken up in subsequent chapters.

Sites of Creativity

Places where famous recordings were made, that hosted internationally famous music scenes or were the homes of famous composers and performers, have been those where the most commercially successful music tourism industries have emerged. Vivid myths of place are linked to music there, and local identity is partly constructed in relation to unique musical sounds or successful people. Such identifications rely on a sense of 'authenticity' being created in relation to the music and to place, so attracting audiences for a musical style or fans of a performer to experience the social and cultural environment within which that music originated. The resultant tourism assumes that those places are indeed the authentic 'birthplaces' (and intermittently deathplaces) of an artist or style; in many cases particular cities or neighbourhoods had a critical influence on the musicians and the music that was made there. However, the cultural politics of 'authenticity' in music and tourism are more complex, and the 'authenticity' upon which music tourism relies is certainly not uncontested. Those issues are dealt with in greater detail in Chapters 5 and 6.

This chapter initially considers four places where some notions of authenticity are assumed and traded upon: Liverpool, England, and three examples from America's South: New Orleans, Memphis and Nashville. They represent some of the most obvious and well-known cities that host music tourism, hence their transformation (and the issues surrounding them) are discussed in greater detail in later chapters. Each are places of musical creativity and largely share roles as meeting points (often ports), centres of immigration and cultural diversity; all are places where music has played a vital role in civic life, but also where, at different times, those musical heritages have formerly been denounced, ignored or downplayed by city authorities, only to be reinvented when the financial benefits of tourism had become obvious. Both New Orleans and Memphis now rely on districts or precincts associated with vibrant music scenes, and other activities, as the core of tourist industries. With the partial exception of Nashville, all four have experienced the negative impacts of deindustrialisation and economic restructuring, with unemployment and other social problems. Music tourism plays an important role in the revitalisation of these cities, against a backdrop of industrial decay.

The Beatles' Liverpool

The lives, itineraries, songs and stories surrounding John, Paul, George and Ringo have become a multi-million pound industry in the United Kingdom, in particular in Liverpool, their home town and source of the 'Mersey-sound' of the 1960s. Liverpool figured heavily in the music of the Beatles; song titles and lyrical references to actual and mythical sites mapped out what would eventually become a tourist trail: Strawberry Fields, Penny Lane's barber shop, the bank and a shelter in the middle of the roundabout. Indeed, beyond the music itself, part of the success of the Beatles is attributable to their city; being from Liverpool authenticated their music as fresh and original, coming from a northern provincial city (in opposition to supposedly bland southern pop), to create a storm of critical and commercial success in London, New York and elsewhere. The Beatles were always known in relation to Liverpool;

it grounded the band in place, gave them roots amid 'authentic', working class, Scouse-accented, masculine youth culture, and added to the mythology surrounding the band as it went from success to success. This mythology became even more pervasive with the subsequent emergence of The Searchers, Gerry and the Pacemakers and other acts from Liverpool, in the eyes of music critics and fans constituting a 'Mersey sound' that seemed to capture and reflect the city's local culture.

After the 1960s Liverpool experienced significant changes as deindustrialisation diminished the role of heavy industry and port activity. Liverpool's population fell by a third and unemployment rose dramatically. By the 1980s Liverpool's social and economic fabric was effectively in tatters: riots in 1981 spurred government authorities to seek new possibilities for investment, which resulted in a comprehensive (and, at the time, controversial) redevelopment scheme for the docklands area, and a new focus on music and tourism as potential panacea for industrial decline (Cohen, 1991). Liverpool's musical heritage was an obvious focal point for such strategies, and music tourism, primarily related to the Beatles, began in Liverpool in the 1970s (Cohen, 1997), although it was largely confined to one small souvenir shop and occasional tours organised by a group of fans in the area. After John Lennon's death in 1980, interest in visiting Liverpool increased; yet it was only when, in the early 1980s, one individual employee of Liverpool City Council, 'working largely on his own initiative and without the support of his colleagues' began organising a regular Beatles Walk, a guidebook, coach tours and a package weekend, that the city began to capitalise on being the 'birthplace of the Beatles' (Cohen, 1997). At the time, chronic social issues – unemployment, homelessness and poverty – understandably prevented city authorities from diverting core public sector funding away from social welfare programmes towards tourism development. Fifteen years later, after the advent of Thatcherism and the popularity of 'arts as industry' discourse in British local economic development planning, chronic social problems still persisted. Yet the city had now changed tack, and tourism strategies were formalised around the Beatles and musical heritage. As Mike Wilkinson, Head of Liverpool Tourism Arts and Heritage, emphasised:

> The importance of the Beatles, and indeed of the whole of the Mersey sound, cannot be overstated where tourism is concerned . . . . When you ask foreign visitors what they know about the city before they came here, it boils down to football teams and pop groups. Pop related tourism has developed a lot already but there is clearly scope for a great deal more. New Orleans has jazz, we have The Beatles, it's definitely an important way forward. (quoted in Wheeller, 1996: 339)

Beatles heritage is now sold in souvenir shops, in a Museum of Liverpool Life (featuring many Beatles artefacts) and *The Beatles Story*, a museum and interactive display of 'authentic' scenes – such as a replica Cavern Club – the legendary venue where the Beatles began their English career. This venue itself has also been reconstructed (after being demolished, perhaps foolishly, by Liverpool City Council in 1973 to make way for an underground railway construction site), and hosts organised tours and performances. So successful has this been that the owners, Cavern City Tours, announced plans in 2003 to reconstruct identical venues in Australia, the United States, Brazil and Spain.

Beyond direct musical associations, but as an acknowledgement of the importance of this tourist market, Liverpool eventually renamed its airport the John Lennon Airport in 2002, and tourist authorities produced publications linking the various Beatles-related sites (such as Strawberry Fields and Penny Lane), thus integrating music tourism infrastructure in the city. These included a Beatles map of Liverpool, social histories and brochures, some directed at overseas tourists (Figure 3.1) and organised Beatles tours – including the Magical Mystery Tour (see Box 3.1). Local music traditions formed the basis of plans to reshape the city's image to the outside world, generating more cultured representations of place counter to the myths of 'rust' and 'roughness' that accompany industrial decline. There is some debate about the extent to which such efforts have come to fruition (see Chapters 4 and 7), though belatedly Liverpool now recognises and celebrates its musical past, seeking to attract others to the city to 'enter a previous time, culture, world' (Cohen, 1997: 76). It has become one of Europe's major destinations for music tourism, just as music has become an indelible marker of local culture and tradition.

New Orleans

In a remarkably parallel case, but in a quite different historical context, New Orleans, another port city, but in this case the famous 'birthplace of jazz', experienced a major scaling-back of its port facilities and offshore oil industry in the 1980s, prompting city authorities to take tourism and music more seriously. In its heyday it was like no other city in the United States. As Atkinson (1997: 93) described it, New Orleans was

> probably the most Africanised city in the United States ... with its French and Spanish, rather than English, colonial background, its Mediterranean culture and Catholicism, its history of a black majority population, racial ambiguity, and native American integration, it is a part of, yet distinct from, the American South.

Figure 3.1 This flyer translates as follows: 'The popular Liverpool Beatles Tour. The six reasons to tour with us: each tour lasts up to three fulfilling hours – far longer than all the other tours. Receive our free information packs and make it an exciting adventure. Enjoy thorough walks in and around the legendary live house, The Cavern, Matthew Street, and more. Your personal tour guide will ensure every scenic moment is captured on film – even you enthusiasts who have been to Liverpool twice, you have not seen it all. We guarantee you an unforgettable experience!'

Box 3.1
Ticket to ride

Rain descended from dark urban skies as the psychedelic blue and yellow tour bus pulled out of the refurbished Albert Dock in Liverpool. The Magical Mystery Tour – with a mixed bag of old and young, British and foreign (from Japan to Belgium), linked only by some degree of fascination with the Beatles – or perhaps a desire to escape the rain – had begun.

Les at the wheel, and Eddie – our tour guide – were a determined double act, constantly interrupting bursts of Beatles music, with laconic scouse observations, fragments of wit – in which Kylie Minogue, rotweilers, mothers-in-law and Gerry and his pacemaker played a prominent role – and microscopic knowledge of the city.

A hundred metres outside the Dock, a frisson of excitement grips us – a bus to Penny Lane crosses our path. Instant reality: this is the Beatles hometown. Even the rain relented: 'blue suburban skies' at last?

We passed the stadium where Paul McCartney had recently played on the 'Rio to Liverpool' tours, where Stevie Wonder was to play later in the year, but such events were transient and recent. We sought substance: history and heritage.

The Blue Angel Club, where the Beatles played in the 1950s and 1960s, passed by, followed by Brian Epstein's record store (now the Bella Pasta restaurant) and the store next door where George Harrison first worked as an electrician before it all happened. Round the corner was Casey Street – Pete Best's first residence. Pete Best, the drummer displaced by Ringo Starr, still lives in Liverpool and tours with his Pete Best band. Liverpool proved a small place; something seemed to have occurred on every corner.

After other workplaces (the Britannia Adelphi where John's mother worked: no minutiae was allowed to escape us) and clubs, barely recognizable from the heady days of the 1960s, we moved on to more solid ground. That was No. 64, Mount Pleasant – a 19th century terrace, less pleasant now than a century ago – where John Lennon's parents married, and he too had married Cynthia in 1962, with the ring paid for by Auntie Mimi. Camera shutters clicked for the first time.

Liverpool Art College (where John 'failed with honours' each year, as did his first wife Cynthia after she met John), Paul's high school (now the Liverpool Institute of Performing Arts) and a statue to a Liverpool woman, Florence Nightingale, who appeared to have been famous in some other sphere and century, all flickered by as we left the city center for inner suburbia.

The depressing terraces of Dingle, once an area of historic Irish settlement, gave us Ringo's birthplace, the Empress Pub at the end of the street (which featured on the cover of Ringo's first solo album and, in turn, features the Beatles on its façade . . . though none were known to drink there) and St. Silas's primary school – where Ringo shared a class with Billy Fury . . . and Les' wife. We stayed on board: 'in the pouring rain, very strange'.

Houses became larger, trees and parks appeared and suddenly we were in leafy Penny Lane – capturing on film the most photographed street sign in Britain, though it had long been simply painted on the wall, after dozens of metal versions had disappeared . . . . Timed to perfection, a meter maid – surely lovely Rita – went by. Dutifully she waved, we photographed.

At the other more commercial end of the lane, beyond Pete Best's fruit shop, the 'shelter in the middle of a roundabout' had become Sergeant Pepper's Bistro – for this was the epicentre of the tour. The barber too waved – our psychedelic bus demanded it – but though there were no bankers or fire machines – we had found the authentic Liverpool, where Paul created his famous lyrics, while waiting for the eternally late John. It was Getting Better All The Time.

Lyrically we moved onwards, to George Harrison's birthplace – another terrace, where impenetrable lace curtains gave contemporary residents privacy (though they took their holidays during the overkill of the annual Beatles convention week) and inevitably reached Strawberry Field (not Fields) – the former Salvation Army children's home, behind John's Aunt Mimi's home. Graffiti on grimy gate posts testified to the enduring love and global spread of Beatles fans. It was the first place that Yoko Ono brought Sean Lennon after the death of his father. And it was not far from the graveyard where Eleanor Rigby was buried.

Suburbia followed: 251 Menlove Avenue, where John lived in semi-detached anonymity between the ages of 4 and 21 (no 'working class hero' was he), and the present residents had been forced to put up a sign: 'Private, No Admission'. Brian Epstein's nearby detached home put Menlove Avenue in its place. Neither had however become a National Trust property, as had that of Paul McCartney – open 'by appointment only' with a plaque proclaiming National Trust, but no hint of the Beatles – a stately home in terraced miniature. I'm looking through you, perhaps at another time. At least the lace curtains moved; a disembodied hand gave us a thumbs-up. Three doors down the road, an animated toy gorilla did another through the curtains performance: the Magical Mystery tour was clearly on schedule.

At the corner of the street, we identified the bus stop where Paul got on the school bus, and met George. Eddie reminded us, as he did at regular intervals for similar convergences, 'And the rest is . . .'. We were able to call out the missing word and receive our prize, the appropriate Beatles song on the bus speakers.

The reconstructed Cavern Club, our final destination, prompted more nostalgia and more statistics. The Beatles had played there 292 times, and there were 1801 bricks in the new walls, with the names of every performer that had ever played there. We soaked up the statistics; after all we were there for the fine print of the Beatle's lives and world. Definitely not Day Trippers.

There was just time to sign the visitor book (what other buses have visitor books?), time for more lyrics and more clichés – from simply 'magical' to the disappointed 'memories are better than the real thing', or those of dissidents 'Up the Reds' and 'I love Elvis, but it was good anyway'. Otherwise we promised to remember it 'When I'm 64'. After all 'There are Places I'll remember all my life'. A final chorus of Magical Mystery Tour brought our quest for roots and authenticity to an end.

Preserved in a timeless 1960s, the 'people and things that went before' gives a fascinating sense of the urban world that shaped the Beatles – from the mean streets of Dingle and dingy clubland to suburban sterility . . . the intricate networks and real places that stimulated and nurtured a sound, and a band, that took them and Liverpool to the world.

For some this was only a start. After all the Beatles had been here, there and everywhere – in London, Abbey Road (whose road signs meet a similar fate to those of Penny Lane) is similarly engulfed with Beatles fans (though not the annual 500,000 that Liverpool claims are drawn there by the Beatles). Two days later I, at least, was still humming the classic Beatles songs. One of them was 'I'll Follow the Sun'.

Source: John Connell (November 1998)

Situated in an unusual geographical location – between Lake Pontchartrain and the Mississippi River,

> Cultural activities brought in by the Africans, Italians, Spanish and French flourished unchecked in this isolation, and merged with those of the indigenous population to produce rituals and cultural events largely unique to the United States, such as second-line parades, jazz funerals, Mardi Gras Indians, and Carnival. (Atkinson, 1997: 93)

New Orleans had always been a minor tourism destination because it was a major port and a crossroads of cultural influences. New Orleans' long-held reputation was as a city of sin, a notorious place for drinking, gambling, prostitution and jazz. The city long had a tourism economy connected to these possibilities; moreover it was, and still is, a meeting place for migrants, itinerants, seamen and wanderers. Port cities have always performed this function, with red-light districts home to many venues, bars and clubs that became places of musical expression and creativity, as well as places where musical styles and influences were shared or blended in new ways, as at Memphis, San Francisco, Hamburg, Oran and Liverpool (Connell & Gibson, 2003: 103). As early as the mid-18th century, New Orleans was already a tourist destination, well known as 'America's foremost Opera city' (Wade, 1994; Atkinson, 1996), particularly for French opera. By contrast, for decades the association between New Orleans and jazz was downplayed by city authorities for fear of the negative connotations associated with the term (since 'jazz' had its origins as a slang word for sex and was closely linked to the 'wild' and 'unruly' activities of black Americans). In the 1940s, however, these attitudes were reversed; in probably the first example of formalised strategies for music tourism, New Orleans sought to market itself as the 'birthplace of jazz', at just the time that jazz had reached unparalleled popularity internationally, with big band jazz, Dixieland and other more 'white' styles of jazz performance constituting the orthodoxy of 'popular music' (Clarke, 1995). However, these marketing efforts remained conservative, organised around 'safe cultural channels' such as 'traditional jazz museums, archives, newsletters, performance halls and festivals', while the Franco-African dimension of New Orleans music-making and performance, 'still alive in the black neighbourhoods, went unsupported and ignored' (Atkinson, 1997: 95), as a European performance aesthetic of the concert hall prevailed.

By the 1970s, New Orleans sought to become a major centre for convention tourism, linked to the offshore-oil industry, though the collapse of that industry in the 1980s encouraged authorities to look past the less than 'salubrious' reputation of the French Quarter (and of jazz) and embrace the city's musical heritage as part of a wider push into domestic and international visitor markets. New Orleans has since developed a more formalised tourism economy based around its musical heritage, emphasising the city as a place apart, a unique place and one that witnessed the birth of jazz, and was home to Louis Armstrong. As the New Orleans tourist board director has argued, 'Music is integral to our marketing plan. Our theme is "come join the parade" and all our television and radio spots use New Orleans music. The whole spirit of the city is summed up in its music' (quoted in Atkinson, 1997: 96). Of importance in New Orleans' ability to become a music tourism destination has been the presence of a particular district in the city associated with music – the French Quarter – with its heritage architecture, bars, clubs and plentiful open public spaces that clearly mark out tourist space. The Quarter, owned by the French and then Spanish until 1803, was the original setting for New Orleans' red-light district and later gay precinct, and it remains a transgressive part of town; though utterly transformed, the French Quarter has never been wholly sanitised for tourism consumption, as has perhaps happened in other places (such as Times Square in Manhattan, New York, after its transformation by Disney Inc. in the 1990s). Nonetheless, music is a formal tourist attraction in New Orleans, and the French Quarter is where the vast majority of visitors flock to hear and see jazz. (Sting, the former singer of English group The Police, assisted through his popular song 'Moon Over Bourbon Street', with its jazz clarinet solos from Wynton Marsalis, marking the song, and New Orleans, with a sultry jazz air. The famous James Bond film *Live and Let Die* (1973) that opened dramatically with a jazz funeral, provided earlier valuable marketing.) Heritage, food, music, alcohol and sex combine in the French Quarter to create the ideal 'authentic' site of music tourism. Descriptions by travel writers thus wax lyrical about its atmosphere:

> It's a heady mix of bars, bonhomie and jazz, of fused cultures, of streets full of quaint French-inspired architecture, of expensive antique stores … of restaurant after restaurant offering the local delicacies – Cajun and Creole shrimp, crawfish, catfish, gumbo and jambalaya – and the mysteries and secrets of the voodoo. (Wockner, 2001: 12).

The French Quarter's reputation serves two purposes – it attracts tourists seeking excitement and nocturnal activities, but it also maintains the claim to authenticity that connects music to place – it legitimises its transgressive air (cf. Dimanche & Lepetic, 1999; see Chapter 5). Beyond the music, tourism is also now very big business in New Orleans – the city has over 30,000 hotel beds, and significant proportions of the city's economy and employment are now linked to tourism, but the benefits are not uncontested. Over the same period that tourism boomed poverty has increased and the urban population has declined, alongside white flight and increased racial segregation (Gotham, 2002). Over the century since jazz was first played in the city, New Orleans has reinvented itself, and reoriented itself towards a tourism that plays upon its musical past.

Memphis

If New Orleans represents an iconic example of a commercial tourist industry linked to musical heritage, it is not alone in America's South. Scattered in the broad region spanning an arc from Louisiana in the south to Virginia in the north-east are other places with rich musical histories. Many have given rise to tourism industries linked to music. Memphis is famous as a centre for rhythm and blues, soul, and as the 'birthplace of rock 'n' roll', linked to Elvis Presley, who recorded his first hits at Sun Studios and lived most of his life in the Graceland mansion. The city's musical past is, much like that of New Orleans, linked to its geography, as a crossroads, situated on the Mississippi River and at the meeting point of major travel routes between the east, Chicago and St Louis in the north, Texas in the west and the Gulf of Mexico in the south. It became, almost by default, a centre for the delta blues, a style of music adapted from African traditions by labourers in the region's cotton-fields. Delta blues provided an early sphere of solidarity and expression for musicians and audiences alike, and an occupation that allowed respite from dreadful working conditions (Hall, 1998: 570). Many of the earliest blues songs, by artists such as Robert Johnson, Son House and Skip James, articulated intimate attachments and reactions to physical places; migratory and transient experiences were littered throughout blues songs dedicated to themes of escape, travelling and leaving home. By the turn of the century, black workers who had migrated from across the Delta had taken up residence in the low-rent housing on and around Beale Street, to the south of Memphis' downtown, a precinct that by the 1920s was a major social centre for black communities throughout the South. As Perry and Glinert (1996: 128) describe it, 'The city's black businesses were segregated into surrounding side streets, and all manner of vaudeville theaters, clubs, juke joints, and gambling houses had sprung up. By day guitarists would busk along Beale, while at night the area swung to a sophisticated big-band kind of blues'. Beale Street, like New Orleans' French Quarter, held a reputation for vice, gambling, prostitution and sin: 'The respectable black citizens of Memphis, every bit as dedicated to their churches as their white neighbours, viewed Beale Street with God-fearing suspicion. They most definitely wanted to keep their daughters as far as possible from its dens of sin' (Werner, 1998: 62). Segregation was extreme in the only state in the union with a black majority (Hall, 1998: 554, 559), but especially in Memphis which had a reputation for violence and debauchery.

By the 1940s, jazz and blues musicians had migrated north, along with a substantial proportion of the South's black population, seeking more sympathetic communities and better-paid work in cities such as Chicago, Detroit and New York. Many musicians moved into Memphis during this period, on their way northwards, triggering a revival on Beale Street, which had suffered during the Depression. The resulting musical mixture created rhythm and blues (R & B) from a combination of blues scales, up-tempo jazz beats and electric amplification. Memphis' function as a crossroads also enabled a vast array of musical styles to emerge; by the

1950s blues, jazz, hillbilly, folk, bluegrass and other country styles could be all heard in the city. At the same time, deeply segregationist politics, entrenched by the manipulative city mayor, Edward 'Boss' Crump (who reigned for over five decades in Memphis, at times with black support), meant that Memphis had a tense social environment, with harsh enforcement of racial segregation, entrenched private (white) business interests and endemic racism. In this environment, ground-breaking hybrid musical forms emerged, partly because it was a place where cultures came together, but also because music had the potential to resist and negotiate discrimination more effectively than formal politics. A hybrid, transgressive air surrounded the city's music, as Gordon (1995: 2) has argued:

> The evil behind that word ['niggers'] lives and breathes in Memphis. The city was built on that word. Rock and roll was a response to that word. Rock and roll rejected the idea of enforced segregation, mixing cultures as it mixed musical genres. On the streets today, the populations mix, but it's a surface politeness, a charming civic trait. Oppression is not unique to Memphis, though it is neatly encapsulated here. It's the sort of environment where great art develops in obscurity. The ideas are strong because, like weeds growing in a concrete sidewalk, the must force themselves through.

Somewhat ironically, it took a white performer, schooled in the finesse of blues, but with a parallel heritage in country music, to capitalise on this atmosphere and creative intensity. Elvis Presley's rise to fame, from Tupelo and the Sun Studios in Memphis to Las Vegas, has been discussed in detail elsewhere (Guralnick, 1994; Gordon, 1995; Hall, 1998). In Memphis, par excellence, the success of one individual transformed the public image of a place forever: it is now virtually impossible to think about, or read about, Memphis without some reference to Elvis. The story of the 'birth of rock 'n' roll' in Memphis is, however, much more than just this one man's music; the city became a centre of creation, production and recording, with a trail of famous artists following in Elvis's footsteps to Sam Phillips's Sun Studios and nearby American Studios, complementing those black musicians already established in the city's musical scene:

> Memphis's impact on white pop music was equally profound. Penn and Moman's American Studio became a Mecca for a range of singers that have little in common except that they made their best records in Memphis: Neil Diamond, Dionne Warwick, Lulu, the Box Tops, the Sweet Inspirations, Dusty Springfield, Bobby Womack, B.J. Thomas, James and Bobby Purify, jazzman Herbie Mann . . . . (Werner, 1998: 74)

A revival in Beale Street accompanied the early days of this success, though it was sadly short-lived. Police crackdowns in the 1950s resulted in the closure of its clubs and gambling dens; the area remained depressed and, after the riots that followed Martin Luther King's assassination in Memphis in 1968, made worse by the recession of the 1970s, Beale Street was effectively razed to the ground (see Chapter 5). Musicians continued to work beyond racial lines – most notably with the emergence and success of Stax records in the 1960s, with its vibrant southern soul sound made famous by Isaac Hayes, Otis Redding and Wilson Pickett, all backed by their multiracial house band, Booker T and the MGs – although musical activity virtually ground to a halt in the 1970s and 1980s. Consolidation of Memphis' independent record labels within the publishing and distribution empires of larger companies, as well as poor signing decisions and heightened race relations in Memphis itself, all contributed to the downfall. In 1976 Stax went bankrupt, and in 1989 the converted art-deco cinema that was Stax Studios was demolished 'to make way for a soup kitchen' (Rodman, 1996: 109).

Twenty years later, in contrast to this history of general disregard for black musical heritage, Memphis belatedly embraced its past, in part fuelled by necessity – the city lagged behind other regional centres in prosperity and economic development – and began to promote itself as a centre for blues, R & B and rock 'n' roll music. Memphis naturally claimed Elvis Presley (discussed in more detail later in this chapter), and also recast itself as a more general home of American music, given the many artists, from B.B. King, Ma Rainey and W.C. Handy to Isaac Hayes, who found success there. The city is now designated 'Home of the blues, birthplace of rock 'n' roll', according to the Memphis Convention and Visitors Bureau.

Music-related tourism began soon after Elvis's death in 1977, with the founding of Elvis Presley Enterprises in the same year for Lisa Marie Presley to manage the Graceland mansion and her father's estate. Meanwhile, the renovation of Beale Street took shape in the early 1980s, opening for tourists in 1983. Much criticism was made of the resulting tourist landscape in Beale Street that replaced the so-called 'black main street of America' (see McKee & Chisenhall, 1981; Brown, 1993: 53; this is discussed further in Chapter 5). Other subsequent attractions and renovations, including the still active Sun Studios (see p. 63) and the Centre for Southern Folklore, were undertaken with a more careful and subtle attitude towards heritage. Aside from debates over the cultural impact of music tourism in Memphis, it has taken on an unprecedented scale in recent years, with the construction of shopping malls, museums and hotels, both in Beale Street and adjacent to Graceland; the Memphis Pyramid (a 32-storey edifice facing the Mississippi River), host to the

American Music Awards Hall of Fame, as well as a plethora of smaller attractions including the Memphis Rock 'n' Soul Museum, B.B. King Blues Bar and Soulsville USA, a museum, performance centre and community outreach facility located on the site of the original Stax Record Studios. Within Soulsville is the Stax Museum of American Soul Music and the Stax Music Academy for inner city youth. Memphis is also now a location for major festivals, including Elvis Week in August on the anniversary of his death, with some 75,000 fans attending. Memphis well exemplifies a place that has at various times oppressed segments of its population, inadvertently created the conditions for extraordinary levels of creativity, failed to preserve important sites associated with that musical history, but has also belatedly commodified musical heritage as part of tourism campaigns.

Nashville

Nashville, Tennessee, has also become a major tourism destination in the American South, in this case based on its famous country 'sound', though its musical history is somewhat shorter than that of Memphis. Although Nashville always maintained a healthy music scene, it only began to capitalise on its reputation as 'the home of country music' after business interests and the major labels centralised activities in the city during the 1950s (Cusic, 1994). Despite a reputation as the capital of the country music world, Nashville has been important to the growth of music across many genre boundaries, serving as a focal point for blues, R & B, rockabilly and hillbilly. Its association with country music goes back to the beginning of the Grand Ole Opry show, first broadcast on WSM Radio in 1927, although the actual term 'country music' was not then widespread. The show, originally broadcast from the Ryman Auditorium in downtown Nashville, became the longest running show in American music history. (The Opry was later moved to its present location within the Opryland theme park, though the latter was replaced by the Opry Mills shopping mall complex.) By the 1930s, Nashville had become a country music centre, a reputation solidified in the 1950s with the emergence of a 'Nashville sound'. The Nashville sound stripped down instrumentation and smoothed out the rough edges of hillbilly styles, but, as Blair & Hyatt (1992: 71) argued, 'What country music did retain was its emphasis on simplicity, heartfeltness and sincerity'. The 'Nashville sound' is generally described as a blend of country and accessible rock ballads: 'somewhat mellow . . . it is not nasal or twangy, and does not include a steel guitar, fiddle or banjo' (Blair & Hyatt, 1992: 71). Nashville's sound became recognisable, not so much because musicians gravitated towards a particular style, or because features of Nashville's physical or cultural landscapes suggested certain musical accompaniments, but because various session musicians recorded a string of famous songs during the city's boom years in the late 1940s and early 1950s:

> Actually the Nashville 'sound' was the jingling of money in the pocket – as Chet Atkins has wryly pointed out – because these musicians were economical . . . . The 'Nashville sound' became a buzzword to describe country music in general and though the term could never really be explained by those inside the industry, it served as a handy, convenient term for journalists and others in the media to hang on to when discussing country music. The result was a built-in promotion for Nashville every time country music was discussed. (Cusic, 1994: 48, 53)

Since then the city has attracted millions of visitors, keen to see the home of this now highly internationalised genre, to bootscoot, line-dance or visit some of the various museums, performers' homes and souvenir shops. Nashville has been shaped by music and, somewhat different from New Orleans, Memphis and Liverpool, has become a city of the music industry itself, with recruiting and publishing offices built for the recording companies, and whole districts specifically catering to the industry. Thus, what the other cities could not achieve in sustaining a vibrant and dynamic music industry, Nashville was able to do because it fostered a cluster of publishing firms, record labels, recording studios, and management and promotional companies, effectively monopolising country music business activities. Unlike the other major music tourism cities, Nashville has also not suffered from critical economic restructuring and shifts in domestic economic conditions; indeed, somewhat in contrast to Liverpool, New Orleans and Memphis, Nashville has become a 'sunbelt' city, with a growing population and an economy connected with high-tech, publishing and information industries.

Somewhat distinct geographically from Nashville's music industry is country music tourism. In addition to the Ryman Auditorium, open for daily tours and occasional concerts, the famous 'Music Row' includes the commercial glitz of the Country Music Hall of Fame. Nashville's 'Music Valley', centred on the Opryland complex, as well as hosting the Grand Ole Opry, has museums, souvenir shops and cafés, and one of the world's largest hotels, built around an interior landscape of mammoth proportions, replete with faux-Southern streetscapes, canals, lush tropical plants and shops (see Chapter 4). Nashville's tourism economy was given greater vitality following the revival of country music in the 1990s, led by popular 'cross-over' acts such as Garth Brooks, Shania Twain and The Dixie Chicks. Synonymous with the genre's re-entry into the mainstream charts was an ever-increasing number of tourists making their way through Nashville as part of road tours, or visiting specific sites associated with country music. Linked to this is a complex cultural politics of tourism, music and identity, one result of which was the emergence of music-making in Branson, Missouri, a town that claimed to be closer to the true country tradition than Nashville (see p. 101). While Memphis has attempted to reflect its mixture of black and white musical heritage in tourism, in Nashville country music, and much of the tourism supporting this, evokes particular versions of 'whiteness', and a set of conservative ideologies surrounding rural, Southern attitudes. Such issues are discussed in greater depth in Chapter 6.

Sites of Production: Recording Studios

The four cities discussed above represent the largest scale examples of popular music tourism: cities whose whole identities are linked to musical histories in unequivocal ways and which have used those associations to launch economic development strategies based around music tourism. These cities, and other much smaller places, trade on similar associations – as places of creativity and production – particularly through recording studios, promoted as 'authentic' locales where timeless music was made.

The attention granted to recording studios as places of production, and thus, as tourism sites, belies the 'apparatus' that enables recorded music to be produced and distributed. As many commentators on the music industry have argued (see, for example, Aksoy, 1992; Sadler, 1997; McLeay, 1998), the industry involves a whole chain of production, from the artist to final recording, and includes a myriad of players, from music publishers, venue booking agents, artist and repertoire (A & R) staff, recording engineers, record producers, advertisers, graphic designers, artist managers, to record company executives. The process that occurs in a recording studio is just one of a set of activities associated with producing and distributing a record, that involve various cultural gatekeepers, each potentially influencing the sound, image, publicity material and track listing of a release. Moreover, as Sanjek (1998: 173) has argued, 'Today, the music business is but one element of a global media economy and cannot be examined apart from other industries with which it is integrated'. Music production is linked to movies, television shows, computer games and sporting events. Thus, somewhat unsurprisingly, when recording studios become tourist attractions – because they are seen as the places where a record was 'made' – less glamorous and visible elements of the production process are ignored or downplayed.

Unlike other elements in the production process, recording studios are concrete spaces where it is possible to imagine (in perhaps a romanticised way, often assisted by films and videos), musicians experimenting, toiling with their art and inspiration to produce the final product. Studios are more permanent reminders of an important stage in the production process, and myths and images of recording have turned them into seminal spaces, each with their own harmonic qualities of reverberation, echo and silence. Musicians have repeatedly argued that there is an inexplicable 'magic' to certain recording rooms, which has drawn them, time and again, to particular studios. Consequently, some of the more famous recording studios have taken on an importance as tourist sites, through their associations with famous recordings. None is probably more well known than London's Abbey Road.

Beatles tourism has expanded in many other places beyond Liverpool where the band spent its early years, with the band's tours, recording sessions and reputation providing the catalyst for many tourist initiatives. In London, Beatles 'sites' are incorporated into an international tourism market that is a major income-earner in the capital, absorbed as one small part of the unofficial 'circuit' traversed by tourists, along with the Tower of London, Big Ben and Buckingham Palace. Abbey Road Studios, made famous through the Beatles's album of the same name (and the famous image of the four band members using the nearby zebra pedestrian crossing) is now celebrated on postcards, T-shirts, and replica street signs. At Abbey Road Studios, souvenir hawkers encourage visitors to scribble their messages to the Beatles on the whitewashed walls; many contain religious overtones, linked to love and pilgrimage, and are testimony to the diversity of places from which visitors have come (Figure 3.2):

> I have been waiting 20 years for this moment. John, Paul, George and Ringo you have touched my life forever. From New York to London, I have finally made it.
> Lennon is God.
> The Beatles will never die as long as the Abbey [Road Studios] lives.
> (Graffiti, Abbey Road Studios, London, 1998)

Abbey Road, a site of pilgrimage and production, thus captures in physical space a musical period, a band, and more than a generation's memories and meanings, long after the Beatles' career had concluded.

The Abbey Road Studios have refused to transform the complex into a tourist attraction; the studios remain active and are considered to be one of the highest quality production and mastering locations in the world (for anything from popular music to the Royal Philharmonic Orchestra). The actual recording spaces themselves are concealed from the public – hence the tourist scene surrounds Abbey Road rather than invades it, constituting an informal, but nonetheless powerful drawcard for international and domestic tourists. However, a number of websites are devoted to the Abbey Road Studios, offering virtual tours of the complex (e.g. www.abbeyroad.co.uk) and stressing the significance of

Figure 3.2 Abbey Road Studios have become a mecca for Beatles fans, as well as now being part of the wider mainstream tourist network in London. Yet the actual studios, still used by the recording industry, remain closed to the public. Instead, surrounding walls have become shrines to the Beatles, with visitors scrawling graffiti messages in numerous languages, before taking a stroll for a photograph across the famous zebra crossing, as featured on the cover of the 1969 LP of the same name. (Photographs by courtesy of Chris Gibson and John Connell)

Abbey Road for the Beatles (e.g. www.webhome.idirect.com/~faab/AbbeyRoad/main), and linking up to London Beatles walks. The latter website gives a remarkable LiveCam view of the famous Abbey Road crossing.

Studios in Memphis, Nashville, Berlin and elsewhere have similarly become tourist attractions. Memphis was host to a series of recording studios that had a major impact on the popular music industry worldwide: Sun Studios, where Elvis recorded his early hits, eventually became one of the city's important musical resources, still active as a studio, but also connected to tourism through organised tours and a gift shop. Tourists can even record their own efforts there. RCA's Studio B, in Nashville, where a string of famous hits was recorded by artists such as the Everly Brothers, Roy Orbison and Dolly Parton, has similarly become an attraction, included in the admission price to the nearby Country Music Hall of Fame. Across genres, from blues and soul to country, recording studios have become destinations due to their status as points of origin for famous cultural artefacts.

In the 1960s too, Hitsville USA – the house of producer Berry Gordy – became famous as the place where the Motown (MotorTown) sound was created in Detroit (Connell & Gibson, 2003: 97–99). As a recording studio and production facility, it better resembled a family-scale production line: 'Musicians hung out at Hitsville at all hours of the day and night. When a song was ready to be recorded, whoever happened to be around chipped in. No one minded being called out of bed to contribute a riff or lay down another take' (Werner, 1998: 21). Where Memphis' music captured the chaos and raw hybridity of its interracial conspirators, and also ended up as a release valve of sorts for the sexual tension of the times, Motown constituted a much more constrained example of black expression, in an orchestrated and more calculated form of musical production.

The studios have remained the only visible, concrete remnant of the Motown era; indeed, when Motown officially relocated to the West Coast in 1972, 'in large part because of Berry Gordy's interest in the film industry – the magic stayed in Detroit. Motown became, in Nelson George's words, 'just another record company'' (Werner, 1998: 167). The site of production for the Motown sound – Hitsville USA – has remained a tourist icon, the space of production turned visitor attraction. It reopened to the general public in 1985, housing the not-for-profit Motown Historical Museum and an educational programme, and has since expanded into adjacent buildings to house a full tribute to the label and producers. According to Perry and Glinert (1996: 192), 'the key attraction is the tiny 20-by-15-foot Studio A, where the vast majority of Motown's hits were recorded'. Faithfully preserved with instruments and microphones in place, 'it really does look like it's been untouched for over two decades', hence grounding the authenticity of the music in physical space.

Many other recording studios have adopted some measure of tourist appeal; Fame Recording Studios, in Muscle Shoals, Alabama, trades on the phrase 'Where It All Started' because of its long (over 40 years) and continuing recording history in soul and R & B, including hits by Little Richard, Aretha Franklin, Wilson Pickett and Clarence Carter. The nearby spin-off studio, Muscle Shoals Sound, established by disgruntled ex-employees of the original Fame Studios, went on to record Paul Simon, the Rolling Stones, Rod Stewart and Bob Dylan. It, too, is included in tourist guidebooks. In Ireland, younger tourists often include Windmill Lane Studios, where many U2 albums were recorded, as part of holidays in Dublin. As at Abbey Road, the studio walls (and surrounding streets) have become graffiti murals, filled with dedications to the band and other markings of pilgrimage. A newer generation of fans have become music tourists. It remains to be seen whether, with the increasing trend towards home production, and the proliferation of digital recording and mastering suites, newer artists and their studios might also become tourist locations.

Places of Performance

Rather like recording studios, places of performances have also become tourist sites, especially when they are still used for performances (and overtly targeted at tourist audiences) or linked to great eras of the past. Some places of performance are associated with particular musical styles or artists (Nashville's Grand Ole Opry, Liverpool's Cavern Club, Milan's La Scala Opera House); others are simply famous architectural sites, splendours in themselves as much as places of performance (such as the Sydney Opera House, perhaps the best-known and most popular tourist destination in Australia, but poorly designed for opera in a city not famed for this), or Singapore's Esplanades: Theatres on the Bay, which opened in 2002, nicknamed the 'durian fruit' complex because the architecture resembles a local tropical fruit, where diverse international acts perform in a deliberately avant-garde acoustic space. In Vietnam, Hanoi's elegant opera house is modelled after that of Paris. Certain international cultural hubs are lucky enough to have several examples of world-famous venues, places that tourists have heard of and are keen to visit such as London's Royal Festival Hall, Covent Garden, Royal Opera House and Royal Albert Hall. New York does better than most, with Carnegie Hall, an elegant concert space which opened in 1891 (with Tchaikovsky conducting) and later became a famous blues and popular music venue before once again reverting back to a predominantly classical calendar of events in the 1990s; the grand art-deco spaces of the Radio City Music Hall; Harlem's Apollo Theatre, America's most famous black venue and host to a Wednesday Amateur Night that would be won at various times by the Ronettes, Jimi Hendrix and the Jackson Five; the Metropolitan Opera; the celebrated stadium rock venue Madison Square Garden, location of many a 1970s live album; as well as many smaller, but no less famous venues: the original Blue Note jazz club; Café Wha?, where Jimi Hendrix was famously discovered; CBGBs and Max's Kansas City, the original venues of punk music in the 1970s; and Studio 54, the legendary disco club of the 1970s that inspired its own feature film 20 years later. Many of these venues serve resident New Yorkers, but they are also increasingly popular among tourists, listed in guidebooks, producing flyers for distribution in hotel lobbies, and occasionally putting on organised tours. All this is buttressed by New York's stage show industry, focused on Broadway at Times Square, where musicals are increasingly targeted to tourist audiences.

Of particular significance here are the various European centres that have marketed themselves as cities of classical music performance and become key destinations in tourism itineraries. Thus, in the Smetana Hall in Prague, named after Bohemia's most famous composer, according to the Lonely Planet Guide, classical concerts form 'a fine soundtrack to the city's visual delights' (King & Nebesky, 1997: 257). Yet Prague is much more than Smetana; since the Velvet Revolution in 1989 it has become a booming tourist town, in no small part linked to its musical past. Mozart reputedly wrote *Don Giovanni* while resident at Villa Bertramka (now the Bertramka Mozart Museum). The city has managed to acquire diverse trappings of Mozart tourism; visitors to Prague quickly became familiar with the endless stream of 'sweaty Mozarts', as Skřivánková (2001: 26) described the costumed flyer-touts promoting classical music concerts in Prague's Old Town Square. Prague's Stavovské ('Estates') Theatre, where 'Don Giovanni' was first performed in 1787 (with Mozart conducting), has become a regular venue for Mozart performances aimed specifically at the city's burgeoning tourist market (as has the dedicated Opera Mozart Theatre), while all manner of performances are held in churches, particularly chamber concerts, deliberately aimed at tourists. These have prompted Czech government officials to consider applying a system of standards for the quality of performances, as many events have been seen as slap-dash attempts to lure in the tourist dollar rather than genuine classical concerts. (At many such performances, tickets to classical concerts can be as much as 600% higher for international visitors than for Czechs, a situation true also in Russia.)

Vienna has long held a reputation for classical music, and has been a tourist city of sorts since the 18th century, as the grand urban centre of the Austro-Hungarian empire, attracting composers from all over Europe to write and perform there. As one travel writer noted:

> Vienna is a city full of ghosts who live on through their music. The day before I had seen the building where Haydn gave his last concert . . . which is next to the church where the young Schubert sang in the choir . . . which is a stone's throw from the house where Mozart wrote *The Marriage of Figaro* . . . which is just around the corner from the site of the apartment where he composed *The Magic Flute* and his *Requiem* and where he died . . . which is not far from the flat where Schumann lived for a while . . . which is close to the tram stop which takes you to Beethoven's house . . . . The connections go on and on. (Pritchard, 1999: 8)

Now marketed all over the world as a place to visit for classical music and opera, Vienna has both a distinct historical association with music and a vast range of civic spaces that enable it to stage events year round, legacies of the city's imperial past, including famous venues such as the the Konzerthaus; the Musikverein, home to the world famous Wiener Philharmoniker (Vienna Philharmonic Orchestra); the Burgkapelle, home to the Wiener Sängerknaben (Vienna Boy's Choir); Wiener Volksoper and Wiener Kammeroper (Chamber Opera), a reconstructed Staatsoper (state opera house); as well as many other smaller venues, including churches and cafés. Vienna is marketed as a city of music. It hosts a series of renowned classical music and opera festivals, is also home to one of Europe's most vibrant gay and lesbian scenes (now a feature of a specific marketing campaign that emphasises musical attractions), and draws Europeans from surrounding countries to its well-known dance clubs, in part linked to the international success of Viennese electronic musicians such as Kruder and Dorfmeister, with their distinct new-jazz sound.

Further west in Austria, Salzburg, also an artistic destination in the 1800s because of its surrounding landscapes, has made the most of its status as Mozart's birthplace (and also of its status as the film locale for *The Sound of Music* (1965), starring Julie Andrews (see Hoffmann, 2001). Linz, birthplace of Anton Bruckner, now runs walking tours of the composer's life (as well as hosting the annual Bruckner Festival). More than any other nation, Austria can lay claim to be the predominant national destination for music tourism.

Elsewhere in Europe numerous cities have stakes in music tourism. Budapest restored its State Opera House and is similarly taking advantage of its Gothic architecture and elegance to market classical music; while Venice's baroque and operatic traditions are now tourism attractions, with regular performances delivered in *costume d'epoca* (period costumes) to visitors (flyers for which are distributed around the city in Italian, English and German) (Figure 3.3). Including occasional performances of Vivaldi's (a native of Venice) work, the music scene in Venice itself is wholly wedded to the past and to tourism, unlike the more vibrant contemporary scene of Mestre and the mainland. Many German towns offer musical festivals. None are more controversial than the Wagner Festival at Bayreuth, where 600,000 people compete annually for 60,000 tickets to the Ring Cycle; Wagner's strident German nationalism and his anti-Semitism made him a symbol of Aryan might for the Nazis, and Bayreuth became a Nazi centre to the extent that debate remains over the appropriateness of listening to Wagner's music and even attending the festival. Wagner himself designed the operas to be heard in a festival setting, with time for listeners to wander the parklands between acts, while 'nine of his operas have rustic pastoral settings, with actors silhouetted against geological foundations, forests, vistas of undulating terrain for pilgrimages, or raging seas, all visually believable scenery' (Sternberg, 1998: 327). Leipzig is home to St Thomas's church, where J.S. Bach was composer and organist for 27 years, and Mendelssohn House, where the composer Felix wrote many of his later works, is also open to the public; the city also has a Musikinstrumentum

Figure 3.3 Venice flyer

Museum, with a global coverage, and the dungeons of the 15th-century Morirtzbastei Castle host popular music concerts. Russia too supports a vibrant musical scene from the Bolshoi Ballet to the State Kremlin Palace in Moscow and the Mariinsky Theatre in St Petersburg, home of the Kirov Ballet. Finland not surprisingly maintains Sibelius's house, north of Helsinki, and a museum in Turku, while in Norway, Grieg's house is similarly famous. The list is almost endless.

Exceptionally certain spaces of performance have come to characterise particular places. Manaus in the heart of Amazonia is famous for just one thing, its Opera House, constructed in the 1890s at the height of the Brazilian rubber boom (Figure 3.4). Portuguese rubber barons built the thousand-seat Opera House with expensive material imported from Europe and it opened in 1896 with a programme of miscellaneous Italian opera excerpts. One unique feature was the rubber roadway outside so that late arrivals would not disturb those already inside. No more than a decade later the end of the boom saw its decline, but it was refurbished before its centenary as a working concert hall. Although José Carreras performed at its centenary and the Amazon Symphony Orchestra are based there, concerts are relatively rare, despite subsidies for cultural development in the Amazonas region. In a vast region with few, if any, other buildings of distinction, it is, however, a major tourist destination.

Figure 3.4 Manaus Opera House (Photograph by courtesy of Gary Cook: www.garycook.co.uk)

Places of performance are not only grand buildings or exotic clubs, such as the Privilege club in Ibiza that can cater for 10,000 visitors. Sites of festivals, notably Woodstock, have similarly become destinations, even though there may be little to see: places of nostalgia and pilgrimage (see Chapter 7).

Show Towns

Destinations such as Vienna, Memphis, Woodstock and especially Venice are places that trade on history; although all have contemporary concerts, part of music tourism is nostalgically tied to the past and even to architectural splendours. By contrast, a series of places have more recently emerged, sometimes solely for that purpose, where music plays a part in contemporary tourism but without overt links to a past scene. Las Vegas is perhaps the quintessential such destination – a place virtually without a musical heritage (despite the latter days of Elvis Presley), where other parts of the world (including the Eiffel Tower and the Egyptian pyramids) have been replicated as pastiche and where grand shows are integral to tourism:

> Fun City? Sin City? Las Vegas, with its 24/7 of glamour, glitz and gambling is different things to different people . . . . Headlining nightly shows at the hotels are the cream of American showbiz: singers, dancers, comedians, magicians . . . . In Vegas the spirit of Elvis is everywhere, from statues to poker machines featuring the King's portrait, to an Elvis museum complete with impersonator and memorabilia including the original blue suede shoes . . . . Thinning the ranks of casino players in the evenings are many stage spectaculars, starring showbiz topliners as well as ever – popular Vegas veterans, such as singer Wayne Newton. . . . [or] *La Femme*, featuring 13 sinuous female dancers from Paris and *Spirit of the Dance*, a footstomping Irish show. (Shrimpton, 2003)

The glitz and glamour of Las Vegas were enhanced through a series of films (such as *Ocean's 11*) and songs (and the movie) such as Elvis's 'Viva Las Vegas' ('Bright lights city gonna set my soul on fire'), and it is his legacy and music that is remembered (unlike the version of the song recorded by the Dead Kennedys or Sheryl Crow's 'Leaving Las Vegas', both of which saw a troubled city). Ironically the index of Gottdiener *et al.*'s sociological account of *Las Vegas* (1999) has seven references to Elvis Presley but none to music! There is a statue of Elvis and his guitar in the lobby of the hotel where he performed, poker machines where three Elvises win the jackpot and the Elvis-A-Rama Museum, with guitars, blue suede shoes, three daily live shows by Elvis impersonators and non-stop video clips. Las Vegas also has the Liberace Museum, which houses 18 of his 39 pianos and his white llama fur coat with its five-metre train. Nonetheless, Las Vegas remains the dominant contemporary city of performance rather than a place of production.

On a totally different scale, numerous holiday resorts, such as those of the British coast, have been closely identified with a range of musical events. Almost a third of all tourists to Blackpool rated entertainment as the most important attraction, ranging from variety shows and talent quests to musicals and ballet, in facilities varying from the 3000-seat Opera House to open-air events on the beach (Hughes & Benn, 1998). Around the Mediterranean, clubbing has totally transformed a handful of destinations from Ibiza to Ayia Napa (see Chapter 6). In quite different ways, summer holidays are inseparable from musical entertainment.

In a more specialised way, several towns in the United States have similarly devoted themselves to music performance. The Missouri town of Branson, about 500 kilometres west of Nashville in the Ozark Mountains and once a local rural resort town, became a regional and later national centre of country and western music after 1959, when a series of music venues were constructed along Highway 76 ('The Strip' or '76 Country Boulevard') dedicated to 'the preservation of Ozark country music' (Carney, 1994: 20) and subsequently to creating venues for veteran artists. Eventually, stars such as Loretta Lynn, Kenny Rogers and Charley Pride invested in the town. By the 1990s for some 'Branson has become the "Toyota" of the country music industry (i.e. it's a great copy, less expensive and more efficient') (Carney, 1994: 25). For others its rapid, unplanned growth made it the 'Las Vegas of country music' (Cook, 1993: 2). Within three decades, a town of less than 4000 people was attracting over four million tourists a year.

The success of Nashville and Branson in attracting tourists led others to copy the formula. In 1998 Virginia and Tennessee Representatives applauded the passage by the United States Senate of legislation that designated the twin cities of Bristol as the official 'Birthplace of Country Music', largely on the basis that phonograph recordings there in 1927 launched the careers of the Carter family and Jimmie Rodgers. As the Virginia Representative noted: 'Tourism holds great promise for our region, and this federal recognition will not only assist our efforts to preserve our cultural heritage but will also boost our efforts to attract a larger share of the traveling public to the region' (Jenkins & Boucher, 1998: 1). Elsewhere, towns such as Myrtle Beach, South Carolina and Pigeon Forge in Tennessee (the birthplace of Dolly Parton) encouraged country music stars to build theatres (as Alan Jackson, Alabama and Louise Mandrell did) and embraced Dollywood, a theme park dedicated to the town's most famous citizen. Pigeon Forge's official website in March 2003 proclaimed itself bursting with springtime excitement – from the international pageantry of Dollywood's Festival of Nations to the homespun appeal of annual events like the city's Mountain Quiltfest and Smoky Mountain Traditions . . . . Even history is fun on a Pigeon Forge family vacation with entertaining and educational exhibits on display at Carbo's Police Museum, Dinosaur Walk Museum, Elvis Museum, National Freedom Museum and the Smoky Mountain Car Museum . . . . The city's theaters present all styles of music, high-energy dancing and magical illusions. You'll see amazing horsemanship, racing ostriches, mind reading pigs, fire-eaters, jugglers and the best Elvis impersonator this side of Graceland! (www.mypigeonforge.com)

By then the town was getting as many as 11 million tourists a year. Country music was the primary catalyst for both tourism and the expansion of a handful of towns that could claim some semblance of links to a music scene. That expansion, and its dependence on country music and older tourists (see Chapters 4 and 6), has been a particularly American phenomenon.

Other towns have also established themselves as festival sites so successfully, as in the case of Aldeburgh (England), that music performance, even seasonally, has come to shape the local economy (see Chapter 7). Much smaller places, such as Glyndebourne (England), have been defined by their musical programmes, although the house and its gardens are open throughout the year. In a quite different context, and a different cultural setting, the Japanese city of Takarazuka, the 'city of music', is a remarkable and unique music tourist destination, mainly for national visitors but occasionally as part of an international tour. Takarazuka, an otherwise anonymous town (near Kobe), became famous in the interwar years following the establishment there in 1914 of the all-female Takarazuka Revue as a deliberate response to the dominant all-male Japanese Kabuki theatre. Spectacular stage shows, sometimes with hundreds of performers, perform everything from Western music (including versions of such shows as *West Side Story*) to manga (comics), but are dominated by extravagant musicals with rotating stages, trapdoors, apron stages and a range of special effects. The 3000-seat theatre is integrated into a cluster of restaurants and elegant stores, and a giant entertainment complex: Familyland. Fans and visitors are mainly women (Robertson, 1998). Quite differently, the small town of Santiago de Cuba, at the eastern end of Cuba, and home town of some members of the Buena Vista Social Club, has become the hub of Cuban music and dance, surpassing Havana as the definitive destination for music tourists.

Beyond places such as these where contemporary performance has deliberately enabled music tourism, almost all large cities have a panoply of venues that may stimulate tourism, even if that is not the most significant urban economic activity. Berlin, for example, has literally hundreds of clubs, theatres and opera houses, ranging from contemporary techno (clubs such as Tresor, in an old bank vault, or Blu) to classical music (as at the Konzerthaus, home to the Berlin Symphony Orchestra, or the State Opera House). All world cities have huge entertainment districts. Many also now have Hard Rock Cafés, a syndicated network of themed restaurants based around the collection of rock 'n' roll memorabilia. Such networks have become global, and now include hotels, including that in Bali, where one travel brochure notes 'Asia's first Hard Rock Hotel covers a 3-hectare site ... 418 tribute rooms and suites are situated in 6 blocks named after different musical styles: rock 'n' roll, blues, reggae, psychedelic, alternative and rock'. Music tourism extends beyond merely the acoustic.

Evident in almost every tourist destination are buskers; their numbers are in some places a measure of success, and they are often closely regulated and controlled. Buskers on street corners, cathedral steps, underground stations and even on the trains themselves respond to existing markets, but occasionally become part of the advertising backdrop for destinations, as in Montreal (see Figure 3.5). Particularly popular tourist venues, such as the steps below the Sacré-Coeur basilica in Paris or outside the Sydney Opera House are contested areas for buskers of different kinds. (On one grey January morning in 2001 one of the authors witnessed in just a few minutes, on different steps outside the Sacré-Coeur, Andean pan-pipers playing James Galway tunes and a harp player performing Frank Sinatra's 'I Did it My Way' as mobile accordionists and violinists passed through, none performing any French music.) As in this example, and a rather similar one a month earlier, when the same author heard a Swiss didgeridu player in Granada, Spain, buskers are not necessarily representative of local music, but tend to play popular music with some universal appeal. Local representativeness may even be illusory, as in Croatia:

> Every day during summer, at the northern end of the ancient walled city of Dubrovnik, stands a bear of a man wearing traditional Croatian dress and plucking out folk tunes on an exquisite hand-made instrument known as a lijerica. In his thick woollen socks, heavy black knee length pants, white peasant shirt and bright yellow cummerbund, the man taps his toes in time to the music. After three songs the giant takes a bow and the mesmerised tourists toss spare coins in a basket. It is the consummate ethnic busking moment in one of the most perfect and picturesque towns in Croatia .... Turns out the giant is from New Jersey and makes a two-month pilgrimage to the homeland of his parents every summer to practice the ancient art of Croatian folk music. (Lee, 2002: 301–302)

Figure 3.5 Live music, busking and street performance have become important ways of enlivening tourism landscapes, although in some places buskers are considered a nuisance. In this advertisement for the festival season in Montreal, street performance has become part of the city's official marketing. (Reproduced with permission from Tourisme Montreal)

The best buskers create 'transitory communities of spontaneous human contact, across ethnic and linguistic boundaries' (Tanenbaum, 1995: 105–106). More often they are commodified in the sense that the famous mariachi bands of Mexico (and also New Mexico), and especially of Guadalajara, mainly stroll the plazas, tune their guitars and chat until someone is willing to pay to hear a song. Much the same is true in San Telmo, Buenos Aires (known as the birthplace of the tango), and of the musicians in the main square, Djemaa el-Fna, of Marrakesh, Morocco, where 'photo-opportunities' of them (and also snake charmers and water carriers) can be similarly expensive (Figure 3.6). By contrast, in the Piazza San Marco in Venice, the music is free but the cost of lingering over coffee and food is expensive. In most world cities busking is carefully regulated to enhance rather than detract from the experiences of tourists and local residents alike. In France busking was illegal on the Metro until 1997 when six-monthly licences were granted to successful applicants; about 300 buskers are officially sanctioned out of a thousand who apply after passing auditions that included in one brief period in 2002 'a koto player from Japan, a gypsy group from the Ukraine, and folk musicians from Haiti' (Sage, 2002: 12). The London Underground followed suit. Several buskers earn significant incomes (see Chapter 4) and others go on to greater success in a more formal context.

Music in Tourism Campaigns

A different kind of connection between music and tourism occurs when the music itself, and visual images surrounding that music, are used in tourism campaigns to promote locations and attractions. Music then becomes a powerful soundtrack to television campaigns, a potent way of constructing authenticity (see Chapter 5) and perhaps also a tourist attraction itself. Using music in promotion may not be primarily to attract tourists because of any local musical traditions, although these may become part of a tourist's itinerary simply because of raised expectations of hearing music there. Rather, music's evocative qualities are used to add credence to the visual images, to convey excitement, tradition, continuity with the past, elegance or escape. Why music is powerful in this regard is in part simply because of its ability to elicit emotional responses from audiences – excitement, energy or melancholy – while music, and popular culture more generally, may be perceived as providing more credible images of places, in contrast to more 'controlled' promotional campaigns, brochures, paid advertisements, where the audience is usually aware of absorbing one-sided, deliberately constructed and positive images explicitly geared towards selling a product (Prentice & Anderson, 2000). By contrast, music, as well as other informal means (such as word of mouth), is more powerful for its apparent distance from control by tourism promotional authorities.

Figure 3.6 This Moroccan busker in Marrakech is playing an *amzhad*, a Berber single-string violin, made with goatskin over a wooden frame, and played with a horsehair bow. (Photograph by courtesy of John Connell)

Music has been particularly prevalent in promotions of countries and regions whose musical traditions constituted part of the 'virtual tourism' discussed in Chapter 2 – locations such as Hawaii, Italy, Austria and Ireland – and whose music (or a certain sanitised and standardised version of it) became imaginary identification for place in emerging international mediascapes (Figure 3.7). The same images and sounds from record covers and records that conveyed a sense of place, even virtually transported listeners to another place, might also be used later on, once tourism had become more accessible and affordable, to lure those consumers to the physical place.

Such 'evocation strategies' deviate from 'traditional' tourism marketing (with its more direct advertising of actual tours, vacations, experiences) by using more emotive ploys:

> The evocation strategy recognizes that visitation may depend upon imagery other than that commonly thought pertinent to tourist promotion . . . . The strategy (here termed 'evocation') seeks to manipulate imagery with much less explicit reference to products, but rather by evoking an emotional response to the 'brand' of the destination . . . promotion is in effect shown as a means not of product positioning, but of re-positioning. Whereas positioning is a means of creating appropriate images for destinations in the minds of potential

Figure 3.7 Tourism advertisements from Ireland and Jamaica (Source: Bord Fáilte and Jamaica Tourist Board)

consumers in targeted market segments ... repositioning is the attempt to change imagery. (Prentice & Anderson, 2000: 494–495)

Ireland is one country where music has been used in this way. Until recently, most tourists to Ireland from Great Britain were motivated to travel for reasons 'other than the culture and history of the island' (Prentice & Anderson, 2000: 497), such as family links, sightseeing and scenery, with Ireland being perceived as an 'easy' place to travel, with no language barriers and left-hand driving on roads. Although visitor surveys confirmed that tourists often appreciated Irish culture and heritage, related images had not been used in marketing to attract visitors for those specific attractions. Hence, 'a marketing niche ... had been overlooked in terms of tourism promotion and thus offered opportunities for supplemental repositioning' (Prentice & Anderson, 2000: 498). In the 1990s Irish tourism promotion increasingly repositioned imagery towards cultural history and heritage, including music: 'Tourists are attracted here to discover our distinctiveness – all those facets of the natural, human-made and cultural heritage which give us a unique identity. These features, reflecting character, authenticity, and sense of place, all combine to create a distinctively Irish image' (Bord Fáilte [Irish Tourism Board], quoted in Stocks, 1996: 252). Thus, in the 1994 National Development Plan, music became explicitly connected to tourism campaigns and Ireland's attempts to reposition itself as a destination of cultural authenticity:

> Irish music, both modern and traditional, is spreading throughout the world with the able assistance of performers such as U2, the Cranberries, Hot House Flowers, The Chieftains, Clannad, Enya and many more. Many people's first exposure to Irish culture is through such musicians which in turn inspires them to visit Ireland. (Department of Tourism and Trade, quoted in O'Donnchadha & O'Connor, 1996: 206)

Subsequently, there were two ways in which Irish music became connected to tourism promotion – through the performance of 'traditional' Irish music, and its use in television and print media campaigns for tourism in Ireland, and in relation to well-known 'contemporary' Irish music such as that of Sinead O'Connor, U2, the Cranberries and Boomtown Rats, whose fans might seek out attractions in Ireland connected to the performers. 'Traditional' Irish music, including fiddles, harps, pipes and accordions, was increasingly used in ways that emphasised its 'authenticity' as an example of living Gaelic culture to be consumed by tourists.

The folk music revival of the 1960s brought success to a number of bands, not only in Ireland, that invoked a Celtic tradition, such as the Chieftains. Their apparent authenticity was emphasised on record sleeves especially, by depicting the band playing in rural settings, stressing the Irish descent of band members, the family legacies of musical performance and the 'traditional' instruments. A Gaelic heritage was frequently invoked and the Gaelic language sometimes used. The context of musical performance laid claim to continuity and links with community: an older Ireland of Celtic rural values – an image for a nation divorced from the troubles in the north and the economic growth of the 'Celtic tiger'. This invention and stimulus of heritage was paralleled in other cultural arenas (dance and film) and seized upon by the Irish Tourist Board as the backdrop for national advertising campaigns.

By the mid-1990s music was clearly an influence on tourism in several ways, from the subtle 'repositioning' of music as a means of 'evocation', to the more deliberate focus on particular performers and genres. Some 69% of all visitors to the Republic of Ireland rated traditional Irish music as 'a very important' or 'a fairly important' determinant of their visit, while over 45% of overseas visitors had witnessed musical performances in Irish pubs (Quinn, 1996: 386–387). Bord Fáilte (1996: 3) argued that 'success in music, literature, theatre, film and dance enhances Ireland's current international fashionability'. The popularity of both Riverdance, a dance stage performance which developed from a five-minute interlude in the 1994 Eurovision Song Contest into a full-blown international touring show tracing 'the story of Ireland and its people in music, dance and song' (Prentice & Anderson, 2000: 500), and The Corrs, a group fronted by three photogenic sisters that has fused traditional with contemporary music – vividly brought 'Irish' music to a global audience, constituting an incidental but inevitable promotion for Ireland whenever and wherever the music was played and consumed. The rapid expansion of themed Irish pubs around the world at around the same time may also have had an impact. The growth in tourist numbers seeking out 'authentic' Irish music as part of their holidays subsequently increased and was translated into specific tourist promotions, that played a part in the revival and tourist reorientation of districts such as Temple Bar in Dublin, where its plentiful pubs now commonly feature 'traditional' performances for tourists. Meanwhile, Irish popular music is considered stylistically different from that of England and Scotland; U2, The Corrs, The Cranberries and Van Morrison, who seemingly epitomise an 'Irish' sound in music (McLaughlin & McLoone, 2000; Rolston, 2001: 52–54), have spawned their own tourism sites, including the Irish Music Hall of Fame and the Dublin 'Rock and Stroll' tour (see p. 000), and the Belfast street 'Cyprus Avenue' (a song on Van Morrison's famous *Moondance* album) is the location of the most-stolen street sign in Ireland. National tourist promotions that utilised music, both formally and informally, for evocative purposes have thus created demand for actual attractions on the ground.

In Latin America and the Caribbean, music has been heavily used in tourism writing and promotion, as in Jamaica and Trinidad (where lively reggae encapsulates the required image), Brazil – where the Rio carnival is the greatest musical event on the continent – and in Cuba. Salsa, Cuba's main musical style, has been popular throughout Latin America and parts of the Western world since the 1960s, particularly when Cuban populations migrated after the revolution in 1959 to Miami, New Jersey and New York. Cuban music again found popularity in the 1990s, linked to the 'rediscovery' by Ry Cooder of artists such as Ruben González, Ibrahim Ferrer and Compay Segundo, sometimes known as *los super-abuelos* (the super grandfathers), and the subsequent recordings of The Buena Vista Social Club. Links to tourism were inevitable. Here was a 'preserved' musical heritage and dance form, cut off from the outside world and its modernising, commercial influences, seemingly untouched and 'pure'. Cuba was rapidly opening up to foreign interests (though not American) following the collapse of aid from the disintegrating Soviet Union in the early 1990s, and urgently needed foreign currency. Not only was tourism the single most important source of foreign exchange by the end of the 1990s, but tourist numbers grew faster than anywhere else in the world until September 2001. As Cuban music was finding new global audiences, tourism became central to domestic transformation.

Travel writers flocked to Cuba; feature articles appeared in national newspapers, while salsa classes expanded in dance schools across the world. The film *Buena Vista Social Club*, directed by Wim Wenders, opened in cinemas across the world in 1999, and Cuban music and culture quickly became globally renowned (Figure 3.8). As one music writer observed 'The *Buena Vista Social Club* would have us believe that Cuba is a land where time has stopped: a country of elegantly decaying buildings, '50s Chevys and ageing musicians playing the music of years gone by' (Wilder, 2002: 4). Another observed that 'the Buena Vista phenomenon is connected to the rediscovery of Cuba, the quintessential land that time forgot. In this sense it's as much cultural fetishisation as musical appreciation' (Slattery, 1999: 7). Nevertheless,

> With Wim Wenders, who made the film on the making of the album, Cooder reminded the world that Cuba had always been the home of truly great and vibrant music. He helped make Cuba, isolated by successive US governments since 1959, one of the hottest and hippest destinations on the planet. Young Americans and Europeans, eager to see what life was like 50 years ago and to hear the music of pre-revolutionary Cuba, snubbed the embargo and put Havana back on the tourist map. Cuba became as hip as New Orleans in the 1930s or Chicago in the 1960s. It was where the real musical action was. (Elder, 2003a: 5)

Figure 3.8 Cover of Lonely Planet Guide to Cuba (Illustration by courtesy of Robert Leon and Lonely Planet)

The expansion of tourism was spontaneous and somewhat accidental. Cuban tourist authorities continued to emphasise a variety of cultural attractions in the country and only belatedly seized the opportunity that exposure of the national music had given them.

A range of other countries, now including China (Rees, 1998), have similar associations with music, and music – such as Chinese opera – plays a part in tourism campaigns and authenticating attractions for tourists in those locations. Argentina has become an increasingly popular tourist destination, and the tango, its national dance/musical form, which 'had humble beginnings in the city's brothels, where it was once the vulgar dance of prostitutes who moved to the sounds of peasant verse and Spanish and Italian music' (Ryle, 2000: 3T). Tango invariably appears as the focal point of travel articles and tourist promotions, as well as being a common feature of street and café performances in the touristy San Telmo and La Boca districts, Buenos Aires and in the square outside the Recoleta cemetery where Evita (Eva Perón) is buried (e.g. Mitchell, 1998; Ryle, 2000; see Goertzen & Azzi, 1999):

> Nothing brings a smile to the face of an Argentinian like the national dance. Energy and passion abound in the Caminito area located in La Boca district. It's tango-ville, one long pedestrian street without sidewalks, unique for its houses made of metal sheets painted in bright colours. Tango bars hazed with the tang of cigar smoke sit beside treasure-filled antique shops. (Kell, 2003: 6)

Tourists seek both to observe and participate. Similar associations abound between music, dance and tourism; as Daniel (1996: 780) has put it, a range of dance styles have been shaped for, and by, tourism performance, as well as featuring in overseas tourism campaigns, from

> Brazil's *samba* and *lambada*, Jamaica and Trinidad's *limbo, calypso,* and *reggae,* Haiti's and the Dominican Republic's *merengue,* Senegal's *sabar,* Zimbabwe's Kalanga *mabisa* and Ndebele war dances, South Africa's *boot dance,* Mexico's *hat dance,* Hawaii's *hula, powwow* dancing from the Apache and Comanche traditions, and *disco* and *hiphop* from the United States.

The Iceland Tourist Board has sought to build on the recent popularity of star performers such as Bjork and, more recently, Sigur Ros, as both indicators of the cultural wealth of the country (alongside references to the Icelandic Symphony Orchestra and others) and invitations to travel. Conversely, Bjork's own website (www.Bjork.com) has linkages to Iceland Tourism pages in an unusual reversal of more common advertising practices. At the very least the high profile of these performers has given Iceland new media coverage.

Classical music has been less evident in tourist promotions. Austria's tourism industry was boosted in the 1950s through *Heimatfilme*

(German-speaking sentimental films set in idealised regional settings), in which popular songs were prominent, then to be catapulted into the international tourism market through the huge success of *The Sound of Music*. Only rather later was classical music seen as a means of drawing in visitors thus, in one account, 'Mozart's birthplace, Salzburg, with the house the composer was born in, the old city and the spectacular fortress towering above it, has won its fame as a tourist attraction through its image in the global entertainment industry' (East & Luger, 2001: 230), rather than as a centre for classical composition and performance. The film of *Amadeus* (1984), even though it was filmed in Prague, may even have been more important than Mozart himself. So too the Cape Verde Islands are virtually never discussed or portrayed in terms of tourism without reference to their most famous musical performer, Cesaria Evora, who almost literally placed the nation on the map as she sung soulfully of her 'Petit Pays' ('Small Country') and 'Paraiso di Atlantico'. Cape Verde tourism, however, has barely benefited from the nation's newfound exposure. Crowded House's famous hit 'Don't Dream It's Over' (1986) became a soundtrack to New Zealand government-sponsored tourism promotions; Bali is consistently portrayed with a gamelan soundtrack (although gamelan performances are often truncated in Bali for tourist audiences with their shorter attention spans) and gamelan music is used as a representation of all tourism in Indonesia. New South Wales Tourism, somewhat oddly, used Chuck Berry's 'No Particular Place to Go' (1962) in one of its marketing campaigns. Australian television tourism campaigns feature the ever-present trance-like sounds of the didjeridu, an instrument that has formed the basis of a tourist economy of performance and craft production in the Northern Territory, especially targeted at visitors from Europe.

Niche Package Tours and Itineraries

As the diversity of possibilities described above indicates, the extent of specialisation in music tourism is profound. Numerous locations have chosen to construct musical trails and tours, some taking advantage of genuine musical history, others with, at best, fragmentary physical sites for tourists to gaze upon. Some, like Pigeon Forge and Parkes, New South Wales, have created something out of virtually nothing, as towns and nations have increasingly sought to capitalise on cultural heritage, in whatever form it can be marketed. The rise of niche tourism in the latter decades of the 20th century enabled an amazing array of musical tours and attractions. Cities such as New York, Liverpool and Dublin developed city walking tours of important music sites – the 'Music Trail', 'Liverpool Beat Route' and 'Rock 'n' Stroll' tours (Figure 3.9) respectively, through a series of plaques on walls of prominent studios, venues

Figure 3.9 Dublin tourist authorities have sought too capitalise on the city's musical heritage and the high profile of Irish popular music on the world scene by constructing a musical trail of dedicated signage, with accompanying publication and map available at Tourist Information offices. Signage alerts passers-by to sites where famous bands such as U2 played in their early years, or where artists worked prior to their musical careers. In a fortuitous moment in Dublin in 1998, one of the authors literally bumped into Bono, U2's lead singer (resulting in two-way apologies), when walking the Rock 'n' Roll Stroll Trail – a new twist on the concept of 'authentic' cultural tourism. (Photograph by courtesy of Chris Gibson)

and company headquarters (Halfacree & Kitchin, 2000). Specialist companies now conduct tours of country music sites throughout the American South, taking in the major attractions in Nashville, Branson and Memphis; travel writers have charted out itineraries of Laurel Canyon, Los Angeles (once home to, and immortalised in songs and on albums by Carole King, Joni Mitchell, Frank Zappa and Jim Morrison). Elvis Tours of Hawaii and Memphis have been run from Australia. In 2003 EIN were offering a 'Blue Hawaii' tour which promised the spirit of 'rock-a-hula', with visits to Blue Hawaii film locations, alongside concerts and films, and coincided with 'Elvis Week' in Hawaii; a year later Travelscene offered the Elvis Presley Tribute Tour, focused on Memphis and Las Vegas. Australian classical music radio broadcaster Peter Egan has for a number of years lead musical tours of Europe 'for lovers of fine music and students of history and culture' aspiring to classical delights, social distinction and elegance, taking in Prague, Salzburg, Vienna and Budapest. These contrast somewhat with Salzburg's other (probably more numerically successful) tours: those of the Sound of Music, retracing the scenes from the movie of the same name. Other tours, such as the Cuba: Music, Plants and Healing Tour, are rather more esoteric. In Britain and the United States a handful of travel agents and tour operators, such as Pro Musica Tours and Great Performance Tours (both in New York), specialise entirely in music holidays, ranging from individual festivals to major tours.

In the United Kingdom, the British Tourist Authority published its own music tourism guide, the *Rock and Pop Map: One Nation Under a Groove* (1998), which directed tourists towards a plethora of rock sites: from the Luton home of Jethro Tull and the Hertfordshire school at which Wham members George Michael and Andrew Ridgely met, to UB40's recording studios (an ex-abattoir) in Birmingham. The various sites were marked on a map of the UK, shaped not by topography, but in the image of an electric guitar, with nearby Ireland the amplifier. The UK itself was thus portrayed, even defined, as an island of rock and roll locations, an island of music:

> THIS ISLAND ROCKS: If you don't own anything by a British band in your record collection, you ain't into music . . . . This map gives you a guided tour of the cities, towns and places that have inspired and shaped British pop makers. Whether you're into The Beatles, Bowie or Blur, The Stones, The Sex Pistols or The Spice Girls – Britain is where the beat is. (British Tourist Authority, 1998: 2)

In this way a whole host of sites associated with the lives of popular musicians and singers have become tourist attractions, whether in birth or death. No classical parallel has ever been developed. For lovers of classical music, Schubert's birthplace in Vienna is now a tourist attraction, as is Mozart's Wohnhaus in Salzburg, which has a museum dedicated to the city's most famous son. Egypt has an Umm Kulthum Museum, celebrating its most famous diva; Paris has its Edith Piaf Museum. In Loretta Lynn's birthplace, Butcher Hollow, Kentucky, there is now a museum. For rock 'n' roll enthusiasts, Lubbock, Texas has a statue, constructed to commemorate its best known citizen, Buddy Holly.

Cemeteries have become attractions too, notably Père Lachaise Cemetery, Paris, which houses Jim Morrison's grave, that of Edith Piaf and of many other distinguished individuals (including Bizet). Morrison's grave is usually adorned with graffiti, flowers and the occasional spliff from adoring fans, many of whom also visit Edith Piaf. Northwards in Montmartre cemetery, Offenbach, Berlioz, Adolphe Sax (creator of the saxophone) and the famous dancer, Vaslav Nijinsky, whose grave is adorned by a statue of him dressed as a clown to resemble the title role he danced in 'Petrushka', all draw visitors. The mausoleum of Evita in Buenos Aires (and a museum on her that opened in 2003) became more important after the *Evita* stage show and the movie starring Madonna, despite Evita's less than stellar career as a singer and actress. Evita's tomb, like Gardel's, has also become a shrine (Standard, 2004: 9). That of Carlos Gardel, in Chacaritas cemetery in Once, Buenos Aires, who died in a plane crash in 1935 and was arguably the most famous tango dancer in the world, draws thousands of visitors a year, including tourists from Brazil, Germany, Japan and the United Kingdom. The tomb of the legendary Portuguese fado singer, Amalia Rodrigues, in the National Pantheon in Lisbon, remained covered with floral tributes five years after her death in 1999 and was much more popular than that of nearby Vasco da Gama. Similar sites are John Lennon's Imagine memorial at Strawberry Fields (Central Park, New York) and the nearby apartment block where he died; Jimi Hendrix's resting place at Greenwood Memorial Park, Seattle; the site of Kurt Cobain's suicide death in 1994 (much to the annoyance of his family who still live there); and even Room 8 in the Joshua Tree Inn on Twenty Nine Palms Highway in California where Gram Parsons died; but, above all, Elvis Presley's Graceland, Memphis (see pp. 88–91). The music of the late English folk singer Nick Drake, who committed suicide in 1974, has similarly inspired visitors to his grave in the tiny village of Tanworth-in-Arden. Testimonies in church guest books and graffiti at such sites suggest the depth of tourists' nostalgia, attachments to the particular performers and claims that their lives have been influenced, even transformed, by their music and by the 'pilgrimage' to the final resting place. Verdi's tomb at Casa di Riposo, Milan, is an attraction, although Vienna's Zentralfriedhof (central cemetery) is by far the capital of death for classical musicians, where Beethoven, Hugo Wolf, Brahms, Schubert, the Strausses and Schönberg are all buried; curiously, Mozart's grave in St Mark's

Cemetery, across the city, is unmarked and unadorned, only 'surrounded by scented lilac and the roar of autobahn traffic' (Pritchard, 1999: 8).

Tourists are not merely passive observers and audiences of musical scenes. Some such as the followers of the Grateful Dead, the 'Deadheads', travelled almost as much as the band to witness its performances (Chapter 6). Many tourists participate, perhaps taking their own instruments with them or simply singing along in pubs or, as the Lonely Planet Guide encourages tourists in St Petersburg to do, sing along with the guitarists along the banks of the Neva river well into summer nights. The New Zealander Peta Mathias travelled around Ireland in search of 'relatives, good food and music', and subtitled her travel book *How to Eat, Dance and Sing Your Way Round Ireland* (2000) which also included a CD of her own Irish songs.

Participation may be the point of travel. A loose circuit links the dance club scene through a series of international destinations, of which Ibiza (in the Balearic Islands) and Goa are the best known. Ibiza became a major destination for dance-club fans at the end of the 1980s and expanded rapidly as international DJs and superclubs moved to the island; vast numbers of tourists came primarily to dance (and consume), creating some conflict with local people (see Chapter 6). Israel has sought to link itself into this scene and its tourism website proclaims that 'Israel's club scene – particularly in Tel Aviv and Jerusalem – is part of the Ibiza–Amsterdam–London scene, drawing DJs and club fans from North America and Europe to all-night parties', and that Tel Aviv also has a Love Parade (www.goisrael.com). Ayia Napa in Cyprus has become another alternative to Ibiza, in the constant quest for new destinations linked to shifts in the dance-club market.

Guided Tours

The simplest way of marking the rise of music tourism is to survey the range of guidebooks now available to music fans seeking to retrace the steps of their favourite artist or band, or hoping to catch a performance in a world-famous venue. Probably the first of these was Popkin's *Musical Monuments* (1986), which catalogued a vast range of classical music sites in Britain, from Mendelssohn's tree in Burnham Beeches to hundreds of portraits, statues and plaques. Music tourism guides became popular in the mid-1990s, which was some measure of the prior rise of popular music tourism, since rock music, rather than classical or jazz, has spawned most of the guidebooks. Many are purely of local interest, cheaply produced in limited runs by printing companies rather than publishers. Specific guidebooks now map out places associated with particular artists (such as Farren's *The Hitchhiker's Guide to Elvis* (1996) and Hazen and Freeman's *Memphis: Elvis Style* (1997)), key music locations (see Fry and Posner (1993) on Cajun country) continents (Plantamura, 1997) or nations, as with Fodor's *Rock & Roll Traveler USA* (1996) and its British equivalent. The former, whose subtitle *The Ultimate Guide to Juke Joints, Street Corners, Whiskey Bars and Hotel Rooms where Music History was Made*, emphasises the mythology of the industry, provides a comprehensive, highly detailed guide to every contiguous state in the United States, filled with information regarding famous sites (such as the Apollo Theatre, Harlem) and much more obscure locations such as the New York college which the Beastie Boys attended; the Boston clubs where the Pixies and Lemonheads first played; or directions to the tiny Roy Orbison museum in Wink, Texas. Britain has been particularly well served (Bianchi & Gusoff, 1996, Frame, 1999). Particular guides cover large cities such as Paris (Simeone, 2000), Los Angeles (Fein, 1998) and London (Lee, 1995), the last being unusual in focusing only on classical music rather than otherwise more popular sites. At an even more localised scale, Scanlon's (1997) esoteric account of rock sites in Camden Town included the Roundhouse venue (the home of early psychedelic 'raves' and performances by Pink Floyd and Soft Machine in the 1960s); the stalls were once run by Annie Lennox and Dave Stewart of the Eurythmics at Camden's weekend markets, and even the fish 'n' chip shop was frequented by members of ska band, Madness.

The guidebooks themselves represent a tiny proportion of possible tours. Vast numbers of leaflets add to these, such as the curiously titled *Liverpool Beat Route*, produced by the University's Institute of Popular Music, and many places offer conducted tours of physical sites and live venues. Copenhagen, which claims to be one of the 'jazz capitals' of Europe and where jazz in the 1940s was a symbolic reaction to German occupation, now has many jazz venues. Copenhagen Jazz Guides, founded in 1995, offer regular weekly tours, including three or four clubs per night, where the history of the club and of the musicians are discussed, alongside stories of the particular inner city neighbourhoods. Cape Town has similar jazz tours that focus on the black townships; indeed, tourists in Cape Town and Johannesburg are advised not to undertake musical tours on their own for security reasons. The first formal Hip-Hop Cultural Sightseeing Tour of the Bronx and Harlem began in 2003, involving seminal DJ Kool Herc who aimed at 'giving back to the kids that don't know their history (Associated Press, 2003), as relatively new music genres began to develop a sense of history.

Lyrical Places

Vast numbers of places have been immortalised in song lyrics. In a handful of contexts such places have been seized upon by tourism organizations to confirm the merit of particular destinations. A very small number have actually resulted in new forms of tourism. Perhaps the most famous of such songs and places is 'The Mountains of Mourne', written by Percy French in the late 1880s. Like so many songs of Irish emigrants, it expresses nostalgia for the home country (in this case from London) with every verse concluding that it would be better to be 'Where the mountains of Mourne sweep down to the sea'. The song has made the Mourne mountains the best known mountains in Ireland, and the song is featured on the website of the Northern Ireland Tourist Board. On the other coast of Ireland, 'The Rose of Tralee' has boosted Tralee and, in a quite different context and time, Marty Robbins benefited the 'south-western town of El Paso'. More recently, Paul McCartney's 'Mull of Kintyre' with its chorus, 'Mull of Kintyre. Oh mist rolling in from the sea/My desire is always to be here', has had a similar impact for the Scottish peninsula that culminates in the Mull. This isolated area, hitherto neglected by tourists, has used the song in various tourist promotions and gained increased tourist numbers. The Australian band, Cold Chisel's most famous song, 'Khe Sanh', has brought a trickle of fans to the Vietnamese town of the same name (e.g. Rollins, 2004).

It is only exceptionally possible to trace the manner in which positive lyrics actually influence tourism, even in the most general sense, but one personal Japanese website tracing a 1997 journey, in its entirety, gives some indication of just how influential a single song can be (Box 3.2). Such single-minded long-distance travel is rare in any kind of tourism.

While Kintyre, Mourne and Route 66 (see Chapter 6) have certainly attracted tourists because they are the subjects of popular songs, other places from 'down Mexico way' to 'Paris in the springtime' and 'Georgia on my mind' or 'Moonlight in Vermont' have at the very least acquired positive images from their particular depiction in songs. Classical music, such as Charles Ives's evocations of New England, Elgar's reflections of England and Richard Strauss's Alpine Symphony may have similarly, but more subtly emphasised their landscape qualities. The extent to which such places, alongside the Blue Canadian Rockies, Copacabana, New York, Acapulco Bay, various islands and a host of others, have gained tourists can never be known. Positive images will certainly not have deterred visitors.

Finally, musical allusions are often part of tourism promotion. Bohemia is rarely advertised without some reference to rhapsody (e.g Skřivánková, 2001), even if that advertising has nothing to say about music. Others have used music to symbolise supposed charms, such as 'In Limbo Land', the bold type of which declares that 'Puerto Rico boasts a romantic Latin heart . . . remote villages swinging to the sound of salsa' (Perrottet, 2003), and 'Living is easy to a mariachi beat' in central Mexico (Grimwade, 2003), but the text describes a more familiar landscape of routes and hotels. In such places the music itself is unimportant.

Box 3.2
Wanderlust

'Paul McCartney/Mull of Kintyre'. When I heard this song's title I presumed it referred to a place in Africa because it didn't sound like English. However, the sound of the bagpipes made me realize the song was about Scotland. The strange song title and sweet, peaceful melody tempted me to travel to Scotland without me noticing. When I came to love the song and decided I wanted to go on a trip to Scotland someday, I gradually found out how to get there. At first I checked the location of the place on the map. I had thought Mull of Kintyre was a very famous tourist resort, but few Japanese articles dealt with the place. According to 'Blue Guide: Scotland' the place is at the top of the Kintyre peninsula of Scotland. At first I had thought that the Mull of Kintyre was on the Isle of Mull in Scotland, but it was the lighthouse. OK, so I decided the destination of my journey, it was the lighthouse.

Consulting books etc. about Scotland so like that and with help from members of the PC communications forum for UK lovers in Japan, I realized that the cape Paul had sang about was very far away. I heard that there was no railway station near the place. I checked railway and coach timetables, began to prepare for travel, felt a touch of anxiety and left Japan.

The places I travelled to Mull of Kintyre are as follows:

(1) Japan (Kansai airport) to London Heathrow (about 16 hours).
(2) Heathrow – London (Kings Cross) – Glasgow (4 and a half hours by a limited express 'Flying Scotsman'). I was so tired that I stay for one night in Glasgow.
(3) Glasgow to Campbelltown (took 4 and half hours by coach). There are no railways between the two points.
(4) When I got in Kintyre peninsula I found the sightseeing board that said 'one of the most exciting roads to the Mull of Kintyre, immortalised in song by Paul McCartney'. I felt his lyrics; I'm getting closer.
(5) Campbelltown to 'End of the Public Road' (20 minutes by taxi). Campbelltown is a small town, however I didn't get the impression the town was inconvenient for daily life, because there is no large city near the town. I checked in a B and B and took a rest. A few hours later I took a taxi in main street of Campbelltown. The taxi went through the green grasslands. There was no cars coming from the opposite direction.
(6) End of the Public road to Mull of Kintyre (20 minutes on foot).

The end of the road was a small park. I had to get off the taxi. There was a board for sightseeing; it had the sentences 'Made famous by Paul McCartney's hit single in 1977, the Mull of Kintyre is strictly speaking, the rounded headland making up the south-west corner of the Kintyre peninsula'.

At last I could see the sea and the lighthouse here. I went down to the lighthouse on the winding road for a while.

Soon I saw a very beautiful and wide landscape: deep blue sea, brilliant green plains. The landscape had a splendid view, because there is no tree. Rabbits sometimes ran across walking path. The very fine weather made the place surrounded by a gentle light.

There is no people, like the Mull of Kintyre was reserved for me. So I sang 'Mull of Kintyre' sitting on a small bench near the Mull lighthouse. I could hear Paul's song with my MD [MiniDisc] player and a ripple without the player.

I could see the land of Ireland dimly over the calm sea.

At 8 pm the taxi I had on the way there came to pick me up. We went back to Campbelltown behind string west sunlight. When I told her to take thirty pictures for the Mull of Kintyre she smiled.

Source: www.yositeru.com/macca/mull

Graceland: Bringing it all Back Home

Graceland is arguably the most famous music tourism site in the world, the home of the 'King of rock 'n' roll' and a focal point for the quasi-religious cult that has surrounded Elvis since his death in 1977. It has become part of a tourism empire. Tours are conducted of the mansion itself, operated by Lisa Marie Presley's company, Elvis Presley Enterprises. There are other related ventures: the Graceland Plaza, the Sincerely Elvis Museum and showcases dedicated to his cars and jet planes, among the ubiquitous souvenir shops and nearby re-created fifties-style diners. Graceland operates as an archetypal music tourist site, but it was also central to constructing Elvis as a star in the first place. Even while he was alive, Elvis's seclusion behind the mansion's gates and his often bizarre activities (including six-month binges on meatloaf) served to separate him from fans' everyday lived experiences. Graceland intensified the Elvis myth because it located all that Elvis encompassed in an easily identifiable, specific site: 'this heightened sense of permanence helps not only to render Elvis's stardom unique, but also to make his posthumous career possible' (Rodman, 1996: 123). The processes through which this site has been transformed into a music tourism centre are multifaceted: Graceland is the 'authentic' site of Elvis, providing a focal point for a large community of fans that continually reproduces the mythology and sanctity of Elvis: 'an environment where the type of 'extreme' adulation that fans of other stars can't openly express is able to flourish comfortably with relatively little fear of public censure' (Rodman, 1996: 127). Some commentators have read further into the mythology that has surrounded Elvis in his afterlife and the pilgrimages conducted to Graceland:

> It's a way of coming to terms with our own sense of loss, with what's become of us as a nation – the transition America has made from the young, vital, innocent pioneer nation we once were (the young, vital Elvis we put on our stamps) to the bloated colossus we feel we've become: the fat Elvis of nations. (Rosenbaum, 1995, quoted in Rodman, 1996: 114)

At one level, as one graffito said, 'Elvis, it's been 20 years and we still can't fight our tears . . . I made it here, love always . . .'. At another, accounts of Graceland by travel writers have captured both this sense of religious awe and highlighted the contradictions of the star's excesses: 'A small bus carried us up the drive to Graceland itself. We entered with the hushed reverence of visitors to the Sistine Chapel, except that here was not symmetry, beauty and the spirit in flight, but heinous taste, berserk ostentatiousness, the evidence of a soul unhinged' (Brown, 1993: 55). At Graceland, fandom, and the successes and excesses of a star performer have come to represent much more than either pilgrimage or crude commercialism, by entering into popular national mythology. Indeed, Graceland has not just become a site of pilgrimage for Elvis fans but, unlike most music tourism sites, it has become part of an American tourist itinerary (Alderman, 2002; Marling, 1996; Rodman, 1996). It is thus a major part of Memphis' tourism campaigns, an international icon, and key to the city's attempts to market itself as the birthplace of rock 'n' roll.

However, Elvis-related tourism spans a much wider circuit than just the Graceland mansion and surrounding commercialism. Graceland itself has spawned a Mobile Graceland that travels to various cities in the United States, appearing at various casinos and chain stores; it constitutes

> a museum quality exhibit featuring authentic Presley memorabilia, much of which has never been displayed outside Memphis that spans the superstar's unparalleled career. The collection, housed in an ultra-modern 53-foot long 18-wheel semi, contains jewelry, clothing, instruments, and other artefacts as unique as the man who owned them. (www.elvis-presley.com)

Elvis tourism incorporates a wide range of places that Elvis frequented and some to which he had no immediate connection in his lifetime. The extraordinary *Elvis Atlas* (Gray & Osborne, 1996) provides a cartography of every facet of Elvis's life, from his family genealogy and tours, to places he visited in Frankfurt and Paris, culminating in a map of the 28 Elvis museums in the United States. Loyal fans in Paisley, Scotland, have called for local acknowledgement of possible Scottish roots. In Bad Nauheim, Germany, the tourist office offers two- or even three-day guided tours of places with Elvis associations, such as the preserved bed in the Hotel Grunewald where he slept and even the wine store of the Pressler family who claim to be descendants of Elvis's German ancestors. Elvis tourists have also been drawn to Kauai, Hawaii, where Elvis had his honeymoon and made the film *Blue Hawaii* in the 1960s (Keane, 1999; Hopkins, 2002). In Tupelo, his birthplace, Elvis's mark is stamped all over town: the first Elvis Presley Day was held in 1956, still early in his career. Town authorities have certainly maximised the association, with the official city website emphasising that 'The most significant landmark of Tupelo's modern history is a modest, two-room house where the king of rock and roll was born' and providing a brief driving tour of a range of urban Elvis sites, including the hardware store where he bought his first guitar (www.tupelo.net). Indeed,

> Elvis's birthplace – tastefully restored, next to a peaceful chapel and a simple museum – stands on what is now Elvis Presley Drive, near Elvis Presley Park, in an area known as Elvis Presley Heights. The 850-acre Elvis Presley Lake and Campground are a few miles away . . . The McDonalds's branch has been done out as a mini-shrine to the cheeseburger-loving Elvis . . . One day Tupelo will no doubt be renamed Elvisville. (Perry & Glinert, 1996: 121)

Other sites include several in Las Vegas (such as the Graceland Chapel, where people can be married by an Elvis impersonator for US$200; the Aladdin Hotel, where Elvis married Priscilla in 1967; and the Elvis Presley Suite at the Las Vegas Hilton where he stayed for four weeks during his 57-show residency in 1969; displays at the Cleveland Rock n Roll Hall of Fame; Market Square Arena, Indianapolis, the site of his last performance in 1977; NBC Studios, Los Angeles, site of Elvis's comeback special in 1968; the Alabama Music Hall of Fame at Tuscumbia (including a display of Elvis's contract with RCA Records which he signed on leaving Sun Records in 1956), and, perhaps the pièce de résistance, Portland, Oregon's 24-hour Church of Elvis, replete with one-dollar slot machine Elvis wedding rings. Elvis tourism is now also international: as far away as Parkes, in inland Australia, the annual Elvis Revival Festival is held, attracting impersonators and fans from all over the country (see Chapter 7). One Elvis-related site escaped commodification, but only by accident: WHBQ, the Memphis radio station that gave Elvis his first radio airplay that led to record company interest from RCA, eventually moved to the suburbs, and now plays 'sports and talk, having abandoned music after DJ Rick Dees assaulted the pop world with his 1976 single, "Disco Duck"' (Perry & Glinert, 1996: 131). Nonetheless, nostalgia, tourism and, on occasion, ironic or subversive pleasures combine to create Elvis tourism in Memphis, throughout the United States and around the world. These sites, collectively, are the prime example of the scope and scale of music tourism, yet, unlike many others, they are now the locations of tribute artists and impersonators rather than 'authentic' live performance, and the adulation of Elvis is unique.

Resounding with Diversity

This chapter has introduced the multiple ways in which music is connected to tourism in a range of places, from those with famous styles and artists (Liverpool, Memphis) to those lesser-known locales that have nonetheless seized on an association with a performer, style or recording to attract tourists. Some forms of music tourism take place on a grand scale – whole cities with musical histories, where such heritage is part of professional, coordinated tourism campaigns and is central to urban economic development, as in New Orleans and Liverpool. Similarly, music is used in national tourism campaigns, as in Argentina, Cuba and Iceland, providing emotive links to imagined pasts, colouring landscapes with aural codes to evoke the exotic, the sensual or the nostalgic. At a smaller scale, sites have become music tourism locations, from recording studios to wedding chapels, and from birthplaces to museums. Such museums range from tiny memorials to almost forgotten singers (such as John McCormack in Athlone, Ireland) and even instruments (such as the Museum of Greek Popular Musical Instruments in Athens) to glitzy excuses for merchandise sales and the enormous Cleveland Hall of Fame (Chapter 4). Specialist tours have developed for all types of music and musicians, from Wagner to Elvis, and buskers have attached themselves to famous tourist sites. In many respects the evolution of music tourism has paralleled that of other forms of cultural tourism, such as that of literature and film, particularly in its association with sites linked to creative individuals and the places they made famous, from Wuthering Heights to the Bridges of Madison County.

The global push for cultural tourism, linked to heritage, with its broad focus on the arts, has resulted in the deliberate creation of music tourist destinations, some with only the most tenuous link to the actual performer. Parkes never had any link to Elvis Presley and Glyndebourne was merely a country house, but by acquiring an extra dimension that links heritage to music, they become new tourist destinations. Equally tenuous are Prague's links to the Beatles, while the massive statue of Frank Zappa in the centre of Vilnius, Lithuania, is a symbol of his anti-establishment songs which paralleled Lithuania's own resistance to the Soviet establishment, although Zappa never went there. Yet not every place has embraced music tourism enthusiastically. Some places have refused to celebrate the lives of those perceived as subversive or immoral; Winchester, Virginia, was ashamed of Patsy Cline during her lifetime, and as late as 1986 (23 years after her death) the town refused to name a street after her and only belatedly decided to capitalise on her largely posthumous fame. When it was finally decided to build a Patsy Cline museum, the principal supporter stated: 'It's not just to raise money, but she deserves recognition and her rightful place in history in her home town' (quoted in *The Sun Herald*, 5 May 2002). The song of the beer 'What made Milwaukee famous has made a loser out of me' had no local resonance (Brown, 1993: 90). Hibbing, Wisconsin, had no time for Bob Dylan, just as Bob Dylan had no time for Hibbing. When George Harrison died in Los Angeles in 2001 there was some reluctance to record the actual address on the death certificate to avoid it becoming a macabre site for fans and paparazzi. Other sites, such as Mozart's grave, are strangely neglected; still others, like that of the legendary blues singer, Robert Johnson, have never been found, a fact that 'probably keeps driving fans like me down to the Mississippi Delta every year, trying to get a hold of a ghost who keeps slipping from our grasp' (Johnson, 1998: 36). Tourism is also idiosyncratic and selective; almost every visitor to Abbey Road must pass the elegant house of the distinguished composer, Sir Thomas Beecham, where a Georgian blue plaque commemorates his life. Few even notice it.

Music tourism is not therefore just a straightforward story of commodification and tourism. As the following chapters discuss, economic impacts and uncertainties, as well as more complex cultural trends and issues, surround music tourism. Its impact on places and people varies enormously according to the kinds of tourists, whether retirees or ravers, and whether they are visitors to the newer destinations such as Koh Phangan (Thailand), show towns or old European centres. The following chapter examines local and regional economic impacts.

Chapter 4

Music in the Market: Economy, Society and Tourism

Music tourism has direct economic impacts on places and people, and there are many intangible benefits in terms of image and marketability that come from associations between music and place. Music tourism has an economic dimension in the simple sense of monetary impacts – primarily the expenditure of tourists and employment generation. More qualitatively, it is bound up in different kinds of local and regional economic growth and decline. Such economic dimensions are examined in this chapter before a consideration, in Chapters 5 and 6, of the more complex issues of culture and politics. Music tourism and its impacts are also invariably caught up in wider cultural and political debates about authenticity, ethnicity, gender and class. In this chapter, though, we consider more immediate socio-economic impacts.

We begin with an analysis of who are music tourists, and when, why and how they have an economic impact on places. At a very simple level, what attractions are sought and what kinds of investments have been made in the production of tourism sites? Remarkably little quantitative data has captured the economic impact of music tourists, in part because music tourism is generally subsumed within statistics on cultural tourism, which is itself somewhat neglected in terms of economic analysis. This chapter examines both types of data where available, but in addition, it also explores more qualitative evaluations of music tourism economies. These include the changing roles of musicians as workers, and distinctions between the large-scale forms of economic development that surround music tourism, and the roles played by not-for-profit institutions in maintaining musical heritages and contributing to local and regional economies. At various points, parallels and distinctions are drawn between music tourism and other forms of travel, but the key objective is to discuss what is distinctive about music tourism and its impacts, as well as to identify circumstances and experiences similar to other forms of cultural tourism.

At the outset it is useful to consider the social characteristics of music tourists and to sketch a picture of their motivations. As the diversity of possibilities set out in the previous chapter implies, no cohesive group can be considered 'music tourists'; travellers cannot be defined in some singular way in relation to music, or any travel activity that includes music. There are too many kinds of music and experience. One standard definition of the cultural tourist, used to generate economic statistics, is 'a person who stayed more than 40 kilometres away from home for at least one night and attended a cultural venue'. Cultural tourism, by extension, is defined as attendance at those cultural venues (NCCRS, 2001: 1). If music is seen as a subset of cultural tourism in this definition, then some measure of initial impact is possible, although this cannot capture the complete picture of music tourism's economic impact or its qualitative dimensions. Throughout this chapter we discuss available statistics on music tourism, both in terms of attendance, spending, income and employment for host places. Limited discussion is made of multipliers from music tourism – a measure of the flow-on effects in particularly communities – but all these have limitations. The Australian National Centre for Culture and Recreation Statistics, after considering working definitions of 'cultural tourism', concluded that 'the feasibility of developing an agreed definition for cultural tourism is not high' (NCCRS, 2001: 3). This also applies to music tourism.

Ultimately, music tourism is a social phenomenon that cannot be neatly bounded off from other forms of tourism or from other pastimes and pursuits for the purposes of determining its economic impacts. Music tourism activities are multiply-embedded in and across geographical scales (Milne & Ateljevic, 2001). Some places draw tourists from other countries, linked to the presence of musical associations in global mediascapes (Appadurai, 1990); others are well known within countries for particular musical events or styles, with tourism economies linked to this (hence Tamworth, Australia's 'country music capital', and Gore, New Zealand's equivalent – so much so that they have proclaimed themselves 'sister cities' – are mostly unknown outside these countries, but are successful national tourism destinations). Others are even more modest, drawing tourists from immediate hinterlands, or for a single festival or performance, or are sites, such as opera houses, within cities.

At any scale, music tourism is linked to other industries – entertainment (including recorded music, television and radio), hospitality (food and accommodation), events management, legal services, transport – just as all music tourism sites require infrastructure provided by various levels of government. Music tourism activities are also subject to regulatory mechanisms that govern tourism activities in general. Consequently, any attempt to distinguish music tourism as a discrete economic (or social) phenomenon can only be hypothetical or artificial. Given that very little is formally known about music tourist activities in an economic sense, this chapter seeks to respond to this lacuna, not by trying to 'add up' in crude quantitative fashion the various economic dimensions of the sites of music tourism (since that would be impossible), but rather to use selected examples where studies exist to demonstrate the diversity within music tourism, and the quite different ways in which it is entangled in local and regional economies.

The Tourists: Demography, Tastes, Expenditure

Some indication of the diversity of music tourists is revealed by the links between musical styles and their audiences, whether those audiences are tourists or not. While certain genres have general appeal across several social groups, others are certainly not widely embraced, resulting in niche audiences and tourist groups. Numerous studies have attempted to understand in a general sense the dynamics that underpin audiences for the arts and for various musical genres. This has been especially so for the broad distinctions between 'classical' and 'popular' music (the former equating to orchestral music, opera, ballet and other instrumental composers, the latter generally referring to post-war music influenced by rock, pop, dance and R & B, as well as country). Audience studies have sought to correlate the consumption of classical or popular music with social indicators, including income, education and previous experience in the performing arts (see Baumol & Bowen, 1966; Throsby & Withers, 1979; Abbé-Decarroux & Grin, 1992; O'Hagan, 1996; Prieto-Rodríguez & Fernández-Blanco, 2000; Bennett *et al.*, 2001). Their findings are mostly straightforward: classical concerts and products (and those of jazz) tend to have older, more educated, professional audiences (and some students); popular music attracts younger people; country music tends to be more popular among rural audiences (but also with the urban working class); 'world' music is popular with young, urban, upwardly mobile residents. Folk music cuts across many such divisions. Other studies have differentiated audiences for particular forms of popular music, from Bruce Springsteen to heavy metal (Cavicchi, 1998); in Tokyo, Japanese music has been more popular among manual workers and proprietors, while administrative and professional workers preferred classical music (Kurabayashi & Ito, 1992). With less emphasis on statistics, Bourdieu found similar results in his sociology of cultural knowledge, *Distinction* (1984), when examining linkages between forms of cultural capital – the knowledges of taste, creativity, refinement and fashion – and the maintenance of class hierarchies and divisions in contemporary French society. More simply, music is a cultural form in which social relations are reproduced and reinforced. Classical music implies distinction, refinement and educational capability, and thus becomes a marker of class differences, constructed in opposition to other styles such as country and popular music – the music of the 'masses'.

Inevitably, such distinctions have been contested, and at the very least they overlap and interact.

Music tourism suggests parallels with these studies of audience structures and their crude distinctions between classical, popular and country music. In Australia, Peter Egan's classical music tours of Europe, for instance, are very much marketed to the educated elite as tours to 'cultured' European capitals known for music (and priced as such, at over A$10,000 (US$7,000) per tour, largely preventing low-income earners from participating). However, at Salzburg, the scale of music tourism means that visitors span all ages and income groups, beyond the more elite crowds who might visit other classical music museums or festivals. Particular kinds of music are used to attract particular visitors in various contexts. Jazz is increasingly thought of as a highbrow music, despite its origins in New Orleans and the speakeasies of prohibition America, where it was a black music of abandon, freedom of expression and subversion. In the Hunter Valley, Australia, an increasingly popular wineries district, both opera and jazz festivals have been used to draw tourists; similar trends have occurred in most world wine-producing regions, even including Texas (Brown *et al.*, 2002). Opera is now universally seen as an elite form of musical entertainment, although it has been performed in a vast range of locations and contexts, from *Aida* in the deserts of Egypt to a range of 'opera-in-the-desert' festivals from Death Valley in the United States to the Northern Territory of Australia. Glyndebourne personifies the elitism attached to opera in its demand that visitors wear formal dinner dress, despite taking picnics on the lawns alongside the performance (Figure 4.1). Numerous studies (see, for example, Horowitz, 1985; Tighe, 1985; Saleh & Ryan, 1993; Americans for the Arts, 2002) have demonstrated that cultural tourists at arts events tend to be predominantly professional groups, with above-average income and graduate or postgraduate university education (see also Chapter 7). In contrast, the Grand Ole Opry, according to its parent company, attracts primarily 'adults, 45+, married, blue collar, home-owner, $45,000 household income' (Gaylord Entertainment, 2003: 1). 'Snowbirds' also dominate at Branson (Figure 4.2). Rock festivals, like much of the rock-and-roll tourism in Memphis or Liverpool, probably have younger, everyday audiences from diverse socio-economic backgrounds. Tourists at Abbey Road in 2002 were aged from 19 to 65, with a mean age of 40, and tended to be either students or from high socio-economic status occupations (Maiden, 2002). A similar age range at the Bob Marley Museum (Stanley-Niaah & Connell, 2004), and at Jim Morrison's grave (Dobbin, 1998), emphasise the wide age range of visitors, but also the fact that many were not alive or very young when these performers died. Visitors to the 2003 Elvis Revival Festival, in the Australian country town of Parkes, were older still, with over 60% being

Figure 4.1 Glyndebourne, Sussex, UK (Photograph by courtesy of Mike Hoban)

older than 45, as might perhaps have been expected (Brennan-Horley *et al.*, 2003). By contrast, dance-club tourism is almost exclusively targeted at the young, with brochures specifying the 18–30 age group, and 22 the average age of participants (Sellars, 1998: 612). But this is exceptional as tourists are usually rather older.

Such generalisations are always contradicted and such distinctions transgressed, particularly in the tourism context. Music appreciation, and music tourism, are far more complex than any simple 'classical versus popular' or 'high versus low culture' binary, and whatever generalisations are made about consumption patterns, audiences rarely conform to the desires of statisticians in rationalising their choices. Popular music fans, for example, may well often enjoy classical music, folk or jazz at various times and in relation to specific performers. This overlap has become more common because of the much wider range of media covering the diversity of cultural production, and through the 'popularising' of hitherto seemingly 'highbrow' music forms through releases such as operatic arias performed by the Three Tenors. Personal desires rarely stay bound by normative class categories. Honeymooners in New York may seek a classical recital in Carnegie Hall without really knowing the composer or performer, because such music might embellish a romantic holiday. Australian backpackers in Munich are drawn to the Oktoberfest for beer, but may, even if inadvertently, absorb traditional

Figure 4.2 Branson, Missouri, famous for its Highway 76 strip of performance venues, and more specifically country music venues, has a thriving tourist market dominated by snowbirds. 'Snowbirds' are a discrete segment of the domestic North American tourist market. Places seeking to attract snowbird tourists often create specialised attractions and offer tailored services, with RV parks, senior discounts, daytime performances, etc. (Photograph by courtesy of Rob Freestone)

German music without any interest in notions of cultural heritage. Nonetheless, there are parallels between audience preferences for certain styles of popular music and the form of music tourism. Festival attendance enables audiences to confirm their commitment to a style or artist, beyond listening on the radio or purchasing a CD – hence music tourism usually favours loyalty to the most loved artists and genres, rather than innovation, and to conform to existing social values. Audiences at Australia's National Folk Festival, Canberra, for instance, are more likely, on the whole, to be left wing or radical in their political beliefs than tourists visiting Dollywood in Tennessee; yet such generalisations are never entirely accurate.

The few studies that have been conducted on music tourists illuminate some of the subtleties in music tourism, particularly where the musical style involved is intimately connected to images and associations of actual places and nations. Prentice and Anderson (2000) conducted a survey of people attending a Riverdance show in Scotland, illuminating both numbers of tourists at that event and their perceptions of Ireland, including Irish music and dance. Tourists made up 50% of the audience. Those attracted to 'traditional' Irish music were 'generic consumers of the performing arts and thus representative of the type of target market for Irish contemporary cultural holidays'. Those interviewed were predominantly female (74%) and from professional/semi-professional, middle-class backgrounds (Prentice & Anderson, 2000). Educational background appears to have an important impact on participation in cultural tourism (see also Lohmann & Mundt, 2001). Most people frequently attended a range of performing arts, were well-travelled and strongly asserted that they did not expect to 'learn' about Irish culture through the performance, but that the show was simply 'consumed as spectacle' (Prentice & Anderson, 2000: 502). Other studies of cultural performances and museums in large cities demonstrate that concerts have substantial national and international drawing power; in Broadway, New York, at least 10% (and usually rather more) of theatre and concert audiences have been from overseas, while in the West End of London a third of theatre audiences are from abroad. Many of these audiences were in the city specifically for particular cultural events and attractions, which, without such tourists, would not otherwise have been viable (Hughes, 2000: 111–113, 152). In this way the largest cities tend to gain most from music tourism, even though a few regional centres and small towns (and large corporations) may also benefit substantially.

Because music tourism is diverse, so too are the demographic profiles of tourists. Visitors to Ireland seeking traditional music are very different from young English tourists in Ibiza, keen on hedonistic clubbing adventures. Travellers to Graceland or many country and western sites are often older and retired. Most visitors to Branson constitute retirees in winter and families in summer, and exemplify Gritzner's conclusion that typical country and western fans are blue-collar, rural 'just plain folks' (Gritzner, 1978; Carney, 1994). Backpackers, similarly, fill a particular niche of music tourists, often visiting places that are well known for electronic dance music such as Byron Bay (Australia) and Goa (India), and relying heavily on both guidebooks and informal 'word of mouth' networks for information (McGregor, 2000; Murphy, 2001). In general they travel for much longer periods – up to 12 months in many cases – utilising hostels and campgrounds rather than hotels and motels, seeking a more communal social environment in which to meet others and 'discover' local cultures. Such backpackers may constitute subcultural, or 'neo-tribal' social formations (Maffesoli, 1995; Gibson & Connell, 2003), where shared identities – visible through general appearance and the activities undertaken – are *performed*, in the sense that identities are socially constructed and continually reproduced by everyday actions, attitudes and understandings (Edensor, 2000; see Chapter 6). Associated with this is a particular version of a 'taste culture', where certain activities, destinations, fashions, styles of music and languages are popular: dreadlocks, deep tans, techno music, didjeridu or surfing lessons, 'natural' beaches, African drumming, particular brands of clothing or 'tribal' tattoos. This taste culture represents a field of social reproduction in which 'subcultural capital' (Thornton, 1995) is pervasive – the knowledge of trends, fashions and appearances which inform the social practices and scripts played out in tourist spaces created by and for backpackers.

The places visited by backpackers are thus connected to constructed identities and the subcultural capital bound up with them; in terms of music, particular locations are sought out because the music played there or associated with that location is credible within backpacker subcultures, hence the popularity of house and techno clubs in Ibiza, Spain, first with British backpackers, then with tourists from elsewhere in Europe, with it eventually becoming a mainstream mass-tourism location, particularly after a 'reality' television series exposed the antics of British tourists (Chapter 6). Travel agents, tour companies, music venues and airlines have become acutely aware of the lucrative nature of this market. Large-scale providers of dance music (such as Ministry of Sound, Cream, Gatecrasher, Manumission and Renaissance – venues and labels that promote album and single releases as well as fashion items, some directly linked to the Ibiza music scene) now operate within this tourist network, staging events in night-clubs in Australia each summer, alongside venues in London, Liverpool and Ibiza. Tour operators have sprung up to cater for this specialist market, capitalising on the commercial success of dance music, particularly in Britain, where one company sent over 65,000 people per year to Ibiza alone (Sellars, 1998). STA Travel Australia now runs a separate tourism campaign aimed at those intending to travel to well-known club locations, while reviews of local club scenes appear widely in guidebooks and backpacker magazines such as *TNT*. What began as a form of 'off-the-beaten-track' travel by intrepid hippies in search of the ultimate drug-related escape, has become a major market, staged by sizeable businesses on a scale more akin to mass tourism than to a low-key, 'alternative' pursuit.

At the opposite end of the demographic spectrum, but in parallel to backpacker tourism, are other nomadic tourists who, at least intermittently, seek out locations known for music. A social group particularly common in the United States, but emerging in both Australia and Canada, are 'snowbirds': retired travellers, so-called partly because of the common hair-colour, but also because of the tendency of people from this age bracket to travel south, from colder northern states in the cases of the United States and Canada, in a broad migratory pattern towards the west, south and desert interior. (In Australia similar groups are known as 'grey gypsies' and 'grey nomads'). Snowbirds are typically users of 'RVs' – recreational vehicles – essentially large, converted buses with all the trappings of a domestic home, often replete with satellite television and gas heating. RVs are often purchased on retirement with the sale of the family home, then taken around the country on extensive trips, sometimes including lengthy stays in specially allocated RV parks. Many places have become popular destinations for RV tourists, from museums and national monuments to state parks and Native American reservations (particularly those with casino developments). RV snowbirds tend to steer clear of big cities, staying on the fringes of metropolises. Also attractive to RV travellers are places associated with country music, notably Nashville, Branson and Pigeon Forge. Some motivation for these destinations is derived from nostalgia – country music had a huge period of popularity in the 1950s and 1960s – when Nashville was the centre for country music through WSM's Grand Ole Opry broadcasts, in the heyday of performers such as Hank Williams and Patsy Cline. Many RV tourists were then in their youth, hence a simple explanation for their contemporary enthusiasm for related tourist destinations. Snowbird tourism, however, represents much more than just nostalgia for a musical style; although 'neotribal' or 'subcultural' may be terms considered too youthful for RV travellers, there is a sense of shared and *performed* identities among RV tourists, with associated ideologies, values, events and activities. Country music locations may also be ideologically and culturally 'safe', where a conservative, home-centred – and largely white American – heritage is celebrated (Chapter 6). Nostalgia for country music is closely related to nostalgia for places and social contexts, emptied of the troubled racial and gendered politics of the time.

In economic terms, snowbirds are now increasingly incorporated into tourism strategies and recognised for their contribution to local economies. The Australian Tourist Commission has identified retirees as a target market because of their propensity to travel longer, with extensive retirement financial packages to draw on – far greater than was available to previous generations (ATC, 2001). Whole infrastructures have emerged to support RV transport and accommodation – specialist camp sites, RV sections of petrol stations and RV-friendly attractions. In the South of the United States, cities and towns such as Nashville, Pigeon Forge and Branson have adapted to this emerging market. Pigeon Forge, birthplace of Dolly Parton and now a centre for RV tourists, has purpose-built country music theatres connected to individual performers such as Alan Jackson, Louise Mandrell and Alabama – largely unknown outside America – which feature extra-large parking lots with dedicated spots for RVs. More purpose-built music theatres have sprung up in other locations popular with snowbirds, but which have less, or nothing, to do with music production, such as Myrtle Beach, South Carolina, and

Daytona Beach, Florida. The numbers of tourists attracted to country music destinations are considerable, and give some idea of the economic flows associated with snowbirds (who are a significant proportion of country music tourists): in Nashville the Grand Ole Opry attracts 600,000 attendees annually and the Ryman Auditorium (home of the original Grand Ole Opry) attracts 350,000 (Gaylord Entertainment, 2003), contributing to Nashville's annual tourism economy of over US$2 billion.

Music tourism sites and attractions generally attract two kinds of visitors: those particularly drawn for whatever reason to the memory or music of a particular performer, composer or genre (most obvious for festivals), and those who are there because the place fits into an itinerary devised for other reasons or because the visit is likely to be enjoyable (especially if linked into a performance). Thus, at Abbey Road, a place identified in many general guidebooks, most visitors were there because they had some (often not very much) appreciation of the Beatles' music, but others were there simply because it was part of an agenda that included a range of obvious London landmarks (Maiden, 2002). Particular links to music sites are, however, much more idiosyncratic and dependent on personal musical taste. Wider cultural and national links may also be evident. New Orleans and the Cajun region are popular with French tourists, 'keen to explore this quirky outpost of the Francophone diaspora' (Lenthen, 2000: 4T). For French tourists, travel to New Orleans in part allows an experience of Francophone identities in the New World, just as it is more likely to be Americans who visit Jim Morrison's grave in Paris.

Major sites, most obviously Graceland, attract a global market – even if by far the greatest number of tourists are predictably from the United States – as does the Bob Marley Museum in Kingston, Jamaica; over a one-month period in 2003 visitors came from over 50 countries, although mainly from North America, Europe and the Caribbean, and from every continent (Connell & Stanley-Niaah, 2004). Abbey Road is similar: a survey of just 22 visitors to Abbey Road in 2002 recorded tourists from some ten different countries, alongside the United Kingdom (Maiden, 2002), and the graffiti on the walls further emphasise the global spread. Even then there are differences: most Graceland visitors have at least some interest in Elvis Presley, as do visitors to the Bob Marley Museum for Bob Marley, whereas many Abbey Road visitors are there out of curiosity because it is an easily accessible site close to central London and quite different from most other metropolitan tourist destinations. Salzburg and other great cities of Europe also have a global reach but, again, music may not be the sole rationale for visiting such places. Similarly, although music is an important part of the tourism economy in Las Vegas (and is a desired cabaret venue for many major artists), establishing how many tourists actually come to Las Vegas for music, as opposed to gambling, golf (or even marriage!), remains difficult. McHone and Rungeling's (2003) analysis of the impact of an art exhibition suggests that local tourists are more likely to visit a destination for a specific event, performance or museum exhibition than national and international tourists who may well decide on that location for its mix of entertainment and attractions, of which music is just one component. Australian statistics suggest a similar situation for festival attendance: at best, 1% of inbound tourists listed a festival or carnival as the factor influencing visitation (NCCRS, 2001: 5), and less than 10% eventually attended a concert or festival (Bureau of Tourism Research, 2000). Nonetheless, impacts vary enormously from place to place. Visitors to the Parkes Elvis Festival in Australia were primarily local, but with significant 'outliers' in the cities of Canberra and Sydney, and barely 2% of visitors were from outside the state or country (Brennan-Horley *et al.*, 2003), a function of both the lack of alternative tourist activities there and limited publicity. Tourists travel to Hawaii for beaches, sun and scenery rather than for Hawaiian music, even though that music may be part of their specific experiences once there, and may have played a crucial part in providing a 'soundtrack' for tourist promotions and a lure to travel.

Most music tourist destinations are less significant for the number of visitors, the distance they have travelled and the extent to which that destination has attracted distant visitors, although even the Mull of Kintyre clearly attracts at least some long-distance visitors (Chapter 3), and, perhaps, also the extent to which they remain there and influence local economy and society. Festivals especially draw visitors for an extended period in comparison with the relatively fleeting visits – perhaps no more than ten minutes – that visitors make to such sites as Abbey Road where there is no active performance or formal means of selling a product to tourists.

Impacts of tourist visitation and expenditure

Few studies have examined the economic impacts of music tourism, although several trace the economic impacts of the arts in general (e.g. Cwi & Lydall, 1977; Mulcahy, 1986; Frey, 1994), and issues surrounding the public and private financing of arts activities (e.g. DiMaggio, 1986; Cummings & Katz, 1987). Since specialist studies are largely absent, observations on the impacts of music tourism must first be extrapolated from studies of cultural tourism in general. Research by the Travel Industry Association of America (TIAA) shows that those who attend musical performances, art exhibitions and other cultural events as part of a trip, on average spend as much as 30–50% more than other tourists (US$631 versus US$457); are more likely to spend in excess of US$1000 per trip; travel longer and are more likely to shop (Table 4.1; Americans for the Arts, 2002). This reflects the fact that visitors to arts activities generally come from wealthier, professional backgrounds (the TIAA survey found that cultural tourists were more likely to have a university degree), rather like visitors to Abbey Road or at Riverdance shows. However, such visitors represent 'up-market' arts tourists and may have little in common with many other music tourists.

One possible means of gauging the impacts of music tourism is to examine expenditure at particular events, the flow-on benefits to a local economy and thus how significant an event may be to local stakeholders. General statistics on multipliers for industries do not separate out cultural tourism, let alone music tourism, so to gain a more accurate sense of its flow-on effects it is necessary to consult the available figures on those sectors with the most obvious connections, such as music and theatre productions and the creative arts. The economic impact is higher than most other industries when measured in terms of extra employment generated. In Australia, 34 jobs are created for every extra $1 million of investment in music and theatre productions and 28 in the creative arts (which includes musical composition) (NCCRS, 2002). These compare with 17 jobs per $1 million in the construction sector, 19 in banking and only 9 in the mining industry. Where studies have been conducted on specific music tourism attractions, the results are similarly favourable. In Memphis, where a rare multiplier figure was calculated, 27 extra jobs were created in the city for every $1 million in investment at Graceland, which attracts over 600,000 visitors annually (Gnuschke, 2002: 6). When converted into real dollar and employment impacts on the city, via visitor spending, change in earnings for employees at Graceland and in related businesses, its impacts were estimated at somewhere between US$300 and $400 million every year, with between 4,000 and 6,000 extra jobs created.

Table 4.1 Visitors to non-profit arts events; expenditures per person, per day, residents versus tourists, 2002 ($US)

Category of expense	Resident visitors	Non-resident visitors	All arts visitors
Meals and refreshments	$9.99	$15.12	$10.33
Souvenirs and gifts	$3.49	$4.01	$3.51
Transportation	$2.39	$5.74	$2.63
Other	$5.88	$13.18	$6.40
Total (per person)	$21.75	$38.05	$22.87

Source: Americans for the Arts, 2002: 10

Even single events can have a significant impact. A rare published study, of the impacts of a series of Grateful Dead concerts in Las Vegas, emphasised the various benefits to the local economy of tourists visiting for the concerts. Such impacts included the expenditures of out-of-town Grateful Dead fans who came solely to attend the show; tax revenues (sales, hotel room, fuel, gaming and entertainment) received by the government as a result of fans' expenditures in the local economy; the cost of running the show (e.g. stadium rental, employment at the concerts) and, finally, the expenditures that local residents would have made if they had attended the show elsewhere (Gazel & Schwer, 1997: 45). Three Grateful Dead concerts were held in Las Vegas in 1995, with sales of over 110,000 tickets. Over 90% of the 52,000 individual spectators (many attended two or three of the concerts) were visitors from outside the local area. Gazel and Schwer provided two estimates of the direct and indirect impact on the local economy – one conservative, one optimistic. According to the conservative estimate, the concerts generated US$7 million in tourist expenditure and another US$5 million in additional, indirect spending (of local businesses and individuals who received incomes from the initial tourist expenditure); the optimistic interpretation estimated direct expenditures of over US$9.5 million, with a total impact of over US$22 million. In either case such 'super-concerts' make significant, if short-term, local contributions.

When tourist expenditure at the Las Vegas concerts was disaggregated, the highest figures were for accommodation (between US$49 and US$110 per capita), bar and restaurant purchases (between US$35 and US$88 per capita), although – and typical of musical events – there was substantial expenditure on gifts and souvenirs: music merchandise on sale both formally, inside the stadium, and informally, outside the stadium. Total expenditure on merchandise outside the stadium was approximately US$275,000 over the three concerts. When these impacts were added to those from tax revenue, employment and other operational costs, the total benefits to Las Vegas were between US$17 million and US$28 million. Converting these figures into an employment impact, it was estimated that the Grateful Dead concerts sustained between 350 and 600 jobs. However, some factors make this pattern of impacts unique: Grateful Dead fans often attended multiple events rather than one concert; tended to buy many goods and services in an 'informal' setting (e.g., bootleg cassettes, T-shirts and drugs on sale outside the venue), and probably purchased more merchandise than at average rock concerts, largely because 'Deadheads', as the fans were known, were famous for their commitment to the band (see Chapter 6). The outcome would have been different for a series of classical music concerts or those of contemporary popular performers.

The impact of concerts and musical events on local economies is magnified in the case of more frequent performances targeted towards tourists (as opposed to just three Grateful Dead concerts). However, many music tourism events are infrequent at best – such as festivals – hence, issues of seasonality affect economic benefits, and the tasks of measuring the local and regional impact of music tourism are considerable. Some problems are simply related to measurement, including issues such as 'the proper treatment of the event's induced spending by local residents, the extent to which the event diverts spending from established local visitor attractions, and the isolation of the event's induced spending from spending that was drawn into the area by other activities' (McHone & Rungeling, 2000: 300). What residents and tourists might otherwise do with their income is almost impossible to determine. Similarly, although visitors stay only a few minutes at Abbey Road, their being there may extend their stay in London and increase their expenditure on other goods and services (such as transport).

As the Grateful Dead fans demonstrated, music tourists spend money on goods. Certain commodities are unique to music tourism as purchasable items, in particular instruments (didjeridus, drums), recordings on CD and cassette (both legal and 'pirated'), and other souvenirs such as t-shirts, sheet music, books and videos. Salzburg has developed a 'Mozart industry' of everything from busts of the composer to Mozart teaspoons, postcards and chocolates. Tourist expenditure patterns vary enormously. Grateful Dead fans were more likely to spend larger amounts on memorabilia than fans of other bands, or casual travellers to music tourism sites who, while motivated enough to visit, might not translate this into purchasing commodities specific to that location. Drugs and alcohol may be significant purchases; hence, the most positive response to a 2003 survey on the impacts of the Byron Bay Splendour in the Grass Festival was from the local pub which had secured the exclusive rights to provide alcohol (at inevitably inflated prices) within the festival grounds (Gibson *et al.*, 2004). Classical music tourists may pay considerable sums for scarce tickets or international tours, while international visitors to Russian concerts pay much more than local visitors. At the Sydney Opera House only a fraction of those who visit actually buy tickets for a performance, and are satisfied instead with a photographic opportunity outside the building. At some destinations, such as Memphis, the array of merchandise is extensive, from the usual T-shirts and posters to musical doormats, Elvis furniture and Gibson electric guitars. At others, such as graves, Abbey Road or the Mull of Kintyre, there is little or nothing to purchase.

The expenditure pattern of backpackers differs from that of the older generations, those using more conventional holiday formats and those on package tours. Backpackers stay longer, spend smaller amounts in a wider range of places, often mix travel with work in the destination and are more likely to use local businesses rather than transnationals if choice exists (Loker-Murphy & Pearce, 1995; Murphy, 2001). A survey of over a hundred backpackers in Alice Springs, central Australia, was conducted in July 2000, the peak season for the Northern Territory, when thousands of young people, mainly from the northern hemisphere, descend on the region in search of desert landscapes, Aboriginal culture, adventure tourism and some element of escapism. It demonstrated how, for most people, culture plays some role in tourism, but is only exceptionally central to it and does not necessarily entail significant expenditure. Alice Springs is the town closest to the most popular site, Uluru (Ayers Rock), and all the backpackers were about to embark on three-day tours around the region. The survey aimed to gauge backpacker perceptions of Aboriginal culture, their experiences of Aboriginal music while travelling, and whether these experiences had led to purchases (see Table 4.2.). The largest group came from the United Kingdom (34%), followed by those from elsewhere in Europe (mostly Germany, Ireland, the Netherlands and Italy), the United States and Canada. These figures are consistent with overall statistics for backpacker tourists in Australia. All were staying in Australia for over a month, with over 60% staying longer than three months. Demand for experiences involving indigenous culture was reasonably high: nearly 60% of respondents listed a desire for some experience of Aboriginal culture as a high or very high motivation to travel to Australia (particularly for those from Germany and the Netherlands). A similar proportion had expected more interactions with Aboriginal culture as part of their trip, and indicated the need for more Aboriginal tours and cultural experiences.

Most backpackers had heard Aboriginal music, either before they arrived in Australia, or while on tour, most commonly in souvenir and art-and-craft shops. The majority (63%) had visited shops or other locations with didjeridu workshops and sales, with significant percentages also attending Aboriginal cultural centres, witnessing Aboriginal cultural performances and participating in tours. However, very few (14%) of the backpackers had purchased any Aboriginal music, either in recorded form or through purchasing an instrument such as the didjeridu, partly because many were travelling over several months and sought to minimise their luggage. Those who did purchase didjeridus in Australia invariably took up offers to mail them home (most didjeridus being between 1 and 2 metres long and rather heavy). Meagre budgets that had to stretch over months of travel also discouraged the casual purchases of goods such as CDs that might not be played until a return home. Moreover, as noted by Edensor (2000), some backpackers deliberately do not purchase souvenirs as one means of differentiating themselves from 'mass' tourists. For a group of tourists, who are characteristically limited consumers of material goods and who could not be defined as music tourists, there was some purchase of music goods

Table 4.2 Survey results: international backpackers in Alice Springs, 2000

Place of origin	No.	%
UK	37	34
Europe	33	30
USA/Canada	18	16
Australia	9	8
Japan	6	5
Other Asia	5	5
South America	2	2
Total	110	100
How long in Australia	*No.*	*%*
1–3 months	34	38
3–6 months	20	22
6–12 months	36	40

Attractions experienced	*No.*	*% of respondents*	*% of attractions experienced*
National Parks	63	57	32
Culture centres/museums	39	35	20
Adventure tours	37	34	19
Aboriginal sites	29	26	15
Aboriginal cultural performance	14	13	7
Eco-tourism	11	10	6
Other	3	3	2
Total	196		100

Experiences of Aboriginal culture in tourism attractions	*No.*	*% of respondents*	*% of experiences*
Didjeridu sales/workshops	69	63	34
Aboriginal cultural centres	45	41	22
Arts and crafts	42	38	21
Aboriginal performances	24	22	12
Aboriginal tours/walks	22	20	11
Total	202		100

Table 4.2 continued

Heard Aboriginal music?	No.	%
No	26	25
Yes	79	75
Total	105	100

Purchased Aboriginal music?	No.	%
No	91	87
Yes	14	13
Total	105	100

Statement responses	S. disagree	Disagree	Not sure	Agree	S. agree
(a) Aboriginal culture high priority	1 (1%)	16 (15%)	34 (31%)	45 (41%)	13 (12%)
(b) Never heard Aboriginal music	42 (39%)	47 (43%)	6 (6%)	11 (10%)	3 (3%)
(c) Need for more Aboriginal tours	0 (0%)	6 (6%)	49 (46%)	37 (35%)	15 (14%)
(d) Aboriginal culture is exotic	0 (0%)	2 (2%)	24 (22%)	62 (57%)	20 (19%)
(e) Expected more interactions	0 (0%)	14 (13%)	37 (35%)	41 (38%)	15 (14%)

Source: Fieldwork undertaken by authors, Alice Springs, July 2000
S. = Strongly

alongside a much wider degree of experience and enjoyment of Aboriginal music as part of the travel experience.

Men were much more likely to purchase didjeridus than women, possibly linked to masculine discourses of virtuosity in performance (the didjeridu is now popular among European and Israeli young men as an accompaniment to trance techno music), but reflecting the gendering of souvenir purchasing in general (Kim & Littrell, 2001). Men and women buy different artefacts in different ways for themselves and for others: while women tend to consider others more in purchasing decisions and spend longer in deliberations, men tend to buy for themselves and place less emphasis on careful consideration of the gifts for others.

Although as our results suggested, many backpackers do not buy didjeridus, the instrument has become one of the more important souvenirs (not just for music lovers) of visits to Australia (and, for many Australians, visits to northern and central Australia). The sheer quantity of didjeridus available in tourist shops around Australia is indicative of their popularity, especially so with short-term tourists. Most didjeridus are made at various locations in the Northern Territory of Australia, where concerns have been raised about the environmental impacts of the over-harvesting of hollowed-out trees in wilderness areas for the tourist didjeridu market (Dunbar-Hall & Gibson, 2004). Demand for didjeridus remarkably resulted in the emergence, in the 1990s, of a didjeridu manufacturing industry in Bali. By the start of the present century, in the village of Pengosekan, just south of Ubud, at least four workshops were devoted primarily to the manufacture of didjeridus, many ironically made from Australian eucalyptus, grown through Australian aid programs in Indonesia (Figure 4.3). Didjeridus were marketed at handicraft shops throughout Bali and sold mainly to European tourists (especially from Germany) returning home. A unique industry was seeking to supplant the much more expensive Australian products.

Expenditure patterns outside Australia, and of those other than backpackers, are vastly different and general conclusions impossible. Wealthy tourists are able to indulge in the raft of Elvis memorabilia in Memphis or Mozart souvenirs in Salzburg (alongside staying in expensive hotels and eating at good restaurants); others, less wealthy, 'dedicated' or impressed with kitsch, may make do with a postcard (or the internet café), a campsite and a donation to a busker. Beyond the specific circumstances of certain music tourism locations, little can be generalised about why certain people purchase which commodities, or go to which events or museums.

Consequently, data on the economic impact of music tourism (and projections of possible tourism increases) need careful consideration. There are analytical problems with being able to neatly define the economic impact of activities linked to 'music tourism', particularly when it is based on extrapolations from visitor surveys (Leiper, 1999: 605). It is just as difficult to separate out the effects of 'music tourism' from 'regular' tourism, as if 'music tourism' was, in fact, a discrete segment of the tourism industry (itself difficult to define). While some locations clearly have benefited in a major way from music tourism, and other kinds of travel and industrial investment have been spurred, there are risks involved, particularly as the scale of development increases.

Investment and Uneven Development

Music tourism, like other forms of tourism and economic activity, is geographically uneven. Places with the most significant music tourism economies (in quantitative economic terms) are part of international

Figure 4.3 Didjeridu manufacture in Bali (Photograph by courtesy of John Connell)

mediascapes; music or musicians from such places are internationally known and the music fulfils a role somewhat like that of films in providing some depiction or symbol of that place, through discursive landscapes (song texts, video clips or CD covers), deliberate marketing strategies and emphasis in travel writing. In well-known cases, these meanings form a palimpsest of media and events – news reports, films, newspaper and magazine articles, advertisements, as well as musical texts – and all inform the images of tourist destinations, whether or not tourism promoters are capable of controlling those images (Judd & Fainstein, 1999). Thus, the reception and consumption of the Beatles is connected to the media images and reputation of Liverpool, at the same time that it contributes to those images and reputations. The largest scale music tourism developments are in those locations with famous scenes, styles and individuals, although many others have built on limited reputations or sought to 'invent' music tourism economies where no musical associations previously existed.

Authorities in the music tourism destinations have become increasingly aware of the contribution of music to the urban economy. In New Orleans, 11 million people visit the French Quarter annually (Rodriguez, 2000: 100); by 1999 tourism-related jobs made up 16% of the city's total employment, up from 7% a decade earlier (Dimanche & Lepetic, 1999: 20). The tourism industry had become worth US$3.5 billion annually. Primary and secondary spending attracted by music was calculated at $593.6 million, with music tourism alone creating 38,000 jobs, excluding those of the musicians themselves (Cohen, 1997: 78; Wagnleitner, 2001). Lafayette, 120 kilometres west of New Orleans, has the second largest Mardi Gras in Louisiana; in 2000 tourists came from 46 states in the United States and from eight countries, most staying for at least two nights, and made payments of over US$50 million into the local economy, in addition to substantial expenditure within the town from local participants' own celebrations (Dwyer *et al.*, 2001). In Memphis, more than 8 million visitors arrive annually, with over US$2 billion in visitor expenditure and 48,000 jobs, effectively a doubling of the tourist market in ten years (Memphis Convention and Visitors Bureau, 2002). Graceland alone draws in over 600,000 visitors a year, with over 5000 per day in the summer months; entry to the house itself costs US$10 per adult, with 'platinum' tours incorporating the Elvis Presley Automobile Museum and his personal jets at US$18.50. By contrast, the small town of Branson gets about 4.3 million visitors in the nine-month tourist season – half from elsewhere in the state on two- or three-day vacations. Although Branson is regarded as a 'value-for-money' destination where people can spend less than US$75 per day, their aggregate economic contribution is massive (Cook, 1993: 14). In Austria, the tourism industry generates over 150,000 direct and over 400,000 indirect jobs, constituting 6% of the nation's gross domestic product, a significant proportion of which is influenced by music tourism (as well as skiing and hiking) in Salzburg and Vienna. In Salzburg, almost two out of every three jobs are either directly or indirectly attributable to tourism, but in a diversity of activities since not all nationalities have similar preferences to Americans, three-quarters of whom list the film *The Sound of Music* as the main reason for their travel (East & Luger, 2001). Liverpool, a city not generally associated with tourism, has nevertheless developed an industry that supports 21,800 jobs and generates £604 million (US$1.2 billion) in annual revenue; about 600,000 visitors (about a quarter of the total) came because of the Beatles, and this particular group spent some £20 million (US$40 million) in the local economy. In 2000 some 1300 people bought packages for the Beatles Festival there and remained an average of five nights in the city (The Mersey Partnership, 2001: 5). Even at Parkes, Australia, two-thirds of all visitors to the Elvis Festival stayed in the town for at least two nights, making a real economic impact on a town of barely 10,000 people (Brennan-Horley *et al.*, 2003: 9). This pattern of expenditure, with tourists staying for several days and nights, and purchasing meals, hotel rooms, souvenirs and local transport, alongside attending music performances, contributes most to local economies and explains the recent explosion in the number of music festivals (Chapter 7).

Many cities advertise the success of their arts communities, part of which comes from music festivals and other special events – even if they are not locations well known for music or tourism. Chattanooga has aggressively marketed itself as a place of arts and tourism, as has Edmonton, Canada, with 18 major festivals in its summer calendar which attracts over 2.7 million people and generates over C$75 million (US$65 million) a year (Economic Development Edmonton, 2003). San Diego has similarly sought to reposition itself as a city of cultural tourism, boasting over 1.8 million visitors per annum to cultural events, generating over US$200 million in direct and indirect expenditures in the urban economy (City of San Diego Commission for Arts and Culture, 2002). Even small towns such as Rochdale advertise their cultural and musical delights, while countries with little connection to a classical music tradition, such as the Seychelles, have sponsored festivals.

All this reflects an increasing recognition of the importance of the 'cultural economy' to urban centres in terms of direct expenditure and employment in the cultural industries (such as music, film, broadcasting, fashion) and the cultural tourism linked to them (Scott, 2000; Gibson *et al.*, 2002). This has become linked to discourses of 'the creative city' where culture is a key component of urban development planning, with 'how to' books such as Charles Landry's *The Creative City* (2001), and Richard Florida's *The Rise of the Creative Class* (2002) stressing the virtues of strengthening relationships between economic development and cultural policy. Various levels of government have been convinced of the efficacy of promoting the cultural economy of which music tourism may be a part: the creation of cultural districts, tax and regulatory incentives for cultural producers (such as film-makers and studios), public and joint-venture investment in new facilities, attractions and beautification schemes, and connections to place-marketing campaigns. Urban boosters and commercial elites have worked 'to transform place promotion from a relatively amateur and informal activity into an increasingly professionalised, highly organised and specialised industry to encourage the growth of tourism within cities' (Gotham, 2002: 1735). Much the same description applies to music within this.

Subsequently, some Western cities have incorporated music and the cultural industries into urban development strategies, although Halfacree and Kitchin (2000) found that all but two of eleven major British cities claimed a musical heritage and tradition, and few incorporated music into tourism distinct from other aspects of cultural revitalisation. Nonetheless, many featured festivals as part of tourism strategies and stimuli for urban regeneration. Reading, Berkshire, was particularly prominent in its incorporation of music into place promotion, hosting an annual rock festival and the WOMAD world music festival, as well as a vibrant pub circuit and culture of music consumption. Southampton now calls itself 'Entertainment Capital of the South'; Glasgow was keen to showcase its culture since it became a European City of Culture in 1990; Nottingham sought to connect music (clubs, pubs, street performances and 'youth scene') to sustainable tourism strategies, including the publication of a guide to local nightlife. Belfast, however, was reluctant to promote and use live Irish music because it was 'difficult in the present political climate to use "traditional music" to attract tourists' (Halfacree & Kitchin, 2000: 7), unlike the situation in southern Ireland. Even in particularly disadvantaged sites, such as Harlem (New York), cultural tourism is a potential mechanism for urban regeneration. Tourists, mainly from overseas, including Europe (particularly Germany), Japan and, more recently, Latin America, perceived Harlem as 'representing Black America, its music and entertainment traditions', an interest fuelled by the resurgence of classic jazz in the 1980s and gospel music in the 1990s (Hoffman, 2000: 209) (Figure 4.4). Over time, American heritage organisations shifted attention from more elite communities to celebrations of the ethnic heritage of minority groups. However, local impacts were limited where tourists largely remained on buses, with some local resentment of 'racial voyeurism' or 'whites on safari', little local expenditure and a commercialisation that excluded local residents (Hoffman, 2000: 219). The empowerment of local populations is crucial to the success of cultural heritage strategies.

Success has stimulated a host of imitators and diverse attempts to market sites. In 1997, Nova Scotia launched a C$3.5 million (US$3 million) two-year Celebration of Music to build on the 'distinct sound' of the province's music and create new jobs, centred around a series of festivals. At the same time, Louisiana was developing a Louisiana Music Trail that 'follows a path that meanders through countless cultures and generations of history' (www.crt.state.la.us/crt/yourism/music). Five years later in Perthshire, Scotland, political parties that usually feuded were united in support for 'A Soundtrack for Scottish Tourism' to link traditional

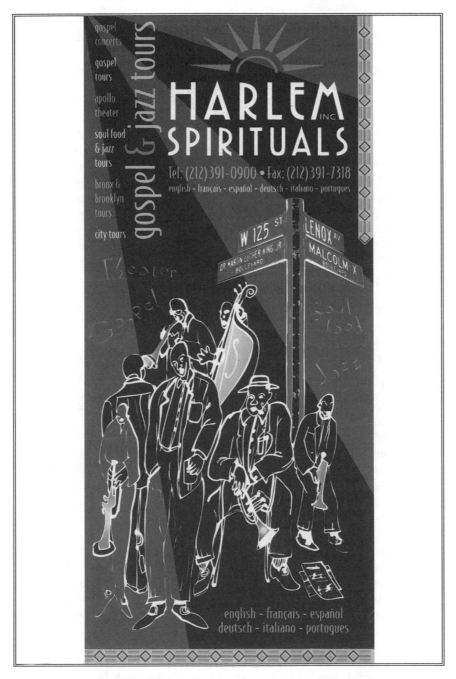

Figure 4.4 Advertisement for Harlem musical tour. It seeks to celebrate and commercialise black American musical heritage. (Source: Harlem Spirituals Inc., www.harlemspiritual.com)

music and tourism, and diversify the tourist industry. In the United States, New Jersey convened a conference to examine whether it could develop Asbury Park, the birthplace of Bruce Springsteen and home of 'Jersey shore' music, that might rival Liverpool, Nashville and New Orleans, and prevent it from becoming more of a ghost town (www. chorusandverse.com/content). In different ways, but drawing on some local context, many places have sought to benefit from music tourism.

The most touted British success story has been Manchester, where cultural tourism formed part of urban regeneration initiatives centred on the city's reputation for dance music and club cultures, growing out of the famous 'Madchester' sound of the late 1980s. Cultural industries and tourism were incorporated into the official development strategies, and local authorities relaxed licensing regulations to encourage more clubs, cafés and restaurants, to catering for the large influx of visitors to the city (Halfacree & Kitchin, 1996; O'Connor, 1998; Haslam, 2000). At its peak, between 65,000 and as many as 85,000 revellers were estimated to come into Manchester on Friday nights, to visit clubs and take part in dance parties. During the late 1980s, at the height of the scene's international prominence, over 40% of young American tourists to Britain listed Manchester as their primary destination, largely due to its musical reputation (Halfacree & Kitchin, 1996). While local councils encouraged new music venues to capitalise on this surge in popularity, there were drawbacks. The decline in licensing regulations, coupled with difficulties surrounding drugs and crime, eventually damaged the original scene that made Manchester a well-known music site. The Hacienda Club (once known within club cultures as 'the Eiffel Tower of Manchester', where artists such as New Order, the Stone Roses and Happy Mondays began to perform), was abandoned, a victim of rising prices demanded by monopolistic door-security cartels and pressure from local crime figures. This created an ironic emptiness, given the 'opening-up' of Manchester to the outside world through marketing musical performance and cultural heritage.

Urban regeneration strategies in deindustrialised cities such as Manchester mobilised cultural industries that promoted a particular mix of 'pro-capitalist' philosophies and deregulation, potentially alienating those people who had suffered most from deindustrialisation: 'the resultant development, while based on images of leisure and consumption and aestheticisation taken up by urban boosterists and sociologists alike . . . had limited cultural resonance, especially among those whose labour would be crucial to the transformation of the centre into a cultural landscape' (O'Connor, 1998: 231; see Chapter 5). In Manchester, as elsewhere, 'a heavy emphasis on the arts may well tend to reinforce and intensify social and economic inequality among residents and, increasingly, to serve as a manifest symbol of that inequality' (Whitt, 1987: 31). Rural areas and small towns have similarly sought to develop tourism to boost declining areas; the small town of Helena, Arkansas, used its links to Sonny Boy Williamson and Muddy Waters to stimulate blues tourism and a successful festival (Rotenstein, 1992), while within months of the death in 2004 of Slim Dusty, Australia's most famous country and western performer, his small home town of Kempsey was planning a A\$12 million Slim Dusty Centre. In urban areas particularly, cultural tourism often brought rising rents and social displacement, as poorer residents were forced out of gentrifying areas. Across locations as diverse as Temple Bar, Dublin; Newtown, Sydney (Carroll & Connell, 2000), Harlem, New York; New Orleans (Gotham, 2002); Memphis (see Chapter 5) and Manchester, renewed cultural precincts, sites of cultural tourism (and gentrification), invariably benefited visitors and upwardly mobile professionals more than the workers for whom economic regeneration strategies were officially intended.

Social costs

Music tourism is no exception to the familiar situation of economic gains coming at the expense of social costs. Tourists inevitably affect the environment (Chapter 7), influence local culture and values, and contribute to the 'staging' of that culture (Chapter 5), produce a demonstration effect and new patterns of consumption (e.g. of dress and food), and even transform sexual practices. Such influences are usually seen as negative by local people and in the scholarly literature, even – and perhaps especially – when incomes have significantly increased. However, uneven development has ensued. Few studies of music tourism have traced the extent of social influences beyond those on musical practice and performance.

Exceptionally, tourist experiences have been negative. Museums, like that at Wink, Texas (McLean, 1997: 112), may be dismal, festivals forgettable, hotels expensive, food poor, touts unpleasant and tourists even robbed, but rarely is this recorded. However, one visitor to Bob Marley's birthplace and burial site in Jamaica noted:

> There are few tourists here, no T-shirt shops [but] the burial site alleged to be free, is actually behind locked gates. A guide must be hired, a self-important 20 year old who unlocks the gates and escorts visitors up the hill . . . The tour ends in what is sadly typical Jamaican fashion. Logan demands J\$40 for his 'tour'. The vaguely threatening group who have rearranged the dust on the car want J\$20 for their unsolicited 'car wash'. And a trip to the gift shop is made to seem a wise idea. The shop holds Marley trinkets . . . The men running the operation are unfriendly, openly hostile when nothing is bought . . . Drugs are offered for sale. (Reynolds, 1992, cited by Dann, 1996: 355–356)

One account of the Liverpool 'Ticket to Ride' Beatles bus tour concluded: 'To say that the actual sites on the tour are disappointing is a wee bit of an understatement' (Goldfried, 1995). However, opinions vary (Figure 4.5). Museums have often attracted criticism; one critic of the National Centre for Popular Music in Sheffield, prior to its closure (see p. 125), observed

Figure 4.5 Tourists at Penny Lane and George Harrison's birthplace, Liverpool, UK (Photographs by courtesy of John Connell)

'It was pathetic. The place was too small to hold much and the majority of the advertising space was taken up with blatant advertising gimmicks for the sponsors. And of course it was all the more disappointing for being housed in a fantastic building' (www.sheffieldforum.co.uk/showthread). Similar experiences are seldom documented.

Buskers may be a menace as much as a pleasure, hence their regulation in many cities. In Cuba particularly, prostitution has been one concomitant of increased tourism (Brennan, 2003). A context of high unemployment lends itself to this, despite the creation of 'foreigner only' tourism zones where Cuban nationals are unwelcome. As one reporter argued, while simultaneously vilifying the local food, 'like music, debauchery never seems far away in Cuba' (Tran, 2003: 1). Hustling is most pervasive where tourists are frequent, and *jineteras* (female escorts) are similarly common (Rundle, 2001). Such issues are rarely more than cautionary phrases in guidebooks, as most travel literature is determinedly upbeat.

The unequal relationship between tourists and local citizens is especially common to developing countries, where economic differentials are greatest and the social impacts of tourism the most complex. There too the cultural implications of music tourism are most significant in terms of apparent threats to 'authenticity' (Chapter 6), but rarely have these issues received detailed attention.

Beyond music tourism?

Not infrequently music tourism has been used to stimulate other forms of tourism, notably conventions and conferences. Memphis and New Orleans have promoted themselves as locations for conventions on the back of an international reputation generated through music; so has Tamworth, Australia's country music capital. These strategies are geared towards increasing occupancy rates in hotels that are booked out in peak season when musical events are being held, but which might otherwise be vacant in lengthy off-seasons. Conventions maximise the tourist capacity of a city, while locations that have become successful music tourism destinations are attractive to conference organisers because of the new cultural status of those cities (in contrast to other nondescript urban centres), and because of available nightlife, restaurants and entertainment options. In the late 1980s in France Montpellier thus constructed a combined Conference Centre and Opera House in the middle of the city in a deliberate attempt to draw cultural events away from Paris (Negrier, 1993: 143). In Memphis, the Cook Convention Center, near Beale Street, was expanded in 2002 at a cost of US$92 million, part of the city's convention tourism strategy. The Convention Center includes a major exhibition space, 31 meeting rooms, ballroom and a 2100-seat performing arts centre. This expansion in turn spawned the construction and opening of over a dozen new hotels in the area (Memphis Convention and Visitors Bureau, 2002). In Nashville, the Opryland Resort and Convention Center, built adjacent to the Grand Ole Opry, now attracts over 4 million visitors annually, 80% of whom are business people.

Similar strategies have been developed for whole countries. Singapore has sought to market itself as a destination for Asian tourists, business travellers and regional conventions to diversify its economic base away from finance, shield the island city-state from the Asian financial crisis of the late 1990s and shake off its authoritarian, staid image, to promote itself as 'fun' and 'funky'. As Prime Minister Goh Chok Tong suggested in 1999, 'people laugh at us for promoting fun so seriously. But having fun is important. If Singapore is a dull, boring place, not only will talent not want to come here, but even Singapore will begin to feel restless' (quoted in Kwok & Low, 2002: 149). In the 1990s the government poured large amounts of money into the arts as part of this strategy, establishing a Ministry of Information and the Arts, and planning for a 'flagship' arts precinct surrounding a new concert hall/music theatre building known as Esplanades: Theatres on the Bay (Figure 4.6). The S$600 million (US$420 million) project took over ten years to plan, fund and build, opening in 2002 with considerable fanfare. Music played a part of Singapore's attempts to become 'Renaissance City', 'a world-class city supported by a vibrant cultural scene . . . a global arts city . . . to provide cultural ballast in nation-building efforts' (MITA, 2000: 4). Singapore stimulated international music concerts, musicals and shows at the Esplanades (such as *Les Misérables*, *Singin' in the Rain*), and conventions, as it became a more attractive place for conferences and work. In contrast to government enthusiasm, local artistic communities expressed reservations about the unintended effects of this expansion, arguing 'that providing the "hardware" (infrastructure and facilities) without concomitant attention to the "software" (creative development) is regressive for the development of local/indigenous arts, and the outcome is that global shows such as the Guggenheim Exhibition, and large-scale performances such as *Les Misérables*, will be quite happy to feature in Singapore, given the many incentives to do so'. Singapore would become 'a kind of emporium for the arts . . . another retail space in Singapore' (Kong, 2000; 2002: 14), while local artforms and artists, unable to compete against international 'big name acts', might not receive equal access to facilities and performance opportunities.

Implementing strategies to develop cultural industries, promote musical (and other) performances, and shift urban and national images have often proved difficult, not least in cities seeking to shake off 'rustbelt' images. In Liverpool doubts were cast over the success of attempts to transform the urban economy through music-related tourism investment. As Cohen (1997: 75–76) argued:

Figure 4.6 Singapore has sought to market itself as an Asian capital of culture and a place for cultural tourism. The cornerstone of Singapore's cultural strategy is the Esplanades: the Theatres on the Bay cultural precinct, which includes waterfront shopping and large performance venues, nicknamed 'durian' after the fruit they resemble. (Photograph by courtesy of Chris Gibson)

> During the second half of the 1980s the small Beatles 'industry' struggled to survive, and Beatles tourism has remained a small-scale affair dominated by a few private sector businesses. Most Beatles visitors are day-trippers with limited impact on the city's economy. Those connected with Beatles tourism describe it as a case of always 'missing the boat', 'a story of missed opportunities', and the city 'shooting itself in the foot', while overseas visitors, particularly Americans, have commented on how badly managed it is.

In one example of failure, a Liverpool commercial radio station, Radio City, built a museum and retail space called Beatle City at a cost of £2 million (US$4 million) that opened in 1984. Less than three years later it closed:

> In a building designed to look like a yellow submarine, and often with the original psychedelic Magical Mystery Tour bus parked

outside, Beatle City made quite an impact on this dowdy backwater of a street [Seel Street]. Within six months 100,000 fans had passed through its portholes. That initial flood soon reduced to a trickle. By the end of the first year its owners began to get that sinking feeling; it was clear that visitor numbers would fall way short of target . . . So where did it all go wrong? Whilst it could have been better, the exhibition itself was not the reason. In my view it was a combination of poor location, ludicrously high visitor targets, and a museum that was extremely expensive to create and run, managed by people who simply didn't have the right 'feel' for the Beatles and, more important, their fans. (Jones, 1991: 34–35)

Its problems derived from commercial imperatives overriding personal and cultural commitments to a band and scene, and underlying economic factors: a bad location, poor management, unreliable and declining tourist numbers, and even uncertainty within the city about the necessity for and the need for a cultural tourism policy (Parkinson & Bianchini, 1993). Liverpool's experience suggests that tourists include musical sites in an itinerary, when and where convenient, but the number of committed fans who will travel substantial distances is rather smaller. As in any form of tourism, particular sites and destinations may not endure, although since these early disappointments Liverpool has supported a more successful tourist industry.

A place for posterity

As music tourism has increased, so too has investment, going beyond developing places of performance to diverse means of enshrining the past. From more humble (or spontaneous) beginnings, some places have secured significant investments in infrastructure and attractions on the back of music tourism. Museums are one common strategy to turn musical heritage into tourist attractions. The vast majority of music museums are small-scale, many operated by non-profit organisations dedicated to an artist, style or era of musical expression, and these, as we will discuss later in this chapter, may perform a vital role in the commemoration of musical heritage. A very small number, notably the Bob Marley Museum in Kingston (Figure 4.7), are of much greater significance.

All manner of music museums have become tourist attractions. In London a music writer embarked on a £5.3 million project to convert Handel's London house into a major museum dedicated to the composer. Curiously the house next door commemorates the life of Jimi Hendrix who lived there in 1968–1969 (Heathcote, 2001). A larger museum complex is dedicated to Handel in his birthplace of Halle, Germany. In Seattle, Microsoft co-founder Paul Allen transformed his passion for

Figure 4.7 The Bob Marley Museum, Jamaica, has become a truly global tourist icon, as this Japanese website attests. (Source: www.purposejapan. com/09history/04bob_marley/bob.htm)

Jimi Hendrix into a US$240 million museum, performance space and multimedia extravaganza dedicated to Hendrix and the region's music more generally (including exhibits on the Seattle grunge scene of the 1990s). The Experience Music Project (EMP), covering more than 12,800 square metres, houses over 80,000 music artefacts, and includes dedicated spaces for museum exhibits, concert halls, a multimedia 'artist's journey', a virtual library and an arts camp for young musicians. Its architecture, designed by Frank Gehry, famous for the Guggenheim Museum in Bilbao, was inspired by the chaotic shapes of Hendrix's smashed guitars, with no right angles in the entire structure. It drew criticism; for one local journalist 'it looks like the Space Needle dropped its clothes in a pile' (Zebrowksi, 2000: 2), while an Australian travel writer likened it to 'cow intestines, a plane crash and a landfill' (*Sunday Territorian*, 5 June 2000: 15). Whatever the aesthetic sensibilities, a museum on this scale represents considerable corporate-driven investment in a city that is well known for its music. Elsewhere in the United States, Nashville has built a new Country Music Hall of Fame to increase tourist flows and revenues. The original Hall of Fame generated more than US$5.4 million per annum to the Nashville economy; the new facility was expected to generate between US$22 and 29 million in its first year and create 600 jobs over a five-year period (Morris, J., 2000). In each of these cases there were obvious links with particular individuals and scenes.

By contrast, Cleveland, Ohio, became the location of the Rock and Roll Hall of Fame, but not because it had a famous musical style or scene; more simply 'The Rock and Roll Hall of Fame is here and not in some other city because Cleveland had the balls to put up the money' (Perry & Glinert, 1996: 212), although it was the home city of Alan Freed, the radio disk jockey widely regarded as the person who coined the term 'rock and roll'. Cleveland's transformation from regional city to rock-and-roll headquarters is an ironic one, given its conservative past: in the 1950s, when rock and roll exploded into the public domain with Elvis's success, in a burst of moral panic, Cleveland invoked a 1930s law preventing young people dancing in public without parental guidance, while in the 1960s the city introduced a 'Beatles ban', barring teeny-pop groups from city venues 'so that teenage girls would not be subverted' (Perry & Glinert, 1996: 212). In the 1980s Ahmet Ertegun, co-founder of Atlantic Records, and other rock-industry moguls established the Rock and Roll Hall of Fame Foundation, a non-profit organisation intended to commemorate rock music's best-known artists, and eventually established a museum dedicated to them. In 1986 the newspaper *USA Today* ran a nationwide telephone poll asking the general public to vote on their preferred location for the Hall of Fame. Cleveland Radio DJs and newspapers took up the campaign, aggressively encouraging local residents to vote. When the count was completed, Cleveland had amassed 110,315 votes, well ahead of Memphis in second place with only 7000 votes. The Hall of Fame opened in 1995; total investment on the project was estimated at US$90 million, with $65 million coming from the City of Cleveland. The Hall of Fame generated significant revenues and helped to double Cleveland's tourist numbers in its first five years. In the first 12 months, the Hall of Fame attracted over a million visitors, although five years later figures had fallen by more than half (Zebrowski, 2000). The local newspaper, the Cleveland *Plain Dealer*, then described the Hall of Fame as the 'rock and roll mausoleum'.

In the United Kingdom, a similar museum opened in 1999 in the northern industrial town of Sheffield: the National Centre for Popular Music, a £15 million (US$30 million) complex with an interactive museum, a 3-D 'sound auditorium' and financed with £11 million (US$22 million) from the National Lottery (Roberts, 1999; Halfacree & Kitchin, 2000). Sheffield, while not then known internationally for a musical scene or style, has many clubs, live venues and a healthy music following, although the decision to locate the centre there was primarily as substantial investment in a region otherwise troubled by industrial decline (made evident in the films *The Full Monty* and *Brassed Off*). Managers of the centre predicted upwards of 400,000 visitors per annum, yet, after 12 months barely 100,000 had passed through the doors (BBC, 1999; 2001), prompting grave concerns about its viability. Despite attempts in 2001 to convert it into a live music venue, the centre was eventually closed as a tourist attraction, although Sheffield city considered other uses, including converting it either into part of a creative and digital industries 'cluster' or as a student union building for Sheffield Hallam University (National Centre for Popular Music, 2003). At the core of its problems were over-inflated estimates of visitor numbers which fell below those required to meet the costs of running a major attraction.

The more successful museums have been those dedicated to individuals and located in places associated with their music, such as those of Bob Marley or Loretta Lynn, rather than grand edifices in provincial locations that sought to cover a range of themes. Specialised museums may be more successful because, although orientated at a smaller potential market, they attract dedicated followers. Larger museums may suffer from the paradox inherent in music tourism – that they are static representations of what were once vibrant, but always fleeting, musical scenes. No matter what artefacts or high-tech wizardry they display, museums by definition institutionalise and formalise what were in essence ephemeral and sometimes rebellious voices. Unless connected to the mythologies and personal lives of key individual performers or styles, music is rarely a good museum theme.

Employment for Musicians

Central to music tourism economies are the musicians: a labour force vital to create and re-create live performances of well-known styles or songs and a crucial component in constructions of authenticity surrounding music tourism sites (Chapter 5). Minimal research has been conducted on the impacts of tourism on the lives of musicians, or how their roles and the industrial relations climate within which they work might be altered through transformations in place and economy brought about by tourism. It is, however, possible to outline several themes.

In many places, whether or not orientated to tourists, there is an over-supply of musicians, and at the same time discourses of 'music as culture and vocation' rather than 'music as work' restrict the remuneration of musicians (Gibson, 2003). The music industry remains under-unionised, although this was not always so, as the musicians' industrial disputes in the United States in the 1930s and 1940s in response to the rise of radio illustrate (Clarke, 1995). In most developed countries, competing entertainment forms (computer games, television, DVDs, etc.) alongside changing demographic structures and urban forms (more dispersed, suburban communities and ageing populations) have reduced the demand for live entertainment; consequently, musicians have experi-enced falling rates of pay for performance since the 1980s. This trend is compounded by the nature of musical creativity; struggling artists are often more willing to perform, at almost any price, to gain a perform-ance space and an audience, however tiny. They may value their work as 'culture' rather than 'labour'. The presence of a cheap labour force encourages promoters to under-pay novice performers whose appeal is uncertain and employ better-known artists who will draw crowds that purchase alcohol (in pub and club gigs) and/or food, souvenirs and merchandise (at stadium concerts and festivals).

Local musicians may be 'crowded out' of performing spaces and oppor-tunities, especially if tourism increases rapidly, attracting not only tourists from distant locations, but also musicians seeking to capitalise on the tourism boom. As they became more successful locations, the Whitsunday Islands (Queensland) used both national and international performers (Hayward, 2001). Similarly, around Byron Bay, on the north coast of New South Wales, Australia, touring musicians have gained better venues and higher payments than local acts of equivalent status, largely because of the perceived extra marketability of 'visiting' musi-cians (see Gibson, 2003). Singapore's strategy to promote itself as a tourist destination for major Western international acts and shows largely excluded local performers. Local musicians can find it more difficult to gain decent exposure once places become well-known tourist destina-tions, as better-known or more professional acts secure the popular venues and prominent slots. Groups playing their own compositions may be displaced by visiting tribute bands or local artists willing to play 'covers' of famous performers. This process is partly offset where visiting musicians generate larger audiences and offer local support roles in concerts.

However, in every context, tourism has increased the demand for musicians, and employment has been created to the extent that in some locations musical activities are formalised in more reliable wage and labour situations. Places such as Honolulu and Las Vegas, and countries that are major tourist destinations, such as Vanuatu, Barbados and Malta, have been major beneficiaries. However, some countries that have gained significantly from music tourism and used music to promote themselves have done little to promote the welfare of the musicians. In several parts of the Caribbean 'traditional' musicians have been ignored in favour of more polished 'Western'-oriented performers:

> [the local performer] is still rejected socially in most islands, because of his [sic] 'lower class' background and limited education; and, as a result, hoteliers continue to exploit his talents, by offering poor working conditions, long working hours for low pay, while demanding preferences of music in the interest of the tourist, and at the expense of creative talent. (Millington-Robertson, 1988: 31)

Such attitudes towards working musicians stretch back to the Middle Ages and the troubadours who were considered the lowest members of society.

Ireland has seen a tendency to assume that some 'trickle-down' effect will support musicians playing in pubs and bars, yet pub music scenes have tended to promote the incomes of publicans and professional musicians (mainly country-and-western duos) rather than performers of Irish music (Stokes, 1999: 146–147). Similarly, in Alice Springs some of the most successful performers of 'Aboriginal' music are Europeans, with stores and theatres located in the main tourist mall. The more local performers may be marginalised and disadvantaged.

Although in some places, such as Aldeburgh, innovation is coveted, in most music tourism locations more sporadic or unplanned, highly variable performances (which characterise some local pub circuits and club scenes) are replaced by the need for regular, replicable performances to satisfy the tourism industry's need for reliability. For some musicians this may mean a degree of repetition that is unacceptable to those seeking their own expressive voices and continual artistic growth (Atkinson, 1997: 101–103). In Cuba,

> artists are appreciative of the regular employment they receive through tourism (although they express frustration when performance becomes too routine). They, like artists everywhere, need

regularity of performance for financial security . . . much like North American jazz musicians who must play 'casuals' (e.g., in weddings and barmitzvahs) to augment their earnings, but who play whole-heartedly in a jazz atmosphere or who are deliriously involved when playing with or singing in an orchestra. Cuban musicians in the tourism environment have opportunities amid many routine perfor-mances to become fully involved, fully engaged. (Daniel, 1996: 792)

In Ireland, the tourism boom has raised demand for 'traditional' Irish music, from urban tourist spaces such as Temple Bar, Dublin, to rural counties. Consequently, but ironically, more informal gatherings of musi-cians in pubs, with no pre-planned line-ups or sets, have gradually been replaced by a more generic performance format for tourists: paid performers, standardised sets, dedicated audiences, sometimes entrance fees to recoup performance payments (as many tourists simply do not drink as much as local audiences may have done in times past), and an emphasis on 'tradition', even though the 'traditional' session format is actually a relatively recent product of diasporic migrant links (Kneafsey, 2002; Chapter 5). Here and in many other contexts the informal is gradually becoming more formal.

Different musical performances have varied impacts on music labour and remuneration. Festivals are both unique opportunities to reach a wider audience, but potentially a limited source of income for most artists who receive a smaller share of the total takings than in a formal concert (see Chapter 7). However, the increasing number of festivals and their organisation into circuits, also evident in the global house music scene (Chapter 6), enable performers to have regular employment and substantially increased income opportunities. Many musicians prefer festivals because they tend not to saturate the market for live perform-ance in any given location (Gibson & Homan, 2004; Dunbar-Hall & Gibson, 2004).

Busking constitutes a distinct form of musical labour that is particu-larly important in relation to tourism with its own distinct economics, being reliant on haphazard audiences – passers-by who might pay for performance if they enjoyed it and/or feel charitable. Buskers have a crucial role in music tourism locations, filling streetscapes with sounds, even authenticating the city and marking out urban space as tourist space: 'music is used to assist in marking spaces where revelry is permitted. Music serves as a signal that a space is open for occupation. Within the French Quarter, where the music stops, tourists hesitate to venture' (Atkinson, 1997; see also Harrison-Pepper, 1990; Tanenbaum, 1995). Busking in effect constitutes a 'public good' in that it benefits a community or society through enjoyment in a public space and because it 'lacks mechanisms to ensure payment by the audience in exchange for consumption of the product' (Kushner & Brooks, 2000: 66). In some cases, though, buskers are backed by local tourism authorities, as in New Orleans, in view of their crucial role in creating atmosphere, adding spontaneity and 'authenticity', and ultimately fleshing out the process of 'place-making' that is crucial to urban regeneration. Such stances vary considerably to those in other locations, often without significant tourist markets, where busking is perceived as a nuisance and safety hazard, an impediment to other 'formal' commercial activities or inappropriate soliciting from the general public. Tourism is one means of counteracting such attitudes on the part of city authorities, reversing perceptions of street performance and enlivening public spaces. Busking is frequently thought of as a desperate means of income generation, often 'not treated as a viable form of exchange by economists, who perhaps think of it as nothing more than begging' (Kushner & Brooks, 2000: 69), but for many semi-professional and even professional musicians it can be a sensible and flexible income-seeking decision, hence the need for it to be regulated in many tourist destinations (Chapter 3). In Paris, for example, the best buskers may earn the equivalent of US$400 a day, alongside sales of CDs (Sage, 2002). At the best sites in Sydney, New York, and other major tourist cities, similar incomes are possible. Some of the greatest beneficiaries of the rise of tourism have been buskers, although they are tangential to music tourism itself.

Music tourism, like other forms of tourism, has created jobs, inevitably for the musicians themselves, most evident in summer 'seaside' tourist destinations where leisure time demanded musical accompaniment from individuals, bands and orchestras that returned to urban centres in the off-season. In several coastal areas of New South Wales, Australia, in the post Second World War years, Aborigines were hired as 'Hawaiian' bands in expanding resorts, and in Fiji indigenous Fijians were drawn into a range of musical activities, performing traditional war dances (*meke*) or playing Hawaiian style music (Figures 4.8 and 5.1), so generating valuable regular, and enjoyable employment outside the agricultural sector. As in Bali and Vanuatu, that income is limited by village musicians and dancers needing to go through commercial intermediaries who may introduce competition between them and impose financial constraints. Nevertheless, much the same could be said of many other tourist destinations in developing countries where the relationship between tourism and music has been valued for employment, artefact sales and in other ways. Tourism is one means for musicians to secure work opportunities in what is a highly fluctuating and unpredictable occupation. Despite low wages, repetition and competition from outsiders, tourism has assisted places in maintaining live musical performances.

Figure 4.8 This postcard from the 1960s depicts Fijian musicians playing in 'island' style, but with guitars and ukuleles, for tourists

The Qualitative Economy: Non-profit Organisations in Music Tourism

Beyond the immediate and indirect impacts of tourist expenditure, the more 'qualitative' impact on the local economy is of some interest – that is, the nature of different forms of accumulation, such as the extent to which music tourism activities are undertaken by profit-seeking ventures or are driven by other types of institutions with non-profit, social or cultural motivations. Where music tourism has become most successful, the particular destinations and the attractions involved have been either established or purchased by large companies keen to capitalise on the potential for tourist growth, or face a situation where more powerful multinational corporations edge in on the market that was previously enjoyed by various small firms. This competitive dynamic, associated with capitalist expansion in general, has contributed to one element of the 'tourist cycle', where small-scale, informal tourism economies make way for larger, mass-tourist orientated attractions and infrastructures as places gain a reputation as a holiday destination, resulting in a potential threat to local incomes (Butler, 1980).

Country music tourism, centred on Nashville (but spreading to many cities throughout the south), is one case where music tourism has evolved in this way and where one particular company, Gaylord Entertainment, based in Nashville, has significantly expanded its empire. Gaylord built its reputation and fortune with the Grand Ole Opry which it moved from the Ryman Auditorium in downtown Nashville to a dedicated complex on the city outskirts in 1974. In what Lonely Planet has called 'a stroke of zoning genius, this premeditated tourist zone was carved from a nearby suburb and built into an American tourist mecca far from where it could sully the original downtown' (Lonely Planet, 2003: 4). Surrounding the Opry, Gaylord invested in a museum, theme park (subsequently bull-dozed to make way for an Opry-themed shopping mall), and the gigantic Opryland Hotel which, according to its press release, has 'a 4.5 acre interiorscape, that rises 15 stories high and includes:

> A flowing river more than a quarter-mile in length complete with four 25-passenger flatboats . . . an 85-foot fountain . . . a 400-seat restaurant, Beauregard's, situated in a 20,000 square foot antebellum-style mansion . . . a spectacular 4.5 acre indoor garden filled with southern live oaks, plants, flowers, a 110-foot wide waterfall. (Quoted in Jameson, 1995: 45)

With 2800 hotel rooms and a major convention centre, the Opryland Hotel was by far the largest hotel development connected to a music-related attraction (and equivalent in size to an international airport). Gaylord owns other hotels, resorts and convention centres, two 57-foot river taxis that shuttle Opryland guests to downtown areas, the General Jackson showboat (the world's largest showboat), Grand Ole Opry Sightseeing Tours, the Springfield Golf Club, the Opryland KOA Campground, the Opryland Music Group, several country music radio stations and cable television interests, country magazines, and the Wildhorse Saloon, a country dance venue in Nashville which attracts 750,000 visitors annually (see Figure 4.9; Gaylord Entertainment, 2003). In 2001 its total assets reached over US$2.1 billion, with annual revenues exceeding US$300 million (although this had fallen from US$514 million in 1999–2000). This expansionary model has been replicated on a smaller but no less commercial scale: country musician Calvin Gilmore estab-lished and still owns the 2200 seat Carolina Opry, at Myrtle Beach, South Carolina, as well as the Historic Charleston Music Hall, in Charleston, South Carolina (well known for its 'stomp' dance style of the 1920s). On Stage Entertainment owns 'Legends in Concert' music theatres in 11 loca-tions including Las Vegas, Atlantic City, Myrtle Beach, Branson, Toronto, Miami, Cancun (Mexico) and, somewhat bizarrely, in Berlin, Germany.

   In New Orleans, the French Quarter was largely ignored for decades by multinational corporations since its seedy reputation did not fit the contemporary, slick appearance desired by large investment firms. But, as tourism has boomed, multinationals have increasingly moved in to the French Quarter and especially the hotel market:

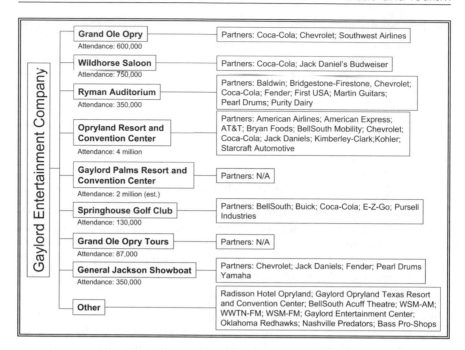

Figure 4.9 Gaylord Entertainment has become one of the largest dedicated music tourism companies, with interests in several attractions, hotels and properties, and partner relationships with several of the largest companies servicing the tourism industry. It demonstrates an emerging corporatism within the music sector. (Source: http://ir.gaylordentertainment.com)

> Though New Orleans has long been a city of small home-grown restaurants, hotels and clubs ... large national corporations have begun to creep in. Within the past few years, a House of Blues, a Virgin Megastore, a Bubba Gump Shrimp Co and a Jimmy Buffett's Margaritaville have all opened prominent locations in the French Quarter. Hotel chains such as the Marriott and the W have taken over and renovated many older buildings. The Harrah's casino, open a year, took up an entire city block at the end of Canal Street, with its huge gaming halls containing 3,000 slot machines and 120 tables for games such as poker and roulette. It is estimated that every person landing at the airport must spend more than $60 at the casino for it to break even. (Rodriguez, 2000: 100; Gotham, 2002)

Similar events occurred in Harlem, New York, where Disney, Sony and AOL Time Warner sought to invest in the gentrifying neighbourhood, including a plan 'to link the legendary Apollo Theater to a nearby theater to create a complex with performance space, rehearsal studios, a television facility and gift shops' (Hoffman, 2003: 292). Rising rents and reduced black ownership of businesses resulted.

Thus, while it might seem counterintuitive, negative economic impacts on local communities are linked to the growing investment in music tourism. Direct employment at a major new attraction enables city authorities and corporate representatives to boast about job creation, yet unless there are significant resulting increases in total visitor numbers, the market for smaller, local competitors is likely to be reduced, thus threatening the small business sector. Moreover, larger companies affect local economies by transferring profits elsewhere – an economic 'leakage' from the region. The extent to which 'first-round' spending by tourists benefits a local economy 'depend[s] on the local average propensity to consume domestically produced goods and services' (Gazel & Schwer, 1997: 43). Because larger ventures, including hotels, may themselves import goods and services (from central warehouses or from other branches of the same companies), a greater proportion of tourist profits leaks from a locality. This is compounded when profits return to owners and shareholders elsewhere. The presence of multinationals is detrimental in two ways: first, in their own transfer of profits outside the region and in centralising logistics and distribution, which constitutes a blow to the propensity to consume locally, and second, because the presence of multinationals results in a greater proportion of the domestic consumption of goods and services by local residents being captured by these multinationals (in, for instance, fast-food restaurants and chain retail stores). This is evident in the partner firms associated with Gaylord Entertainment properties (Figure 4.9) which have a stake in Gaylord, supply various products and endorsements to Gaylord attractions, and emphasise leakage from the local economy.

In contrast, non-profit organisations have greater propensities to consume domestically. They are usually smaller and more effectively embedded in webs of local relations with suppliers and service providers, as well as being staffed by local people. Moreover, as the case of New Orleans' casino illustrates, size brings both economies of scale and potential instabilities. As one commentator argued in relation to Seattle's Experience Music Project, 'EMP faces many challenges. Its image must remain current and exciting, to lure all those tourists each year. The day it becomes known as the Excessive Monotony Project, there's trouble' (Zebrowski, 2000: 1). Non-profit organisations, on the other hand, neither share the same impulse towards maximising profits, nor have shareholders to whom they must deliver dividends. Consequently 'nonprofit firms, in effect, employ a system of voluntary price discrimination, [thus] can often survive in areas of the performing arts where for-profit firms cannot' (Hansmann, 1986: 360). They are often more resilient and in the long run better able to cope with fluctuations in tourist numbers.

Recognition of the role and significance of non-profit forms of economic institutions is becoming increasingly apparent. Previous understandings of regional economies, steeped in a political economy framework which pitted workers against the activities of capital (and the state), have underestimated the extent to which alternative forms of economic exchange, including non-profit firms, exert a stabilising influence because of the intensity of local flows of money, greater capacity to address labour issues and the higher priority placed on social equity, affirmative action and other cultural goals (Gibson-Graham, 1996; Amin *et al.*, 1999). The contribution of non-capitalist economic forms has been greatly underestimated, but they are increasingly seen as having policy relevance, especially in relation to the arts. Several studies of the economic contribution of non-profit organisations to local economies and creative industries emphasise the real gains. San Diego's non-profit arts sector is worth more than US$375 million per year (in non-profit organisation spending, and audience spending at venues and events staged by such organisations). Equivalent figures for other cities with strong music heritages and tourism industries are similar: over US$300 million for New Orleans, US$100 million for Memphis and $430 million for Detroit (Americans for the Arts, 2002). In these three centres the full-time equivalent jobs created by non-profit arts organisations exceeded 35,000.

Beyond this quantitative impact, non-profit organisations involved in music tourism (such as fan clubs) warrant particular attention since it is they that initially seek to commemorate musicians' lives or the music of a particular era, and so transform particular sites into tourist attractions. With an emphasis on fostering 'community' and their greater capacity to absorb risk, they have pioneered music tourism in many locations through the establishment of monuments, museums, walking trails, tours and commemorative festivals. Public tourist authorities have further encouraged these developments.

Furthermore, non-profit organisations play a vital role in cultural policy. Divorced from profit maximisation, such organisations have a capacity to support more experimental, innovative or, indeed, 'traditional' cultural expressions, and often such aims are written into their constitutions and vision statements. Better-known examples in music tourism include Memphis' Centre for Southern Folklore and Staxville USA; Cleveland's Rock and Roll Hall of Fame and Detroit's Motown Historical Museum in the original Hitsville building. In Australia, the Central Australian Aboriginal Media Association, which runs a radio and television station, records Aboriginal musicians and operates a tourist shop in Alice Springs, provides an alternative to the non-Aboriginal-owned didjeridu shops in the town's main precinct. The Centre for Southern Folklore's charter requires it to provide an educational role, alongside its touristic purpose. Thus, its public shopfront has regular exhibitions on all aspects of Southern politics, music and culture, as well as free performances by Memphis' older blues and folk performers (in contrast to the more standardised rock cover bands who play at nearby 'blues bars' in the tourist section of Beale Street). Its annual Memphis Music and Heritage Festival, well known for its commitment to original, high-quality blues and roots music, has become a major event on Memphis' events calendar. Non-profit organisations provide support for musicians with different power dynamics from those regularly experienced in both the music and tourism industries. They play a role in nurturing performers and preserving musical traditions, while opening up space for greater creative freedom. In this respect, then, they are more capable of guarding 'authenticity' against the worst commodifying elements of the tourism industry.

Money, Money, Money?

Music tourists are as diverse as the destinations and events they go to and participate in. So too is their pattern of expenditure, yet as tourism has increased in volume and duration its impact has been greater, especially in once more distant locations, such as Guinea where hardy groups of drum enthusiasts have pioneered new destinations (Chapter 6), or Bali where didjeridus are now manufactured. It has been particularly significant in such primary tourist destinations as Graceland, Hawaii, Salzburg and the Caribbean. Urban tourism, centred on cultural tourism in destinations such as New Orleans and Memphis, has been a vastly more powerful means of income and employment generation, despite conflicts over uneven development and the status of participants as beneficiaries; Harvey has even perceived the use of cultural policy in urban restructuring as no more than a 'carnival mask' (1989), concealing growing social inequality, polarisation and conflict within cities. As expenditure has increased, so places and corporations have sought to capture larger markets and market shares, extend the duration of music (and other kinds of) tourism through festivals and festival cycles, and link tourism to hotel chains and related enterprises. In several regions there has been intense competition. At the start of 2003 the two neighbouring Australian country towns of Parkes and Forbes had jazz and Elvis Presley revival festivals on the same weekend, actively competing for a similar market. New museums have similarly been developed and become highly successful when focused on a single performer, as music has become part of their heritage. Nonetheless, as the experience of such exhibitions as those at Cleveland and Sheffield has demonstrated, music tourism is fickle and fraught with uncertainty. As with other components of cultural tourism, it continues to expand rapidly and stimulate employment in a range of arenas, although its geography and impacts are uneven. Similarly, like other forms of tourism, music contributes to 'tourism cycles' that spur fluctuating investment and accumulation, so altering the working lives of musicians and those who depend upon them. In that process, as in Ireland, the music itself has changed, as has the cultural context in which it is performed. Such changes are examined in the following chapter.

Chapter 5
Music, Tourism and Culture: Authenticity and Identity

Previous chapters have examined the emergence of music tourism in historical and geographical contexts, and have explored the economic impacts of music tourism. As with other types of travel, music tourism is also bound up in a range of debates and conflicts that are inherently cultural. Such debates and conflicts involve questions of local or global cultures, the meanings and identities involved with music tourism, debates about the validity of images, attractions or campaigns, and discussions of relations of power. This chapter examines the cultural politics of music tourism, engaging with three distinct, but interrelated concepts – authenticity, identity and performativity – that trace the manner in which musical expressions and tourism industries combine. These three concepts shape a cultural geography of music tourism in and across places, and determine the extent to which music tourism is celebrated or even contested. This cultural geography is more complex and contradictory than might be expected.

'Authenticity' in Music and Tourism

The notion of 'authenticity' permeates most forms of tourism (Cohen, 1988; Wang, 1999), and is simultaneously a concept that is central to the production and consumption of music, irrespective of the extent to which it might be linked to tourist activities. 'Authentic' music is usually seen as that which is deemed credible, central to the genre, original and true to the artist's intentions. For instance, 'black' music played by black musicians is often considered more 'authentic' than that of white musicians playing a similar style (Gilroy, 1993; Lauret, 1996). Audiences ultimately enjoy music because of the sounds themselves – the notes elicit feelings, create excitement, emphasise moods – but authenticity demands more than the arrangements of notes in particular ways. A whole infrastructure surrounds music as a cultural industry, enabling production, distribution and consumption (Frith, 1989; Negus, 1999; Connell & Gibson, 2003). This context, which is not immediately obvious when listening to either recordings or live performances, shapes the image of performers, while also seeking to reproduce the artist's musical intentions and inspirations. It involves talent scouts, promotional agents, publishing firms, recording studio engineers, record producers, recording companies, advertisers, graphic designers, photographers, publicists, radio DJs, reviewers and retailers. All create an image or a reputation and inflect the final delivery. Audiences as well as producers also invest in shared meanings – making myths come true and creating, substantiating or wrecking reputations. Music-making is as much about the discourses that surround an artist or genre, as about a recording process that captures and sells the essence of creativity.

Even genres purportedly distanced from modern technology and commerce, such as folk music, still rely on amplification equipment, instruments and notions of authenticity and style. They too are influenced by the stages of production, just as other genres that might appear more 'produced'. Notions of authenticity in music rely on an 'imaginary identification' with audiences, a belief in the music as unmediated by commercial concerns and forces (Bloomfield, 1993; see also Bourdieu, 1993). Opinions about authenticity are one component of cultural capital – the knowledge of tastes that audiences acquire, and that performers and producers seek to create and replicate for commercial purposes.

Such authenticity is always constructed, in often deliberate ways by marketing companies and record labels, and 'made' real by artists and audiences who believe in it and invest in the myth. No music style, artist or expression can easily maintain a claim to authenticity because even music with the most apparent 'authenticity' – perhaps 'world' and 'classical' music – is nevertheless mediated by an industry, and packaged and promoted in particular ways. Authenticity is an illusion, especially when it is equated with distance from commercialism. It embellishes melodies, lyrics and instrumentation. It provides musical releases with critical currency and credibility essential to sales figures, but it is always a social construction.

Authenticity is not, however, only constructed through perceptions of authorship, but is also linked to place. Much is made of the 'roots' of music in particular locations, eras and in social 'scenes' – the 'psychedelic' scene of San Francisco in the 1960s, jazz from New Orleans, waltzes from Vienna. Places become known as authentic sites of musical creativity, where 'musicians came together', where the 'magic took place'. Settings for the myths of classical music, rock 'n' roll, hip-hop and other styles are made authentic through discussions of the places and people surrounding musical creativity and production (Connell & Gibson, 2003). Thus, audiences come to know places that they have never visited through music: Frank Sinatra's 'New York, New York', the mythological

'California Dreamin'' of the 1960s counterculture, Haitian voodoo, Argentinean tango and the bluegrass twang of Appalachia.

Parallels are evident in the versions of authenticity that are apparent in tourism. Tourism marketing usually demands that places are portrayed as distinct, unique and home to authentic cultures, original landmarks or events (Waller & Lea, 1998), but how that 'authenticity' is created provokes much debate. MacCannell (1973; 1976) argued that tourists seek experiences beyond the ordinary: an escape from the drudgery of everyday life, searching for places and cultures that are 'authentic'. Consequently, authenticity becomes quickly commodified, as tourism producers stage 'authenticity', creating tourist attractions, preserving heritage or reproducing tradition in order to entertain or to enhance the appearance of 'escape' and 'otherness'. Events and customs are re-enacted for tourist consumption. Tourists may deem an event or attraction 'authentic', even when it has been wholly staged to appear that way. A converse situation might also occur, in what Cohen (1988) called a 'denial of authenticity', when tourists are suspicious about an event or attraction, although for the person providing the experience, it may indeed be 'genuine'.

However, the quest for authenticity is far too narrow a foundation for explaining contemporary tourism (Urry, 1991: 51). Tourists themselves interpret authenticity in many ways and place varying importance on authenticity in their motivations for travel (Littrell *et al.*, 1993; Hughes, 1995). As Bruner (1994: 408) has put it: 'No longer is authenticity a property inherent in an object, forever fixed in time; it is seen as a struggle, a social process, in which competing interests argue for their own interpretation of history.' Authenticity thus 'can no longer exist in the sense of the "real" or "original" thing standing outside of cultural interpretation' (Fawcett & Cormack, 2001: 689; see also Wang, 1999). Music is associated with place in ways that can be marketed and authenticated by promoters and tourists. However, many other places with no, or merely dubious, associations with musical styles, artists or scenes have also successfully generated tourism.

Authenticity as isolation: Cuba

Tourism in Cuba and the re-emergence of Cuban music in international markets illustrate both how authenticity is articulated as discourse, and how musical expressions become tourism resources. In its reincarnated form, since being 'discovered' by Ry Cooder in the mid-1990s, Cuban music has been marketed as 'world music', most notably on the World Circuit label (with Buena Vista Social Club, Ibrahim Ferrer, Omara Portuondo and the Afro-Cuban All-Stars). Supposedly 'authentic' world music is associated with the criteria of the perceived distance of non-Western artists from the capitalist music businesses, the 'emotion-ality' or 'feeling' that is absent in Western music, the healing properties and appeals to the 'primal' in an unchanging past:

> What is of concern to listeners is that the world music they consume has some discernible connection to the timeless, the ancient, the primal, the pure, the chthonic; that is what they want to buy, since their own world is often conceived as ephemeral, new, artificial and corrupt. (Taylor, 1997: 26)

Appeals to unchanging pasts are simultaneously desires for unchanging, and usually distant and exotic sites that are less likely to be corrupted by market forces (Connell & Gibson, 2003; see also Chapter 3). The ways in which Cuban music has been described in marketing material rein-forces this discourse. Ry Cooder, for instance, on the inside sleeve of *Buena Vista Social Club* (1997), argued that Cuban music was 'nurtured in an atmosphere sealed off from the fallout of a hyperorganised and noisy world . . . the music flows like a river. It takes care of you and rebuilds you from the inside out'. Cuban music is thus 'authentic' in its geography, its origins are free from Western commercial intents, and it has healing and 'rebuilding' properties.

This same discourse informs tourism in Cuba and the ways in which music figures in depictions of the country as a destination. For one travel writer, Cuba was 'shaped like a giant cigar which, metaphorically, is encased in a cylinder preserving conditions as they were when Castro came to power . . . a country caught in a time capsule' (Masters, 2000: 4T). Cuba is cast as an isolated cultural experiment, reflecting a Western longing for something beyond the corrupting influence of contemporary society. For another travel writer,

> This is a report from a parallel universe. Our time-warp traveller saunters past first one lovely old colonial house, through whose windows a string ensemble were spotted playing Bach, then another with a battery of African drummers and leaping dancers in the court-yard, then an otherwise deserted theatre with a dance band playing in the foyer. In every case he, or she, feels instinctively free to enter and listen. The leader of the Bach players invites him as their guest to their next concert in the capital. The Africans explain that their group is called Abbure Eyé, 'brother's blood' in the Congo language. The dance band thrust an instrument into his hands and asked him to join in. (Ottaway, 1999: 1)

Cuban music is made 'authentic' because the tourist journey it entails transports visitors 'back in time' and more simply because of the percep-tion of the difficulty of getting to Cuba. Cuban music, and tourism, does not appear to be mass produced and 'staged'. Thus, 'Discovering Cuban jazz must be similar to the experience of a wine connoisseur finding a bottle of rare Grange Hermitage selling in an outback Australian pub for $10' (Masters, 2000: 4T). In this instance, though, claims that Cuba's cultural isolation gave rise to its distinctive soundtrack of salsa, rumba and jazz are inaccurate. Cuban music incorporates African, Spanish and American influences; thus it is, and has always been, a transnational musical idiom. Nonetheless, local infrastructures have also been impor- tant. Cuban music, and increasingly tourism to Cuba, relies on the spaces in which music and dance performances are organised and performed in Cuban cities and towns, in *trovas* – 'immensely companionable, semi- outdoor places where local musicians drop in to jam' (Ottaway, 1999: 2) – and in *casas de la cultura* and *casas de la musica* – venues organised by the writers' and artists' union that are commonplace in towns and cities across Cuba. These spaces enable public performances, encouraging participation and spontaneity, and providing ready-made venues for tourist-host interactions.

Despite mythologising, music is constructed and commercialised, even in this distinctly non-capitalist setting: 'If Cuba's geriatric musicians are on celluloid, the next generation is in Havana's hotels, moving hope- fully from table to table, offering a selection of songs from their own CD. Show more than a flicker of interest and you'll immediately be offered the CD for sale' (Masters, 2000: 4T). Cuban music is dynamic and tourism has played a role in making it so. One dance style, *batarumba*, for example, combines drum rhythms from sacred contexts with more modern ones – Yoruba, casino and rumba dance styles – and musical accompaniment, creating a new style. Given that Castro's government has been secular in orientation, sacred music and dances have been marginalised. However, these musical expressions were permitted, even encouraged, when tourist numbers increased in the 1980s, as they appeared more 'traditional' and thus appealed to tourists:

> It was through the emphasis on touristic dance performance that religious drum rhythms and dances were developed as source mate- rials for the creation of a new form. It was the Cuban tourism of the 1980s that provided the time and ambience where artists were freed for expression, where such creativity could gain momentum and acceptance. (Daniel, 1996: 794)

Tourism added to the dynamism of music, rather than merely seeking to preserve it.

Threatened authenticity?

Authenticity in music and tourism is invariably revealed as historically and geographically contingent, even when it is defined as the pursuit of 'historical, geographical, and cultural accuracy' (Daniel, 1996: 783). In Tahiti, for instance, pre-European dance and musical forms were replaced after colonisation with European musical structures, instrumentation and performance; these in turn became a 'historical', 'traditional' style re-created in airport arrival halls for tourists, so that 'the "new" became "authentic", a radical change that was accepted by the Tahitian community' (Daniels, 1996: 784; Kaeppler, 1973). In Fijian villages the *taralala* dance, performed for and with tourists, and perceived as traditional, was introduced by missionaries in the 19th century. In Haiti, voodoo ceremonies were truncated and exaggerated for foreign visitors when they were incorporated into hotel performances. In many contexts performances are shortened, enlivened and decontextualised for tourists' benefit (see pp. 146–9).

In New Orleans authenticity is, for many, a desired element of the tourist experience, and a musical dimension fretted over by older musicians, some of whom bemoan the demise of 'traditional' jazz and its corruption by tourism. For Michael White, a clarinet player:

> Most of what you hear in New Orleans is nothing to do with traditional jazz. It is a pathetic commercialised pastiche of it. . . . In the French Quarter are the tourist traps where a ghastly parody of New Orleans jazz is inflicted night after night on the unsuspecting public. It is an irony that you stand a better chance of hearing New Orleans jazz, a genuine attempt at the real thing, like it was, in Tokyo, London or Madrid than you do in New Orleans itself. . . . There are some signs of America waking up to what it has all but lost. New Orleans jazz has been declared a 'national treasure', the city is celebrating the centenary and they are putting a 60-foot high painting of one of my old clarinets on the side of the Holiday Inn – but I fear it is too late. (Quoted in Tyler, 2002: 14–15)

Similar complaints are legion. In Jamaica,

> We are guilty of catering to mediocrity and stagnation, as we have given visitors the easy-to-take pap, the familiar western harmonies and rhythmic style, the non-Jamaican forms (such as fire-eating) we think they are prepared to cope with, rather than what they believe they should have – a real taste of Jamaica in the form of our authentic, traditional music forms. (Williams, 1988: 17)

Such local observers may be formalising – and inventing – the elusive 'authenticity' and the unchanging 'traditional'. Nevertheless, it may be the fate of many musicians and performers in tourist destinations (but not only there) to have their work transformed and traduced, and their creativity stultified, to meet transient commercial requirements. Yet, as the Cuban example demonstrates, in particular circumstances tourism may simultaneously stimulate creativity, enable continuity and encourage hybridity.

Both Tibet and Mongolia provide examples of cultural transformations in musical practice from Chinese influences and because of Han Chinese migration, the introduction of modern sources of electrical power, less mobility for local people (as sheep-herders and nomads found it difficult to survive in 'traditional' ways), urbanisation and the arrival of Chinese and Western tourists. For one travel writer, music played a crucial part in 'threatening' the Mongolian way of life:

> What was once the terrain of nomads is now the equally well-trodden domain of the Asian tourist. And where there are Asian tourists by the bus-load, there will be karaoke. . . . Mongolians are now a small minority in their so-called autonomous region. Three million lived there in 1992 – twice the number in 1947. In that time the number of Han Chinese has grown 29 times, to 19 million. . . . Trips for outsiders to stay in the canvas huts with the herdsmen start at about 350 Chinese renminbi (£29/US$60) a night – a lucrative and badly needed alternative to shepherding. But the combined influx of migrant and karaoke culture is permanently diluting a serene way of life. (Palmer, 2001: 6)

Similarly, in Tibet,

> For many Westerners visiting Tibet, but particularly for those involved in the movement to free Tibet who have come to Lhasa to validate their time-consuming intentions and efforts, karaoke is usually discussed as a sign of the 'decline' of Lhasa and the 'loss' of an authentic Tibet at the hands of the Chinese. . . . For some Westerners, this sentiment emerges from a larger narrative about the loss of a premodern and sacred civilization, one among many other narratives that define Tibet in the Western imagination. (Adams, 1996: 14)

Yet, ironically, many Tibetans enjoy karaoke, not simply as an unfettered absorption of Western influences, a pandering to tourists' desires, nor as resistance to tradition and conservatism:

> Pastiche and blurred boundaries are for many not simply an aesthetic commentary on resisting modernity but an accurate representation of the experiences of modernity. . . . Karaoke may in fact be an indicator of how important it is to not efface modernity but to acquire, participate in, and benefit from modernity rather than be oppressed by it. . . . Karaoke tells us that sites of authentic Tibetanness may be nothing more than sites for scripted simulation. (Adams, 1996: 537–538)

Karaoke is not incompatible with being Tibetan. Musical traditions and performances change. They cannot be preserved indefinitely, nor can culture be reified, however much the most colourful moments of past musical styles are presented for tourist consumption as definitive statements about indigenous musical cultures.

While changes in musical performances are most evident in the developing world, they are ubiquitous. Tourist destinations, whether they involve folk, popular or classical music – particularly where they involve festivals and performances – are 'packaged'. Unlike more overtly popular and 'commercial' styles of music, classical music too is about 'the production of belief', and the perceived authenticity of events is vital to maintain the prestige, distinction and allure of opera, ballet or symphonic performance. This authenticity in some ways parallels that for Cuban music, relying on an assumption of its distance from 'cheaper' commercial considerations and the 'rarity' of an event. Similarly,

> ballet performance in New York has much in common with touristic dance performance elsewhere in terms of intentions that frame the 'exotic other' in traditional or extravaganza dance style, motivations that conserve and present national or ethnic cultures, and packaging that creates visible, mesmerizing products that generate profits. (Daniel, 1996: 781)

When performances take *Aida* into Egypt or Verdi into Milan, the commercial construction of authenticity becomes even more evident.

Classical music festivals, venues and performances are linked to tourism, but both authenticity and innovation are sought-after qualities of music performance. Authenticity in classical music is partly 'a logical elaboration of the concept of a museum of musical works. It involves the attempt to recreate a musical work as it would have been heard at the time by recreating the original event, or something like it, just as a work of art is (supposedly) better appreciated when restored to its 'original' condition, erasing the work of time' (Keen, 2001: 38). The promoters of 'high culture' are just as aware of the importance of tourists to their audience figures as any Hawaiian *hula*, country music or rock-festival organiser, and maintaining a sense of 'authenticity' is crucial for success. If not in dinner jackets, classical music performers (and occasionally promoters) may even dress in 'period' costume, maintaining one crude temporal notion of authenticity.

Social constructions, in places as different as Mongolia and Venice, reveal that music and dance in tourist contexts are inevitably inauthentic, and that a cultural politics of authenticity is itself false. As Trinh T. Minh-ha has argued, 'Authenticity as a need to rely on an 'undisputed origin', is prey to an obsessive fear: that of *losing a connection*. Everything must hold together . . . the real, nothing else than a code of representation, does not (cannot) coincide with the lived or the performed' (1989: 94). At the same time that music might be perceived as 'authentic' in its rigid adherence to traditional styles of expression, it is also more fluid and interpretative than first impressions might suggest. Thus, Native Pueblo Americans, performing 'traditional' ceremonies, actually incorporated into their music and dance certain movements and passages that ridiculed tourists. In many developing world contexts, stability and change go largely unrecognised by tourists.

In Ireland too, for one 'traditional' Irish performer, 'most tourists don't know the difference between tunes, so it doesn't really matter what he plays' (Kneafsey, 2002: 355). Tourism had changed the format and economics of Irish musical performance in other ways: tourists drank less alcohol and videotaped performances, encouraging publicans to start charging entry fees; the more collective and informal 'session' was replaced by a format of 'star' players, with an emphasis on virtuosity in more regulated, paid performances. But even staged authenticity produced complicated interactions and negotiations between performers and audiences. As Daniel (1996: 785) has put it, 'The tourism setting, then, provides the space and time for ideal definitions to expand, for play and experimentation at the edges of boundaries with combinations of styles and traditions that reach for innovation, invention, and creativity'; thus, in one Irish music performance,

> the tourists really helped to shape the music. For instance, Frank asked me to play the bodhran, which I did. Then the tourist with the video camera shouted out 'play another song with the drum'. So we did some more reels and jigs. Then Jack sang Woodie Guthrie songs for some Americans and later, a group of six or seven Swedish people sang an uproarious folk song. In return, Maura sang a song in Irish. I wonder if the visitors know that some of the musicians were also visitors? Or, did they think it was all local people playing, in some time-honoured ancient way? I wonder if they know that the session is actually a comparatively new invention, imported into Ireland from America and England by emigrant musicians of the Irish diaspora? It struck me that most of the musicians tonight were from other places – I think only Seamus was actually born in the county. Yet this has nothing to do with its authenticity – it's easy to fall into the trap of thinking that if it's not being played by the local-born Irish, then it's fake. Ultimately, whether authenticity is endowed on an event depends on the meanings that musicians and listeners attach to it. (Kneafsey, 2002: 356)

At the same time the tourist experience may have little to do with the extent to which the music is in some sense authentic, but more to do with the aesthetics of the setting, the flow of alcohol, the mood, the enjoyment and enthusiasm of the performers and the overall pleasure of a good night out. Authenticity is 'relative rather than absolute and, like beauty, is in the eye of the beholder' (Xie, 2003: 5). If not false consciousness, it is at best a constructed set of shared meanings – contingent and often contested – by audiences, promoters and participants.

Towards inauthenticity?

Not only do many tourists, even those who proclaim a clear interest in musical heritage, fail to distinguish between 'real' Irish music and modified forms (Kneafsey, 2002), but they may also have little interest in doing so. Tourism is a journey for entertainment as much as for enlightenment. Nonetheless, distortions may be enormous, as one of the authors experienced when seeking advertised 'Traditional Irish Music' in a Dublin pub and being confronted by an electrified cover band exclusively playing the music of the Eagles. Here some notion of entertainment had utterly overwhelmed any claim to authenticity and even integrity. However, change and destruction are rarely so absolute. Although tourism was criticised in the 1970s as 'demeaning and distorting culture, inciting the pillage of artwork and historical artefacts; leading to the degeneration of classical and popular dancing; profaning and vulgarising places of worship and perverting religious ceremonies; and creating a sense of inferiority and cultural demoralisation' (Wood, 1998: 235; see Greenwood, 1977; Shepherd, 2002), it has not normally been so devastating.

Not all music, especially from places with unfamiliar styles, such as Asia and the Middle East (see Connell & Gibson, 2003: 146), is easily accessible to Western ears and tastes. Musical performances have been modified for tourist audiences, as in indigenous contexts in Australia, where tourists expect a particular instrument and context associated with a time and place other than that of the performance itself (see pp. 159–60). In China, Chinese classical orchestral performances for tourists are introduced as 'traditional', despite the form of the performance (in an auditorium, before a foreign public) being barely a decade old (Lau, 1998: 120–121). In Malta, 'traditional' folk dances that were no more than a year or two old were performed for tourists (Boissevain & Inglott, 1979: 282), emphasising that all traditions are at some point invented. In Australia in the 1960s, Aboriginal groups would dress as Polynesians and perform hula dances for tourists (Figure 5.1). In Nouméa (New Caledonia), the capital of a territory whose indigenous population are Melanesians, Melanesian music is rarely performed for tourists and almost never in hotels, since promoters regard it as dreary and monotonous. Instead, migrant Wallisians and Tahitians from Polynesia perform dances and music, which is seen as more lively. However, Tahitian performances incorporate fire-dancing and are more dramatic than

Figure 5.1 The 'Hula Girls' from Burnt Bridge, performing at the Kempsey Spring Festival, 1962, in New South Wales, Australia. At that time indigenous Aboriginal music was unknown to, or unappreciated by, white audiences. Hence, ironically, Aborigines were expected to perform as more familiar Hawaiian dancers.

Wallisian dances, some of which are performed sitting down – hence, Wallisians have reduced the number of sitting dances and Melanesians have 'livened up' performances and adopted more exotic attire. In general, Tahitian dancing and drumming have led to the 'homogenising of the South Seas image [and the] Tahitianization of Pacific Islands music and dance' (Stillman, 1988: 162). Parallel processes, as in Trinidad, where steelbands virtually disappeared during carnival because of competition from electronic sound systems (Nurse, 1999: 672), have contributed to homogenisation in the Caribbean islands.

Such transformations towards tourist needs and expectations are commonplace – usually, as in New Caledonia, reducing the length of performances, minimising less exciting parts, incorporating audiences into the show, emphasising exotic and unusual acts (such as fire-dancing) and dressing more colourfully and less comprehensively. In Bali, after tourists found a three-hour dance performance, which included dancers entering into a state of trance, stabbing themselves and devouring live chickens, too demanding and disturbing,

> a special hour-long story was devised ... designed to transcend linguistic and cultural barriers, so dialogue was kept to a minimum, and more slapstick humour was promoted [and] female dancers have been incorporated in place of the males who previously danced female roles. Tourists see a shorter play, which uses a different story,

and leaves no room for musical or dramatic improvisation. The trance
dance that occurs at the climax of the performance is simulated,
well-controlled and brief. (Sanger, 1988: 93)

Similar transformations, all reducing length and complexity, have
occurred in Korea (Man-young, 1988), Hainan, China (Xie, 2003) and the
Philippines (Trimillos, 1988). In Hainan, this followed demands by local
vendors that tourists be allowed more time for shopping (Xie, 2003: 11).
In Fiji the *meke* is a combination of dance, song and theatre, partly
designed for performance in hotels, with particular prominence given
to war clubs and dramatic spear challenges to audiences. In most of the
Pacific, the weekly 'Polynesian Show' is a fixture in which a small group
performs a range of Pacific dances that are invariably centred, irrespective of location, around the 'flashy hip-gyrating dances identified with
Tahiti and Rarotonga'. The social context has been thoroughly lost, but
'for many tourists this reader's digest approach is sufficient as an experience of island cultures' (Linnekin, 1997: 232; Hayward, 2001). In Hawaii
the struggle to retain a hula that differed from Hollywood stereotypes
(associated with a slim half-caste – *hapa haole* – look) or Tahitian influences has been long, difficult (Tatar, 1987; Desmond, 1999) and only
partially successful.

While musical change is a necessary part of creativity, it is not generally welcomed by tourists who prefer more familiar versions of the past.
In the interest of profitability, tourists are usually given what they are
believed to want. Participants in tourist performances become 'tourees',
where behaviour is constructed in the image of what tourists wish to
see and hear. This is particularly so where the cultural distance between
performers and tourists is considerable:

> The touree, in short, to the extent that he [*sic*] responds to the tourist,
> makes it his or her business to preserve a credible illusion of authen-
> ticity. He fakes his art, his dress, his music, his dancing, his religion,
> and so on, to quench ethnic tourists' search for authenticity at the
> very same time tourist invasion assaults his culture and subjects it
> to the homogenising process known as 'modernisation'. (van den
> Berghe & Keyes, 1984: 346)

Tourism is by its very nature unusual and largely outside the sphere of
daily relations, hence some pretence and transformation is inevitable.

In every setting transformations linked to tourism have been highly
complex, none more so than in Bali, where many classical features of
Balinese dance and music have been shaped by more than 75 years
of interaction between Balinese and tourists. Balinese performance has
become thoroughly intertwined with alien influences. The famous kecak
dance emerged through collaborations between Balinese and Europeans

in the 1930s, yet retained its strikingly distinctive cultural ambience. Indeed, the creation of the kecak dance was part of a constant process of innovation and change in Balinese music, as in art, involving some Western intervention. Change has been so substantial that in the late 1960s Balinese authorities commissioned a new 'secular' welcome dance to avoid what was assumed to be the desecration of sacred dances through their tourist performance. Change was also perceived as desirable 'to save tourists the discomfort and long waits characteristic of performances – quickly tiresome for non-Balinese spectators [hence] it was recommended that dance performances be organised especially for tourists, freely transposed from the traditional forms and adapted for a diverse foreign audience' (Picard, 1996: 46). Villagers accommodated change because of communal gains, village social cohesion was enhanced and performances remained respectful and aesthetically imposing (Sanger, 1988). Moreover, nightly performances became part of a standard tourist itinerary that fluctuated according to villagers' financial needs, but produced a new tourist-influenced timetable of daily life. However, the new secular dance proved so popular that it was quickly introduced into the temples for sacred ritual purposes (Dunbar-Hall, 2001: 216; Dunbar-Hall, 2003: 14). Attempts to distinguish between the sacred and core elements in Balinese culture and tourist forms of cultural expression have therefore been unsuccessful, in some part because they have attempted to impose distinctions (such as sacred/profane), which is alien to most Balinese. Furthermore, tourism is so ingrained in what Balinese do that it has become central to life, culture and ethnic identity, and a living heritage of islanders (Wood, 1998: 228; Johnson, 2002: 16) within a Balinese tradition of transformation.

A similar transition has occurred among the indigenous ('aboriginal') Li people on Hainan island, China, where bamboo-beating dances, originating from funeral ceremonies, were turned into festival celebration and integrated into the contemporary tourist system, following directions from the Chinese government. Other changes in the dance context evolved in parallel; the importance of the bamboo colour and its religious significance disappeared, while new rhythms, teamwork and smiling faces were incorporated. The new dance emerged as 'authentic' for the Li people – an important part of cultural identity and held in high esteem by tourists (Xie, 2003: 11), as a religious ceremony became secular and 'cultural' within a socialist nation. A later phase of change resulted in a more simplified performance of the final part of the 'show' to enable spontaneity and improvisation, enabling more effective tourist participation without their inappropriate and unfortunate blundering. Xie argues that this is a positive mechanism in the pursuit of authenticity and 'ultimately a route towards genuineness: a reborn cultural identity', just as more commodified and entertaining dance performances are 'an effective vehicle for cross-cultural understanding' (Xie, 2003: 14). Such performances, however, take place in 'purpose built folk villages' rather than in the Li villages.

Much as performers appear to have become 'tourees' and music has occasionally been transformed beyond recognition, most host societies have adapted to tourism, made accommodations, linked tourism into aspirations for modernity and material goods, and used it as a vehicle for change. In vibrant cultural contexts, musical performances change. On Hainan, tourism has created a new form of 'cultural involution' that has turned commodified dance performances into an 'authentic' indigenous cultural expression (Xie, 2003: 6). Both on Hainan and Bali the hybrid music and dance created for tourists has been a means of spreading and validating that musical culture and emphasising cultural identity, even as it changes. External commentators may bemoan inauthenticity, but this is as elusive a concept as authenticity, while the erosion of borders between tourism and other social and economic activities at the very least means that the rationale and basis for change and stability are harder to determine. Tourism and changes in musical performance do not occur in a vacuum.

'Identity' and 'Performativity'

Beyond authenticity, further insight can be gained by examining issues surrounding the identities created and interpreted within music tourism. Interest in identity politics has emerged from the popularity of post-modern, and in particular post-structuralist and feminist critiques. Prior to the 'cultural turn' in the social sciences in the 1980s, the identities of individuals or groups were invariably presented as coherent 'units' of meaning, assumed to be fixed and definitive. Efforts to classify places and people(s), individually or into groups, were effectively assigning identities to individuals and communities. Neat and stable categories were created – indigenous peoples, social classes, women and men – that enabled generalisations and social analysis.

The post-modern turn, however, has questioned this standardisation; indeed, identities were revealed not as objective, but as polymorphic. Individuals could be perceived (and see themselves) as female in one situation (for instance, in gendered workplaces), but elsewhere their identity could be perceived as aged (in a dance club), indigenous (in a cross-cultural setting) or poor (when attempting to secure a loan). Identities are dynamic and never static. Identities must be made and maintained (or are intermittently challenged and contested) through the continued attitudes of others and in self-perception. Identities are always in a process of becoming, even when they are perceived by others as 'natural' or being. In other words, human identities are not objectively 'natural', but are created and continually reproduced through a repetitive enactment of expectations and appearances.

Social identities are therefore constructed and performed:

> Social actors produce distinctive gaits, ways of speaking, dress and demeanor that articulate shared forms of understanding. Moreover performance of identities does not occur in an ideology-free context in which individuals are completely free from manipulation; rather 'what is 'appropriate', the order of action, who should participate – is frequently regulated by key personnel, who monitor and instruct participants and maintain key scripts. (Edensor, 2000: 323)

Tourism spaces are often highly controlled and managed, particularly where larger commercial interests are involved (Lefebvre, 1991: 384). However, such regulation can be evaded or negotiated by tourists through criticism and irony. The nature of performance and identity is inevitably fluid.

Performing and reinventing tradition

Identities are always performed in the production of a tourist attraction; for instance, tourism workers are trained to enact certain roles, conveying attitudes regulated by the institutions of employers, the host culture and clients. Tour guides perform 'eagerness to please'; characters dress up in 'authentic' costumes (in theme parks or developing world villages); restaurateurs may perform the role of culinary expert and local eccentric, with their knowledge of tourists as customers, creating 'meaningful settings that tourists consume and tourism employees help produce' (Crang, 1997: 143). At one level this is banal and obvious – tourists expect service and show. At another, it reveals how culture is reproduced and contested in tourism settings.

In music tourism, performativity is ubiquitous; beyond service, its most obvious manifestation is in costume. In Venice, performers (and ticket touts) adopt 'authentic' Renaissance costumes, a feature heavily promoted in advertisements for performances. In the Cantal region of central France, villagers dress up in 'traditional' smocks and clogs to perform dances for tourists, invoking images of an idealised rural past, as recorded by folklorists in the 1890s (Abram, 1997). The distinctive clothes, bells and performance of Morris dancers symbolise 'olde England', although Morris dancing was introduced from continental Europe. Even relatively contemporary country-and-western performers often adopted the manner and garb of 'country bumpkins', rather than city slickers (Connell & Gibson, 2003). Pressures to conform to dress codes are particularly common in developing world contexts and among indigenous peoples. Aboriginal performers are encouraged to wear red loincloths, even though such attire was never worn by pre-contact societies, and tribal groups favour Western fashions. Despite disturbing and humiliating consequences, in Papua New Guinea participants in cultural dances at the Goroka Show were encouraged to 'take off bras and underwear because they are not recognized in PNG traditional culture', according to the festival director, Mewie Launa, because 'this is not what our culture demands. Our culture is unique. It is in our blood. We should be proud of it and not mix modern culture with what we have always learnt' (quoted in *Sydney Morning Herald*, 20/9/2002: 1). In Xi'an, Chinese classical musicians 'went as far as putting on historic costumes and make-up and playing on replicas of period instruments', while implying that the music descended from the 6th century (even though the names of contemporary arrangers were given in the programme), in performances aimed at tourists who 'preferred seeing "historic stuff" rather than improved modern Chinese music' (Lau, 1998: 122–123). The 'traditional' is thus a very common identity in the tourist context; and dress, deportment, music and the languages of tourist/host contact all play a part in reinventing tradition for the tourism market, a 'kind of first-contact moment, a nostalgic tribute to a bygone age' (Johnson & Underiner, 2001: 48). Forms of tourism may thus recall a range of colonial and imperial desires.

Performances may also cherish, and invent, a version of history. In Malacca (Malaysia), the Portuguese settlement, dating from the 16th century, has been officially designated a key tourist destination in the city, conferring on it an aura of authenticity and timelessness, different from reality. A weekly cultural show is given, the performance centred around music and dance derived from Portuguese folk tales. It was first created in Malacca in the 1950s, when dances were learned from a book and costumes were created from its illustrations. The eventual outcome of this 'invented tradition' (Hobsbawm, 1983) was that local residents managed both to earn tourist income and transform their wider image from poor, lazy, music-loving fisher-folk to glamorous, hardworking folk-dancers and musicians. Tourists often accept the performances as Portuguese, although they are eclectic as 'the "tradition" is opportunistic' but, only 40 years after its establishment, the younger generation and tourists see it as 'an unbroken tradition stretching back to the 16th century' (Sarkissian, 1995: 41). While the original performance was planned by a Portuguese priest to entertain a passing Portuguese minister, its invention – and distinctive imported content – has proved a boon to the tourist industry and to the local residents.

Tourism contexts reproduce and reinforce images of indigenous peoples as exotic 'others', a process that reaffirms unequal relations in colonial (and post-colonial) power (Johnson and Underiner, 2001: 44; see also Jones, 1988; Fusco, 1994). When commercial imperatives are involved and are non-indigenous, such activities, performances or destinations can be interpreted as having appropriated native expressive forms – these are cultural theft (or cultural imperialism): 'People have always shared ideas and borrowed from one another, but appropriation is entirely different from borrowing or sharing because it involves the taking up and commodification of aesthetic, cultural, and, more recently, spiritual forms of a society. Culture is neatly packaged for the consumer's convenience' (Root, 1996: 70). At Tillicum Village, a theme park near Seattle that presents local Native American traditions as part of a musical/theatrical performance entitled 'Dance on the Wind',

> rituals and entertainment normally conducted in the open air or in dimly lit longhouses for a surrounding circle of spectator-participants are here framed by a double proscenium in a very Western-style production for an audience literally fenced off and enjoying after-dinner coffee. Moreover, here the disembodied wisdom of a legend is heard not in the soul of the seeker, but over a loudspeaker system from a pre-recorded tape written by two white men. (Johnson & Underiner, 2001: 52–53)

In such performances, representation of 'otherness' becomes substantially divorced from past or contemporary social contexts.

Parallel processes have occurred elsewhere; promotional campaigns using Australia's indigenous cultures have resulted in increased demand for Aboriginal music, particularly 'traditional' music associated with didjeridu performance (with solo vocal and clapstick accompaniment). One of the more successful ventures seeking to capitalise on this has been the Tjapukai Aboriginal Cultural Park in Kuranda, far north Queensland, where traditional performances, occurring in ceremonial circumstances, have been altered and incorporated into a multi-media 'extravaganza' of indigenous culture, including 'traditional'-style performances, contemporary songs and story-telling. The particular format of the performance – didjeridu and occasionally solo vocal accompaniment – has become pervasive across the continent wherever tourists converge, whether at Circular Quay, Sydney (the tourist space between the Opera House and the Harbour Bridge), at festivals and sporting events, such as the 2000 Olympic Games, or in outback towns where tourism economies exist. Yet this format of Aboriginal performance, in its ceremonial context, had a much more limited geographical scope than suggested by its tourist transformation, being originally limited to far north Queensland and parts of the Northern Territory, and certainly not in Sydney or Alice Springs (Neuenfeldt, 1997). Nevertheless, tourists have walked out of Aboriginal dance performances in central Australia simply because didjeridus were missing (Burchett, 1993). Beyond the questions of authenticity are economic issues. In many places, Aboriginal musical expressions now include contemporary influences – reggae, rock, hip-hop and country (Gibson, 1998) – yet tourist expectations demand didjeridu performance. While some heavily truncated performances have gone from ceremonial context to a means of earning income, other forms of indigenous musical expression, in which local Aboriginal populations actively participate, remain distant from tourism economies. They are, somewhat ironically, mostly the domain of informal, spontaneous performances in remote communities, with little regulation, no paid remuneration, and intense links to local cultural concerns. Thus, the 'traditional' and 'contemporary' in Aboriginal music have become inverted in relation to tourism.

While some Aboriginal people gain economically from tourism in a limited number of accessible places, even financial benefits may be less than expected. For the Djabugay people, whose community is an equity partner in the Tjapukai Aboriginal Cultural Park, the complexities are considerable. The benefits of tourism included the revival of Djabugay culture (Henry, 2000), employment opportunities, especially through working with other community members, increased cross-cultural understanding and improved material welfare. However, the disadvantages include what many Djabugay see as a degradation of their culture. The preparation and performance of dances is incompatible with short-term tourist itineraries, while dances are adjusted periodically in accord with surveys of what tourists believe to constitute Aboriginal culture, notably through the incorporation of the didjeridu (Zeppel, 1998) – a modification and commodification of Djabugay culture some cannot accept. Other Djabugay nonetheless argue that tourism had enhanced pride in local culture and language, and combated negative stereotypes of lazy Aborigines. Moreover 'you can feel the spirit around you when you dance' (quoted in Dyer *et al.*, 2003: 91). Economic gains are disappointing because of limited local equity in the Park, weak management capacity and minimal opportunities for the effective investment of profits beyond short-term material goals. Beyond the economic consequences, dance performances raise complex questions about identity and intellectual property, particularly in a place of considerable tourist significance, where alternative economic opportunities were few.

Sustaining traditions?

In Hawaii, music and dance cultures have been deliberately encapsulated in the tourist experience, with large hotels and cruise lines offering and funding cultural experiences in attempts to sustain and even revive indigenous cultural practices. One consequence has been that the tourist industry has provided employment for some of Hawaii's most respected musicians and dancers, and thus helped to sustain those practices. At the same time tourist presentations are usually framed as part of the 'soft primitivism imaginary, a nostalgic evocation of the past' (Desmond, 1999: 273). Tourist performances simultaneously both conserve and dissolve cultural experiences to ensure a particular exotic, and often gendered, representation of the past. The most commercial tourist shows emphasise the disjuncture between performance and 'reality'. Young performers are usually slim *hapa haole* (part-Polynesian); few possess the usually larger body sizes of Polynesians and rarely are they white or black, neither of which image would fit mainland Americans' perceptions of Hawaiians. Women often wear coconut-shell bras. By contrast, local hula performances and troupes are more multi-ethnic, a reflection of Hawaii's Asian and European population. Indeed, the hula, 'the social practice most strongly and most visibly identified with Native Hawaiians, is, paradoxically, performed by Hawaiian residents of all backgrounds' (Desmond, 1999: 27). In the tourist marketing of heritage, evolving complexities of who and what are Hawaiian has been lost, while simultaneously shaped into an essentialised image of what promoters would prefer ancient Hawaii to be. An idealised past is preserved in performance and music in a way that denies historical change.

Among the Pataxo Indians of Brazil, dance and song had largely disappeared, despite its being regarded as central to their spiritual world. The emergence of tourism in the 1970s led the local municipality to request that the Pataxo present a 'representation of their culture' through dance. This coincided with the Pataxo's own wish to become more visible as a 'legitimate Indian' population, while simultaneously earning new income (Grunewald, 2002). Tourism, and the role of dance, enabled the Pataxo to reclaim their culture, express their identity and earn money, a situation similar to other places where people have used tourism to reinforce their uniqueness. At the same time the actual musical performances were transformed to emphasise variety – for example, through the incorporation of the samba.

More prosaic are instances where tourist demands have enabled the retention of dances and musical traditions that might otherwise have been lost. In Fiji, in two nearby villages, the one that was most locked into the tourist economy (in employment) and had the 'more capitalistic economy' had retained the *meke* for entertainment purposes, whereas the dance had lapsed in the other village (Ulack, 1993: 5). Yet ironically, the *meke* was a dance created for tourist consumption. Similar ironies are repeated in many contexts. In Malta, for example,

> The tourist demand for folk music has unquestionably helped preserve the limited traditional instrumental and vocal music that existed. It has also helped to make this music acceptable to some

young educated Maltese who might otherwise have copied the middle-class disdain with which their parents regarded this 'peasant music'. Patriotism has also played a role, for the music has provided an authentic item of local culture to a newly independent country in search of its identity after four centuries of heavy handed foreign rule. (Boissevain & Inglott, 1979: 282)

In the Seychelles, tourists' interest in local dances, notably the *sega*, have stimulated local pride in, and enthusiasm for, the Creole culture that was beginning to disappear (Wilson, 1979: 230). Returning overseas Chinese have been particularly influential in supporting performances of traditional opera. Their financial support has allowed musicians to be employed, and enabled opera to withstand the onslaught of popular music, karaoke and dance music imported from Hong Kong and Taiwan (Lau, 1998: 129). In numerous destinations authorities have supported both the music and tourism industries by sponsoring festivals or subsidising cultural activities of various kinds. In Cyprus, the Ministry of Education encouraged and supported folkloric dances and other performances related to the island's history. This led to increased tourist numbers and to these performances becoming part of a national cultural scene, enjoyed by local residents as well as foreigners (Andronicou, 1979: 253). Performances also served as a means of strengthening national identity. At one level such changes constitute cultural survival, even revival; at another, they demonstrate the commercial construction of tourist economies.

Inevitably, there are exceptions to these trends and considerable complications in the tourist-led transformation of music. In Yunnan, southwest China, for example, many backpackers travelled to Lijiang to hear amateur musicians of the Naxi ethnic minority group play Dongjing music. Unimpressed with professional musical performances that had adopted Western-style harmonies and 'glitzy' staging, backpackers preferred the apparent authenticity of the Naxi musicians' conservative heterophonic style, local tuning, sober gowns and dignified demeanour. For the local musicians their 'strongest ally has been the hundreds of obviously fabricated so-called "folk" or "traditional" performances their audience has encountered elsewhere in China' (Lau, 1998: 149). Moreover, 'the location is picturesque, free of the concrete and plastic otherwise so ubiquitous in China, and the proceedings are marked by dignified solemnity' (Rees, 1998: 138). However, Naxi musicians have deliberately developed 'traditional' tourist concerts that constitute a new form of Dongjing music by selectively borrowing from disparate historical contexts to create a staged timelessness that emphasises tradition and reverence: 'to be able to claim "exotic" minority credentials can be a selling point in today's minority-conscious world' (Rees, 1998: 146).

Ironically, what Rees describes as 'truly "authentic" traditional musical gatherings' flourish, without audiences, in nearby Naxi villages seldom visited by tourists, where experiments are made with music in a way that is both authentic and innovative (Rees, 1998: 153–154; see Xie, 2003: 14). In other contexts, from Hawaii and New Orleans (Regis, 2001) to Ireland (Kneafsey, 2002), 'real' music is played away from the tourists. In Yogyakarta, Java, tourists who had observed a performance of the Ramayana Ballet were later told that it was a recent creation, further shortened and edited for tourists, but none expressed any loss of enjoyment, believing that 'it was a good show, they were the only persons present, that it was stimulating being in an Indonesian home, seeing all the old Dutch and Javanese pictures and memorabilia, that the food was fine and the performers were superb'. A day later the tourists witnessed a similar performance of the ballet in the Bali Hyatt Hotel but disliked it, arguing that it was too much like Miami or Honolulu since 'they were in a room with three hundred or four hundred other tourists; one Hyatt hotel is much like another; it was too crowded; the buffet lines were too long; there was no feeling of intimacy and they were too far from the performers to take good photographs' (Bruner, 1996: 174). As the Chinese, Javanese and Balinese experiences indicate, changes may be exceptionally complex, while what convinces and entertains tourists depends on wider contexts – the physicality of tourist spaces themselves, their intimacy and appearance, and the tourists' own knowledge and expectations.

The identities constructed in tourism destinations are as much defined by what they exclude as by observable elements in their production. Music tourism identities are framed within selective scripts shaped by silences, and by aspects of history and experiences that are not communicated. As Abram (1997: 29) has argued: 'If we are to consider how identities and ethnicities are revealed, expressed or exploited through tourism, then the presentation or negation of history must be foremost in our analyses'. Tourist commemorations of artists and their work in museum displays may erase histories of the exploitation of the artists, while positive identities are portrayed for industry figures who 'discovered' artists and brought them to fame. Colonel Tom Parker's role in Elvis Presley's career is invariably presented as positive in Elvis's route to fame, even though Parker manipulated the artist for his own profit. That many blues and jazz musicians were never paid properly is almost invariably ignored; references to the often hostile, racist climate in which black music was made and performed are often absent (see McKee & Chisenhall, 1981; Kofsky, 1998). Where indigenous music and dance is incorporated into tourism, 'references to contemporary Native American culture are hidden ... in nostalgic visions of an untroubled past. The history of the colonization of land, traditions and people is never mentioned, yet the entire [tourism] enterprise seems underwritten by that history' (Johnson & Underiner, 2001: 53). Moreover, what is also invariably hidden is the whiteness of the authors of tourism productions, usually non-indigenous promoters who undertake what Root (1996: 75) describes as a 'salvage paradigm', rediscovering, or saving 'lost' or 'dying' cultures from extinction: 'Those doing the saving choose what fragments of a culture needs to be "saved" [so that] ... having done this, they become both the owners and interpreters of the artefacts or goods that have survived from that dying culture'. Confronting elements of the histories of places and peoples may be excluded from tourist experiences and the identities performed in these locations.

Negotiating identities

Pacific Islanders, Native Americans, Aboriginal Australians and others are participants in tourism performances (either reluctantly or willingly), and variously engage with the identities presented. At Tillicum village (Seattle), tribal elders have veto control over the dances and music performed for tourist audiences, and have been known to refuse permission in some instances. Sometimes sacred content, crucial details of a performance's origin or personal elements are kept from tourist display. Humour in performance sometimes helps to negotiate the expected identities of the 'serious' native or 'noble savage'. In Kiribati, in the south-west Pacific, expectations of the musical content and dress of performance have similarly been debated to take note of past 'traditional' performances, the expectations of local and international audiences, and the feelings of the performers (Marion, 1988). The musical stage is also a space from which to dismiss assumptions about indigenous peoples, even if those keen to do so are partly involved in constructing and performing stereotypical identities.

At Iweniar village (Tanna Island, Vanuatu) 'traditional' dances are performed at approximately weekly intervals for tour groups (mainly from Australia) by villagers dressed in grass skirts and other elements of traditional dress, with faces and bodies painted in bright colours now enhanced by certain store-bought make-up. Collectively, in 2003 the village earned barely a hundred dollars from each tour and performance, but this enabled households to meet school fees and other modern needs. Performances included other facets of 'traditional' culture – from the consumption of village foods to the demonstration of local games – reinforcing the value of these customs, so that the 'custom village' (as it was touted by travel agents) had become a museum or archive for musical culture not performed in other Tannese villages. While what was performed is inauthentic, since dances otherwise are rarely performed even once a year, it constitutes a 'strategic inauthenticity' where tourists capture some semblance of the Melanesian past and

Melanesians perform the past as a means of generating much-needed cash incomes (Figure 5.2). Local (European) promoters have sought to 'maintain tradition' by demanding female toplessness – on occasion promising 'plenty of bums and tits' to visiting tourists – and excluding villages who 'become too modern'. Villagers have increasingly rejected this ploy (and toplessness) and those promoters who demanded a form of 'tradition' they no longer welcomed. Villagers performed an identity with which they were comfortable, whether invented, borrowed or preserved, and which ironically, though a version of tradition, moves them further away from it.

Contested identities are also evident in central Australia. Musicians, managers and promoters connected to contemporary Aboriginal music in Alice Springs have been highly resentful of tourist caricatures of indigenous culture and the ways in which 'traditional' musical performances pander to stereotypes. Contemporary Aboriginal musicians, most notably reggae, rock and country groups, receive virtually no support from the tourism industry, while their music is largely alien to the tourists who overwhelmingly expect the performed 'traditional' identity rather than contemporary hybrid expressions (Bonamy, 2001). For others, by contrast, performing 'traditional' identities allows a safe distance between lived indigenous culture and a version presented for tourists. Because contemporary music scenes remain largely disconnected from tourist audiences, this also protects an expressive terrain as a

Figure 5.2 Tourists dancing with Iweniar villagers, Tanna, Vanuatu (Photograph courtesy of John Connell)

'backspace', distinct from tourist areas and free from their incursions. That 'backspace' enables Aboriginal identity as lived experience, where there is no pandering to tourist demands, and there may be little or no relationship to tourist expectations and 'new' musical identities that include hip-hop and country music – possible anathema to those tourists who seek didjeridus and boomerangs. 'Traditional' indigenous musical shows have become a means of negotiating tourist economies and influences, a deliberate identity performed for tourists, while another space for musical creativity, expression and community interaction is shielded from tourist influence.

Even where global cultural diversity is celebrated in music tourism, as at world music festivals such as WOMAD, the politics of cultural identities is complex. At WOMAD and similar festivals, an array of exotic sounds is brought together. Here world music becomes 'a kind of commercial aural travel consumption, where the festival . . . assembled from "remote" corners of the world, could be a reconstructed version of the Great Exhibitions of the nineteenth century' (Hutnyk, 2000: 21). While origins in developing countries seemingly conferred local authenticity, tensions remained in the placelessness of certain forms of consumption: world music constituted 'the ubiquitous nowhere of the international financial markets and the Internet' (Erlmann, 1996: 475) since, rather differently, 'we no longer have roots, we have aerials' (Wark, 1994; see also Connell & Gibson, 2004b). Therefore, the construction of ethnic diversity, within a context that was established for consumption by Western cosmopolitan audiences, separated those identities from the field of meaning from which the musicians and their songs emerged: 'The utterly eclectic mixing of cultures in this tourist economy has the troubling effect of suggesting that all cultures, from Norwegian to Native American, are equally consumable, providing one has the economic wherewithal to take advantage of these offerings' (Johnson & Underiner, 2001: 45). Commerce and culture are entangled in a dialectic produced by deliberate and unconscious constructions of identities performed for, and consumed by, tourists. Ultimately, however, as Grunewald (2002: 1016) has suggested, tourism, through its creation of new patterns of consumption and identification, indeed of 'new traditions', may well be positive and welcomed. Various indigenous communities perceive the very existence of tourists as proof of the continuity and presence of authenticity, a means of validating uniqueness and distinction (Wood, 1998: 224). Indeed, whether subverting or sustaining tradition, tourism has largely been welcomed, even demanded, not least among relatively impoverished ethnic communities which, again ironically, may be most changed by it.

Celebrated and Contested Heritage:
Beale Street, Memphis

If Beale Street could talk ... Beale Street would cry
Nat D. Williams, quoted in
McKee & Chisenhall, 1981: 10

Just as individuals and groups perform, accept and challenge identities, so too are places imbued with various social meanings, which are entangled in the cultural politics of race, ethnicity, gender and class. The ways in which Beale Street, Memphis, has become a music tourism location exemplify this phenomenon, and provide insights into the politics of authenticity and identity that is cut across by racial politics.

Memphis was long plagued with endemic racism, and the interracial climate in the city was the formative background to the music produced from the 1930s to the 1970s, when various styles, from blues to soul and rock and roll, all had their genesis (see Chapter 3). Indeed, although the musical *Annie Get Your Gun* was banned from the city in 1947 because it starred a black man in the role of a railway conductor and showed scenes of blacks and whites dancing together, music became a means of political statement for musicians who, despite rigid social norms, eventually transgressed racial boundaries to create music. For James Brown, 'The word soul ... meant a lot of things – in music and out. It was about the roots of black music, and it was kind of a pride thing too, being proud of yourself and your people. Soul music and the civil rights movement went hand in hand, sort of grew up together' (quoted in Werner, 1998: 72). For white drummer Jim Dickinson, who played on much of the recorded music at Stax records, 'The Memphis sound is something that's produced by a group of social misfits in a dark room in the middle of the night. It's not committees, it's not bankers, not disc jockeys. Every attempt to organize the Memphis music community has been a failure, as righteously [*sic*] it should be. The diametric opposition, the racial collision, the redneck versus the ghetto black is what it's all about, and it can't be brought together. If it could, there wouldn't be any music' (quoted in Werner, 1998: 75). Such transgression did not occur on an equal playing-field because of the subtle powerplay of white producers directing black (and white) musicians: 'Sam Moore of Sam and Dave isn't alone in his belief that Stax – at least before black executive Al Bell became a major figure in 1965 – amounted to a new kind of plantation where the black singers did the work while the white management made the decisions' (Werner, 1998: 75).

The racial politics of Memphis' music was not, however, limited to powerplays within the recording studio. A wider set of tensions in the town, in particular the governance and control exerted over Memphis' most famous black precinct, Beale Street, indelibly shaped the contexts within which the music was made. Blacks were initially forced into Beale Street through segregation, but vital community links were forged there and expressive spaces carved out – clubs, theatres, parks, streetscapes. The spaces were transformed through both community presence and music. Beale Street became a place for the inversion of enforced identities of segregated African-Americans who became owners of a physical and cultural space in the city:

> The white man had said the black man couldn't go certain places, that Beale was the place for blacks; and the black man turned it around and said Beale was the *only* place to be. It was more than a collection of stores and saloons, pawnshops and lodge halls and church headquarters. Beale was Main Street and back alley and the Rialto and Courthouse Square; Christians, hypocrites, heathens, gamblers, the upright, and the uptight; harlots and mothers of the church; professional men in their black suits and dark ties; country folks in overalls and flour-sack dresses; easy riders in their box-back suits, Stetson hats, and silk shirts, with diamond stickpins and gold chains, glittering symbols of Beale's glamorous wickedness; wandering minstrels singing their blues; itinerant preachers shouting a hell-fire-and-brimstone blues of their own; conjure men and con men; voodoo and hoodoo women. It was a melting pot of black America. (McKee & Chisenhall, 1981: 6)

At various times white city authorities sought to rid the precinct of its perceived sins – the vice, prostitution and corruption associated with the black informal sector that had sprung up in the neighbourhood behind segregation lines. Urban renewal was touted as early as the mid-1960s, but would take another decade to begin. Beale Street constituted a 'dangerous' space for whites and one that was at the core of Memphis' black community, imbued with deep connections and social meanings. As W.C. Handy, the 'father of the blues' commented in an interview in the mid-1950s, 'The white people of Memphis have never understood just what Beale Street really meant and means to my people' (quoted in McKee & Chisenhall, 1981: 2). Beale Street was the site where city riots in 1968 erupted after the assassination of Dr Martin Luther King Jr, leaving many buildings vacant and shop-fronts smashed. The deterioration of buildings continued, in part because of neglect by white landlords, but also, some have argued, because of the lack of attention from black leaders, such as those in the Negro Chamber of Commerce. This neglect, as well as racism on the part of city authorities, led to Beale Street's eventual demolition (Figure 5.3). Even Beale Street's part in the story of Elvis Presley, Memphis' most famous white export – Presley spent many hours on Beale Street, buying clothes, listening to music and

Figure 5.3 Beale Street, Memphis, has undergone several transformations from black business precinct to urban renewal site and finally music
tourism locale. Above left, Nat D. Williams, Memphis radio DJ and
writer, stands in front of the ruins of the famous Palace Theater, 1973,
at the height of the urban renewal phase. Meanwhile, above right,
present-day Beale Street has become a pedestrianised tourist landscape
of blues bars, souvenir shops and restaurants. (*Above left* Photograph
by courtesy of McKee and Chisenhall, 1981; *above right* photograph by
courtesy of Chris Gibson)

impersonating the blues musicians he heard there – could not prevent
the demolition. Thus, the Memphis Housing Authority, 'after years of
talk about razing Beale and rebuilding it, began to act. Down came the
Panama, the Midway Café, the Palace Theater, and other landmarks.
Rubble and empty lots were about all that remained' (McKee &
Chisenhall, 1981: 96).

For the blues disc jockey Nat D. Williams, demolition of the district
had tragic consequences: 'He looked again at the ruins of the Palace, at
the old black man sifting through the debris, and reflected on the irony:
black men had made Beale world famous under the watchful eyes of
white men, and black men under the watchful eyes of white straw bosses
had wielded the iron wrecking balls that tore town the framework of
Beale, had manned the bulldozers that shoveled up the bones of their
street' (McKee & Chisenhall, 1981: 6). Early hints at a tourist-oriented

future were evident when, despite the demolition, on 15 December 1977, Beale Street was officially declared the 'Home of the Blues' by an act of Congress, even if more accurately the blues had its genesis throughout the Delta region, as a development of the 'field hollers' and calls on cotton plantations. A little later, Edward 'Prince Gabe' Kirby, a famous Memphis saxophonist, stated: 'Once Beale Street is restored, hopefully the blues will regain its full life in the city again. As a neighbourhood, however, Beale Street can never be restored' (Kirby, 1983: 42).

The plans of the Memphis Housing Authority (MHA) for urban renewal, when announced in 1966, were to convert 'drab Beale Street into a glittering jewel, complete with its own revolving-tower restaurant at the Mississippi River, a riverfront freeway, high-rise apartments, a plaza along Beale, and a huge, covered commercial mall' (Worley, 1998: 24). The subsequent election of the Nixon government and shifting priorities for public investment in urban renewal meant that the US$200 million required for the MHA plan never materialised. The reconstruction of the Beale Street precinct was 'by the mid-1970s, dead in the water' (Worley, 1998: 24). Joe Raffanti, owner of the Midway Liquor Store on Beale Street, said in 1973 that 'they keep tearing buildings down and boarding them up, but nothing is ever built' (quoted in Worley, 1998: 26). More than 8000 residents had either moved on or been relocated since Beale Street's heyday over a decade earlier. Even official city maps printed between 1973 and 1977 'simply omitted the four liveliest blocks of Beale Street. Sadly, no public official or citizen with enough clout to be heard even noticed the error' (Worley, 1998: 26).

In 1982, without Housing Authority backing, a consortium of local interests formed to redevelop the street, mostly made up of developers, local proprietors and city promotional agencies. Their aims, according to redevelopment director John Elkington, were to 'return commerce to the street . . . Beale Street would become the music and entertainment center of the community . . . it would become a place where there would be no barriers, real or imaginary, and where citizens of all races would be welcome' (quoted in Worley, 1998: 35). Beale Street Management (now known as Performa Entertainment Real Estate Company) lobbied for licensing changes that would allow alcohol consumption in the open street (vital to staging festivals and open-air events), changed opening hours to allow Sunday trading and encouraged new businesses in the precinct.

A renovated and smaller, tourist-orientated section of Beale Street opened to the general public in 1983. Subsequently, W.C. Handy's childhood house was moved to Beale Street from its original location a few miles south as part of a 'museum-opening craze' (Perry & Glinert, 1996: 131). Some, though, argued that Beale Street's designation as a US National Parks Historical Landmark should be rejected, due to the demolitions and relocation of the residents, although reconstruction made more tenable the link between tourism and heritage. A string of changes followed the redesignation of Beale Street as a National Historical Landmark in 1987: the Centre for Southern Folklore opened in 1989; B.B. King's Blues Bar began in 1991; Elvis Presley's Memphis restaurant and live music venue opened for business in 1997; other museums, nightclubs and attractions, such as the Beale Street Blues Museum and the Memphis Music Hall of Fame all sprang into life. Beale Street had gone from black America's Main Street to a reconstructed tourist attraction based on the black cultural expressions that were the core of the original place identities developed earlier in the century.

In more recent years, Beale Street, along with other attractions in Memphis – most notably the National Civil Rights Museum at the site of the Lorraine Hotel where Martin Luther King Jr was assassinated – have become part of an African-American tourist network. Whereas in the early 1990s Beale Street's attractions seemed geared towards a predominantly white tourist audience, ten years later black tourists had become more common. This trend brought new complexities to the cultural politics of music tourism in Beale Street. On the site of a once segregated black community was now a simulated landscape of former (musical) glories, packaged for tourist consumption and too antiseptic to ever again pose as the place that B.B. King once called 'college for blues men' (Winegardener 1987: 81). Although much of Beale Street's black cultural heritage was jettisoned in demolition and urban renewal schemes, its contemporary role as an emerging focal point for new forms of black tourism suggests that, despite demolition, black heritage is belatedly being more effectively recognised and promoted. For John Elkington, 'it is one of the few places in the city where whites and blacks can gather. It is a place where, hopefully, we can foster an understanding in the community' (quoted in Worley, 1998: 35), one largely created around music.

Beale Street has become an 'anchor' for the renewal of Memphis' entire downtown, coordinated by the Center City Commission, that seeks to create a wider cultural/entertainment precinct, including apartment renovations and building conversions, a major convention/conference complex, and the construction of new purpose-built stadiums for the Memphis Grizzlies and Redbirds, the city's national league basketball and baseball teams. While such efforts will bring back renewed vitality to the area, poorer residents may be further displaced from the inner city through residential property market dynamics; urban renewal stimulated by cultural tourism, as in New Orleans and Harlem, has had negative impacts on black residents as gentrification has brought greater rents and other costs.

Memphis' experience with music tourism in Beale Street does not necessarily demonstrate that something 'authentic' has been replaced by something 'inauthentic', even if black culture was ignored in the renewal schemes. The process of urban redevelopment in Memphis created a tourist space in which black culture and heritage were simultaneously the means for commodification and sources of musical inspiration for contemporary artists. Beale Street is a site of intense cultural meaning and significance, not just because of its black history prior to demolition, but because of what happened after it – with its reorientation towards commercial activities and eventual incorporation into a black American tourist network. It could be argued that the restoration of Beale Street produced a 'themed milieu' (Rojek, 1995), designed with a limited range of motifs derived from media cultures, rather than a continuing space of lived black culture. It had been transformed into a place of heritage, just as, in an even more antiseptic and saccharine manner, has been Graceland (Chapter 6). Beale Street's new tourist function could never hope to replace its role within the community, but the version of American musical culture that would eventually be presented in tourism attractions, despite certain silences in the landscape, provides some belated recognition of the importance of black musical expressions and what were, particularly in their time, radical cross-racial musical alliances.

Tourism as Theatre

The meanings and identities ascribed to music tourism locations by those who work in the tourist industry, whether as performers or entrepreneurs, or who visit, with whatever objective, are varied and always fluid. Music provides one means through which places are perceived, and often these links are reliant on the invention or reinvention of tradition, or even strategic inauthenticity, where musical styles and codes of dress and behaviour from particular eras come to represent the 'authentic' history of a place. In this way, as in Tanna, Memphis, Hainan and Bali, particular places become represented as 'a type of living museum that is imagined in both the minds of the performers and the audience' (Johnson, 2002: 14), despite the context and nature of performance having substantially changed.

Tourists have usually sought out exotica, or at the very least distinctiveness and difference, and music has inevitably been part of this appetite. Tourism thrives on difference and also on pleasure. Music was not expected to be commonplace, nor were its performers – hence the need for essentialised *hapa haole* 'Hawaiian' performers and Aboriginal didjeridu players, or even the simple caricatures portrayed in the *Black and White Minstrel Show*. In most such contexts there is some notion of history, heritage and the quest for 'roots'. Yet such essentialisms have usually been challenged, especially where indigenous performers have achieved their own forms of accommodation within the music and tourist industries. Such accommodation is never complete, as the experience of Aboriginal performers or the reconstruction of Beale Street demonstrates, since tourism exists within a wider and evolving political economy.

Music tourism has also demanded some local specificity. In Liverpool, tourists seek out associations with the Beatles, the very phenomenon that made Liverpool apparently unique, just as in West Africa they sought out Djembe drummers (Chapter 6); in Hawaii they craved steel guitar or ukulele peformances. Vienna could never escape the classical heritage of Mozart and the blue Danube. In some cases history was denied, but in others, spaces were effectively stabilised around the time that they created a particularly distinctive musical product. In Vienna:

> The past has been sanitised, disinfected and altered to conform to a sentimental view of a culture or a heritage which no longer resides in reality but engages with images of fantasy . . . as in all good theme parks, the past is spruced up to appeal to the sensation-seeking tourist. (Riemer, 1993: 34–35)

This stabilisation of a particular moment in time and place is more generally true of heritage tourism.

Western audiences' demands for cultural authenticity or 'purity' have sometimes required local performers to dress up and perform as caricatures of a culture that probably never existed outside the representational frames set up in Hollywood and Broadway. Nevertheless, Hollywood itself has contributed to some of the most successful – and wholly inauthentic – music tourism activities, in Salzburg's Sound of Music Tour and Mozart tourism (Figure 5.4). In other contexts 'authenticity' is perceived as being under threat because of tourism, which is seen to 'dilute' local cultures with foreign influence (even if local people themselves have welcomed it, especially in places such as Bali and Iweniar village, where it is a key means of earning income and embracing change). Many authorities and scholars have railed against the 'debasement' of music and culture by pandering to tourism, but efforts to control 'purity' have challenged aspirations for income, performers' notions of what is appropriate and, in the end, tourists' desires for entertainment. In 1969 the government in Austria issued a law about the use of the name 'Tyrolean Evening' and about the performance of authentic Tyrolean folk music, folk-song and folk-dance. However,

> this law did not change the situation because most tourists do not know authentic folk music, and they do not like to hear and see authentic folk traditions. They like to have fun; they like to laugh about the primitive folk of the Alps, the yodeling Alpine herdsman and the dairymaid, the sooty poacher and the rustic woodcutter. (Suppan, 1988: 169)

Figure 5.4 Getreidegasse no. 9, Salzburg, is where the Leopold Mozart family lived from 1747 to 1773. Wolfgang Amadeus Mozart was born here on 27 January 1756. Today, the rooms once occupied by the Mozart family house a museum – one of the oldest dedicated music museums in the world. The International Mozart Foundation first set up a museum here on 15 June 1880. Since the 1984 film *Amadeus* rekindled awareness of Mozart and subsequently expanded the tourism market, Salzburg tourism has spawned a range of related, but somewhat less 'authentic', Mozart industries, including chocolates (pictured right), T-shirts and umbrellas. (Photographs by courtesy of Natascha Klocker)

Moreover, the hosts are well capable of distinguishing between this kind of superficiality, the music they might prefer (and may be performed elsewhere) and the economic realities of a tourist economy. Neither music nor culture can be stabilised, and while entertainment always threatens notions of authenticity, it is an impossible task to measure and evaluate changes in culture and tradition.

The quest for authenticity demands 'that one is always looking elsewhere, over the shoulder or around the bend' which prevents enjoying and understanding the actual performance as a performance (Bruner, 1996: 176). Authenticity becomes an 'arbitrating mark' (Shepherd, 2002:

190), perhaps even the perfect simulation of one moment in history, but one that is subjective and against which everything must be judged. Yet in every context performances are altered for tourists; many are shortened, made more accessible in language, rhythm or familiarity, so meeting the need of tourists for the entertaining, exotic or nostalgic. They 'chart a course between 'exoticism' and comprehensibility' (Edensor, 2001: 70). Not only is theatre the basic metaphor of tourism, but tourists willingly enter into some degree of suspension of disbelief, so collapsing the issue of authenticity into a problem of verisimilitude and credibility (Bruner, 1996: 176). Isolation, few other tourists, ethnic integrity and the role of place all assist in emphasising mythology, and even credibility may quickly disappear under intense scrutiny. In this sense much of contemporary music tourism may indeed be post-tourism, where performance and pleasure are more important than authenticity.

In places such as Memphis, urban renewal and tourism development have given rise to complex cultural meaning and politics. Such issues continue to be played out. In 2000, another black music precinct – Maxwell Street, Chicago, home of the city's most vibrant African-American community, and also considered the birthplace of the electric blues scene – fell under the wrecker's ball, with its historic theatres, churches and stores demolished to make way for an expansion of the University of Illinois campus. A local action group, formed to represent the community and prevent destruction of the precinct, called on the authorities to preserve its built and cultural heritage, appealing to the National Register of Historic Places to list the precinct because of its legacy of the blues. Among the recommendations from the Maxwell Street Historic Preservation Coalition was that of renovating the area as a tourist district, with a blues museum and regular performances. Ironically, the plans compared it with Beale Street. Nonetheless, demolition continued, drawing criticism from activists, who see it as another manifestation of state-led racism:

> The agenda of the University of Illinois and the City of Chicago is to continue to largely ignore the African-American and Blues history of Maxwell Street so poor minority people of color will no longer come down to the old Maxwell Street area. UIC spends hundreds of thousands of dollars to perpetuate the notion that the proper place for history is on websites and in libraries not in historic sites where ordinary folks can see, smell, taste, and listen to their own history from the people who made it and their descendents. (Balkin, 2001: 30A)

Music tourism is thus both an agent of change, which can in the case of Beale Street enact new forms of urban development, and a means for political action, which the Maxwell Street protesters used as a tool to

prevent the further destruction of a black neighbourhood. It also represents a means of consolidation, where tourism acts as a critical force
ensuring continuity with the past, even as 'museum' or 'archive', despite
contemporary tourist displays in quite different social contexts having
only limited resonance with those of the past. In Memphis, Liverpool
(Brabazon, 1993) and elsewhere, 'authenticity' is not merely a cultural
concept waiting to be discovered, observed and heard, but is a social
construction, firmly linked to political issues of who has the power to
develop and promote particular representations. At the very least,
tourism necessitates some compromise between authenticity, however
defined, and interpretation. This situation is further complicated because
tourism is about some degree of entertainment. Hence, tourists may well
prefer to be complicit in a version of history that ignores dissonant
elements. Tourists are not usually anthropologists, historians or musi-
cologists.

Chapter 6
On the Road Again: Nostalgia and Pleasure

Tourists undertake travel for a number of reasons. Music is sometimes one of these, but it is also a part of tourist experiences triggered by other motivations. Tourists seek sand, sun, sex, or more cerebral delights such as architecture and heritage sites. Some tourists are driven by informative, self-educational or experiential motives, others undertake to fulfil what might be perceived as more 'bodily' desires. Music can be a part of all these configurations. In places where music and tourism come together, it most simply facilitates 'having a good time': an essential for dancing, a major feature of stage performance, a background to socialising and interacting with other tourists and local hosts. Music is entertainment and relaxation, as in seaside and show towns, and 'social lubricant', as in such backpacker locations as Ibiza, Goa and Koh Samui. Music is a major attraction in some of these places, in others no more than an accompaniment. In certain contexts where particularly committed music tourists dominate, some degree of nostalgia for past times and places is invoked. Such circumstances have often given rise to the 'heritage industry' and the reconstruction of place, alongside demands for authenticity about places and performances.

This chapter examines the rationale for music tourism: where tourists go and what they seek to do. It focuses especially on those who are, in some sense, more willing to travel to particular destinations because of music. Travel has been particularly extensive for some music fans; music plays an important part in their lives (sometimes most obviously for musicians themselves), and thus tourism connected to music may be thoroughly memorable. This chapter therefore traces different patterns of travel, particularly among the more committed music tourists, whether for sheer pleasure or even out of some sense of duty. In the most dramatic cases, music tourism has involved notions of religious awe and even pilgrimage – an extreme intensity of experience.

Song Lines

Notions of more idyllic places elsewhere are embedded in lyrics, the words of songs and arias. These musical constructions of place have stimulated travel. Country music, for example, has expressed distaste with the city and celebrated, often critically and ironically, rural spaces, as in John Denver's 'Country roads, Take me Home/To the place I belong/West Virginia . . .'. Much country-and-western music portrayed a 'nostalgia for a rural paradise, symbolised by a yearning for a simpler way of life, a looking back to an uncomplicated place' (Kong, 1995: 187). Simultaneously, it stressed individualism, loneliness and self-reliance, alongside working-class and Christian values and the virtues of hard (usually outdoor) work in opposition to urban anomie and radical change, so nourishing 'sacred places and times' (Woods & Gritzner, 1990). Home was 'more than a locale and site of family and friends [but was] the essence of the natural world', the 'Tennessee mountain home is nature itself, the Emersonian center of authenticity in America' (Tichi, 1994: 25). Such places represented alternatives to the city, 'a landscape of nostalgic rural salvation and refuge from the cold impersonal nature of the modern cityscape' (Lewis, 1997: 167). In essence, country music was the music of poor white folk struggling against authority, fate and challenging environments.

While a sense of space and mobility pervades country music, most genres of popular music envisage physical escape from restricting confines, especially in the United States. Music contributes to a celebration in literature, film (the road movie) and art of the American road (and the railroad) – a prominent aspect of American culture and symbol of mobility in a particularly mobile nation. Blues music traced journeys out of poverty and oppression, while rock music spoke of freedom and adventure, born of emerging affluence, and access to cars and motorbikes. Truck-driving songs offered a parallel 'fakelore' of endless highways, strong coffee, speed and smoke (Jarvis, 1985: 102), an elusive and transient culture that transformed the highway into home.

Tracing the legacy of the blues and Jack Kerouac's Beat Generation, road songs emphasised the simple pleasures of escape and freedom, restlessness and divorce from weary, conventional lives: 'It is hard to think of the early Dylan or Guthrie or the Delta Bluesmen without seeing a picture in your mind of a lone male figure walking away down a neverending road with just a rucksack and a guitar for company' (Heining, 1998: 106). Highway songs offered a promise of better places somewhere down the road, as railroad songs similarly craved distant delights and temptations, places that offer escape, adventure or, alternatively, security. No highway song was more famous than the much recorded 'Route 66' which emphasised the extent to which road songs were quintessential

American songs, linked to a particular sense of space. While not just a specifically American dream, notions of escapism were more muted elsewhere, in both song and experience, although voyages of escape and discovery tended to be linked to discourses of 'frontier' landscapes in large continents such as North America and Australia.

Rave and house music went beyond this to spin dreams of alternative places – fantasy and pastoral landscapes where participants could escape the confines of urban life and temporarily 'drop out'. According to Greil Marcus, 'it may be that the most interesting struggle is the struggle to set oneself free from the limits one is born to' (1975: 19). This has resonance in music and tourism, both intermittently offering experiences beyond the mundane. Music tourism has cherished lyrical themes, such as the notion that country music pictures a distant and idyllic home, and the more nebulous 'struggle' for a different identity beyond the confines of daily life. Music enables contentment within expressions of identity. Such quests have also taken on the characteristics of relaxed, if commodified, modes of entertainment.

Into the Music

The most demanding music tourism requires substantial immersion not just in the music but in the wider economic and social environment of the host culture. Specialist tourist companies operate lengthy tours to West Africa (Figure 6.1), where tourists engage in month-long village experiences in Guinea and other nearby states, aimed at their learning African drumming and dance. Similar tours, advertised as ecotourism, operate from Europe and North America; the Netherlands-based Arafan Tours, led by Arafan Toure, formerly the main djembe (drum) soloist of Les Ballets Africains, advertises:

> Our tour with Arafan starts at Wonkifon, the village where his mother was born, and where we'll be staying as the guests of local families. Deep in the bush and not far from the river we'll meet families living much as their forefathers used to. ... The musical instruments in this area have been played as far back as anyone can remember. They include the Balafon, Kondi, Flute, Bells and Drums. Djembe amongst them. The rhythm of the women is known as Yogui, whose music and dance will be familiar to us after nine days there. ... It's a journey to learn (insight and knowledge) one month in Guinea playing and/or dancing singing and looking at people (and join them singing and dancing). On working days in the morning and in the afternoon there are lessons by members of the National Ballet (dance) and 'Percussion de Guinée' for 4 or 5 hours a day. Before the journey one decides what one wants to learn: percussion,

Figure 6.1 Drumming tours in Guinea

balafon, kora, dance or singing and Arafan Tours will organise the proper teacher for you. The journey is for dancers and percussionists-singers and during the trip we learn customs and rituals from different cultures and you see the artists working. (www.gofree. indigo.ie/~djembe/guinea)

Similar tours emphasise wider cultural experiences, including learning the medicinal values of local plants, soap- and salt-making, basket-weaving and mud-hut accommodation (as Tribes Fair Trade Travel does in Gambia). In Cuba music tours may be combined with esoteric know-ledge as in the 'Cuba: Music, Plants and Healing' tour organised by Plenty-Canada, a Canadian First Nations non-government organisation (www.nativeamericas.aip.cornell.edu). Most stress themes akin to the British-based Drum Doctor tours: 'We offer you the experience of the reality of the Gambia, not some superficial, concocted, artificial, "tribal" presentation to be found in hotels and "cultural centres".' Other tours undertake similar journeys in places well beyond Africa, such as Karamba Experience tours to Cuba (where tourists learn music, dance and singing with the Danza Libre group), and India (with tuition in Gujarati drums bells, castanets and/or singing); Brazil hosts capoeira (martial dance and music) and drum tours. Especially in West Africa, but also in Bahia (Brazil), small-scale music tours have contributed to local development where otherwise tourism had limited significance.

Australian participants in Guinea drumming tours were 'usually obsessed drumming students', previously involved in Sydney drum and dance classes taught by migrant African musicians. Some were students in university dance and music classes. Some West African drum tourists were on the 'fringe of the alternative movement', but all were working in order to cover the cost of the tour (about A$3500/US$2500) and their earlier classes (K. Buchan, personal communication, 2002). These music tourists were serious about their intent to learn West African drumming styles, seeking to overcome the particular complexities of Guinean polyrhythms and the difficulties of mastering the instruments without years of experience. They had no interest in overtly 'constructed' tourist promotions and the lack of substantial earlier tourism to rural Guinea suggests that modification of local musical styles and practices, in the light of tourism, had been limited. As one Australian woman on such a tour noted: 'I want to become, in a month, a little bit African' (Brown, 2002: 7), a pious hope that is unrealistic, but illustrative of the desire to 'connect' with places through tourism in rather greater depth than is possible in conventional beach holidays. Tours provide musical and cultural insights and knowledge, rarely available in the West. Travel creates the opportunity for intensive learning through immersion in an 'authentic' context, much like the artists and architects who travelled to Paris to immerse themselves in alternative lifestyles in the early 20th century.

Drums have been much the most popular of indigenous African instruments among tourists – although the *mbira* has attracted tourists to East Africa – and have similarly been popular among backpackers in contexts far removed from Africa, such as Byron Bay in Australia. African drum workshops in Byron Bay, oriented to tourists, are described as 'a dynamic and powerful way to access your inner joy and celebrate your being, using African movement to make you move, groove, sweat and smile all over' (quoted in Gibson & Connell, 2003: 179). The rise of drum workshops has been stimulated by the reverse migration of West African drummers, conducting courses, lessons and workshops, in Australia, Europe and North America, and in key back-packer locations such as Byron Bay and Bali. These are as much as any cultural factor, a means of earning money, often to send or take back to Africa.

The indigenous Australian didjeridu has similarly attracted specialist interest and tourism to the Northern Territory among enthusiasts. It is

> the latest stage in the yidaki's [didjeridu] long cultural journey; a journey that at first led outwards, across the Top End's plains and stringybark forests, to the great cities of southeastern Australia and even beyond, into the wider world of new age beliefs and spiritual fashions: then back in a slow, returning arc towards Yirrkala [in Australia's far north], as its western enthusiasts gradually learned how much of the instrument's strength remains bound up with the secrets and depths of Arnhem Land. (Rothwell, 2002: R4)

Enthusiasts travel from Europe and urban Australia to participate in workshops and master classes, to absorb the didjeridu's role in the ritual world of east Arnhem Land and to 'use the instrument to investigate themselves'. Such 'yidaki tourists . . . feel themselves close to the heart of the mystery: here they are at the source of the yidaki's plaintive throb-bing call'. This obsession with the didjeridu is a 'form of imperialist nostalgia: you glorify what your culture once destroyed' (Karl Neuenfeldt, quoted by Rothwell, 2002: R6), although many tourists might not think of themselves in this way. Tourist numbers remain relatively small – a handful of individuals in search of a means of learning and contextualising distinctive musical skills.

This desire for rhythm has certain spiritual overtones, linked to changed states of consciousness, as at Byron Bay where this involves 'using ritual, rhythm and dances from all over Africa to excite and inspire you and let your wild side out to play' (quoted in Gibson & Connell, 2003). Participants in drumming sessions, whether in an Australian resort or the 'real' space of West African villages, search for access to knowledge, times and places that have escaped the transformations of modernity, in all its guises.

Parallel quests for authenticity are most evident in developing world contexts where ideas surrounding 'world music' have intimated that distinct musical forms exist, untarnished by modernity and isolated from contact with alien musical traditions. While such ideas are now evidently mythological (Connell & Gibson, 2003, 2004b) they have provided a basis for some contemporary travel. For the small town of Lijiang (Yunnan, China), English-language (including Lonely Planet) and Chinese guidebooks emphasise concerts of 'traditional Naxi music' frequently performed by this particular ethnic minority group. These concerts have been sought out by 'backpacker' tourists who expressed delight in the performances, being impressed by the dignified elderly musicians, their determination to maintain a longstanding tradition, and by the fact that no obvious concessions were apparently made to a Western audience (Rees, 1998; see Chapter 5). Tourists used words like 'traditional', 'genuine', the 'real thing' and frequently 'authentic' to describe the experience. Naxi performances were explicitly compared with more 'sanitised "folk" music performed in a restaurant – comely maidens and youths in too-bright minority costumes pranced and posed with all the authenticity of the cheerful Cockneys in Lionel Bart musicals, and to a background of largely re-recorded music' (Rees, 1998: 149). For the tourists who reached remote places such as Lijiang, electric pianos and organs, strobe lights, identical sequined bodices and corny Western harmonies were immediate turn-offs. Tourists at Lijiang concerts were thus perceived as 'existential tourists' who sought to abandon modernity and draw closer to indigenous peoples and their cultures.

The kind of 'existential tourism' that opened up remote areas of China and Vietnam, enabling some survival of declining traditions, is somewhat uncommon (and linked to a particular 'backpacker' scene); moreover, it is tangentially linked to music. More accurately, only in a handful of cases, such as travellers going to West Africa seeking to learn particular musical skills, is music central to the existential quest, which is more likely to be about abandoning the Western world than acquiring the ideologies and culture of other places. Nevertheless, tourists have deliberately chosen places where they might experience musical traditions close to their heartlands. Such interests contributed to tourism in Cuba in the last years of the 20th century, took tango enthusiasts to Argentina and, in larger numbers, resulted in the booming folk-music scene in Ireland. While such tourists have come from Europe and North America, Japanese tourists too have sought to learn tango, jazz and folk music in distant destinations.

Ireland has consistently advertised itself as a place of music, a trait that regional tourism organisations have emphasised in a manner that attests to the continuity and informality of the musical experience. The Ring of Kerry Tourism Office states that 'the remote and beautiful Ring of Kerry is an important destination for those wishing to hear Irish

Traditional Music at its best' and that 'Perhaps the best way to hear the music is at a "Session" – usually a group of local musicians who just turn up at a pub and play – just buy a drink and sit and listen – one of life's great experiences' (www.ringofkerrytourism.com). Galway tourist authorities note that the region

> is a hotbed of musical activity. From the old masters singing ancient songs unaccompanied, to the young pretenders of the rock scene, there's music galore to be found here. If you're after a musical experience, tracing the roots of Celtic song, or if you just want to dance the night away it's here. And not forgetting ceilidh. Rince – pronounced rinka – the Irish for dance, is something altogether less slick and heartfelt than the river dances you might be familiar with. But the emotions expressed in the movement of the body: a word-less evocation of the Celtic spirit that will stay with you forever. (www.galwaytourism.ie/ch)

Stress on continuity and informality, the involvement of the bodily senses and the apparent absence of commercialism, emphasise the potential for genuine experiences that are unavailable elsewhere, but to be found at the core of Irish culture. Similar themes have drawn tourists to Brazil, Argentina and Cuba in the demand for enjoyable and credible experiences. Although Irish music, like any other, has constantly changed, its image has attracted – and been used to attract – tourists in search of credible performances that appear to have links with Celtic history. Indeed, diasporic performers such as Moya Kneafsey argue: 'When you play traditional music you are enmeshed into all these very emotive issues to do with roots, belonging, place' (Kneafsey, 2002: 356). Exactly these dimensions have stimulated tourism, not only in Ireland, but more generally among a musically literate population.

Classical musicians have similarly travelled in search of authenticity – for example, in the desire to hear Wagner's operas performed in Bayreuth (as Wagner intended) or to hear the great orchestras or opera companies play in their home concert and opera houses. Individuals too have travelled widely to be involved in the 'master classes' that distinguished musicians have organised. Here too there is a quest for authenticity, history and personal involvement. Among those who have sought to learn jazz in New Orleans or bluegrass in Appalachia, there have been parallel searches for both meaning and participation.

Get Your Kicks on Route 66

> If you ever plan to motor west
> Travel my way, take the highway, that's the best
> Get your kicks on Route 66

It winds from Chicago to LA
More than 2000 miles all the way
Get your kicks on Route 66
You go through St Louis, Joplin Missouri
And Oklahoma City looks oh so pretty
You'll see Amarillo, Gallup, New Mexico
Flagstaff, Arizona, don't forget Winona
Kingman, Barstow, San Bernadino
Won't you get hip to this timely tip
When you make that California trip
Get your kicks on Route 66
(Bobby Troup, 1946)

No other road in the United States is as famous as Route 66; no other road has become part of national culture and mythology or more treasured in memory. The original Route 66, opened in 1926, covered more than 3800 kilometres from Chicago to Los Angeles, through the heart of the United States, crossing prairies and plains, through hills and deserts, becoming part of the land and of the cities that it linked. Unlike other roads, it was not linear but wound through the countryside, stimulating a unique roadside culture in an age before franchising and corporate uniformity, as thousands of gas stations, cafés and motels were established alongside. In the *Grapes of Wrath* (1939), John Steinbeck called it the 'Mother Road'; it was the 'road to opportunity' as migrants travelled to California to escape the dust bowl. As Steinbeck put it, '66 is the path of a people in flight . . . from the desert's slow northward invasion, from the twisting winds that howl out of Texas, from the floods that bring no richness to the land . . . 66 is the mother road, the road of flight'. Others later used the road to escape the declining rust-belt cities of the Northeast. It eventually had a blend of petrol named after it, its own television show and a major pop song. That song, written in 1946 by Bobby Troup, a former pianist with the Tommy Dorsey band and a marine, who had himself migrated west along the road, declaimed the route and geography of the road, and captured expectations of post-war prosperity (Krim, 1992). The song was sung by Nat King Cole, later recorded and performed by many, including Chuck Berry, and made famous for a second time by the Rolling Stones in the 1960s.

In the post-war years the road – sometimes known as America's Main Street – came to symbolise freedom, excitement and endless promising horizons, exemplified in Jack Kerouac's *On The Road* (1957), a book reputedly inspired by his having heard the song and then setting out on his own travels (Krim, 1998). Travellers can retrace Sal Paradise's steps on www.litelit.com/kerouac.html. Yet in the late 1960s new, modern interstate highways began to replace Route 66, its roadside attractions and stores gradually closed and the last small stretch of the road closed in

1985, ironically at the same time the television series *Route 66* was broadcast weekly to American households. Local organisations in each of the eight states it crossed campaigned to keep the road alive, through websites and guidebooks (detailing every mile of the original route), marking the road with Route 66 historic signs, setting up museums and eventually securing a Route 66 Preservation Bill in 2000 seeking to respect the 'idiosyncratic nature' of the road.

Tourists, especially from Europe and Japan, began visiting sites along the road in larger numbers in the 1980s, drawn by the promise of open spaces, the history of opportunity, ever-present small-town America and their immortalisation in book and song. For Americans the television series *Route 66* was both restless and bleak, an existential search for escape and meaning that echoed *On The Road* and preceded *Easy Rider*: a tale of both search and flight (Alvey, 1997). Route 66 in song offered the freedom of the open road, new possibilities and a hint of sexual emancipation. The song's continuing success helped to promote international interest in America's highway culture. In later years respite from the freeway, and the emergence of heritage sites, museums and festivals became additional attractions. Clinton, Oklahoma, for example, houses the Route 66 museum, and the Trade Winds Motel where travellers are urged to 'sleep where Elvis slept', while at Erick, there is the Roger Miller Boulevard (inspired by his truckin' anthem, 'King of the Road').

Route 66 became not just a means of getting across America, but a destination in itself. The Route 66 Association has an annual two-day drive along the Chicago–St Louis section and maintains a Route 66 Hall of Fame. American travellers on the Illinois section 'profess to deep affection for the road, combined with nostalgia and longing for a simpler time. It seems that the road serves as a time machine, transporting travelers, however temporarily, back to prosperous and happy days' (Ryburn-Lamonte, 1998: 128).

Overseas visitors, recorded from at least ten different countries (but particularly Germany), whose average age was in their thirties, had heard of the road from Steinbeck and television documentaries, but especially from the Rolling Stones version of the song. Most saw their trip as a means of visiting the 'real America'; some saw it as 'my youth fulfilled', 'feeling the past, seeing the past, smelling the past' and as not 'a usual road, but a state of mind'; others sought to return to do the trip by motorbike or vintage car. Overseas tourists were equally driven by nostalgia and the longing for an earlier America (Ryburn-Lamonte, 1998: 128–131). Associations between popular culture and mythologised American history are precisely those touted in travel articles and brochures (Figure 6.2). Thus the Australian Jennifer Berry found herself humming Woody Guthrie lyrics – harking back to the Dust Bowl ballads that effectively set Steinbeck's novel to music – as she drove in search

Figure 6.2 Route 66 (STA brochure) (Illustration by courtesy of STA Travel)

of America's lost road culture. Others who have travelled the road have drawn in Buddy Holly on deserts and Bruce Springsteen on cadillacs in their own search for the link between music and freedom (Hitchens, 2002). Advertising campaigns of various kinds have focused on similar themes. The National Historic Route 66 Federation suggests:

> Take the offramp into a bygone era. Discover the 2400 miles of Route 66 and see how America traveled in the 1920s–60s. Visit the wonderful old trading posts, filling stations, motels, tourist traps, diners and villages along the scenic 'Mother Road'. Slow down and enjoy the scent of new mown hay and hickory drifting from the pit barbeque chimneys. Stop and stroll through villages which haven't changed since they were bypassed by the interstate highway decades ago. Sample a real American hamburger and a rich, creamy malt that taste the way they're supposed to. Experience Sky City where native Americans live exactly like they have for hundreds of years. Pull over on a deserted stretch of the Mojave and listen to the hum of millions of wheels that have passed this way. (www.national66.com)

Cruisin Route 66 promises:

> No road has more appeal than the legendary Route 66. It is 2400 miles of a uniquely American phenomenon that beckons fans from all over the US and the world to follow its path. Why? Because Route 66 is more than a strip of pavement – it is a state of mind. It is a fascinating mix of nostalgia, adventure and the open road. It's family vacations, mom and pop diners, and neon lights. It's rolling plains, prickly deserts and funky architecture. And it's small town America, peopled with friendly folks who still know the meaning of the word 'hospitality'. (www.cruisinroute66.com)

That it is a state of mind as much a highway is evident in the adoption of the name for various products, such as Route 66 Rockabilly, sunglasses and a clothing label. There may be some truth in Krim's idea that 'cartographic reality sets an accuracy in the lyric verse that trusts the authenticity of the song as a musical map into the *terra incognita* of the west' (1998: 58). Route 66 has long offered the promise of adventure, freedom, escape and, increasingly, nostalgia, although with little of Steinbeck's poverty and hardship.

Going Home?

Nashville's tourism growth in the 1990s substantially capitalised on the country music revival that propelled artists such as Garth Brooks, Trisha Yearwood, Shania Twain and LeAnn Rimes into mainstream charts, and the city has continually been tempted to reproduce the 'codes' of country-and-western music in its attractions. Conservative themes of family, religion, wholesome lifestyles and 'home', common in country music, have been transplanted into the built landscape, prioritised and celebrated as 'quintessential' elements of an American lifestyle. In particular, the notion of 'down home', central to country-and-western songs, was idealised and captured in physical structures of tourism, as performers opened up their homes to the public as tourist attractions. Many country song titles play on the idea of a utopian 'home' as a site of solid values, prescribed domestic roles and a permanent 'haven' from chaotic, urban landscapes. As Blair & Hyatt (1992: 80) suggest, 'the home is a universal symbol of love, security and family. It is the one thing we would all like to go back to, somehow expecting that it will still be there, just as we remember it'.

Themes of home and domesticity are (re)presented in the homes of country music stars such as Conway Twitty; in Patsy Cline's complete, re-created lounge room in the Country Music Hall of Fame and personally sponsored displays such as the Willie Nelson and Friends Showcase. These are designed, built and decorated to reflect particular ways of life, reaffirming morals and values that the music itself parades:

> Between the rows of cheap souvenirs and the trophies of success, one could read a deeper story. At a time when America was fragmented, seemingly spinning inexorably out of control, country music was a touchstone of more reassuring times . . . a buffer, and a consolation, against the giddying uncertainties of modern life, embodying a vision of America of unchanging and dependable values. There was a reassuring simplicity in the songs about loving, cheating and drinking too much – everyday human frailties and emotional dilemmas whose very familiarity offered a kind of comfort in itself. (Brown, 1993: 218)

Although the texts of country music are diverse, it is through this particular set of ideologies that dominant gender, class and ethnic identities are produced and performed in Nashville, for both the tourist industry and for tourists themselves. The identities portrayed are gendered in that they reinforce stereotypical roles for men and women, idealising a lifestyle and romanticising the music of an era (the 1950s and early 1960s) prior to feminism and its social impacts. Those identities are also profoundly, and almost exclusively, white. This whiteness is both immediate and physical, and also ideological. Country music has always been considered a white music, with an establishment often criticised for its exclusion of black artists, even though it was heavily influenced by black expressive forms (Joyner, 1996). Indeed, country music has even been likened to 'the aural equivalent of white flight, the phenomenon of whites leaving mixed-race areas for comfort and security

of suburbia [and thus] the security of country' (Bull, 1993: 89). Tourists
who visit Nashville's country music attractions and also such sites as
Dollywood (Figure 6.3), are also almost exclusively white and from a
particular demographic group: older couples, often from working-class
backgrounds, frequently 'snowbird' tourists. Not only are white tourists
the norm at Dollywood, but the whole park has been designed to be
'rooted in the historical traditions of the Smoky Mountains', with a replica
of Dolly Parton's tiny wooden childhood home, and a 'whole zone given
over to the preservation of local crafts, where men and women, dressed
in dungarees, carved wooden furniture, forged tools by hand and made
all sorts of things out of leather' (Middleton, 1999: 160). This inauthenticity is part of a process through which the history of the American
South, and of country music, is straightened out, whitened and made

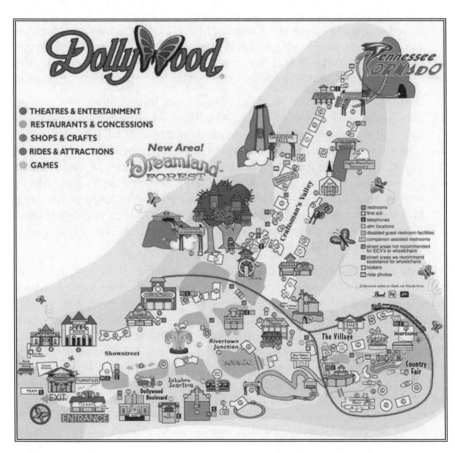

Figure 6.3 Dollywood, Pigeon Forge, Tennessee (Illustration by courtesy
of Dollywood)

ideologically safe for nostalgic tourists, more generally evident in heritage sites (Bruner, 1994). For one writer, 'Country music was about creating a community for working-class white people in the way that soul music had been for blacks ... walking around Opryland ... it appeared to have been modeled on an idealized small-town America, a village of clapboard buildings and cottages, but in this case housing not a hardware or feedstore, but the inevitable gift boutiques' (Brown, 1993: 218–219). In this way the notion of 'country' – as in 'country music', as well as 'country' as a signifier of rural lifestyles and values in America – becomes a marketing catchphrase and semiotic device of heteropatriarchy and whiteness. Here it differs from how 'country' (and rurality more generally) is constructed in other places, as exotic or chic when 'French country' or 'provincial', aristocratic in English 'country life'. 'Country' changes in the imaginary of the beholder and the tourist. In America in particular, this merges with ways in which 'country music' is understood, and has been incorporated into tourist experiences.

In suburban Memphis, Graceland grew as a tourist attraction with museums built around the mansion site – one dedicated to Elvis's cars, another to his planes – followed by shopping malls and a new hotel (named Heartbreak Hotel). In contrast to Beale Street's history of transgression and subversion, Graceland had always been a heavily controlled tourist attraction. Careful attention is paid to representations of Elvis whose posthumous identity continues to be shaped by tourism promoters who present the mansion and its interior in a controlled manner. Tickets are purchased in a purpose-built facility which incorporates Elvis museums and souvenir shops on one side of Elvis Presley Boulevarde, for the series of tours that begin every hour. Tourists wait (for up to two hours) in the complex, wandering through other displays, exhibitions and souvenir shops, until the tour number for that hour is called. All participants are equipped with digital audio players of a pre-recorded guided tour narrative, spoken by Priscilla Presley, which offers a manipulated image of her former husband. Buses then take visitors from the Graceland bookings/shopping/museum complex to the front entrance of the mansion. Segments of the audio tour are timed to synchronise with traffic flow throughout the mansion's various rooms (including Elvis's television room, kitchen, pool room, even his uniquely decorated 'jungle' room), with the narrator making suggestions to move onwards from room to room, thus enhancing management's ability to both direct the tourist gaze towards particular features and displays (such as Elvis's philanthropic work, thank-you letters and gold records) and maintain a steady, high-volume traffic through the mansion. The whole tour is stage-managed and it is impossible to visit Graceland without being corralled into this scenario – visitors are not allowed to wander freely or deviate from the intended tour, video cameras are banned, and several security staff control the booking complex, buses and entry to the mansion, as well as all the individual rooms. Such control is in part intended to manage the large crowds that move through Graceland in peak periods, as well as stop crowds invading rooms and damaging the interior decorations and artefacts. But it also adds to the intended solemnity of the occasion. The soundtrack also allows music to filter through Priscilla's voice-over, introducing emotive triggers to the visitors who are expected to treat the mansion and its contents with appropriate respect; the music is a manipulative device to emphasise solemnity. The tour ends at Elvis's grave – designed to elicit appropriate responses of silence, reflection and nostalgia. Tourists are just as much part of the attraction; fans cry at the grave, look on in horror at the stale meatloaf on Elvis's kitchen stove, with the occasional younger tourist bemused at the others around, but refraining from laughing or commenting. Tourists at Graceland draw on the performance and social codes learned in other contexts – in churches, museums and mausoleums – and undertake in what is considered to be morally appropriate behaviour.

The highly regulated tourist experience at Graceland did not emerge without criticism from locals and commentators. For one writer,

> The contrast between the increasingly antiseptic glitter of the Graceland giftshops and the nitty-gritty, slightly run-down, working-class flavour of much of the rest of Memphis ... is striking: wandering around town, one gets the distinct impression that the average Memphian would be quite happy to see all the 'Elvis Zombies' wither up and blow away so that the city could get over Elvis already and go about more interesting business. (Rodman, 1996: 108; cf. Middleton, 1999: 197–204)

In line with these reactions, a local record store, Shangri-La, published an alternative music guide to Memphis which actively avoided references to Elvis sites and offered a radically different perspective on the musical heritage of Memphis, beyond the 'line of 800 Elvis Zombies waiting to shell $15 out to smell Elvis' bicycle seat' (quoted in Rodman, 1996: 108). Visitors to Graceland, especially Elvis fans, are also overwhelmingly white (though increasingly Hispanic as well); moreover, 'fan understandings of family, loyalty, respect and identity are often tangled with abiding habits of American racism' (Doss, 1999: 166). In certain contexts Elvis is the 'fulfilment of southern history' with 'old fashioned southern values' (King, 1994: 99), despite his own absorption of, and support for, African-American music. This is particularly so because the South has itself moved on: for the professional corporate classes and cosmopolitans of Miami or Atlanta, there is at best a bemused nostalgia for Elvis, not so much for the values he represented, as for the distant youth of themselves, their parents or even grandparents.

Some fans 'extend Elvis's whiteness to his (and their own) idealized working-class image' embodying values such as sincerity, self-improvement and perseverance, with work presuming whiteness (Doss, 1999: 186–188). Although Graceland is in a predominantly black neighbourhood, few blacks take the tour (or belong to Elvis fan clubs). However, African-Americans staff nearby shops and restaurants:

> Neither Memphis, despite its 'birth of the blues' reputation, nor Graceland, despite being the caretaker for the King of Rock and Roll, projects an image of a 'color comfortable' public space ... most [blacks] believe that Graceland, and Elvis Culture in general, is a white thing ... organized as a distinctive, deified even, site of whiteness ... Graceland mostly remains an island of whiteness, a white mansion and a dead white rock star, attended by legions of white fans. (Doss, 1999: 195, 203)

In stark contrast, as discussed in the previous chapter, other parts of Memphis are now major black tourist destinations.

At Graceland tourists express not just nostalgia for a dead performer but also nostalgia for a past life that is out of tune with contemporary times. In Hawaii too tourists are predominantly white and African-Americans are underrepresented. Indeed:

> the Edenic vision of Hawai'i was built up over the years and clusters around heterosexual assumptions of sensual enjoyment and 'the natural' associated, for whites, with the icon of the hula girl and brought to life vividly in the mass-market lu'au shows. The embeddedness of these assumptions and the linkage of nation, race and sexuality with idyllic nature sutures these components together as 'pleasure', naturalizing and reinforcing a conservative vision of social relations. (Desmond, 1999: 141)

In some contrast, at the Bob Marley Museum in Jamaica, which celebrates the life and times of the nation's most famous reggae performer, although many tourists are white, there is a very substantial minority of black tourists. Those who are expatriate Jamaicans perceive their visit to the museum as a means of coming home from an alien experience since, as one stated, his music and life 'gave pride as a Jamaican and his messages give black people respect in contrast to American music' (quoted in Stanley-Niaah & Connell, 2004). Particular images are created, celebrated and performed in the practice of tourism.

Exceptionally, tourists may not only have previous experience of destinations, but they are returning to places that were once 'home', even after the passing of generations. Here tourism plays a very particular role in its powerful emphasis on a past that may have been lived, rather than a nostalgia for an idyllic past or place that was either never experienced or wholly mythical (like those of the 'country'). Tourists who are also return migrants have particular expectations of music and of other cultural expressions, where a sense of 'home' has been imbued with the sounds and smells of past times.

Second or third generation Chinese migrants, 'returning' as tourists from Thailand and Singapore to the town of Chaozhou in south China, constantly frequented one park where Chinese opera was performed. Such performances 'speak to their heart' and made them feel 'close to home' and 'emotional'; indeed, those who were born in Thailand found that the performance helped them 'to affirm their Chaozhou identity' (Lau, 1998: 125). The musicians, enabled to play operas through tourist support, were thus performing for a tourist 'us' rather than the more common tourist 'them' (Lau, 1998: 126). Their performance 'is a process through which memory of the past and a collective identity is established' (Lau, 1998: 129). In a wider sense, tourism thus celebrated past glories as it affirmed for participant and observer alike the idea of the nation as eternal, ancient and sophisticated.

In such contexts tourism emphasises the continuity of musical performance, embalming the past around the time of migration; tourism also demonstrates the significance of home in shaping memory and music, and underlines the role of nostalgia in the more existential searches of others. Many tourists in Ireland, for example, see folk music as an integral element of the Ireland that is part of their heritage (however many generations removed) and thus seek to experience it during what is arguably a 'return'. Returning Jamaicans particularly celebrate both the spirit and music of Bob Marley. The 'return' may be less positive, however. Dancers in Cajun groups in California, on a first visit to hear and dance to Cajun and zydeco dance music in Louisiana were largely disappointed because of their belief that 'the home locale could mean only one thing: authenticity', whereas what they found were 'boozy and cigarette filled dance halls' where the music seemed less exciting than in California (Stokes, 1999: 142; de Witt, 1999). In almost every context the music has 'moved on' and the past can only be re-created through tourism.

'I'm with the Band . . .'

While much of music tourism implies a physical site, these may be existential, such as Jimmy Buffett's imaginary and idyllic Margaritaville, but music tourism takes other forms where place is either relatively unimportant, or is essentially a good site for recreation, rather than somewhere that is imbued with history. For a few bands, music tourism subcultures have emerged, centred on fans who travel with the tours. This is no new phenomenon. By the mid-19th century, when brass bands in Britain were central to urban life, many had followings like those of contemporary football teams. Local people attended rehearsals, wore the band colours, followed them to distant contests, gambled and fought with other supporters and judges over the outcome, and saw victories and losses as part of their own and their town's existence (Russell, 1997: 225–227; Smith, 1997: 513–514). A century later groups of highly committed fans ('groupies') followed performers from concert to concert, creating a similar sense of community (Sardiello, 1994; Reist, 1997; McCray Pattacini, 2000) through shared experiences, fan clubs and traditions. Famous examples of this rather particular form of music tourism include 'Deadheads', fans of the San Francisco rock group the Grateful Dead, a subset of whom, known as 'tourheads', traversed the United States with the band (until its demise in 1995), developing new practices, words and symbolic devices of their own. Original Deadheads kept in touch via newsletters ('Grateful Dead Almanacs') and established a utopian subculture, exchanging tapes of Grateful Dead performances (a practice sanctioned by the band) and travelling from concert to concert as part of an 'alternative', drop-out experience. Audiences established zones of exchange and experimentation outside gigs; venue parking lots became spaces where fans camped out, 'colourful street fairs' where some subsidised their trip by selling T-shirts, tapes, hash cookies and necklaces, and 'the culture outside the concerts became a ritual, a homecoming, almost a religion' (McCray Pattacini, 2000: 2). The concerts themselves were also a 'ritual that closely resembles a religious festival' (Sardiello, 1994: 15). The Haight-Ashbury precinct in San Francisco, California, original hang-out of the band in the late 1960s, was subsequently transformed into a key tourist site, largely because of its significance in the counter-culture 'summer of love'. Deadheads thus had a place for pilgrimage that later filled with cafés, souvenir shops, record stores, graffiti, and an ice-cream store advertising flavours such as 'Cherry Garcia'.

After the death of Jerry Garcia (the band's leader) in 1995 and the demise of the band, many Deadheads turned to the Internet to keep ideas and subcultural traditions alive. Others followed newer groups such as Phish (whose fans were known, in a deliberate paraphrase, as Phishheads). Like the Grateful Dead, Phish were primarily a live band whose concerts included experimental improvisation and unusual antics, but whose recordings gained limited success. Performance was almost everything. Phish phans saw themselves as different from most music fans, even to the extent that

> for many the shows are less important than the tie-dyed, counterculture community. Phish heads reject American society, a culture they say is poisoned by prejudice, violence, consumerism, conformity and environmental degradation. Their community, they say, is built

on freedom, environmental awareness and unconditional love. Jarrod Wright . . . said being a Phish head is more satisfying than joining the rat race. 'A lot of people in Babylon (mainstream culture) just jump into jobs and buy houses but they're not happy' . . . Irie, a high school dropout, said Phish heads are the latest wave of travelers and naturalists that trace their roots to the Gypsies, bards and witches of mediaeval Europe. (O'Keeffe, 1996)

Phish-devoted Internet sites continue wordplays with Phish Net and Pholktales: The Ophishal Tour Story, contemporary versions of fanzines provide information, enabling Phishheads to plan journeys around the country – and into Europe – in ways that are reminiscent of 1960s counter-cultures. Female fans, the Phunky Bitches, organise special women's meetings and tours, while overseas groups, such as the Phriends of Phish Europe, coordinate overseas tours.

Thus, a different generation of wandering music fans had revisited a distinctly American alternative tradition, although many ex-Deadheads complained that Phish attracted a 'jocky, punky element' – evident in the wordplays – creating 'a haven for overindulged white kids who were looking to rebel against their parents, but not rebel so far as to never be able to return at the first sign of trouble' (McCray Pattacini, 2000: 3–4). Even among Deadheads and Phishheads, subcultures often characterised as sharing, peaceful and generous, particular distinctions sought to separate the credible from the inauthentic and emphasise even smaller subcultures.

Not surprisingly, most bands attract loyal fans to concerts and see themselves a part of a dispersed community, with shared loyalties, connected via an 'invisible magnet' and a sense of belonging together (e.g. Cavicchi, 1998; Carroll & Connell, 2000). Concerts are rituals and performers are sometimes akin to deities, but only rarely does this extend to extensive travels. Both the Grateful Dead and Phish fans specifically saw themselves as separate from the mainstream, with characteristics of new age travellers (both in travel and attitudes to the environment); most were white, middle-class and young, with Grateful Dead fans averaging around 24 years (despite a wide range in ages). Deadheads perceived themselves to be acolytes of the counter-culture, having sought to distance themselves from material comforts, oppose conservative political positions and attain community with others (Sardiello, 1994), a legacy that many Phish Heads similarly seek to take up.

Rave and House in Ibiza and Beyond

In contrast to quests for authenticity that have taken 'existential tourists' to distant corners of the world, the emergence of house music spawned a hedonistic tourism that transformed the Mediterranean island of Ibiza, and to a lesser extent the chain of sites that were part of the house-party world. Ravers were not just with the band, they *were* the bands – performance was central to recreation, with obvious links to ritual. In the 1990s, raves, clubbing and other types of dance parties became common youth practices in many Western countries and to some extent elsewhere, including Thailand and Israel. These scenes followed earlier precedents such as gay (and straight) discos in the 1970s in major cities such as New York and Montreal. Dance-party spaces were deliberately created to give credibility to particular scenes that were often secluded and remote, attesting to the transgressive and inclusive nature of raves. Advertisements for raves, given names such as 'Utopia', 'Field of Dreams' or 'Tribal Gathering', and, later, the decorations of inner-city clubs, enhanced the illusions of escape that are evident in images of tribalistic societies or futuristic 'other worlds', Celtic symbols, mandalas and depictions of Krishna, all suggesting links with spiritual states or simply altered states.

Following its initial northern European genesis, rave culture spread rapidly to such places as Rimini (Italy), Koh Phangan (Thailand), Israel, Goa (India), coastal Mozambique and, most dramatically, to Ibiza (Balearic Islands, Spain). All were coastal resorts but with no particular musical connection, other than at Goa, where classical Indian music was an attraction for some. At Ibiza, 'the Mediterranean haven of hippie tribalism and drug taking in the 1960s' (Gore, 1997: 59), and a gay mecca in the 1970s, a dance-club scene emerged in the late 1980s due to unrestricted licensing hours, late-night dining and socialising, and the easy availability of drugs, especially ecstasy. The booming resort town of San Antonio offered cheap alcohol, plenty of small clubs and bars and a party atmosphere; it also offered jobs for those seeking longer stays. Those who were most involved regularly returned, and by the late 1980s

> there was real element of loyalty in the scene that was suddenly materializing. We all stuck together, went out clubbing together and ended up spending summers together. It was more exciting, more colourful, more worldly. ... The madness and extravagance and outwardness of gay people you never really saw in Britain. Those scenes were separate. Ibiza brought that all together. (Quoted in Garratt, 1998: 96)

Ibiza became an 'escapist paradise' (Garratt, 1998: 98) for the young – parties, music, drugs and sex, sustained for some by a range of illegal activities. DJs were happy to spend extended periods on the island, 'superclubs' holding over 5000 people opened and turned their dance floors into circus tents, with entertainment ranging from dancers in fetish costumes to jugglers and acrobats. Cheap package tours boosted the tourism industry, and companies like Club 18–30, whose advertising ran

'Danceathon, drinkathon, bronzathon, partyathon ... don't do Ibiza unless you can do extreme to the moon and all the way back', were targetting young people. Most went to extend weekend pleasures over a full week or longer, with friends and like-minded others, and had no desire for new experiences (Khan *et al.*, 2000: 221). Ibiza retained a special allure for many, like one Danish record producer who settled there: 'There's something uplifting and positive about Ibiza. A joyous final escapism from the cruel world up north where there are hard cities and you run away and this is paradise that you find. In all this music's the predominant factor' (quoted in Botsford, 2001).

At one level 'cosmopolitan subjects' had tried to break away from the stress, boredom and meaningless of 'mainstream' society, to create an 'aesthetics of existence' manifested in various 'spiritual, creative and hedonistic practices, cultivating values of freedom, pleasure, tolerance and self-exploration' (d'Andrea, 2003: 239). However, as one British DJ put it: 'People go to Ibiza, do loads of drugs, have rampant sex with loads of people, have a really good time and a fantastic holiday, then go home' (Steve Lawler, www.tranzfusion.net/hownews.asp). Advertising emphasised hedonism and ignored local sites. Tours were oriented to the young:

> 2wentys night action is legendary. With us you can turn your summer holiday into an assault on the senses. We've got foam parties, strip karaoke, pirate shows, 70s nights, reps taking their clothes off, pre-club parties, live bands, jousting, comedians, drink driving ... and lots of stuff we're not allowed to print. No 2wentys holiday is complete without a major portion of club action. All the resorts we feature have top notch clubs with major UK DJs. Have you ever tried coming out of a club, stripping off on the beach and running into the sea at 5 am in the morning? You can't do that in Scunthorpe. (2wentys Holidays, 2002)

Its rival, Club 18–30, promised

> Non-stop 100% full on hardcore dance Mecca. Staying in San An, you'll be right in the heart of the action, surrounded by restaurants, bars and designer shops. Your time in Ibiza will be one big blur as it rocks 24/7 and there's definitely no time for sleep. From cruises to the bar blitz to the best clubs you're sorted. The most in your face sorted dance scene in the Med. So hardcore there's just no going back. This is clubbers paradise. (Club 18–30, 2002)

By the end of the 1990s two million tourists (twenty times the resident population) were visiting Ibiza every year, about a third from Britain, most intending to be there simply to party. As one commentator observed: 'Drugs are ubiquitous and are the engine that drives the club scene. E-commerce has a completely different meaning in Ibiza. This is hedonism on a grand and industrial scale. Ibizan clubbing is not for the prudish, fit or fainthearted' (Sorrenti, 2000: 22). The island had then become notorious, yet for many clubbers it remained the ultimate holiday experience:

> Ibiza has it all and does it better than London. There is something about that place, the hype, its eminence as the clubbing capital of the world, the incessant 24 hours a day partying, its smouldering melting pot of cultures and people, all united under the ever growing global religion of house music, one of the most powerful forces drawing together the youth of 21st century Earth. (Shrik, 2002)

Ibiza's notoriety grew after a British television series followed a group of partying tourists. Local authorities sought restrictions on noise levels in clubs and introduced on-the-spot fines for drunkenness. San Antonio's authorities were loath to curtail and regulate an industry that brought in US$939 million a year, but many sought to win back their island. In 2001 Ibiza introduced a 'green tax', oriented towards environmental projects but indicative of an attempt to move into more upmarket tourism.

Dance tourists, whether in search of new and different venues and scenes, frustrated with increasingly crowded (and regulated) Ibiza, or desiring something more than the 'cheesy Eurotrance' that had come to dominate Ibiza, moved elsewhere, including such Asian sites as Goa. To a much greater extent than Ibiza, Goa had been part of a global hippie circuit in the 1960s, and tourism at places such as Anjuna centred around drug-taking, nude swimming and rock music, especially of bands such as Pink Floyd and the Grateful Dead who produced soundtracks for getting stoned. Two decades later the music had become more electronic, linked into club circuits in the West, yet distinctively local; it was now christened Goa (or 'psy' – psychedelic) trance. Goa was repositioned as the rave capital of Asia and perhaps the world, with a party season centred around dance parties in the forests, in the hills or on the beach. Three-quarters of the participants were Indian tourists rather than either travellers or the long-term foreign residents – the 'Goa freaks':

> The presence of sand, red rocks, ocean, paddyfields, vegetation (notably palm trees), even other people's gardens, makes it all the more exciting and authentic. Any Goa freak will tell you that dancing in Goa is the real thing, with the stars and moon above, the sea wind, the fluid boundaries of party space. No roofs, no walls – how unlike the indoor happenings at home. No entry charges, queues, bouncers, guest lists, surveillance cameras, cloakroom, fire extinguishers, first aid. This is clubbing in the wilderness. (Saldanha, 2002: 50)

Travellers came from Europe, but also from Japan and Israel – one part of Anjuna beach becoming known as Tel Aviv beach. As in Ibiza, but dramatised in the developing country context, conflicts arose over space and noise, drugs and drunkenness, bribery and corruption, pollution, and complex tensions between impoverished Indians, affluent Indian tourists and various Western tourists, and several episodes of moral panic, in opposition to what is seen as both neo-colonialism and the worst excesses of Western counter-culture (Saldanha, 2002; 2003a; Routledge, 2000; 2001; Wilson, 1997).

This 'acoustic tourism' brought 'an articulation of music, dance, drugs, internationalism and pilgrimage not so different from Woodstock, Ibiza or the Berlin Love Parade . . . except that Goa lies in the Third World' (Saldanha, 1999: 2). Bodypainting, drug taking (mainly LSD and cannabis rather than ecstasy and alcohol) and sexual tolerance have contributed to an image of Goa as a timeless, workless place of tolerance and permissiveness, where tourists can project their fantasies. Westerners, when asked why they have come to Goa, usually refer to the state's 'idyllic' quality; a group of Englishmen called it 'a great place to party' and a typical English female perspective was that 'I want to get away from everything, and this is the perfect place. It is like paradise and I am here for the culture'. An American admitted: 'In Goa I can escape India' (quoted in Routledge, 2000: 2652). Travellers were coming to Goa as much to escape as to arrive, while their self-images were boosted by having visited Goa's beaches, taken drugs and attended acid and rave parties: 'a certain symbolic capital for tourists upon returning home' (Routledge, 2000: 2653). Satisfaction was centred in the music and the drugs rather than in 'the spectacle of an exotic other' (Saldanha, 2002: 59). Goa, like Ibiza before it, was becoming a place of 'global' performance rather than a destination that emphasised distinct local characteristics.

The islands of southern Thailand, but especially Koh Phangan, presented an alternative to Goa as it became overcrowded, welcomed charter flights (bringing the arrival of British 'lager louts') and suffered environmental degradation. Koh Phangan emerged as a tourist destination in the 1980s, after the nearby island of Koh Samui became more expensive, a target for drug busts and a site for 'mass tourism'. It was initially synonymous with reggae and marijuana, but by the end of the decade a house music scene was evident, with the arrival of members of the British rave culture from Goa. These party tourists saw Koh Phangan as a new and liberal party site. As at other rave sites, the youthful visitors simply sought to participate in 'the ultimate pursuits for many of their age group: sex, drugs, freedom and adventure' (Westerhausen, 2002: 7). Police crackdowns in the mid-1990s slowed growth and ensured that new locations were sought elsewhere, but monthly Full Moon Parties have continued to draw crowds of up to 10,000 people to Hat Rin beach:

The party begins at dusk when the round yellow moon makes is appearance over the white sand beach. In twilight small tables are lined up on the beach and thousands of lamps are lit. As the evening progresses the beach explodes into a dancing frenzy as different m.c.'s take their turn on the decks. There is something for everyone here, trance, techno, drum and bass, commercial dance and reggae, no-one is disappointed. Jugglers and fire eaters entertain the crowds as the night goes on and with the brilliant impromptu fireworks display, the party atmosphere is complete. After a few hours it could be time for the chill-out for a while, maybe grab a drink or a bite to eat from one of the many beach traders and wade out and sit down in the warm surf of the Gulf of Thailand, pure, pure heaven. (www.kohphangan.com)

Other subsequent venues for house music included Faliraki (Rhodes, Greece) and Ayia Napa (Cyprus), a different scene from Ibiza, where beach resorts are as important as the club scene, and there is greater official control over drugs. As one promoter has explained: 'Ever since about 1990 many resorts have tried to recreate Ibiza on a different island but places such as Tenerife, Miami and others have not come close [but] Ayia Napa is now the undisputed club capital of Europe' (www.2step-garage.co.uk/ayia_napa). By the end of the millennium Ayia Napa was receiving about half a million tourists a year, including numerous black tourists who preferred Ayia Napa's garage music to Ibiza's rave scene, but as in Ibiza the pressures of rapid growth and partying were causing tensions and frustrations (Morris, S. 2000). A new trance scene also emerged in some Himalayan valleys of northern India (d'Andrea, 2003). Bali too had a house scene, with regular monthly moon parties, at different locations in the south of the island, providing an opportunity for residents 'to meet up with the usual crowd' (*Rendez-Vous*, 1, 2001). The 'usual crowd' included house-party fans who had met in other house venues in the world, and who could access new events and clubs across the globe through websites such as the rather appropriately entitled www.globalhedonism.com that provides listings for more than fifty countries. Many house DJs similarly work through a global circuit. Thus, Graham Harding, the English DJ at the Double Six Club in Bali early in 2001 had worked a circuit including Jakarta and Bandung (Indonesia), Korea, Australia, New Zealand, Singapore, Hong Kong, Las Vegas, Los Angeles and Hawaii. Circuits of tourists, clubs and DJs, some influenced by climate, linked destinations from Brazil to South Africa, from Israel to Ibiza, and from Bali to Byron Bay.

Dance music tourism had a distinctive influence on many destinations, often perceived as particularly negative. As one journalist has written of Koh Phangan:

What is Koh Phangan if it isn't the embodiment of the globalisation we all profess to despise? Twenty years ago before the full moon parties, Hat Rin Nok was a tiny fishing village unchanged in millennia. A generation later – our generation – and the streets are paved with Internet cafes and the fishing boats conduct all-you-can-smoke ganja cruises. Backpackers Inc has become a franchise, too, a prefabricated worldwide formula that is constructed wherever two or more Germans are gathered. It exploits the disparity in Third World wages just as surely as does Nike. Cultural imperialism? Don't blame McDonald's or Bill Gates. They didn't bring the satellite dishes and Premier league soccer. They didn't demand the right to have Celtic rings tattooed around their biceps. Nor did they put sausage and eggs in every breakfast menu from here to Honduras. Equitable distribution of wealth? Not in this place. Many of the bars, restaurants and bungalows are owned or leased by *farangs*, foreigners who came for a holiday and never left. The only locals who can get jobs are those who can speak English. Environmental vandalism? You betcha. And no evil, oil-spilling, faceless corporations here, just a bunch of rich and spoilt people who can't be bothered cleaning up their own rubbish. And what of the full moon party? There is nothing in the slightest bit indigenous about it. Phangan locals are originally from the Chinese island of Hainan, but the hip-hop, trip-hop, garage and reggae – as well as the DJs – are from the clubs back home. 3,4- methylenedioxymethamphetamine does not occur naturally on the island so ecstasy too needs to be shipped in. (Smith, 2002: 6)

Dance music tourism, just as so many other kinds of tourism, exemplifies the manner in which itinerant tourists search for different sites and sights, often to escape the crowds and pollution (ironically produced by the last dance tourism wave), simply to enjoy a taste of the new or experience distinct sounds. At the same time others are simply in search of familiar experiences. Indeed, for many,

to call them tourists at all stretches a point. What elements of 'touring' were there? . . . At the best of times travellers cannot see much out of an aeroplane window: at night, as for this group, nothing at all. When they were there being in another place was not the desired end, neither did it much live up to expectations: the important expectations they held related to consuming passions and substances. (Khan *et al.*, 2000: 234)

Dance music tourists may travel as part of a 'spiritual journey' or to achieve self-realisation, but others may interpret this as introspective and hedonistic, in search of instant gratification rather than about notions of identity, memory and nostalgia, or any link to place. Somewhat similarly, Finnish tourists have created Finnish bars in the Canary Islands, where they can listen to popular Finnish music or engage in Finnish karaoke, to the extent that the Playa del Ingles (ironically 'English Beach') is an 'extension of the tourists' home culture and could be considered the southernmost province of Finland' (Selanniemi, 2001: 82). For such 'tourist bubbles' actual places provide only venues.

On the other hand, this is more complicated than just a narrative of insensitive Western middle-class kids rampaging across the vulnerable spaces of others. There are always interactions between tourists and locals, and intimate relationships established, no matter the extent of perceived cultural imperialism (Malam, 2004). To some extent, global backpacker tourism creates musical spaces where obvious cultural difference is downplayed, 'internationalised' spaces such as clubs that can benefit locals as much as tourists, most simply in terms of creating opportunities for intimate or sexual exchange with foreigners. Music clubs are the spaces where these intimate ethnographies may be played out.

Performing Tourists

As is evident, tourists themselves are both engaged in some elements of performance, whether drumming or dancing, where identities are created and re-created, so expressing some sentiments about the worlds and spaces in which they live or seek to live:

> Tourist practices are enframed and informed by different discourses which provide practical orientations and cultivate subject positions, specifying what actions should take place at particular places and times. . . . Thus for instance, tourists look at symbolic attractions in distinctive styles, communicate and consume particular narrative interpretations and move through tourism spaces in specifiable ways. (Edensor, 2000: 325)

One mode of tourism involves the idea of 'letting go', or 'letting one's hair down', where activities from the tourist's home environment are cast aside in favour of other practices – hedonistic, escapist, lurid, emotive – deemed to be repressed by the conventions of everyday life. Dance holidays in Spain may have yet more dramatic effects: 'For people travelling alone salsa helps break the ice; it allows you to sidle up close to someone, perform a sexually charged dance and then walk away once the song stops – if you so desire. Alternatively you could continue to be dark and naughty. Perfect, really.' (Gillan, 2002: 2). This mode of tourism is one that usually includes music – whether at clubs in Ibiza, tribal drumming lessons in West Africa, tango dancing in Argentina, line dancing in Nashville or classical master classes. Music distinguishes a particular time and space, 'that of the extraordinary from that of the mundane, a period of relaxation and play which marks release from work and duty' (Edensor, 2000: 325), although in several contexts learning may be both pleasurable and intensely challenging. Performed identities can be deliberately constructed where 'tribal' musicians dress up – or down – for tourist performance, or can be more subtle, ingrained identities of the subconscious, where tourists themselves enact identities through their understandings of expected behaviour, rituals and exchanges. Dress, attitude, activities and bodily appearance are shaped by desires to emphasise subcultural identity. Thus, backpackers, as 'neotribes', demonstrate identity through appearance, dress sense, bodily adornment and even their type of luggage (Elsrud, 2001), while most tourists share some group identity with others. Interactions between the tourists as both audience and performers, however limited this may be, convey a sense of belonging, cultural difference or an assertion of ethnicity, gender and nationality.

Identities are negotiated in music tourism sites, rather than simply imposed. Dance performances provide one illustration of ways in which tourists negotiate the identities of their home environment within newly encountered tourist spaces. In Cuba, tourists are commonly encouraged to participate in rumba dances opened up by the tourist context, and in these spaces, as Daniel (1996) argues, tourists are forced to challenge their habits. Some refuse to participate, not happy with the sensuality involved in the rumba, thus reaffirming already existing moral codes and beliefs (while others may simply be shy). Others, in contrast, are 'taken outside themselves'; thus,

> tourists and performers are immersed in a complex of multiple, simultaneous sensory stimulations in Cuban touristic performances ... often, not knowing the rules, they do not wait to be invited to dance, but spontaneously join in ... for many tourists, the dance becomes their entire world at that particular moment. Time and tensions are suspended. The discrepancies of the real world are postponed. ... Tourism, in moments of dance performance, opens the door to a liminal world that gives relief from day-to-day, ordinary tensions, and, for Cuban dancers and dancing tourists particularly, permits indulgence in near-ecstatic experiences. (Daniel, 1996: 789)

As an Australian tourist noted:

> A dance course I took at the performing School of Arts in Havana, Cuba, was amazing, just like being in *Fame*. As a result of lessons over two weeks I must say I can now salsa really well. I danced with so many Cuban men and cannot begin to explain how well they dance and move their bodies; they just flow with the music. Sometimes I felt I was in a trance, at one with the music and my partner. (Quoted in *Planet Talk*, 45, April–June 2001: 7)

At the same time, Cuban musicians and dancers themselves also negotiate their own performed identities. For one instructor, 'when I dance
in performance with the drums, and the music, something real comes
out – something genuine, authentic, more organic and pure than what
I know is in the tradition. My gestures are free . . . All the possibilities
are there, movements are creative, beautiful, corporeal, and enriching
the dance. . . . Someone, some other actor inside me makes those movements – those other things – come out when I really dance' (quoted in
Daniel, 1996: 789). This notion that music embodies the real and that
only the 'real' is authentic, underpins the search for authenticity and so
influences tourism. At the same time it also emphasises that the
'authentic' cannot be pinned down in any one time or place.

While tourists may seek authentic manifestations of culture, they may
also challenge the identities of the performers themselves, resulting in
deviations from expected norms. Tourists seek experiences that may have
little to do with authenticity, evident where tourists breach social codes
expected of them in a dance situation,

> because tourists do not usually know the rules thoroughly, they are
> often indulged when they mistakenly cross boundaries, by dancing
> their versions of imitations of dance sequences and traditions, by
> entering a dance that prohibits certain personnel, and by not
> following the musical or gestural leads. These 'mishaps' and the
> responding behavior that attempts to make the guest feel safe and
> free from embarrassment, allow spontaneity and improvisation to
> flow. (Daniel, 1996: 793)

In such contexts cultural meanings are collectively created for and by
musicians, dance instructors and tourists, and necessarily divert from
previous performances. In many cases, tourists are encouraged and
expected to participate. Thus, at Iweniar village (Vanuatu) tourists were
exhorted to join in dances they were unlikely to have seen before, in
any media or context – hence their own performances could only be at
variance with previous ones. Here, and in so many other contexts, what
begins as formal performance, linked to some version of history, is transformed into entertainment, with the pleasurable (or embarrassing)
outcome, as much for the benefit of the hosts as for the guests.

At Takarazuka, Japan, performances inspire 'both a spirit of resistance
to normative gender roles and expectations and also a distinct and significant sexual subcultural style . . . among fans' and contribute an
essentially 'strategic ambivalence' (Robertson, 1998: 175, 209). On a much
grander scale, transformed meanings permeate Carnivals and Mardi Gras
– whether in New Orleans, Rio de Janeiro, Havana, Venice or Sydney –
where the politics and assumed identities of everyday life are inverted
in a temporally and spatially contingent context, where music is either

soundtrack or catalyst for celebration. Meanings are frequently and irregularly transformed in performance, yet within certain limits that do not challenge particular versions of the past or present social relations. During the Magical Mystery Tour of Beatles sites in Liverpool, the tourist guide narrates the 'accepted' history of the Beatles and sites associated with them. After an initial period, these stories (of, for example, Paul first meeting George at a particular bus stop) are invariably concluded with 'And the rest is . . .' with tourists expected to yell out 'history' (Chapter 3). Audiences participate, and in a small way corroborate to consolidate the 'true story'. At Abbey Road, almost the only thing to do is to walk across the famous pedestrian crossing and take a photograph.

Tourists do not necessarily seek authentic sites, recognise that much of what they see is inauthentic and are not perturbed by that. As Rees (1988) has pointed out, the 'existential' tourists at Lijiang were clearly not witnessing a musical performance that had any real degree of continuity with the past, but one that was self-consciously traditionalist and externally oriented. Tourists nevertheless perceived it as authentic in relation to other performances of Chinese music, so that for them it was credible and convincing. Authenticity itself can be interpreted in many ways. What is deemed in some respects 'inauthentic' may in fact become credible as subversive identities are played out – lesbian tourists in the Dollywood theme park invert the meanings of 'home', 'domesticity' and heterosexual consent imbued in much of Dolly Parton's music and in the theme park itself, and so transform a place that some tourists might perceive as authentic and others as simply 'tacky' into a humorous or even credible place (e.g. Woods, 2003). Much Elvis tourism can be interpreted in a similar fashion. While most Elvis tourists are fans, and are thus 'serious' about travelling to particular sites such as Graceland, others travel to the sites for their schlock value, revelling in the tacky, celebrating it, rather than dismissing it as an inauthentic, and thus deficient, experience.

Tourism as Pilgrimage?

Despite music tourism being about entertainment and pleasure, in the context of many forms of tourism, and much of that linked to music, the question of whether it 'constitutes a kind of sacred or ritual experience in modern society' (Stokes, 1999: 148) hangs over much analysis. Such debates in turn stem from MacCannell's *The Tourist* in which he argues that tourism is 'a ritual . . . a kind of collective striving for a transcendence [that attempts] to overcome the discontinuity of modernity, of incorporating its fragments into unified experience' (1976: 13). Cultural tourism in a broad sense, and some elements of music tourism, have been said to provide the capacity to enhance 'self-actualization, self-enrichment, self-expression and regeneration or renewal of self, feelings of accomplishment, enhancement of self-image, and interaction and belongingness' (Stebbins, 1996: 949). While elements of this may be true for many tourists, some of these themes emerge in the concept of pilgrimage.

Music tourism is as much an individual as a collective experience, but whether for individuals or groups, the languages of ritual, travel and pilgrimage are key elements. So much of music tourism is linked to the past, to bearing witness at the places that Mozart, Elvis Presley and others made famous, and especially at their graves – places to reflect on past lives. In key contexts these represent travels to sites associated with those who have not just given individual lives particular direction and meaning, but have been part of a nation's heritage.

Music tourism is not, though, necessarily tied to the past. Fans of the Irish country-and-western star Daniel O'Donnell travel from various parts of the British Isles to Kincasslagh in Donegal, where they drink tea with the star, attend a concert and stay in his hotel, an experience which his biographer describes, with a degree of hyperbole, as 'like a cross between a church fete and a pilgrimage to Lourdes' (Vaughan, 1999: 94; Stokes, 1999: 151). Broadly, similar situations occur in Pigeon Forge, Tennessee, where concerts, hotels and personal experiences of stars are tied up in a single package. Bruce Springsteen fans are similarly seen to be engaged in pilgrimage:

> one of the major activities among fans is making a 'pilgrimage' to the New Jersey Shore and locating all the different streets and sites mentioned in his songs ... the sites are typically located in New Jersey although some fans have made pilgrimages to other places mentioned in Springsteen's songs such as the Badlands. Pilgrimage stories are always about achieving a goal and emphasize both the commitment of fans in the face of adversity and their special status as pilgrims. . . . It is portrayed as an ordeal, an activity which separates true fans apart from mere audience members. Many fans plan for years to go to Asbury Park [hence] pilgrimages take on an even greater importance for fans living in the Midwest or West. (Cavicchi, 1998: 70, 170–171)

Beyond such travel, Springsteen fans, like others, used metaphors of religion (such as concerts being 'religious experiences', 'his songs are my bible' or 'converting' others to his words) to explain their actions. Several had Springsteen picture galleries that they referred to as 'shrines' and others argued that his lyrics offered a sense of values (Cavicchi, 1998: 186–187). At the Bob Marley Museum almost all visitors emphasised the religious and political connotations of his life (almost to the exclusion of the music), some claimed that he was 'a visionary spreading a world message of love' and others hailed him as a religious leader and prophet (Connell & Stanley-Niaah, 2004). In Liverpool, somewhat more prosaically, American Beatles fans found that 'before it was two dimensional; now I can actually see three dimensions it's fantastic' and exulted in the possibility of chance encounters with people who might have a particular, undocumented personal insight into the Beatles; as one fan stated: 'Lennon's music was crucial to me. It gave me hope at a time of depression. I just want to come back and sit and think at Strawberry Fields for hours' (quoted in Style Tribes, Foxtel TV, 16 March 2002). Within the Liverpool 'Beatles industry', Beatles visitors who make a once-in-a-lifetime trip are regarded as 'pilgrims' (Cohen, 1997: 79). For an Australian fan who toured Britain through U2 concerts: 'It was a spiritual pilgrimage. A consummation of her passion. A rite of passage for any big U2 fan. And an enormous strain on her wallet' (Israel, 1999: 92).

Similar themes have not surprisingly referred to Elvis Presley and the pilgrimage to Graceland, which has legitimately been compared with the shrines of medieval European saints, through the similarities in validation and devotion felt by the pilgrims, especially on the anniversary of 'the King's death' (King, 1994; Figure 6.4). To Mick Brown, Graceland 'felt like a low-budget Lourdes, but then what was Elvis anyway if not a modern-day saint?' (1993: 56). The 'holiness' of Graceland stems more from the attitudes, behaviour and actions of fans rather than any intrinsic merit in the life of Elvis or even the architecture of Graceland (Rodman, 1996: 117), although his own religious music (such as 'Crying in the Chapel') has contributed. That behaviour includes writing messages, praying, delivering wreaths (and other offerings), especially on days of particular significance, and simple contemplation: 'Hundreds (of tourists) linger on until the dawn breaks on the actual anniversary of his death, lighting a succession of candles. Throughout the year, tour operators present visitors with the Elvis experience. Tourists are invited to walk where he walked, sit where he sat, see what he saw' (Rojek, 1993: 143). The chapel at his birthplace in Tupelo is similarly perceived as 'sacred' (Rodman, 1996: 121). Where others are simultaneously engaged in devotional practices, and Graceland is the quintessential example, such sites become 'a physical point of articulation where a global community of Elvis fans could regularly congregate and acquire a true sense of themselves as a self-defined community' (Rodman, 1996: 103). At the same time the First Presleyterian Church of Elvis the Divine challenges through kitsch the reverential awe of 'true believers'.

Graceland, the Bob Marley Museum, Abbey Road and other similar sites have become secular shrines. At both Graceland and the Bob Marley Museum (within the house where Marley lived and died) some or all forms of photography are banned, so heightening the sense of their being special places. Graffiti at all such places celebrate affection, love

Figure 6.4 Elvis Presley's grave, Graceland (Photograph courtesy of Chris Gibson)

and life-changing experiences. At anniversaries they are decorated with wreaths and welcome even more visitors. Specific memorials, such as graves, almost inevitably have religious significance, and become places of memory and meditation. Strawberry Fields, the memorial to John Lennon in Central Park, New York, quickly became a site of secular pilgrimage, notably on the anniversary of his death. While some visitors to the monument believe that John Lennon 'is with us' here, others see it as both a place of some religious significance and 'a shrine to the youthful idealism of the 1960s ... a place of pilgrimage that binds together the past, the present and the future of the generation that was most affected by the Beatles' (Kruse, 2003: 159). Exactly what sacred or secular meaning might be attached to this site, or to any other place, is both subjective and varied.

Websites for many past performers offer ample examples of what have become virtual shrines. Elvis is well represented. On www.elvis.com/vigilcast/show_messages in 2002, messages of adulation were commonplace; thus Rachel Wolf wrote: 'I love you Elvis. You will be forever the king of rock n roll ... you are so beautiful. Thank you God for letting his presence grace this earth for the short time he was here. He is a treasure to us all. I always go to Graceland at least once a year.' and Lucy Lopez from Puerto Rico recorded: 'Every night I look forward to visiting "elvis.com" and reading the messages written by so many wonderful people at the virtual wall page.'

The home page for the Michael Hutchence Memorial site (www. michaelhutchence.org), which includes information on the scattering of his ashes in Sydney harbour and his funeral service, declares: 'This website is Michael's sacred site, dedicated to his memory and celebrating his life. It is a central location for all who love him and miss him to come together and pay homage to a gentle lovable spirit.' Fans both express their love for and devotion to Hutchence (formerly the lead singer of INXS), but also communicate with each other on the site. Thus, Aidan, from Toronto, Canada, wrote in July 2003:

> Sorry I haven't been on here for a few days. Apologies I miss you all though. Ian once again thank you for maintaining this beautiful site. Not only has it helped me come to some closure with Michael, but helped me remember him in ways I never thought possible. Also I've met the nicest most loving people on here, whom I always look forward to coming here and reading posts. You're forever in my heart. I've said it before and I'll say it again, Michael would be thrilled to know that his spirit has united friendships worldwide. To my Prince in the sky, I love you.

One of the more unusual websites is that for the Joshua Tree Inn in rural California where Gram Parsons died in 1973. The inn has maintained the room as it was when Parsons stayed there and the website has a photograph of the door to Room 8 where he died, captioned 'We have no idea what causes the illumination of the door or the aura of light to the left, and above the visitor's head several claim to see a familiar face or two in the image not to mention the file's disappearance from several computers'. The room, popular with fans, has its own visitors' book, where there are such comments as 'Gram couldn't have chosen a more spiritual place to lie. His spirit will live on in the hearts of many. Room 8 is a very spiritual place'. Many other websites, official and otherwise, enable the expression of similar sentiments by those who have been deeply influenced by particular individuals. And, as messages on Michael Hutchence's site attest, true devotees maintain that devotion at very regular intervals over many years.

Classical music tourism is rarely documented in anything like these terms. Most writers on classical music invoke a 'higher' culture, apart from notions of pilgrimage. As Riemer (1993: 81) has put it: 'the audience at Bayreuth (as in other theatres where the Wagner cult came to flourish) are too disciplined to sway and chant in shamanistic ecstasy; there is nevertheless, something of the possessed in their demeanour, as they sit immobile on their hard wooden seats for two hour stretches at a time in a darkened theatre'. Discernment and detachment were more critical values.

Rave as a collective performance has closer links to ritual, as 'through a tapestry of mind-bending music, the DJ is said to take the dancers on an overnight journey, with one finger on the pulse of adventure and the other on the turntables' (Hutson, 2000: 38). Similarly DJs have been seen as both chief priests and shamans (Gore, 1997: 62; Saldanha, 2002: 51; d'Andrea, 2003). Drugs reduced inhibitions, contributed to feelings of egalitarianism and collective consciousness (or its absence) and, especially where tourists were overseas, differentiated performers and participants from the local population. Ravers themselves have equated raves with religion, spiritual healing and ecstatic experience; as one raver, Megan, confessed: 'The rave is my church. It is a ritual to perform. I hold it sacred to my perpetuality . . . we in the rave are a congregation – it's up to us to help each other, to help people reach heaven. . . . After every rave I walk out having seen my soul and its place in eternity.' Another revealed: 'techno brings us back to our roots . . . [it] sings to a very visceral ancient part of us deep down inside. It draws from the "reptilian" brain, past our egos and beckons us to dance with abandon' (quoted in Hutson, 2000: 38, 42).

Raves have been equated with the trance dances of Native Americans, in the structure of performance, altered states of consciousness and the association with spiritual healing. Rave culture blends homogeneity and comradeship into *communitas*, and 'dissipates the tension of entering the world of wage slavery, underemployment and shrinking opportunity' (Hutson, 2000: 42). Consequently, it has been argued that 'the rave experience might be highly symbolic, but these symbols are fashioned and imbued with such meaning that they far surpass the empty, touristic simulacra that some academic commentators consider them to be' (Hutson, 2000: 46).

Where the rave experience is overseas and detachment is prolonged, the mystical element is intensified. As one raver in Ibiza recalled: 'It really struck me that we had got into some kind of . . . it felt like a religion' (quoted in Collin, 1997: 72). In Goa such feelings were even more common. One promoter, Goa Gill, argued that

> the good thing about when we did come here, and it was untouched, was we created a lifestyle which was the best of the East and West. We developed the concept of redefining the ancient tribal rituals for the 21st century and tried to use the party situation to uplift people's consciousness through the trance-dance experience. It's nothing new; every tribal group since the beginning of time has been practising this thing. You know, use music and dance to evoke the cosmic spirit, and everyone will be rejuvenated and healed by that, and the earth also.

DJ PWRGRRL stated that Goa trance was a 'sonic spiritual journey' while performers were similarly motivated:

> Dance is like an active mediation. You stop thinking. You just become one with your body. If you get a really good guide he takes you beyond thought, beyond mind, beyond individuality into a cosmic oneness with all the people there. It's like bonding with all the spirits of the universe. (Quoted in Noronha, n.d.)

More generally, participants enthused over how nationality, skin colour, class and language ceased to matter as 'all are in trance, become one with music, beach, ocean, palm trees, moon, stars and sun' (Saldanha, 2003b), although such utopian sentiments are as much myth as reality.

Pilgrimage attests to movement in search, or in celebration, of places and times where life was simpler, where identities were both more solid and more spiritual, and where community appeared to have tangible local boundaries. Music tourism especially often provides 'languages of celebratory inclusion . . . framed in a religious idiom' (Stokes, 1999: 150). Journeys, such as those along Route 66, to Graceland or Jim Morrison's grave (Figure 6.5), acquire ritual significance through repetition, the certainty that others with similar interests have made the same journey in the past. Conversely, and quite differently, music is inseparable from pilgrimage: 'The songs of pilgrimage are replete with the metaphors of time and place, the history and geography of human existence' (Bohlman, 1996: 389). Pilgrims turn to music just as music lends itself to pilgrimage.

Concerts, like festivals, can be seen as 'secular rituals' that 'symbolically separate individuals in both space and time from their ordinary social lives' (Sardiello, 1994: 129–131). Both Deadheads and ravers refer to performances as escapes from reality, argue that they experience altered states of consciousness (hypnosis and catharsis) and, in both contexts, dress and dance styles 'work to unify the audience and create a shared text with mythical and philosophical meaning' (Hutson, 2000: 43). Drumming tours that involve temporary immersion in the wider context of indigenous lives take this sense of philosophical meanings into a different dimension.

Especially at festivals, tourism becomes a collective event which for some constitutes 'a matter of a complex and unstable semiotics of self and otherness, a Turnerian drama of communal transformation' (Stokes, 1999: 148). Indigenous families in the Tatra Mountains of Poland use music festivals to 'symbolically and ritually preserve and represent their unique identity in the face of a changing world' (Cooley, 1999: 31), and more generally festivals tend to celebrate and preserve the music of past times and local regions (Chapter 7). The music press, but especially travel journalism, often promotes 'fandom as a kind of spiritual duty' (Stokes, 1999: 151). In a newspaper article entitled 'Pilgrimage for Loretta', the

Figure 6.5 This early gravestone belonging to Jim Morrison has been thoroughly vandalised and replaced by a plainer version without the statue. Yet tourism to the grave is undiminished.

author argues that 'the true test of allegiance is taking the rugged pilgrimage along twisting mountain roads around steep ravines to the place where Lynn's rags-to-riches story begins, the real "cabin on a hill in Butcher Holler"' (Alford, 2002: 7). While this may well be metaphor, the 'cabin' has echoes of stables in Bethlehem and the duty of true fans is implicit. At the very least languages of spirituality have been widely mobilised in both the discourses of advertising and promotion, and both the intents and beliefs of fans and tourism have become more than merely escapism, in a more secular world.

Moving On

At home and in concerts, music allows escape into virtual and more pleasurable worlds, yet certainly such worlds have offered more than mere virtual reality by becoming places that symbolise particular notions – 'home' or 'escape' – and have engendered music tourism. One frequent manifestation of traveller subcultures, an extended trip away to 'find oneself', is broadly evident in various facets of music tourism, from the more obvious goals of actual or would-be musicians, especially in developing world contexts, to the less obvious nostalgia of snowbird tourists.

Music tourists seek to derive pleasure and some meaningful experience through tourism, ranging from learning to play (or play better) particular instruments, which in itself may be related to some spiritual transformation, to simply visiting the home of a favourite performer, and experiencing the context of his or her work. In doing so, visitors are playing their part in re-creating a 'mythical collective consciousness' that reinforces a perception of a place, time and context. In Liverpool, Dollywood or Graceland, tourists may be actively encouraged to reinforce official history, through powerful narratives or even tape cassettes; such emphases are vastly more common than subversive modes of tourism.

Tourism is a symbolic activity, physically and socially displacing individuals to sites of performance and/or memory elsewhere, and enjoining entertainment with some sense of ritual. A recurrent theme is the particular link between music tourism and the dead. Beatles tourism effectively began after the death of John Lennon, and Graceland is much the most visited site of all. Here tourists have obviously departed far from ordinary routines towards ritual devotion, empathy and community with others, a sense of self-realisation and even feelings of being drawn there beyond ordinary volition. More generally, 'particular tourist contexts generate a shared set of conventions about what should be seen, what should be done and which actions are inappropriate. Such shared norms instantiate a way of being a backpacker, a participant on a tour bus or a member of a Club 18–30 holiday' (Edensor, 2001: 60). For Bruce Springsteen fans, 'fandom involves an extension of the performance based feelings of connection and community into daily life [as] fans are engaged in examining themselves and their place in the world' (Cavicchi, 1998: 188). Websites extend such communities into virtual realms. Tourism is one means of performing fandom and sharing in some notion of community, however temporary the experience may be.

Sites such as Graceland and dozens of museums have been constructed and reconstructed to be both informative and pleasurable, linking heritage and nostalgia. Visitors to museums tend to identify such key themes underlying the experience as 'connection to self', 'education and learning' and 'mindful outcome' (Mitchell, 1999), or alternatively information and pleasure, but also 'numen seeking' entailing a personal spiritual connection with the past' (Cameron & Gatewood, 2003). In such contexts and at memorials, pleasure has been formalised. Moreover, music tourist sites are largely visited by those who are 'insiders', willing participants in the histories and myths surrounding performers and scenes, hence highly receptive to positive images. Many sites have thus been invested with national and even ritual significance. Particular images and values dominate places, from Waikiki to Dollywood, but are also evident even in small-town China where stability, continuity, community and integrity are similarly triumphed (Lau, 1998). Such themes are also invoked by those seeking less formal experiences, from drumming in Byron Bay to cruising Route 66, or visiting secular and religious shrines. Indeed, acute parallels function at quite diverse music sites. Yet where nostalgia may shape the activities of older music tourists, pleasure determines those of house music fans; not all tourists are in search of mythological structures, invented traditions, superior musical performance or a deeper understanding of the self. Many are simply engaged in pleasantly superficial relaxation and recreation.

Chapter 7
Festivals: Community and Capital

This chapter discusses music festivals within the context of music tourism. Festivals provide case studies of issues discussed earlier, since they represent what 'might be categorised as cultural *display*, cultural *text* or cultural *product*. That is, the festivals might be viewed as an expression of historic tradition, a statement of social and political identity, or a commodity to be sold. The same festival might be interpreted along all three of these dimensions by different participants' (Saleh & Ryan, 1993: 290). The first section of the chapter outlines the background and history of festivals, while the second deals with their economic impacts and role in place promotion. The third section discusses the politics of music festivals, including issues of regulation, conflict and environmental impacts, and the final section discusses identity construction in terms of authenticity, identity and performativity.

Music festivals are in the broadest sense the oldest and most common form of music tourism. Musicians were invariably a part of community festivities around harvests, equinoxes, village fairs, Mardi Gras and similar gatherings; musicians, often travellers themselves, added a soundtrack to the sense of relaxation of social norms that accompanied celebrations. Just when festivals began to develop a tourist dimension is impossible to trace; the title of 'Europe's oldest festival' is claimed by England's Three Choirs Festival which dates to 1724 (and still continues) in the cathedral cities of Hereford, Gloucester and Worcester, although Antrim's Oul' Lammas Fair at Ballycastle was chartered in 1606. By the mid-1800s many European locations had staged opera and orchestral festivals, important destinations on the Grand Tour. Classical music festivals are ubiquitous throughout Europe in summer months, but now compete with, or complement, other music festivals across all genres, from 'indie' rock to zydeco. Music festivals have become more common features of economic strategies centred on tourism and regional development, since the internationally famous Woodstock, Monterey and the Isle of Wight popular music festivals in the late 1960s, and the earlier Aix, Edinburgh and Bayreuth festivals. Festivals provide places with 'spectacle' and a sense of 'uniqueness' – associating locations with one-off performances, or collective gatherings associated with a style, sound, or genre of music, as with the Brighton Festival '[helping] to project the town's individuality and validity' (Meethan 1996: 188). By the 1980s, festivals had widely become important means of promoting places and regions.

Beyond their particular significance, festivals are often part of wider musical networks through which performers (and sometimes audiences) migrate, connected to particular musical niches: bluegrass, country-and-western and hillbilly festivals in the United States, jazz festivals in Europe and North America; folk festivals in Israel (Waterman, 1998a), Sweden (Aldskogius, 1993), Germany and Britain. By contrast, 'indie' rock and folk festivals such as Lollapalooza and Lilith Fair in North America, Glastonbury in England, Japan's Fuji Rock Festival and Denmark's Roskilde, which attract major international performers and tourists, are more idiosyncratic. Many smaller festivals are aimed at specific audiences from a limited, domestic tourist market or at enhancing the cultural awareness and experiences of local populations, and less explicitly concerned with generating tourist income or catering for tourists' tastes and needs. Some are intended to bring diverse factions of a community into a shared experience (Craik, 1997: 135). Others cater to particular groups, such as women or indigenous people. Festivals may be both inclusive and exclusive.

Festivals often attempt to provide for narrowly defined and otherwise neglected niches of music, often supported by the state and local cultural non-profit organisations, such as the Irish Wexford Opera Festival, which aims to 'be the recognised world leader in the production of rare or unjustly neglected opera and to continue to win for Ireland a reputation as a centre of cultural excellence' (quoted in Quinn, 1996: 391). Like the Kfar Blum festival in Galilee, Israel, festivals may draw many visitors from distant places – hence 'a particular version of cultural tradition and identity is performed or paraded' (Waterman, 1998b: 264). Rather differently, WOMAD – the global network of 'world music' festivals – features a diverse mixture of 'exotic' musicians, with tourists experiencing both the festival as an event itself and as vicarious sonic tourism to a range of places. Others are quite local, even seemingly obscurantist, such as the annual Elvis Presley Revival Festival in Parkes (Australia) or the Nakodu village festival in Fiji (see p. 219).

Since the 1960s a shift has occurred in the perception of music festivals, and in their cultural and economic roles, from community orientation to commercial motives. Indeed, one writer on opera has queried:

> Is the festival idea dead? Democracy, education, technology and a huge rise in living standards have made the arts readily accessible to many. We have more leisure time, more money, more ease of

access to far-flung places. And we have far more music and opera. As cultural consumerism has spread, the idea of the festival as a source of renewal, as break from routine, fuelled by the spirit of artistic adventure, has all but disappeared. It has been swamped by the sheer quantity of events parading under the festival umbrella. Today all the world's a festival. In season, out of season you will search long and hard to find a festival-free zone. (Clark, 2000: 11)

While 'classical' music festivals have been associated with an educated elite and many folk festivals (epitomised in the May celebrations and maypole dances of England) emerged from village or peasant communities, popular music festivals had a more recent genesis in the counter-cultures of the 1960s, as an alternative space for social and sexual interaction, drug consumption and musical expression. Their beginnings comprised part of new social practices rather than a commercial imperative, in some ways building on the format and atmosphere pioneered by jazz festivals such as that at Newport, Rhode Island, begun in 1954. Early rock music festivals celebrated transgressive social and political practices, at a time when the United States was at war in Vietnam, conscription was in full swing and a sense of rebellion swelled among younger generations. One could get away with more risqué behaviour at festivals than in other spheres of life – drug consumption, public nudity, protest and performance – an expressiveness not permitted in domestic and public spaces. Popular music festivals emerged through the challenge to orthodoxy.

The late 1960s and 1970s also marked the expansion in mass tourism, both domestically and internationally, and even the most counter-cultural festivals, such as Woodstock and Monterey, were inherently touristic in orientation, as they sought to attract visitors from across the country and around the world. The emergence of mass tourism coincided with an era of ethnic revivalism around the world, creating demand for Celtic music festivals in Wales, Scotland, Ireland and the United States. Eisteddfod festivals were revived in Wales and new festivals began elsewhere. In Cajun areas of Louisiana in the 1960s, 'music was an essential part of the Acadian revival ... CODOFIL [Council for the Development of French in Louisiana] sponsored 'Acadian Festivals' which proved far more popular than school instruction' (Lewis, 1996: 74), backed up also by renewed interest in Mardi Gras celebrations throughout the state's francophone communities. In 1986, the Festival International de Louisiane in Lafayette was established to celebrate French musical expressions in the South, at the same time that Louisiana itself became an important destination for francophone tourists from Canada and France (see also Esman, 1982; 1984; Trépanier, 1991; Dwyer *et al.*, 2001). Tourism here contributed to the resurgence of ethnic identity.

Most contemporary festivals are explicitly commercial, either from the point of view of tour promoters looking for fruitful markets in which to stage festivals, local planners seeking ways to boost local economies or participants wanting to earn incomes. The growing economic role was accompanied by more comprehensive marketing, such that by the 1990s major festivals were institutionalised as part of formal tourism campaigns and sought increasingly global markets. Balinese promoters, for example, found festivals more difficult to sustain with growing costs:

> the musicians, dancers and other performers can't continue for only the pleasure of the experience. As a result of the soaring costs, a new means of finance must be found. Like most organisations in Bali they turn to the tourist industry for survival. With some help from travel agents, hotels and tour guides they try to promote participation in this wonderful festival. (*Rendez-vous*, 1, 2001: 6)

Even small island states very distant from obvious tourist sources sought festivals to generate tourist income. The Seychelles established an annual classical music festival (Figure 7.1) while, less successfully, Tonga 2000 tried to attract dance music tourists to the central Pacific, on the edge of the International Date Line, to mark the millennium. The Festival in the Desert, north of Timbuktu in Mali, that brings together Turaeg nomads and their camels, with European tourists and occasional foreign bands, is arguably the remotest festival on earth (Newbery, 2004). Just as dramatically, the first Rainforest World Music Festival was held in 2001 in the Sarawak Cultural Village, 'a living museum where the traditional inhabitants of Sarawak's major ethnic groups have been lovingly reproduced'. The festival, 'in the heart of the Borneo jungle', included henna tattooing by 'the Henna queen of Cairo', late-night World Music Disco and performances by Tuvan throat singers from Mongolia:

> This will be one of the most unique and exotic groups to be brought into the festival this year. Not only will they be performing a blend of Mongolian ethno-jazz at one of the night shows, but they will also be taking part in the various workshops that will be held in the longhouses of the Sarawak Cultural Village. Follow the sound of the umzad, open your minds to the khoomei, feel the wind of the Mongolian steppes and imagine yourself horseback riding with the armies of the Genghis Khan. See you there! (www.rainforestmusic-borneo.com)

Such festivals evoke utopian desires for localism and cultural specificity, even when they are collapsed into unusual hybrids with quite different styles featured together on the same stage. Further, festivals can constitute a search for exoticism, while commercialising indigenous worlds, in a vivid demonstration of their ubiquity.

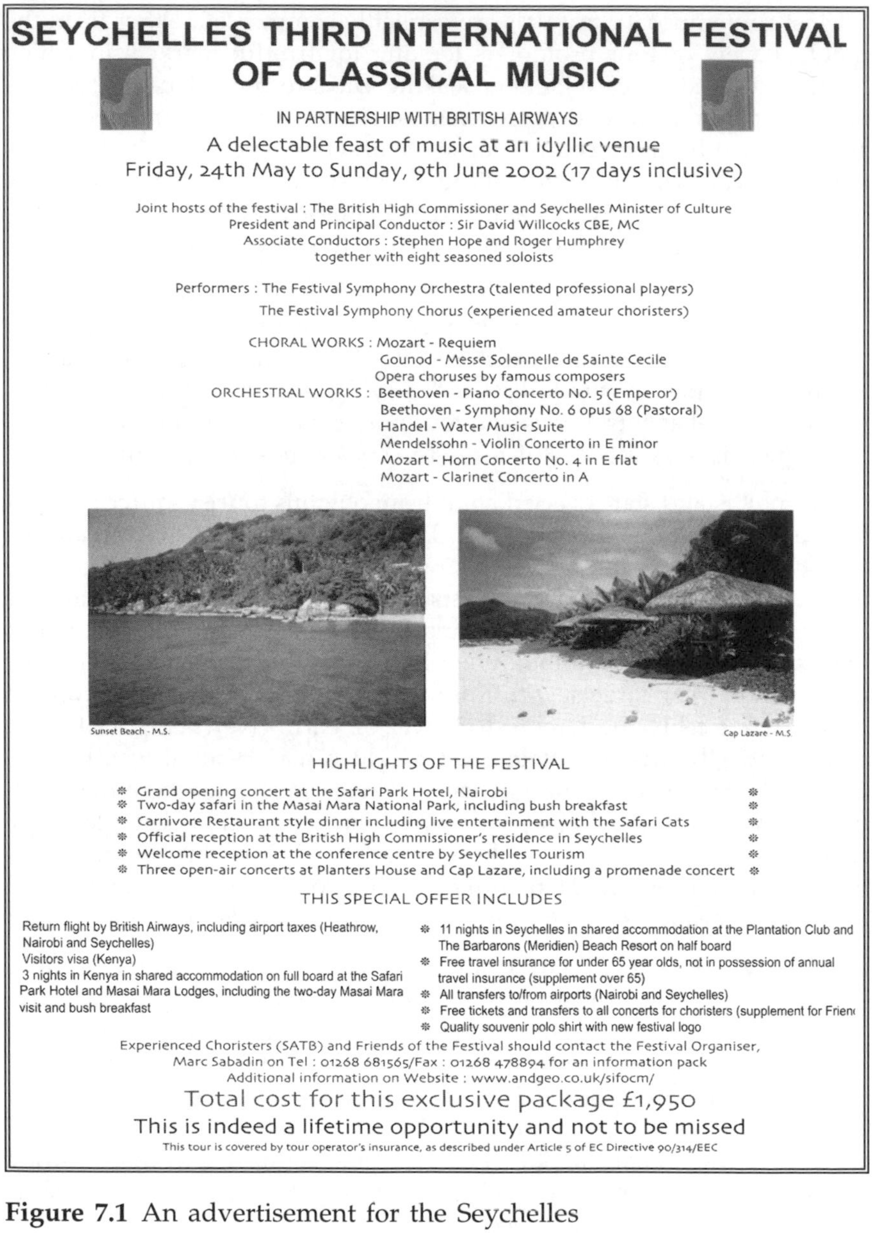

Figure 7.1 An advertisement for the Seychelles

Appeals to a wider tourist audience have sometimes ironically ignored local musical cultures at the same time that they sought to market the locality at an international level. In Ireland, organisers of the Clifden Country Blues Festival attempted to 'package' it for a particular type of overseas tourist with very specific tastes, constructing 'uniqueness' with reference to place, yet defining this uniqueness through repressing local culture:

> The choice of music and of musicians was based at least in part on an expectation of what was most likely to attract visitors to the area. ... There was a deliberate strategy to exclude local bands on the grounds that the quality of musicianship would not be sufficiently high to enhance the event's reputation and to attract audiences to the event. (B. Quinn, 1996: 391–392)

By contrast, the Kangnung Dano Festival in Korea explicitly excluded new residents in the area, and also women and youth, who were considered 'secular' and 'immature', to the extent that one local artist advocated the inclusion of 'vibrant and dynamic culture in present Kangnung society. We can consider pop culture, hip-hop dance and rap music to attract young groups for the Dano festival' (Jeong & Carlos, 2004: 647, 652).

Like all facets of music tourism, festivals are thus not always reflections of local identities and musical expressions, especially as commercial considerations have become dominant.

Music Festivals as Local Economic Strategy

> *There is a new economics, Carnivalnomics. We need to develop . . . a*
> *Carnival Ministry.*
> Alfred Aguiton, Chair of the Trinidad National
> Carnival Commission, quoted in Green, 2002: 283

Since the 1970s music festivals have become common components of local tourism strategies, their growth nothing short of dramatic and their economic significance considerable. At the start of the 1980s, pop festivals had become a 'regular feature of the British countryside in summer' so that at least 29 took place in 1979 (Clarke, 1982: 1). By 1998, the *Guardian* newspaper was advertising over 85 major summer music festivals in Britain. Other estimates suggest that in the United States, there are more than 4000 festivals every year, over 520 in the United Kingdom and over 800 in France alone (Waterman, 1998, Hughes, 2000). In the early 1990s Frey (1994) counted between 1000 and 2000 classical music festivals in Europe every summer. Australia has almost 600 festivals; 'hardly a genre or a geography has been left untapped' (Delaney, 2003). In Sweden, where there had been a similar rapid growth, festivals were remarkably evenly distributed throughout the country (Aldskogius, 1993), a pattern that seems evident elsewhere, suggesting that every region, at least in the developed world, has sought to develop festivals.

The increasing 'niche' marketing of music and the rise of nostalgic tourism associated with individual artists has also contributed to a growing diversity of festivals. For each niche – from folk to trance techno – festivals have grown to meet demand, while festivals increasingly cater to fans of specific artists. In Europe and the United States, with larger populations (and more extensive and affluent middle classes), even the most specific niches can support festivals. The Fleadh Festivals, in both London and New York, re-create Irish culture and music in two diasporic contexts; Budfest in Lubbock, Texas, celebrates the music of Buddy Holly, while Ozzy Osbourne's Ozzfest was originally set up as a showcase for up-and-coming heavy-metal bands. Madstock is the annual reunion festival of London ska group Madness; the annual Cropredy Festival in Oxfordshire centres on Fairport Convention.

While festivals have become a common component of local economic strategies, surprisingly little academic work has explicitly quantified the economic dimensions of festivals. Indeed, there are few studies of the profitability of festivals, partly because such information is often zealously guarded. The rise of music festivals responded to increased demand attributable to a relative growth since the Second World War of both disposable incomes and leisure time, alongside airfares becoming cheaper, freeways more pervasive and tourist infrastructure more sophisticated (Frey, 1994). Since disposable incomes and leisure time were far from equitably distributed, festivals were initially predominantly middle-class pursuits as part of tourist experiences. Festivals are now closely connected to local tourism strategies, evident in their promotion and the way tickets are purchased – through travel agents, rather than mainly at record stores or from festival organisers – and are incorporated into tour packages inseparable from the other basic elements of tourism, such as accommodation and transport.

Various factors influence attendance at festivals, including the quality of the programme (the line-up of 'names'), accessibility (accommodation, transportation, ease of purchasing tickets), flexibility of movement through a festival and its various events, and additional attractions in the surrounding district or city (Saleh & Ryan, 1993), alongside its timing. Visitors to the Woodford Folk Festival in Queensland during the 1990s had relatively low incomes, reflecting the large number of students and teachers, but over half were either undertaking or had completed university studies (Raybould *et al.*, 1999). However, in the United States it has been argued that 'tourists who frequent festivals are younger, earn higher incomes, spend more money, have more education, stay in hotels longer and bring their children more often' (Frierson, 2000). At the Umbria Jazz Festival in Perugia, tourists were certainly younger and mostly professionals and managers, while local visitors were older and from skilled occupations (Formica & Uysal, 1996). As at Glyndebourne, classical music, jazz and opera festivals are still to some extent a pursuit of the elite, but many have become more popular among the middle classes and those with ambitions to upward social mobility, especially when on holiday: 'attending, for example, an opera at Verona's Roman amphitheatre needs very little psychic effort by a visitor booking a trip to Northern Italy, but the same person might not dream of visiting an opera performance during the normal course of the year' (Frey, 1994: 32). However, at the Saskatoon Jazz Festival, Saskatchewan, Canada in 1993, 65% of visitors were employed in professional/managerial occupations, earned over C$40,000 (US$35,000) per annum and held graduate or postgraduate university degrees. In terms of ranked importance to the success of the jazz festival, respondents overwhelmingly listed factors such as 'quality of the programme', 'high-quality product', 'clean facilities', 'quality hotels' and 'good local restaurants' (Saleh & Ryan, 1993; cf. Thrane, 2002). Of importance with classical music, jazz and opera is the symbolic capital associated with those styles of music and their festivals. They imbue a place with 'class' and sophistication, important images used by tourism promoters to attract exactly the demographic group – older professionals, discerning middle-class tourists with higher disposable incomes – that are sought after by many locations as 'ideal' tourists. However, similar groups of tourists attend quite different kinds of festivals; over 77% of visitors to the 1990 King Biscuit Blues Festival in Helena, Arkansas, were middle-class white people (Rotenstein, 1992), different on both counts from those who were performing the blues there. Festival-goers at classical and jazz concerts are of more elite employment status, and potentially contribute more to the local economy than those at popular music festivals, but the absence of credible data means that generalisations may rest as much on prejudice as fact. Nevertheless, if such statements are valid, the attraction of certain festivals for income generation is obvious.

Large festivals with particular themes and in beautiful locations usually attract more distant audiences. At the 1996 Cuban Jazz Festival in Havana, which coincided with Carnival, 30–40% of audiences came from overseas, despite the considerable difficulties of getting to Cuba in the face of American sanctions (www.afrocubaweb.com/jazzfest9796.html). The Edinburgh Festival has comparable proportions with about 42% of visitors from outside the British Isles, mainly from continental Europe and North America (Prentice & Andersen, 2003). By contrast, the much smaller Glenelg Jazz Festival in Adelaide (South Australia) gained 3% of its audience from overseas and the larger Adelaide Festival 13% (Hughes, 2000: 217–218), despite its isolation from international airline routes. The King Biscuit Blues Festival in Helena, Arkansas, managed to draw visitors from 27 American states and also from Great Britain, Japan, Australia, Sweden, Germany and Canada (Rotenstein, 1992).

About 3% of the audience at the Tamworth Country Music Festival in Australia and 2% of those at the Elvis festival in Parkes, are from overseas – but probably none of these came to Australia specifically for these events. Other small festivals, such as the Swedish island of Gotland's music week, get just over a third of festival-goers from off-island and probably none from overseas (Aldskogius, 1993). Out-of-town visitors are much more numerous, especially in tiny places such as Woodford, Glastonbury or Glyndebourne, where there are few attendees from the village or town; but larger festivals – even though they attract more tourist numbers – may also be quite localised. The Riverbend Festival in Chattanooga attracts 450,000 people but gets 80% from the metropolitan area (Frierson, 2000).

Music festivals have underpinned tourism promotions in a number of ways, most obviously as 'special event tourism', but also through creating particular images of place. Festivals are a means of constructing and reinforcing reputations as major events on the calendar of certain destinations and anchors for music tourism economies. Munich's Oktoberfest claims to be the world's largest festival, with six million visitors, although in contrast to beer, music is a minor attraction. Berlin's annual Love Parade, a celebration of club culture and a giant techno carnival, attracts more than a million visitors each year. The New Orleans Jazz Festival draws 400,000 people; the Salzburger Festspiele has an attendance of over 200,000; Liverpool's Mathew Street Festival, with Beatles tribute bands playing across the city, brings together 350,000 people. In Memphis, Elvis Week attracts 75,000 fans every year in addition to the city's half-dozen other major music festivals; Nashville's International Country Music Fan Fair similarly anchors the city's music tourism economy, offering 250,000 fans the opportunity to meet the 'stars' in person. Roskilde, Europe's largest regular pop festival, attracts 100,000 every year. Birthdays and anniversaries are particularly important – hence the candlelight vigil at Graceland and Dead Elvis Ball in Memphis on 15 August (the anniversary of Presley's death) and the three-day celebrations of Louis Armstrong's birthday at the Satchmo Summerfest in New Orleans. Moreover, three years in advance, Salzburg was advertising and planning for the enormous festival to be staged for the 250th anniversary of Mozart's birthday in 2006.

Large festivals generate substantial incomes. In the Caribbean, the St Lucia Jazz Festival has been calculated to make a profit of about US$6 million, while the Trinidad carnival, considered the premier festival in the region, attracts over 30,000 visitors per year, has a general economic impact of around US$50–67 million and earned over US$30 million in foreign exchange (Nurse, 1999: 673; Nurse, 2002). The Australian Festival of Chamber Music in Townsville brings in about A$4 million (US$2.8 million) to the local economy (Morgan, 2003). By some world standards such impacts may be small. The Mathew Street Festival in Liverpool attracts 350,000 visitors who spend £15 million (US$30 million; The Mersey Partnership, 2003). The Edinburgh Festival in 1990 received about £1.5 million (US$3 million) at the box offices, but the total additional expenditure was estimated at £43.9 million (US$90 million). Moreover, 86% of additional expenditure came from tourists who spent at least one night in Edinburgh, rather than either local residents or day visitors. Many tourists also spent money in other parts of Scotland (Gratton & Taylor, 1995; Gratton & Richards, 1996: 81–83). At the other end of the scale, the Woodford Folk Festival makes about A$300,000 (US$210,000) a year (Roberts, 2003) and the Nakodu village festival on Koro island (Fiji), which drew in more than a hundred returning villagers from elsewhere in Fiji who heard 'the best sounds of modern music by the island's renowned pop bands', raised F$14,000 (US$7500) specifically for the upgrading of the village school and other local projects (Kikau, 2003).

There are a myriad of tiny festivals. As in Fiji, struggling towns in rural Australia have promoted festivals both as a community-building exercise and because they can bring wealthy urban visitors: 'For country towns forced to look at different ways of bringing visitors, and money, to their drought-plagued regions, musical festivals have proved a marvellous lure. Many are growing, attracting bigger crowds of new and repeat visitors, and with them, significant funds' (Williams, 2002: 44). In 2003 an annual international music festival was argued to be the only viable means of rescuing the host Shoalhaven River estate from bankruptcy and mounting debts (*Sydney Morning Herald*, 26 April 2003). Later that year the tiny former gold-mining township of Hill End, with just 120 people, launched the inaugural Hill End Jazz Festival, which was expected to bring 1500 visitors and raise enough money to buy a defibrillator for the community (*Sydney Morning Herald*, 24 October 2003). In the small town of Queenscliff, Victoria, tourism income from its modest annual music festival totalled over A$2 million (US$1.4 million). For the festival's manager, Barbara Moss,

> That economic impact is tied to the social fabric of the community. It's directly linked to the social health of the town and confidence is always a big factor in economic growth. A lot of local people become involved in the festival – up to 400 people volunteer to help out each year – and we've found that to be a big long-term stimulant to the economy. Some of those people might otherwise be lying in bed watching Oprah. Now they're out getting involved. That connectivity, the bringing together of diverse elements, is what social wealth is all about. (Quoted in Williams, 2002: 44)

In the United States too 'towns like Helena unashamedly admit that they stage local culture for profit' (Rotenstein, 1992: 139). Festivals thus provide diverse means of grass-roots community development and contribute to social capital.

Some small towns, such as Queenscliff, have been so successful that festivals have substantially contributed to economic and social development, and resulted in those places being known through their festivals. Port Fairy (Victoria, Australia), once a tiny fishing and farming village, and now dependent on second-home owners and tourists to survive, is boosted annually by its folk festival. It also has a Koroit Irish Festival, Rhapsody in June (mainly for local music), a Spring Music Festival and a Singing Up Country Festival (of Aboriginal music). Llangollen in Wales, a town of just 3000 people, is famous for its International Musical Eisteddfod, which usually attracts 12,000 performers from over 40 countries and 100,000 spectators, and also has an International Festival of Jazz. The small township of Tanglewood, in the Berkshire Mountains of Massachusetts, the summer home of the Boston Symphony Orchestra, attracts as many as 350,000 visitors a year to its various concerts. Helena, a town of just 20,000 people in Arkansas, deliberately fostered 'blues tourism' and thus revived its declining down-town area, but, as in Memphis, at the expense of the local context of 'juke joints' replaced by 'parking lots full of blues ghosts' (Rotenstein, 1992: 143).

Festivals are valuable components of tourism strategies because they have lower marginal costs; they require less investment in 'fixed' infrastructure such as permanent performance venues (Frey, 1994). Because festivals rely on infrastructure provided by others, usually rented on a temporary basis, they can better absorb the risk of low attendances. Yet this capacity is contingent on the size and scope of the festival, with many very large festivals, such as Glastonbury in Britain, involving major outlays. In 1998 alone Glastonbury paid £2 million (US$4 million) to performers; £800,000 (US$1.6 million) on police and security; £400,000 (US$800,000) on water, electricity and toilets; and £250,000 (US$500,000) on weather-related damage. In the previous year £1 million (US$2 million) was spent on fencing and local farmers received £170,000 (US$340,000) for renting the land (Hughes, 2000: 224). Since then, costs have risen with increased premiums for public liability insurance. The Glastonbury Festival also seeks to purchase all goods used at the festival from within 20 kilometres of the site to support local businesses, and in 1999 donated £600,000 (US$1.2 million) to local charities, including £125,000 (US$250,000) to Oxfam (which provides 750 stewards) and smaller amounts to women's institutes and sports clubs (Wheat, 2000).

Seasonality and one-off events pose inherent problems. Despite Frey's (1994) claims of their independence from the need for fixed capital, festivals need fixed infrastructure within cities or towns – hotels, transport, retail facilities, cafés, bars and restaurants – that would be under-utilised without a year-round tourism economy. Cities such as Salzburg have responded to seasonality by staging other festivals. In addition to its annual August Salzburger Festspiele, Salzburg hosts the Osterfestspiele at Easter, Mozart Week in late January and Pfingstokonzerte on the Whit Sunday weekend. Memphis stages festivals throughout the year, including Elvis Week, the Beale Street Music Festival, a Zydeco Festival, W.C. Handy's Birthday Celebration, the International Blues Talent Competition and the Centre for Southern Folklore's Memphis Music and Heritage Festival. Smaller towns, however, are hard-pressed to develop repeated attractions; Parkes, for example, alongside the Elvis Presley Revival Festival, organises a Country Music Spectacular, the Australian Marbles Championships, a Motorcycle Rally and Kennel Club Show. Such diversity is exceptional, but none last more than a weekend. Even so, as the experiences of the small towns of Port Fairy and Llangollen show, few places are associated with only a single cultural event.

Music festivals may also fill the void left by seasonality in other forms of tourism; in ski-towns such as Thredbo (Australia), blues and jazz festivals in summer months 'provide a useful top-up in tourist revenue outside the busy ski season' (Williams, 2002: 44). Rocky Mountain cities such as Aspen and Banff and various Alpine cities such as Salzburg have similarly diversified. Indeed, Aspen has had a music festival for more than 50 years. What began in 1949 as the idea of a Chicago industrialist to 'create a haven in the Rocky Mountains for the arts, an experimental hothouse for high culture ... in the tranquil serenity of the great outdoors', in 2002 had 200 events and 100,000 visitors over nine weeks. So successful had it become that it was claimed that 'the music festival is partly responsible for the high level of property values. It's made Aspen a desirable place to live. People come to Aspen for the winter but stay because of the summer' (Peters, 2002: 36, 39). In Jamaica, the Reggae Sunsplash Festival was introduced in the 1980s to revive the dormant summer season in Montego Bay when overseas visitors were few, to the extent that it 'almost single-handedly converted what was a trough in the tourism calendar to a summer season that rivalled the traditional peak season' (Nurse, 2002: 137).

Smaller places that are able to host relatively large events obviously reap the most significant rewards (Mitchell, 1993), but the infrastructure required to host a major event means that the most successful festivals occur in metropolitan centres (Gazel & Schwer, 1997: 52), although large cities with diverse economies need tourism income less than smaller, struggling towns. Thus festivals, despite their allure, can exacerbate processes of cumulative and circular causation that draw people and capital into urban centres at the expense of peripheral locations. Festivals do not always effectively redistribute resources towards smaller centres.

Economic success, paradoxically, has enabled festivals to celebrate some degree of 'purity' and avoid the extremes of commercialism and popular taste. The Santa Fe Opera Festival (New Mexico), Aldeburgh and Glyndebourne have all been able to mount relatively unknown and new operas, in the expectation that this would not discourage visitors. In Adelaide, the early years of the WOMAD world music festivals included local mainstream bands such as Midnight Oil and Crowded House, since organisers felt that 'obscure' overseas performers were not expected to draw crowds. Success meant that by 2003 bands such as Crowded House had disappeared, replaced by more 'exotic' performers from 31 countries, as fans travelled from all over Australia and New Zealand, with 40% being from states beyond South Australia or from overseas (Elder, 2003b). By then WOMAD was supported by the State Ministry of Tourism and had 15 corporate sponsors. In Queensland, the early years of the Australian Festival of Chamber Music were characterised by familiar Mozart, Brahms and Beethoven pieces, but after success seemed assured, more contemporary music was included (Morgan, 2003). However, innovation may also decline in the face of apparent commercial imperatives (or merely conservative planning and management). At Aspen,

> Inevitably we've lost a bit of the improvisation and spontaneity that were part of the original festival. There's been a shift in focus in programming from the esoteric and less heard to more standard pieces. That is contrary to the original plan. People too are worried about creeping commercialism – rising prices, assigned seating and more 'fly-in' performances by well known names. (Peters, 2002: 38)

Salzburg too has long been described as an 'art-shrine' rather than a 'place of creation' (James, 1984: 106). Some commercial classical music festivals have been criticised for being quite routine in their annual reproduction of a narrow canon of composers and pieces, in an 'imaginary museum of musical works' (Goehr, 1992). The repertoire of the Vienna State Opera has been argued to be 'the most conservative in the world, with almost no departure from standard Italian and German works [while] the living culture of the German-speaking people is conducted elsewhere' (Riemer, 1993: 32–33). Predictability is similarly evident in the content of the Seychelles Festival, although many festivals have sought to escape more formal and repeated structures to encourage diversity, flexibility, novelty and originality. Glyndebourne has sponsored new operas (such as *Tangier Orange*) and many festivals have developed innovative links with art, film and food. Success may stimulate conservation as much as innovation.

Beyond their direct and indirect income and employment impacts, festivals influence images of places. One problem with festivals is that 'the "out of region" tourist who is a festival-goer is primarily just that, someone who is interested in the festival. To extend visits beyond the festival, both temporally and spatially, would appear to be the challenge' (Saleh & Ryan, 1993: 297). For smaller festivals, festival-goers concentrate expenditure within the confines of an event or venue, limiting economic flows to surrounding regions and attractions, and do not return at other times. Distribution of economic benefits can vary between two festivals in the same place. Byron Bay's annual winter rock festival, Splendour in the Grass, attracts a younger crowd than its earlier East Coast Blues and Roots Festival. Surf shops and fashion stores fare better during the former, but restaurants are worse off as locals avoid the busy town centre and younger crowds opt for fast food (Allen *et al.*, 2003). Nonetheless, a third of local businesses had enough increased sales to make it worthwhile to hire new staff during the festival period. Even more were hired during the Blues and Roots Festival.

Festivals usually enhance images and make contributions to tourism on a year-round basis. Rather more than with popular music festivals, perceived to have a different (and not necessarily positive) image and market, classical music, jazz and opera festivals have become ubiquitous within tourism and place marketing campaigns, as much for a contribution to image as specific revenue-raising ability. This is particularly true in Europe where cities have some association with a composer or work that can be exploited, such as Vienna's Haydn Festival at the Schloss Esterházy, the Bruckner Festival in Linz, the Bayreuther Festspiele, run by Wagner's grandson, Wolfgang, Nuremberg's Wagnerian Ring Cycle, Prague's Spring Festival, Warsaw's Autumn Festival and Verona's Opera Festival. This has certainly not precluded festivals in more unexpected places, such as an opera festival in the desert at Santa Fe, New Mexico (and others in desert Australia); the Glimmerglass Opera Festival in the Catskills Mountains, upstate New York; or both Jazz in the Vines and Opera in the Vineyards (Hunter Valley, Australia). In such places many promotions emphasise landscape and culture as much as music. The Metropolitan Opera Guild Members' Travel Program advertised the 2001 Sante Fe Opera Festival by listing the operas (most infrequently performed works) and suggesting:

> Experience the splendors of the Southwest and the internationally acclaimed Santa Fe Opera with Desiree May, Santa Fe resident and lecturer for the company. By day discover some of the world's finest collections of European and American art, as well as displays of primitive New Mexico cultures; explore the Museum of International Folk Art and art galleries of Canyon Road, as well as the cliff dwellings of Bandolier National Monument and the Sanctuario at Chimayo, where miracles are said to occur.

Similar descriptions were afforded to the Wexford Festival, where Desiree May was described as 'Irish-born', the Po River Music Cruise (from Venice through Verona, Parma and other cities, with distinguished performers on board) and the Zurich International Festival (www. metguild.org). Morgan Tours, based in Canada, offered tours, including Australia (with the Australian premiere of *Parsifal*, the Barossa Music Festival, the Australian ballet, the Great Barrier Reef and 'from the sacred Aboriginal sites to the unique cities. Fine dining throughout') and Iceland (with two operas, a ballet and a symphony at the Reykjavik Arts Festival, alongside 'museums, galleries, whales and volcanoes. Gullfoss, Geyser, Jokulsargljufur National Park (Iceland's Grand Canyon) excursion') (www.morgantours.com). The Glyndebourne Festival runs a concert series over a three-month period, which draws on landscape, location and music, and

> combines aristocratic surroundings with that quintessential English ritual, the picnic, and fine ensemble opera . . . not to mention the corporate sponsor. Glyndebourne has been called the cultural Wimbledon and seats are as coveted as those on centre court. Keen to impress visiting firemen with a uniquely English experience, London CEOs pop biddable bankers and their wives into Rollers, send them scurrying through south London traffic snarls and down the M25, through the picturesque town of Lewes and out the other side to the turn-off to Glynde and Glyndebourne. (Schofield, 1996: 1)

Brinkburn Music 2001 in the North of England offered similar aesthetics but a greater diversity of music, from orchestras to small choral groups, and advertised: 'Brinkburn Music's summer festival is held in a beautiful 12th century Priory nestled on the banks of the River Coquet. A marquee serves refreshments and traditional Northumberland food. Or you can bring along your own picnic and relax in the idyllic grounds of the Priory before the concert' (*Gramophone*, May 2001: 116). On the same magazine page, the ten-day long Oundle International Festival (which ranged from piano concertos and restored opera to a Gospel and Latin Spectacular with Fireworks) emphasised the charms of 'the lovely Nene Valley in Northamptonshire'. Some degree of musical and landscape diversity has proved a means of commercial success.

Festival success has encouraged promoters to make events regular, revive once-successful events (such as the Woodstock and Isle of Wight Festivals) and create festivals in new places, even without related musical history. There has also been intense competition between sites, and both diversification (as at Oundle) and specialisation. In 2002 the Isle of Wight Festival was revived and sponsored by the trading arm of the island council, Wight Leisure, after an absence of 30 years. The events manager of Wight Leisure observed that 'we are playing off the 1970 festival because we have that musical brand heritage', while one of the organisers of the original festival noted 'any radical event is very quickly taken over by the established sector when they see they can make something of it'. The programme differed from the original format with an 'indie' concert on the first night, followed by jazz, blues, folk and world music events (*Guardian*, 1 February 2002: 12).

Success has resulted not only in the exponential increase in numbers since the 1960s but intense competition to host those festivals. The WOMAD Festival in Adelaide has considered becoming an annual rather than biennial event to prevent a larger Australian city developing a more successful alternative. In England, Newcastle secured the BBC Radio 1-sponsored Love Parade from Leeds. In Russia rivalry characterises the relationship between the Kirov and Bolshoi Ballets and the cities of St Petersburg and Moscow, respectively (von Uthman, 2002), a relationship intensified by tourism.

The proliferation of festivals has meant that fewer have obvious musical links to place, but have emerged from local attempts to develop a valuable cultural and economic activity. Ravello has a Wagner week in its six-week long music festival on the basis that Wagner wrote *Parsifal* there, but Leeds, for no particular reason other than individual inspiration, has benefited both from its long-established International Piano Competition and a Love Parade (modelled on that of Berlin) that brought around 400,000 participants in 2000. Other cities have tried to capture particular markets. Those with an alternative heritage (such as elegant historic buildings) or beautiful landscapes have been most successful. Aix, Beaune and Orange, in France, strongly emphasise food, wine and architecture, including the acoustics of Orange's 2000-year-old Théâtre Antique. Saxony in Germany offers a Festival of Sandstone and Music. The Kowmung Festival in rural New South Wales has venues ranging from caves to cattle-sheds. Bregenz in Austria is famous for its massive floating stage on the waters of Lake Constance (where *West Side Story* was performed in 2003). However, even places with neither cultural continuities nor spectacular landscapes have been able to achieve modest success. The combined role of music and landscape is exemplified in the development of the Schleswig-Holstein Music Festival in northern Germany, an area hitherto associated with tourism to beach and coastal landscapes. The festival brought 'top quality music in the north', so improving and diversifying its image. The festival association was a non-profit organisation that included prominent artists and politicians. The programme included several 'product lines', ranging from famous orchestras to solo performers, used venues such as barns and castles to provide a 'special atmosphere' and developed annual themes such as 'Music of the Baltic Countries'. The apparent key to success was the consistent application of a 'mature marketing mix' and a 'clear corporate identity consisting of a combination of music and the countryside' (Roth & Langemeyer, 1996: 179). Little was left to chance.

Growing possibilities for specialisation, from techno festivals to those for specific instruments, have accompanied rising numbers. Days of Dance in the North of England enable participants to learn some 30 different kinds of dance, from Greek to morris, Klezmer to 'welly', while simultaneously supporting Oxfam and the Campaign for Nuclear Disarmament (Macaskill, 1999). Busking festivals are widespread, Fez (Morocco) has a week-long annual Festival of World Sacred Music (including lectures and films), Cardiff hosts a World Harp Festival, Oulu (Finland) stages the annual World Air Guitar Championship and American Samoa held the first World Fire Knife Dance Competition in May 2003.

Commercial concerns have also led to diversification, with events restructured to cater for more diverse populations (the converse of the greater focus achieved at WOMAD in Adelaide) and parallel attempts to extend the duration. Major festivals, like Edinburgh, acquired Fringe Festivals that catered to more youthful audiences than their supposedly more staid progenitors (and eventually drew larger audiences). Growing diversity has also meant linkage with non-musical activities such as food and wine, the landscape (built and natural), and seminars, lectures or conventions. Conversely, vast numbers of vineyards in every country have established jazz and opera festivals in the vines that both create income and buttress sophisticated identities for rural regions. Festivals have become valuable promotional devices, even in places with few real connections to music scenes.

Parkes, New South Wales: Australia's Elvis town

The emergence of an Elvis Presley Revival Festival in Parkes (Australia) has been entirely the result of a chance local whim, when one individual, devoted to the memory of Elvis, was able to galvanise a committee into action. In 1992 a small group of fans, one of whom later changed his name to Elvis, decided to stage Australia's first Elvis festival in this town of 10,000 residents, 350 kilometres from Sydney. The first annual festival was held in January 1993, coinciding with Elvis's birthday. It attracted 500 people from as far as Adelaide, Melbourne and Sydney, and set the theme for those that followed, with Elvis and Priscilla look-alike competitions, a street parade with vintage cars, shop-window displays of memorabilia, Elvis movies at the cinema (since closed) and concerts, one of which is at the Gracelands Club. Indeed, the previous existence of a Gracelands Club had been one factor convincing organisers that Parkes was the appropriate place for the festival.

The first festivals were largely ignored by the local media (despite the dearth of news in midsummer) as inappropriate or trivial, and that exclusion has not substantially changed. By contrast, the national media have covered the festival invariably because of its curiosity value (Figure 7.2)

Figure 7.2 The Elvises at Parkes, Australia (Photograph by courtesy of the *Sydney Morning Herald*)

and through some claims of the Parkes committee that it was keen to become the 'Elvis capital' of Australia. Ironically, the national coverage, and its celebration of tackiness and kitsch, rather than local promotions, have probably drawn most visitors. Parkes itself rarely mentions the festival in any tourist publications or on its website, preferring to adver-tise itself as the town with 'the dish' (a radio-telescope that figured in a 2000 film) and a prominent regional commercial centre. The festival is nevertheless supported by the Parkes Shire Council through its Music Development Project and profits go to local charities.

In its second year, the festival brought visitors from further afield, including Western Australia and Queensland, and added a clambake at Gracelands, with sand and surfboards brought in to transform the car park. The Parkes Tourism Promotions Officer heralded it a success, and conceded that it had become an integral part of the annual events calendar:

> the event will provide substantial tourism value for Parkes, in terms of publicity and in cold, hard revenue. The revival could well become a role model for other interest groups keen to promote their festival. A hard core of Elvis stalwarts researched and marketed the concept and banded together to form an effective working team. (*Parkes Champion Post*, 5 January 1994: 1)

The two-day festival attracts modest crowds, with 2500 at the street parade, and 100–200 at most of the commercial events, with 400–500 estimated to have come from outside the town (Figure 7.3). A special train runs from Sydney. Over a third of the festival-goers in 2003 came from Sydney with some being from further afield. These numbers are not insignificant given the size of the town, the fact that most stayed for a couple of nights, and usually in hotels and motels, and the relatively small tourist market – especially in midsummer – for inland Australia.

Although some outsiders might see the festival as a celebration of kitsch, most visitors do not. The average age in 2003 – almost 50 years – indicates that many were relatively old, and their comments – many disappointed with some aspects of local support and in favour of a much greater visible presence of Elvis memorabilia – indicate that a substantial proportion were 'true believers' and repeat visitors (Brennan-Horley *et al.*, 2003). Tourist expenditure on food, accommodation and other goods has helped to offset the impacts of drought and rural decline, and prompted some competition from other regional towns to develop comparable festivals and sources of income. In 2001 the small South Australian seaside town of Victor Harbor launched the Festival of the King, this time marking the date of his death, and, for the first time, Parkes had direct competition.

Figure 7.3 Parkes Memorial Gates celebrate the burgeoning association between the town and Elvis. They are a replica of Graceland's gates in Memphis. Each year, a new plaque is added to commemorate an Australian rock and roll icon who also headlined that year's Elvis Revival Festival. (Photographs by courtesy of Chris Gibson)

Country music tourism in Tamworth, Australia

Tamworth, a country town of 40,000 people in the rural New England region of Australia, has seen extensive transformations in its economy and local identity based around associations with country and western styles of music, and thus has a different experience of festival-led economic growth from those places marketing classical, jazz and opera. This occurred partly through a growth in musical 'scenes' in Tamworth, made up of a number of 'grass-roots' participants in country music, from instrumentalists and singers to sound engineers, venue owners and event promoters. However, Tamworth's now accepted status as 'country music capital' of Australia was an outcome of the strategic place marketing that surrounded its annual country music festival. Since the 1970s, but particularly in the 1990s, country music has come to define Tamworth, gaining it unprecedented media attention and creating an intangible but invaluable stock of meanings deployed in tourism promotions.

Tamworth's claims of a historical link to country music date to before the first festival in 1973. Australian country music emerged and became more popular from the late 1940s through to the 1960s, with the growth of its own distinctive style formed by 'pioneers' such as Slim Dusty, Buddy Williams and Tex Morton. This era saw the local radio station of Tamworth, 2TM, incorporate more country music into playlists, as radio stations did in many other rural towns. Tamworth pubs, popular stops on the long highway from Sydney north to Brisbane, became venues to see touring country artists perform. While country music made new incursions into the broadcasting terrain normally covered by other 'popular' music styles, radio suffered major blows in audience numbers with the introduction of television in the 1960s. 2TM started to run special-interest programmes during the evening as a response to changing media consumption. 'Hoedown' was one such special-interest show, first broadcast in 1965; widely listened to, it eventually dominated the evening timeslots on 2TM. The radio station's unusually clear broadcast signal – it could be heard across eastern Australia and some parts of the Pacific – attracted an audience much greater and more widespread than the town's population. Tamworth became an important centre for country music through its radio show.

Executives at 2TM, impressed with the potential to influence a large rural population, began in 1969 to use the tag 'country music capital' to describe Tamworth, mainly to advertise country music merchandise. The establishment of several recording studios also solidified the presence of the country music industry in Tamworth around that time (Allen, 1988: 6), while the Modern Country Music Association (MCMA) established a local group in Tamworth, which later became the Capital Country Music Association (CCMA). The CCMA started a talent show in 1965 and a Jamboree the following year, both focusing on country music. These events were eventually scheduled for the Australia Day January long weekend that in 1973 became the Tamworth Country Music Festival, during which 2TM announced the winners of the inaugural Australasian Country Music Awards. The Australia Day long weekend was chosen because, although January is a quieter time for businesses and for 2TM, it is a good one for tourists and for media short of hard news at that time of the year. The festival hoped to win national news coverage and free publicity (Max Ellis Marketing, 1999). Although the festival was explicitly commercial in intent, only later was it perceived as a boost to the local economy and brought into the broad orbit of local development strategies.

By 2000 the festival had grown from a weekend gathering to a full ten-day programme, with 2400 performances across 116 venues, over 1000 performing artists and an estimated 500,000 visitors over the whole course of the event. The festival covers the range of 'country' music from rockabilly to bluegrass, bush poetry and country swing, reflecting the diversity of country music as it increasingly 'crossed over' with other genres. With growing diversity in music and related attractions, it has widened its appeal, simultaneously pitched as a family event and a musical festival for 'serious' country music enthusiasts. According to the City Council's festival staff, the festival is 'sophisticated, comfortable with itself and provides a wonderful platform for people to celebrate being Aussie' (quoted in Gibson & Davidson, 2004). Visitors from a range of mostly Australian places (including big cities and other country towns) flood local accommodation, overflowing into 'tent cities' along the riverbed and highways in and out of town. There is a mix of snowbird travellers, older working-class couples, younger rural folk (for many of whom the festival is an important meeting place, a place to 'pick up') and other much smaller groups, including lesbians and gay men, punks and college students. Tourists move through the town centre during the day – the main shopping streets are closed off to traffic and commerce is reorientated towards the festival and visitors: temporary souvenir stores open, record shops and bookstores stock up on country music titles and employ extra staff, clothing shops order in more 'cowboy' stock. New hotels, restaurants and cafés have opened up in Tamworth because of the festival.

The larger performances by major artists known nationally and signed to major labels (particularly ABC Country/EMI) are attended by mostly older, polite, but nonetheless enthusiastic crowds. These concerts are fully professional performances, with slick production and merchandise available. Some visitors are city-folk seeking a temporary immersion in a rural context, a conscious attempt to adopt or be influenced by 'country' values, attitudes, hospitality and humour. Hence, many dress up in

Akubra hats (Australia's equivalent to the Stetson), Blundstone boots and R.M. Williams-brand jeans (although the archetypal and rather warm rural Australian 'moleskin' jacket is hard to find, as the festival is held in the middle of the hottest period of the year). Some younger men dress up more elaborately in the full cowboy regalia, but such outfits, although common among performers, are now generally only worn in the audience by some Aboriginal people and white rural working men who come to Tamworth from the remotest parts of the country, or by those 'playing up' a retro-image of cowboys and cowgirls: line-dancers, gay men, younger straight university students, and inner-city country/rockabilly punks who relocate temporarily to Tamworth, enjoying an opportunity to dress up and live out an identity.

Most of the festival's performances, though, are free and in the town-centre streetscapes, designated as busker's alley through the ten days. Hundreds of artists set up, some selling CDs and offering business cards with booking numbers, others encouraging passers-by to join in the jam, learn to play gum-leaves or simply (line-)dance along. Some audiences bring fold-up chairs and camp out in front of their favourite performers, others toss coins at the better acts on offer. This more informal space is where the festival's Aboriginal performers are mostly found and heard. A few individual Aboriginal country artists, such as Jimmy Little and Troy Cassar-Daley, are now successful in Australia and are rarely marketed in terms of Aboriginality. They attract both black and white crowds to large performances in clubs around town. Other Aboriginal bands and performers take part in showcase nights, held in the Town Hall and in other smaller, Aboriginal-controlled venues, which are more overtly orientated towards Aboriginal crowds: rare opportunities for generations of Aboriginal country singers and audiences to come together, in black-friendly, Aboriginal-controlled spaces. On the streets, Aboriginal buskers entertain crowds of both white and Aboriginal passers-by, and are likely to be perhaps the only Aboriginal musicians that festival-goers encounter. Of significance to Aboriginal people throughout the country, the festival provides venues for Aboriginal performance and social interaction, distinct from the older, white mainstream audiences. The festival is not 'owned' by any single company or organisation. Rather, a decentralised management structure – made up of local government, country music associations, tourism promotion boards and private interests – markets and coordinates the event on behalf of the many venues that host performances through the ten-day period. Because of this, Aboriginal country music is a part of the festival and has access to some venues (not always the case in other country towns). But Aboriginal country music also occupies an uneasy space, particularly given the conservative rural culture often celebrated more widely at the festival (and which has historically displayed racist attitudes towards Aboriginal people). Aboriginal country musicians and audiences participate in Tamworth, at many levels, but face marginalisation within it.

Tamworth demonstrates the importance of the social context of consumption for understanding the music and tourism cultures experienced there. Crowds at performances are younger at night. The main performances include big names in large venues, special showcases of grouped artists (as at folk and bluegrass nights, new artists showcases), and stage shows depicting the lives of famous country stars of the 1950s and 1960s (such as Patsy Cline). More rowdy folk and 'roots' country nights occur in smaller pub venues, featuring swing-dancing, rockabilly, bluegrass, bush poetry and 'alt. country' (although alternative country acts that travel up to Tamworth from Sydney and Melbourne have often complained of the festival's inauthenticity). Across these styles of performance at Tamworth, story-telling between songs is a crucial part of the act. The best artists introduce songs with imaginative, captivating inter-song banter, intriguing the audience or convincing them of the value of the song, seducing the audience into the story. This compares with other musical styles, such as 'indie' rock, where minimalist inter-song banter is expected. Country songs appeal to emotions in a direct way; opportunities to embellish them in between numbers flesh out those connections. Humour, tragedy and the strength of human courage are common themes, as are the importance of individualism and collectivism, of both being oneself and sticking together in hard times. At some events, and especially in folk songs, Australian collectivism and unionism are celebrated, a link to a particular brand of rural Australian left-wing politics. In others, songs are linked to hardships of drought, financial ruin, marital breakdown, or the pleasures of home and family.

At Tamworth, much is made of possibilities to 'meet the stars' (as at Nashville's country music festival). Public signings of CDs are common, while musicians seek to interact with audiences when attending other performances and venues, in bars and clubs. This is part of a wider discourse of country music, and Tamworth as a place, by implication, as 'grounded', 'honest', 'direct' or 'no bullshit'. In part because of this, and somewhat ironically, the festival has odd quasi-political overtones, including links to the National Party (formerly the Country Party) and the rural lobby group, the National Farmers Federation, both of whom run campaigns based on the idea that they are 'closer to the rural people' and 'keep it real', in contrast to city-based political parties. Links are established when musicians support campaigns by these organisations, or when conservative politicians attend or get involved in the country music scene. In the most well-publicised example, Pauline Hanson, founder of the briefly successful right-wing party, One Nation, sought to reinvent herself as a country singer and promoter. Hanson, infamous for racist, homophobic and xenophobic attitudes, visited Tamworth and recorded a single there. Such attitudes rarely reach confrontation, although in past years there have been problems with 'bikie gangs' (motorcycle enthusiasts/clubs) and street violence, particularly against Aborigines – the result of an aggressive, alcohol-driven pub culture. This aspect of Tamworth is in direct contrast to the Aboriginal country scene there (a space for self-determination, rather than vilification), and the attitudes of most other performers (if not audience members).

Permanent reminders of country music have been established in the town's built environment to increase year-round tourism, engaging with and attempting to control representations of place to increase commercial benefits. Landscape repackaging, an important component of the place marketing process (see Hall & Hubbard, 1998; McGuirk *et al.*, 1998; Loftman & Nevin, 1998; Miles, 1998; O'Connor, 1998), is particularly important as music is inherently invisible, and in the case of festivals is highly seasonal. Music is often made (almost literally) concrete in the built environment to create reminders of music for the tourist 'gaze' beyond the time of the festival. In Tamworth, country music venues, museums, special walks, parks and memorials all seek to reassure the visitor of Tamworth's status as the 'country music capital'. In 1988, the Golden Guitar, a 12-metre high replica of the trophy presented to the winners of the annual Australasian Country Music Awards, was erected at the southern entrance to the town. The Golden Guitar is clearly visible to people entering the town on the main New England Highway from Sydney and is the most photographed landmark in Tamworth (Figure 7.4). The Tamworth Tourist information centre is also built in the shape of a double-neck guitar. Originally, plans were developed to build a Tourist Information Centre in the style of a colonial house, similar to those in many other Australian country towns. However, this plan was rejected in favour of the distinctive guitar design. Tamworth City Council has adopted a guitar and country music logo that is displayed on street signs, official vehicles, taxis, buses and council signs. Tamworth has also developed country music-related museums and memorials to tell country music stories and commemorate artists. Museums include the Wax Museum, the Australian Country Music Federation 'hall of legends', and the 'walk a country mile' interpretive centre. Each provides information on the history of country music in Australia and Tamworth, and promotes country music artists, especially the 'pioneers' of Australian country music, such as Slim Dusty, as well as reinforcing mythologies of rurality through stories in the songs of these 'pioneers'. There are also memorials in the landscape. These include 'The Hands of Fame' and its spoof, the 'Noses of Fame', the 'Roll of Renown', a songwriter's memorial, and the 'Winners Walkway'. These provide material sites for country music pilgrimages.

Figure 7.4 Tamworth's Golden Guitar statue is a three-storey replica of the annual Australasian Country Music Award presented each year at Tamworth's country music festival. It graces the entry to town on the major highway north from Sydney and is thus a prominent symbol of the town's musical identity to passing tourists. (Photograph by courtesy of Deborah Davidson)

Although the festival is much the most important tourist time in Tamworth, there have been steady increases in visitors to Tamworth for country music outside this period, as Tamworth has invested in infrastructure and promotion, and developed events to provide year-round reminders of country music. Country music has become vital to its economy, largely through tourism (although Tamworth does have recording studios and some record labels) and mainly from the annual festival. Tamworth's experiences demonstrate that it is possible to use music as a means to generate a year-round tourism economy, as festival tourism sparked additional tourism, including conventions and conferences, beyond the specific event itself. While Tamworth is in some respects a model for other locations seeking to generate tourism around a festival or special event, few other locations could replicate its success. Tamworth's claim was based on its country music show, broadcast nationally on a weekly basis; while its location, on a major highway between Sydney and Brisbane, two of Australia's largest cities, and with a regional airport, eased the transport constraints that plague other remote locations. More simply, not every location can become 'country music capital' or 'home of the blues'; there are limits to the extent to that distinct and marketable identities can be fabricated by promoters using festivals as an 'anchor' for music or general tourism. Tamworth does, though, reveal how festivals can create different sorts of economic and social spaces – from the glitzy PR-massaged event to the grass-roots busking scene – and that there are a diversity of uses and roles of a festival by different groups. Social and economic spaces within the festival are part of a wider cultural politics of race, class and gender – hence the varying kinds of participation of urban subcultures, Aboriginal musicians and audiences, and women.

Serendipity and festival tourism: Woodstock, New York

Woodstock, New York, has been a tourist destination connected to the arts for over 100 years, ever since Ralph Whitehead established an arts colony there in 1902. The town was for decades an upstate recluse for 'landscape painters, bohemians, socialists, writers, poets, cranks, dancers, dreamers and musicians' (Hill, 2002: 9). Almost accidentally, Woodstock became a renewed destination for musicians and tourists because of the famous 1969 festival. While the town has been the retreat of many famous musicians (including Bob Dylan, Van Morrison and John Sebastian of the Lovin' Spoonful), the actual Woodstock festival took place at Bethel, 70 kilometres south-west of Woodstock. Indeed, the town of Woodstock actively opposed the promotion of '3 days of peace and music' (as it was billed), forcing organisers to shift the festival to Bethel, 'a quiet, small, economically and spiritually dead redneck town' (Tiber, 1994: 6).

The 1969 festival, recorded in a memorable film, brought almost half a million people to upstate New York in a celebration of music, from Jimi Hendrix, Janis Joplin, The Who and many others, and radical protest.

Woodstock has been the recipient of the festival's heritage, highly reliant on the tourism that has followed the event even after 30 years. Despite its initial resistance, 'the irony is that Woodstock, without investing a cent in any of the festivals, has become a tourist attraction ... where perfumed soaps, handpainted clothes, secondhand jewellery, and home-made pickles are sold in the same town hall which banned the 1969 festival' (Masters, 2000b: 3T). Tourism has become vital. While

> people complained it was a bore having to keep directing them 60 miles south-east [to the Festival site at Bethel], the inconvenience could be partly mitigated by selling them a Woodstock Festival T-shirt, poster or badge ... [Woodstock] has become as dependent on tourism as an addict to methadone: in summer, it was the only part of the local economy that counted. (Brown, 1993: 13, 28)

Now Woodstock has become 'a haven for semi-retired professionals and Manhattan lawyers with weekenders' (Masters, 2000b: 3T), but also David Bowie and film stars such as Robert de Niro, a population attracted by the reputation passed down through festival mythology. Woodstock is integrated into the international tourist industry, but for one travel writer the absence of visual reminders of musical heritage at the actual festival site tainted the tourist experience:

> The mythology of Woodstock seemed to evaporate with every mile that I travelled. Bethel was too insignificant to be marked on my road map and I stopped several times to ask for directions. The replies were polite, bemused and ultimately pitying. 'You can git there, but I don't know *why* you wanna git there. Ain't nothin' there but a field' ... (Brown, 1993: 31)

Woodstock inadvertently inherited the festival's mythology and built a tourism industry around adopted images of place.

In the 1990s, Woodstock revival concerts were held in Wiener Neustadt, Austria, and at Rome and Saugerties (New York) in the United States. Attempts to hold a revival at Bethel itself collapsed because of poor ticket sales for the line-up of 'golden oldies'. A different era brought quite different sponsors, music, drugs and attitudes to the festival experience. Violence marred the atmosphere; at one 1990s revival 'brawling turned the lovefest into thugfest' (Masters, 2000b: 3T). At another revival concert:

> Woodstock 2, from the name down, was an attempt to create an instant myth. Woodstock 2, they said, was going to 'make history'.

It has certainly passed into legend, though not in the way the promoters intended it . . . we joined the 300,000 befuddled souls who were rained on, pissed about, ripped off, spattered with slime and tormented like no other assembly in human history . . . it would take a leaky press tent full of mutinous, muddy, bored, annoyed, sober journalists three days to list everything that was wrong with Woodstock 2. (Mueller, 1998: 11; Samuels, 1999)

Given their failures, the Woodstock revival concerts are unlikely to be staged again in the near future, but the town of Woodstock, without a music festival of its own, somewhat ironically continues to experience a growth in tourism connected to its misplaced (and displaced) musical past.

Festivals can serve as strategic tools to reinvent towns (Tamworth), emerge from quirky ideas based on no obvious musical reputation to create tourism (Parkes) or simply be accidents of history (Woodstock). Although successful examples are many, no formulae – other than good performers and a lack of competition – explain economic growth through festivals.

Festivals, Tourism and Musical Employment

Festivals are linked to the recording industry and perform an important employment function for record companies and musicians. Record sales are likely to be enhanced by festival appearances, and festivals allow emerging artists access to larger audiences than otherwise might be possible. The careers of many musicians have taken off following captivating festival performances: Jimi Hendrix at Woodstock and Monterey, and Nirvana, at the start of their career at the Big Day Out in Sydney, Australia. The success of U2 was stimulated by their appearance at Live Aid. At a national scale, bands gain a reputation by being part of a festival circuit – hence indigenous Australian groups such as Nokturnl and The Stiff Gins developed loyal support well before releasing full CDs. Ben Harper, Jack Johnson and Michael Franti have support well beyond their record sales, due to regular appearances at summer festivals and outstanding live performance.

Festivals represent both opportunities and detractions for musical labour (and the labour of those involved in staging a festival). They provide bigger audiences and new opportunities for musicians to earn an income in an intense period of activity. Wider exposure is possible than in smaller, regular venues, yet festivals can cut into the market for weekly local performances. In Sydney, live venues have struggled in recent years, at the same time that festivals have grown (although there are many other reasons for this, beyond festivals, such as the impact of competing entertainment forms and noise regulations on venues). Performers in their early careers may become marginalised in smaller side-tents at awkward times, or dwarfed by major acts. As the manager of one young Australian band, Defect, commented in relation to the highly tourist-oriented Gold Coast of Australia,

> If you go for the festivals, how many small independent bands are clammering to get on that little local stage, for nothing, and get their twenty minutes? They [Defect] were on the Warped Tour two years ago, they played on the local stage. These guys need to be on the major stage, need to get in the major cities. (Interview, 1999)

The perceived benefits for musicians are limited when there is an over-supply of festivals in the summer holiday period:

> I think that last year there was a real problem with how common festivals were. The tickets cost $70 or $80 [US$50 or 57], and last year between Livid and Homebake there were about six or seven festivals on the Gold Coast – Springboard, Surf Skate Slam, and Warped; some of the numbers were so down. Springboard was a shocker. I think there was 600 through the gate, last year there was 12,000. The thing is that there were just too many big festivals. The kids don't have that kind of money, and they go to one or two festivals that summer, but they can't find that $80 or $90 a month or every three weeks. There's just not enough kids who go to festivals, to spend that money. In America, sure, you've got the population base to handle it. But here it's a problem, we need the festivals, we need the bands to get up and play and the kids to hear them, but at that price and that frequency . . . I don't think it worked well this year. (Interview, 1999)

In some locations, an over-supply of festivals – including wine, food, writing and film – have stretched local and tourist expenditure, the extent of support and festival credibility. The slump in worldwide tourism numbers after 11 September 2001 and the 2003 SARS virus scare, and increased security concerns at large-scale events, seem likely to reduce demand. Thus their attractiveness – at least from a musician's perspective – may be more fragile than in earlier years.

Despite limitations, musicians have on the whole embraced the shift from local pub gigs to the festival circuit, grateful for usually larger audiences and pay-cheques than in smaller venues. Aboriginal musicians in Australia, for instance, who find it difficult to travel great distances from remote homelands in order to tour major capital cities, much prefer to perform at a smaller number of festivals than at numerous, less well-paid pub gigs (where racism might also be experienced). Aboriginal cultural festivals and community celebrations tend to be more inclusive, and have sympathetic directors and management, while festivals with significant tourist audiences – such as Sydney's Festival of the Dreaming – provide opportunities to communicate and educate spectators about Aboriginal culture. Moreover, despite dangers of over-supply, the economics of festivals usually make more sense for musicians: fewer performances for better wages to larger audiences.

Governments have provided cultural grants to stimulate innovation. In France, the government has legislated for the payment of adequate salaries to musicians who perform at festivals, in view of the huge tourist revenues that semi-professional performers produce. Elsewhere, as in Liverpool (Cohen, 1997), however, official concern has supported the view that musicians put little back into the community, a perspective with little empirical basis. Arguments are often made that artistic endeavours are inherently more 'efficient' if they are undertaken in the model of private enterprise (Frey, 1994; 1996), a common belief in the arts industries where the romantic myth of the individual creator as entrepreneur is pervasive (Gibson, 2003). Yet long-term music institutions, funded by government or other non-profit organisations, may provide a much more positive example of how musical labour can be organised, both for performance and within tourism economies (DiNoto & Merk, 1993; Americans for the Arts, 2002). The conditions of work may be more secure, allowing musicians room for creativity (contrary to discourses about public funding as a 'suffocating' influence), ensuring more regular performances (which the tourism industry requires) and remunerating musicians for the effort required to achieve excellence.

Employment and the contribution of tourist expenditure are only the most obvious impacts of music festivals. Even when events create few full-time jobs and only briefly support the local economy, they have intangible and usually positive effects on places. At Skinnskatteberg (Sweden) local people wanted an economically marginal festival to continue, since they believed that the boost to the local image was more important than a short period of overcrowding and noise, and limited direct economic gains (Aldskogius, 1993). The elusive impacts of image are as valuable as the hard currency of immediate economic success.

The Politics of Festivals

Political dimensions of music festivals are related to the contexts within which they occur, as well as the nature of the festivals themselves, as at Tamworth. Popular music festivals have been a part of political struggles, as with Live Aid in the 1980s, and specific festivals have supported independence movements in Tibet, East Timor and West Papua, and raised funds for drought victims, refugees and political prisoners (Denselow, 1989). Denmark's Roskilde Festival is unusual, not only in supporting local charitable groups who provide labour, but in being a non-profit organisation that donates all profits to such charities as Médecins sans Frontières, Amnesty International and the Save the Children Fund. Despite the festival's website noting that for one week traffic in the town of 50,000 people breaks down, it also claims 'The town of Roskilde lives with its festival. Is influenced by It. Profits from It. Demands its continued development and existence' (www.roskilde-festival.dk). Festivals, from Parkes to Glastonbury, often support local charities, although this is by no means standard practice. Exceptionally, even the simple existence of festivals may emphasise national peace and stability. The Festival of the Desert in Mali 'plays a vital role in consolidating and demonstrating that peace'; Mali's Minister of Tourism and Handicrafts has stated that "One goal of the festival is to promote the image of a peaceful country. We want to show that we have no ethnic problems"' (Newbery, 2004: 54). Such overt national politicisation is relatively rare.

Festivals have also been political struggles when they are controversial, with issues such as the operation and control of events, perceptions of public nuisance and environmental degradation, and the apparent incursions of outsiders into quiet communities. They have engendered strong criticism and opposition from local residents: 'The reflexes of most areas unfamiliar with festivals in the locality are those of anxious vigilance, easily precipitating into repression – sometimes a festival is stopped early, banned beforehand, or told that it can go elsewhere next year' (Clarke, 1982: 3). Resistance is probably greater than for other forms of cultural tourism such as literature, film or heritage tourism, in part because music has always triggered moral panic. This has proved especially (almost exclusively) so for pop festivals, notably in relatively remote and affluent rural areas, such as Glastonbury and the Isle of Wight and, more recently, at sites of rave concerts. In the Isle of Wight the local Conservative Member of Parliament brought in an Isle of Wight Act to ensure 'that no such massive happenings would ever disturb the geriatric charms of the Island again' (Hinton, 1995: 94). Fixed sites, however, have been relatively immune to opposition. The history of controversial music festivals is extensive, from the avant-garde Beaulieu Jazz Festival in England during the 1950s (which was eventually disbanded after crowd dissent to overpolicing), to counter-cultural gatherings in the 1960s and techno dance parties in the 1990s in the UK and Australia, frequently closed down because of noise complaints, concerns over illicit drug consumption or 'public nuisance'. Festivals tend to generate more opposition because their congestion and noise impacts are greater than those of particular concerts, even in open-air venues (Chase & Healey, 1995).

For festivals the form of music matters: classical music festivals might have just as detrimental an impact on surrounding noise levels (at least when measured in decibels), local parking and traffic congestion, but rarely elicit the same kind of responses as youth rock festivals or techno dance parties. This reflects the wider privileging of, and discrimination against, certain social groups. A politics of 'music as noise' (Attali, 1985) is articulated in relation to festivals; certain genres, particularly those enjoyed by young people, are portrayed as 'not real music' or simply 'noise', unwelcome sounds to ears alienated by the particular style. In Britain in the 1990s, in response to outrage over the consumption of ecstasy at rave parties – involving techno, trance and house music – the Conservative Government enacted the 1994 *Criminal Justice and Public Order Act* which made the convergence in public space of large numbers of people and lengthy broadcasts of music with repetitive beats punishable offences (Wright, 1993; Sibley, 1994; Gilbert, 1997; Martin, 1998). In Australia, regulatory mechanisms such as noise restrictions, codes of practice for dance parties, environmental protection legislation, fire and safety laws, and alcohol licensing regulations have been used to shut down clubs and turn off disruptive styles (and volumes) of music (Homan, 1998; 2003). Central to invariably negative reactions of local residents to rock, techno, metal or hip-hop concerts are moral panics where residents fear drugs, sexual promiscuity and other dimensions (such as racism in the case of events that took place at the Notting Hill Carnival, for example, which has often been prematurely shut down by police), rather than simply oppose the music.

In these cases, residents react to the music, but also to festival-goers as visitors and tourists, in much the same way that other types of tourism elicit resistance, particularly those involving large influxes of people from very different cultural backgrounds from the locals, as in Glastonbury or Ibiza. Such perceptions might be based on genuine concerns for local social and environmental issues, as was patently the case at the Altamont festival in the United States in the 1960s, where violence culminated in the murder of a black audience member by a Hells Angels gang which had been hired as security, and the Woodstock revival festival in 1999, also marred by violence. Opposition may relate to the fear of outsiders and cultural intermixing, implicit racism and a belief in generalised representations of young people as 'deviant' and in need of state-sponsored surveillance and control (Clarke, 1982; Sibley, 1994; McKay, 1996; Homan, 2003). Moral panics encourage overt policing, increased security measures and arrests, but also encourage participants to 'act up' in a resistant manner (Thornton, 1995), authenticating an event, in the eyes of participants, as subversive.

In the search for distinct sites and venues, tensions arise between festival participants and local residents. The 'original' rave spaces of the late 1980s and early 1990s usually relied on, and transformed, locations associated with purposes other than musical performance (Thornton,

1995). Early raves took place in rural locations, challenging familiar urban–rural disjunctures and destabilising 'the perceived axis between urban location and authenticity' (Gilbert & Pearson, 1999: 23), before later returning to the anonymity of the cities. Beyond the music itself, techno festivals were not without their own environmental controversies. Part of the ethos of dance parties was that they constituted alternative spaces for music, distant from pubs, alcohol and the more masculine rock scenes of urban areas. Often, such events were connected to political agendas, intended to increase environmental awareness, or to promote radical campaigns – hence the importance of staging them in rural environments. Yet unintentionally, many threatened the nature that they sought to celebrate. Some festivals have been notorious for the environmental damage wrought by large numbers of people living, dancing and performing in a tiny area for several days. Others, like Roskilde, have a long-established environmental group organising to reduce consumption and enable conservation. Yet even the most successful festivals (in terms of environmental management), such as Roskilde and Aspen, can never avoid traffic congestion, local frustration and tension. Even the remarkable Festival of the Desert in Mali cannot grow much further because of the limited ability of boats to transport vehicles across the Niger river, and that there are only three water holes for watering camels (Newbery, 2004: 59). How all this is managed and the specific gains within particular places is crucial to longevity and wider success. This is particularly evident in small places, such as Byron Bay, Australia.

Music Tourism and the Environment: Byron Bay, Australia

From Ibiza to Byron Bay, festivals and free techno parties have been linked to environmental degradation, a simple consequence of the numbers attending and their immediate impacts on delicate ecosystems. Yet, as one participant from Byron Bay observed in 1999, it is possible to mitigate such impacts through careful planning:

> It's a huge scene, there's a big forest techno scene here, we do a lot of outdoor parties up in state forests. It is sort of an ethical quandary, in terms of the effect on wildlife, but the effects it's having on humans is pretty damn good! If people are out in the bush, they're getting turned on, they're dosed, they're dancing to the music all night. It's like the oldest religion on the block, for a start. It's what tribal peoples always did, was to get high and dance all night in the forest, and inevitably you have some kind of awareness of your place in that forest. Even if people are a bit heavy footed that day, but they get

blown out and the next time they're a lot less so, and over time they realise the environment's this major, important thing, you know ... The critters will cope with it; doofs [dance parties] are usually held in old logging dumps anyway, spaces that have already been trashed, we don't go in the national parks ... state forests just about always, or private property. (Interview, 1999)

Environmental impacts are linked to the scale of tourism and the capacity of communities to support festivals with appropriate infrastructure. Festivals have been a means through which Byron Bay's identity as cultural mecca and 'alternative' tourist destination in Australia has been created, yet it has paradoxically brought intense commercial pressures to bear on the town (Derrett, 2003). Festivals began with the decision of the National Union of Students (NUS) to host the 1973 Aquarius Festival, a major 'alternative lifestyles' event, at nearby Nimbin. Because of its spectacular surrounding landscapes and physical structures, previously used by the declining dairy industry, Nimbin became a haven for city-dwellers seeking rural refuge; many participants in the Aquarius Festival stayed on, establishing communes and influencing the economic and cultural life of the region (Hannan, 2000; 2003). The trend toward 'dropping out' from large cities brought people in search of 'alternative' lifestyles: permaculture enthusiasts, surfing subcultures, artists, musicians and large numbers of itinerant unemployed young people. Festivals and more regular musical nights (such as full moon parties held in dance halls) provided relatively spontaneous counter-cultural activities for 'drop-outs' from urban areas and growing tourist numbers.

The establishment of key live venues, and new festivals throughout the 1980s, solidified Byron Bay's reputation as a place to experience music, particularly as part of a tourist experience. Two major holiday periods – the January summer break and Easter long weekend – featured major 'alternative' festivals that set it apart from the many family-orientated holiday destinations along Australia's east coast. Byron Bay quickly became the most important coastal destination for students from capital cities, offering good beaches and reliable surf breaks for daytime activities, and numerous pubs, clubs and parties at night: a 'nocturnal economy' that added significantly to the town's already hip reputation. Australian travel companies that specialised in package coach tours of Australia for foreign backpackers, such as the Oz Experience, all scheduled a few days' stop in Byron Bay, billed as a centre of surfing and nightlife. Musicians themselves saw the town as a convenient location to break up busy touring schedules, with well-known national and international bands and artists (including Paul Kelly, Bob Dylan and Ben Harper) choosing to perform there and take time out mid-tour. Professional recording studios were established nearby during the 1990s, encouraging artists to choose Byron Bay as a suitable location for extended stays while working on new material: an antipodean version of the holiday/recording session template established at Montserrat and other Caribbean islands during the 1980s. Festivals and tourism thereby enabled spill-over benefits for music production, establishing an infrastructure that could be used by musicians seeking professional quality recordings and taking advantage of reduced rates in 'downtime', when major artists had finished.

A string of festivals have become major tourist drawcards in Byron Bay and the wider region, including the Homebake Rock Festival, Northern Rivers Folk Festival, the Byron Bay Arts and Music Festival, Nimbin's Mardi Grass festival (a pro-drug legalisation event), the Chincogan Festival, Splendour in the Grass and the Byron Bay East Coast Blues and Roots Festival. The last one, in particular, has become an internationally renowned event every Easter, attracting 60,000 visitors and generating A$40 million (US$28 million) of tourist expenditure in 2001 (Gregory, 2002). The annual East Coast Blues and Roots Festival capitalises on the town's reputation and 'alternative' ethos, positioning itself as 'earthy', in contrast to mass commercialised pop and rock festivals.

Major influxes of festival tourists into a shire of only 30,000 full-time residents placed intense pressure on urban infrastructure, including road congestion (with squabbles over the introduction of parking meters), and sewage, which occasionally overflowed when festivals coincided with rainy spells, pouring raw outfall through residents' backyards (Gibson & Connell, 2003). By 2003 the festival required 160 portaloos alongside several permanent toilets at the key site. Intense debates have followed over how to manage peak tourist periods when the town's population is effectively magnified sixfold. This complex problem is not solely related to festivals, but is caught up in a wider debate about the nature of urban and coastal development, and clashes between its increasing popularity as a counter-urban migrant and tourist destination and images of a small rural 'alternative' retreat. The small urban population (which residents defend as crucial to the intimate, 'special' nature of the locality) has made it difficult for the Byron Shire Council to raise adequate taxation revenue to upgrade the infrastructure to cope with tourism. Through the emergence of a cultural economy based on festival and special-event tourism, Byron Bay has experienced tensions between the images of 'alternative' lifestyles, rurality and distance from the excesses of urban capitalism (that explain why people move there, even if only to establish weekend 'get-away' holiday homes), and its own popularity. Byron Shire's mayor, Tom Wilson, has noted:

> We have a population of 30,000 people and 12,000 rateable properties are paying to maintain the shire and the effect of the 1.65 million

visitors. There is not direct or indirect cash flow from tourism back to council, which has to deliver the infrastructure and services. . . . Tourism is an extractive industry. Everyone thinks it is a benign, beautiful delivery from heaven. Visitors fly in from around the world, they enjoy our lifestyle, they spend their money and they go home. But when you cease to be a community and become a commodity, small towns like Byron Bay lose their essence. We don't want that to happen. (Quoted in Gregory, 2002: 47)

In recent years, such concerns have been magnified: house prices in Byron Bay have grown dramatically, putting the original residents, students, the unemployed and fringe artists under pressure from rising rents. Byron Bay's identity has been transformed by tourism, and festivals have played a major part of this. The politics of music festivals are thus broader again than the music or the moral panics surrounding the events themselves; festivals are bound up in local cultures, economies and environments, contributing to the reputation of the locations, potentially attracting many more tourists off-season. While for most places rapid rates of tourism growth may be seen as a boon for the local economy, the benefits may be offset by other problems, particularly in small places where aesthetics and the ethos of residents are threatened. Indeed, at almost every site of internationally renowned festivals, from Glastonbury to Woodstock, and especially in relatively affluent rural areas, there has been diverse opposition to their presence.

Festivals and Identities: Carnival, Inversion and Regulation

Festivals have powerful symbolic dimensions, which partly explain some local opposition. They represent social practices, constituted within cultural, economic and political actions and networks: 'Festivals are cultural artefacts which are not simply bought and "consumed" but which are also accorded meaning through their active incorporation into people's lives' (Waterman, 1998a: 56; see Jackson, 1993). Festivals are a conduit for the construction of individual and collective identities – a field of meaning shaped and contested by those participating (or objecting to and avoiding them), and by those portraying festivals in the mass media and elsewhere (Saleh & Ryan, 1993: 290; Jeong & Santos, 2004). For participants, the actual meaning of participation, and the pleasure gained from this, may be the most significant dimension of festivals, although this may mean little to promoters, with more narrow concerns of logistics and profit margins.

Contemporary festivals, even in a seemingly more commercial era, are argued to be about personal experiences. According to Briand Sansom, coordinator of Australia's National Country Music Muster, held in Gympie, Queensland, 'I think that the resurgence of popularity of festivals is all about our lifestyle. People are living under a lot more pressure nowadays, and they're looking for different, stress-free forms of recreation. This kind of festival is all about fulfilling fantasies' (quoted in Williams, 2002: 44). Intense experiences linking participants are argued to have been most prevalent in the 1960s – hence in some part nostalgia for that era. For counter-cultural generations of the 1960s,

> rock music came during this period to occupy a pre-eminent position as a common denominator of youth culture: while the highly committed among the revolutionaries and the communes might argue about life-style, politics, commitment and what was relevant, music was there to celebrate common areas of values: anti-authoritarianism, sexual relationships without marriage, drug consumption, togetherness. The pop festival became the venue at which these values and feelings could be celebrated *en masse* with the minimum of interference from straight society. (Clarke, 1982: 26)

As one organiser of the Woodstock Festival observed:

> It was about music and freedom. Music was the medium; freedom was the message. For me the Festival was about free choice . . . values that had been obscured by the rush of the industrial and technological revolutions. [In America] 1969 was the cusp of all the freedom movements of the last part of this millennium. And Woodstock lives on as the call for self-realization on every level for everyone. (Tiber, 1994: 267)

In Britain, the Glastonbury Festival, staged annually on a rural dairy farm property, epitomised such feelings in the early years. First staged in 1970, when 2000 people turned up to see T-Rex perform, the festival has grown to its current three-day format, with crowds of over 100,000 seeing more than 500 bands and solo artists; it 'has come a long way from the days when Marc Bolan played to fewer than one thousand people out in a field next to a farmhouse with free milk being ladled out by the dairy'. At one festival in the 1990s, BBC recordings reached an audience of over 500 million people in over 45 countries, including China (Bianchi & Gusoff, 1996: 46). Despite such global reach, Glastonbury is still considered a festival where 'alternative' identities are formed and played out. As one journalist suggested, 'instead of going to university, people should go to Glastonbury. Consider Glastonbury as a holiday from all normal experience: it has grass, trees, flowers, cows, it's a lovely drive no matter where you come from, and when you get there you can skip around in the garb of a hippy like a demented earth sprite. Glastonbury is a pocket in time where anything can happen. It often feels like a medieval bartering town' (Bussmann, 1998: 16). Indeed Glastonbury has particular iconic significance in mediaeval myths and legends of ley lines, King Arthur and Camelot, and is the centre of the New Age movement in Britain (Riches, 2003).

Yet by the late 1990s, such authenticity was seen as under threat from overt commodification. For one reviewer, 'the gatherings of the nineties are far removed from the laid-back smaller-scale festivals of the late sixties and early seventies. Today's festivals . . . seem to be more about making money, flogging products and squeezing in punters than peace, love and harmony' (Jones, 1998: 2). One company, Mean Fiddler, has become the largest festival promoter in the United Kingdom, with an annual turnover of £30 million (US$60 million), staging the Reading, Phoenix and Fleadh Festivals, as well as operating live venues. One ex-organiser likened Glastonbury to a motorway service station: 'You drive in, consume, leave your litter and drive off. It's become a sort of financial juggernaut – Thatcherism on acid' (quoted in Jones, 1998: 2). Critics, lamenting its loss of authenticity, were alarmed not just by its increasingly commercial nature, but by its routine structure from year to year. Predictability compounded fears of 'selling out', with an emerging view that even the 'alternative' identities performed at Glastonbury had become normative, repetitious and, ultimately, mundane.

With tickets priced at over £80 (US$160, plus booking fees), television coverage and National Express bus services organised to transport revellers from over 30 cities around the UK, Glastonbury became as much a tourist event as an 'alternative' gathering. However, organisers have been quick to defend its intent and sentiment, pointing to £600,000 (US$1.2 million) donated to charities such as Oxfam and Greenpeace; the value for money (given that 500 artists perform) and low-key sponsorship (in contrast to many other festivals, where all aspects are commercialised, including the names of the festivals themselves, such as the Guinness Fleadh in London and the Virgin Cola-sponsored V98 festivals). The longevity of the Glastonbury festival, along with its institutionalisation as a tourist destination and acceptance by the wider British public, resulted in some degree of compromise and balance between alternate scenes, tourism and commerce.

More symbolically and dramatically, certain music festivals became stages for the performance of the identities of 'sonic terrorist': symbolic, non-violent resistance through sound. Wally Hope, original organiser of the Stonehenge Free Festival in the 1970s, argued that 'our temple is sound, we fight our battles with music, drums like thunder, cymbals like lightning, banks of electronic equipment like nuclear missiles of sound. We have guitars instead of tommy-guns' (quoted in McKay, 1996: 8). Similar notions took raves beyond the immediate control of local authorities, emphasising their transgressive nature and suggesting parallels with anarchist concepts of the temporary autonomous zone, and its transitory potential for dynamic liberation in the face of commercial culture (Bey, 1991). In Blackburn, England, dance parties surrounding the acid-house music scene, inspired by New York loft parties, almost all held illegally in empty warehouses and linked to the consumption of illicit drugs (predominantly ecstasy and speed), provided a sense of release, emanating from the collective – almost conspiratorial – use of space, with venues kept secret until the last moment, mainly to avoid the police (Ingham *et al.*, 1999; Ingham, 1999). Actually, getting to the venues and evading detection became central to the experience. In London, 'The derelict locations – warehouses, car parks, railway arches – with their dusty floors and industrial ambience, offer only crumbling walls, a loud sound system, and the potential for anything to happen; unpredictable and unrestrained, the parties are imbued with the thrill of their dubious legality' (Lewin, 1997: 90). As dance parties and techno festivals became increasingly normative, music provided opportunities for conspicuous consumption and brand recognition, necessitating the latest street or urban fashions, footwear, mobile phones and accessories, including drugs.

Festivals were particularly closely linked to ever-fluctuating fashion trends, house music magazines devoted many pages to clothing and footwear, while similar clothing styles – and drugs – occasionally created moral panic (Verhagen *et al.*, 2000; Gilbert, 1997). Techno festivals were further distinguished through the particular languages they created, to differentiate subtly a panorama of musical subgenres that had global resonance and which were impenetrable to those outside these scenes (Connell & Gibson, 2003: 206). Participants in electronic dance music festivals have been perceived as 'neo-tribes' – loosely organised small groups, temporarily but intensely identified with particular styles and attitudes (Maffesoli, 1988; Halfacree & Kitchin, 1996; Malbon, 1999; Gibson, 1999; Bennett, 2000), where opposition from mainstream culture heightened the sense of collective unity and exclusivity.

Although dance music became commodified, threatening the 'underground', community nature of festivals (Weber, 1999), it was used to give new and sometimes radical meanings to otherwise apolitical spaces (McKay, 1996). Techno music underpinned *Reclaim the Streets* events in cities from Stockholm to Bogota, Tokyo to Toronto (Luckman, 2001), where thousands gathered at strategic locations to 'reclaim' major intersections and disrupt city traffic, converting streets into dance venues, with quickly erected public address systems, road-blocks and a range of distractions (including fun fairs, informal market activities and political stalls). Such urban events and impromptu festivals protested against the increasing privatisation of public space and challenged the dominance of cars in urban transport and planning (Connell & Gibson, 2003:

206–207). In other contexts, festivals are oppositional. Dance parties are particularly important among gay men, acting as a means of expressing group identity, meeting partners and, in the 1980s especially, 'permitting expression of psychological coping with the HIV epidemic' (Lewis & Ross, 1995: 42). Dance parties in Sydney, notably the Sleaze Ball, and events that form part of the annual Gay and Lesbian Mardi Gras, were prototypes of subsequent house-party scenes in acceptance of diverse sexualities and as one form of differentiation from mainstream society.

Festivals and carnivals thus challenged the existing order. Sydney's Mardi Gras, the single largest economic contribution of tourism to the city, inverts the sexual order and exemplifies how sexuality is not always distinct from constructions of economic identities. The Mardi Gras, an annual month-long festival of events culminating in a march (attended by between 750,000 and one million visitors), is a key event through which Sydney's gay and lesbian movement demonstrates its presence in the city, alongside marchers and floats from other parts of Australia and beyond. Such gay pride marches (where music has a more muted role compared with spectacle) challenged the heterosexual order of the city, in a manner that combined the political and the carnival. The economic and cultural dimensions of the Mardi Gras, particularly its contribution to tourism and to Sydney's international reputation as a city of culture, are mobilised in arguments against intolerance and homophobia.

Excluded and minority groups, such as Cape Coloured of Cape Town and Aborigines in Australia, have commonly established distinctive festivals to promote their own sense of identity, and many such festivals stand apart from commercial concerns. A network of women's festivals has evolved, primarily in North America, from the 1970s women's movement and from lesbian feminism that sought to establish women's only spaces and genres that might nurture women's creativity and community. Festivals like the Michigan Womyn's Music festival were attended primarily by lesbians, while the three-year Lilith Fair, founded by Sarah McLachlan in the 1990s, offered a more inclusive version. Many participants at core festivals identified as separatists and 'womyn', out of impatience with male hegemony, and Michigan attracted as many as 10,000 participants. Despite occasional conflicts over racism, the presence of male children and transgender persons, festivals enabled women to meet partners, make commitments to them, perform 'rituals of solace and celebration' and, above all, temporarily create women-only spaces (Morris, 1999; Cvetkovich & Wahng, 2001). The creation of a sexual public culture, and a defined and gendered space, was often at least as important as the music.

There are parallels here in the ability of Afro-Caribbean carnivals to create a space beyond the reach of racism, yet which simultaneously expresses 'both alliance and enmity, both consensus and conflict' (Cohen,

1982: 37), where black music has the power 'to disperse and suspend the temporal and spatial order of the dominant culture' (Gilroy, 1987: 210). As in gay parades, such carnivals constitute a 'hybrid site for the ritual negotiation of cultural and practice' (Nurse, 1999: 661) throughout a web-like diaspora of locations where West Indian communities reside. Social practices and trends in the 'original' locations of carnival, such as Trinidad, both inform and are informed by what happens in other parts of the diaspora. Hence, carnivals of huge proportions now take place in Toronto (one million participants), New York (two million) and Notting Hill, London (2 million). Substantial carnivals are also held in 25 American and Canadian cities and more than 30 British ones, as well as in European centres such as Stockholm, Rotterdam and Nice. In such gatherings the usual social order is inverted through mimicry, derision, expressiveness, role reversals and satire, and the social relations of class, gender and ethnicity are confronted (Bakhtin, 1984; Nurse, 1999). Thus, it has been said that

> Carnival embraces an anticlassical esthetic that rejects formal harmony and unity in favor of the asymmetrical, the heterogeneous, the oxymoronic, the miscegenated. Carnival's 'grotesque realism' turns conventional esthetics on its head in order to locate a new kind of popular, convulsive, rebellious beauty, one that dares to reveal the grotesquerie of the powerful and the latent beauty of the 'vulgar'. In the carnival esthetic, everything is pregnant with its oppo-site, within an alternative logic of permanent contradiction and non-exclusive opposites that transgresses the monologic true-or-false thinking typical of a certain kind of positivist rationalism. (Shohat & Stam, 1994: 302)

Such inversions occur elsewhere, from Rio (Turner, 1983) and Toronto (Jackson, 1992) to Cuba (Daniel, 1996) and Pamplona (Ravenscroft & Matteuci, 2003). Even in Muslim areas of Xinjiang, China, religious (*mazar*) festivals are accompanied by more popular music and practices that are normally considered immoral, including taking lovers, smoking hashish and gambling (Harris & Dawut, 2002: 112). In every case the fact that such inversions and challenges to the established order are usually brief, present in marginal spaces and increasingly festive rather than overtly political, emphasises that they rarely substantially threaten that order. Carnivals are also highly codified, even normative – specific colours of attire for each day (as in Martinique), special meals and feasts or the organisation of musicians into highly disciplined bands.

In Cape Town the annual music festival, the Coon Carnival, was largely supported by members of the mixed-race Cape Coloured community, who specifically adopted the name 'coon' to publicly turn a reviled racial slur into a scathing parody. In the early years participants actually blacked up for performances and parades. However, the festival has yet to attract significant white interest and receives little publicity or public funding. In 2001 it was renamed the Minstrel Festival to gain wider appeal and lose the racist nuances that 'coon' implies outside a Cape Town context (Sommers, 2001). Other carnivals, often initiated as symbols of political dissent and celebrations of difference, have become increasingly commercialised. The Berlin Love Parade, for example, established in 1989 by an underground DJ, Dr Motte, when just 150 people took to the streets in affirmations of 'peace, love and friendship', now attracts a million participants from all over the world, and has become a major tourist attraction and income-generating event (Richard & Kruger, 1998; Borneman & Senders, 2000). It is, in fact, one of the largest regular mass events in Europe. While all carnivals, often initiated as symbols of political dissent and celebrations of difference, have become increasingly commercialised, in that commercialism lies some measure of what was initially transgression, becoming part of a transition from 'a temporary spectacle of inversion for a more permanent revolution in the social order' (Mitchell, 2000: 162).

At the same time that their 'subversive power is reabsorbed into dominant structures of power and ordered norms of culture' (Mitchell, 2002: 162), at festivals 'space is territorialised through the use of periodic repetitions that signal ownership to others' (Duffy, 2000: 55; see also Deleuze & Guattari, 1987). Over time such displays and appropriations of public space confer symbolic ownership of territory. Festivals may therefore be interpreted as 'manipulative mechanisms for neutralizing social conflict' which 'enable the politically marginal to express discontent through ritual, thereby restricting their revolutionary impulses to symbolic form' (Waterman, 1998a: 60), and also events where cultural diversity is defended through both economic and cultural means, in what some might perceive as a compromise to the original radical intent of the event (see also Cohen, 1982; Jackson, 1988).

It would be a mistake, though, to interpret the cultural politics of festivals and carnivals simply as a binary between normative and radical or transgressive readings. Such interpretations run the risk of falling into the 'trap of authenticity' discussed earlier, where an 'original' untainted cultural form is commodified and reified, and thus becomes an inauthentic, commercial imitation. The performance of tourist identities is far more subtle, and sometimes more complicated, than these binary readings suggest. More simply, 'the community music festival, then, can be seen as a means of promoting a community's identity, or at least how that community would like others to see it' (Duffy, 2000: 51–52), a dimension of music festivals that inevitably involves constructing a 'sense of place' (see also Waterman, 1998a). Duffy (2000: 59) argues that the relationship between place and the performance of identities is one of territorial possession, meaning both the use of the physical spaces of venues and more generally redefining places discursively through music. At the Top End Folk Festival in northern Australia, folk music's 'inclusivity is a means to create a space of belonging', made more significant by the sheer geographical distances that participants and performers travel each year in order to take part. Yet festivals are framed within the wider scales of identity construction and performance, including that of the local state and national cultural policies, which all influence the intended meanings of events, and regulate festival spaces and bodies. Hence,

> Festivals may be mono-ethnic or mono-art, or multi-ethnic or multi-art. The festival may be an expression of a community's sense of fun, or a statement about its existence and its norms. It might there-fore be a political statement, or be perceived as 'removed' from politics. But as a means of either regenerating or confirming an interest or culture, festivals can have significant political implica-tions. Within a Canadian context, the recognition of multiculturalism by government has generated an ethos where festivals are encour-aged as supporting a national ideology. (Saleh & Ryan, 1993: 289; see also Smith & Brett, 1998)

In Puerto Rico the establishment of a music festival was seen as crucial to the prestige of a colonial state, but the choice of music posed prob-lems since little local music was available (Lisker, 1993). In Australia, state-sponsored festivals like Yeperenye (Alice Springs) unite 14,000 Aborigines from across the country, collectively representing 45 language groups. In remote Arnhem Land in northern Australia, the Garma Festival, established by the indigenous band Yothu Yindi, similarly triumphs local culture and draws in both Aboriginal and non-indige-nous visitors (Gebicki, 2003). Such indigenous festivals are regarded as essential for preserving, maintaining and celebrating Aboriginal cultures, but also provide a means of expressing the social, economic and polit-ical issues that concern indigenous people. As one participant has pointed out: 'It's about our learning and healing and cultural expressions. In most mainstream festivals the artistic control is done by non-Aboriginal people and we slot in however they see the artistic side' (quoted in Albert, 2001: 15). Nonetheless, as one Aboriginal leader has observed, 'Having a festival is a fine thing but where are the structures to help sustain the culture and enable the rest of Australia to have some better insight?' (Patrick Dodson, quoted by Steketee, 2001: 5). Public support for festivals often underwrites important social and cultural imperatives.

The Caribana Festival, an annual Caribbean event in Toronto, exem-plified the extent to which state policies may frame the construction of cultural identities through Canada's official commitment to multicul-turalism. Multicultural policy 'defines the terms and sets the limits of the political potential of Caribana which its participants constantly threaten to transgress. Various territorial issues are central to the political and social geography of Caribana, including the routing (and rerouting) of the parade and the strategies of 'containment' used to police the parade and associated festivities' (Jackson, 1992: 13). The performance of tourist identities is thus mediated by different actors, and in social and physical spaces, from streetscape to live venue. The state, interested in promoting tourism and cultural diversity, but also establishing and policing ideological agendas, is a key actor. So too, wider images of gender and racial identity contribute to the 'containment' of cultural festivals and carnivals, particularly where black expressions might be articulated. In London,

> Through a gendered lens 'black' male participants in the festivals have been portrayed as 'dangerous' and 'criminal'. Female participants, on the other hand, are viewed as 'erotic' and 'promiscuous' ... these modes of representation have come in tandem with heightened surveillance mechanisms from the state and the police. In the case of London, the expenditure by the state on the policing of the festival is several times larger than the contribution to the staging of the festival. (Nurse, 1999: 676)

Racism and sexism cloud representations of carnivals in the wider public sphere, and these discourses mitigate the performance of identities for participants, even when, in the case of Notting Hill, there are fewer reports of violence than at the smaller (and much whiter) Glastonbury Festival (Nurse, 1999: 676). External discourses and actions mediate the identities staged by participants in carnivals.

In New Orleans, 'second line' street parades (which involve black bands and spontaneous crowd interaction) play a valuable role in strengthening the social fabric of inner-city black neighbourhoods, weakened by poverty, unemployment, violence, segregation and racism, as participants 'through the transformative experience of the parade ... *become owners of the streets*', creating 'alternative moral and aesthetic orders' (Regis, 1999: 478, 495; italics in original), though, of course, such participants only ever symbolically reclaimed the streets, which continued to be owned in a legal sense by others. However, such festivals are quite different from those staged for tourists; indeed, 'the minstrel-like appropriation of black cultural tradition by the city's elites and the tourism industry proceeds without any acknowledgment of the popular black street based tradition on which it is based' (Regis, 1999: 473). Tourists and most white residents have no idea what the popular second line tradition is about and those who perform in tourist marches hold back and conceal much of the second line's significance 'at the same time as they represent it to the world' (Regis, 1999: 475). The staged tourist spectacle is quite different from the black working-class parades just a few kilometres away.

Festivals and other cultural events may be staged to stimulate or create elements of national identity, especially in such nations as Mali, Papua New Guinea and Vanuatu where national identity was unknown before independence and nations have to be imagined, and may be performed, into existence. In Tokelau, a tiny group of atolls in the South Pacific, the *fatele* dance was expressly created to foster nationhood and, like other similar dances in the Pacific region, promotes identity, politics and tourism. At a wider scale, when such dances are performed at regional events, they nurture similar goals and enable the 'preservation of diverse identities within a multicultural world promoted by festivals and enjoyed by tourists' (Kaeppler, 1988: 138). Much earlier, by contrast, the 19th-century Salzburg Festival sought 'the denial of ambiguity and diversity in the interest of homogeneity and totality' to the extent that in the 1930s 'existing in the space of official culture, [it] passed into the service of Nazi ideology' (Steinberg, 1990: xiii, 223). In post-war Eastern Europe, folk festivals became common as new Communist governments sought to promote the ideology of a unified national 'folk' (Cooley, 1999: 35). Amateur Chinese street opera performances in Singapore, often in tourist locations, are a recently 'invented tradition' in the post-independence years as opera 'became an appropriate symbol for the cultural ideal of possessing a strong heritage in a rapidly modernising social space because it embodied the imagery of a rural, simple and rustic location' (Lee, 2002: 150). In each of these places, 'traditions' were freely invented to emphasise distinctiveness and continuity with a mythical past.

Despite diversity and creativity within festivals, many are retrospective and enshrine notions of authenticity more than do most other musical contexts. Cajun festivals in Louisiana 'represent what the media and tourist bureau messages have told Cajuns and their visitors about Cajun culture. . . . "Ethnic" tourists want to witness "authentic" ritual in order to participate as fully as possible in the culture they visit, and Cajun festivals are the closest thing there is to public ritual' (Esman, 1984: 460). In Eastern Europe festivals of folk music seek to incorporate the 'picture of it held by urbanites' to be successful (Cooley, 1999: 32). Festivals thus often seek to invert, preserve and invent – or celebrate – established social orders and imagined cultural spaces.

In certain contexts, festivals may be divisive. No musical festivals, if they can be so described, are more political than the sectarian religious marches of Northern Ireland. During the annual 'marching season', exclusively Protestant marchers and performers mark out the urban landscapes of Protestantism, in the guise of emphasising tradition and claiming freedom of movement, and challenge Catholic claims to space. Bands play the pipes and drums, defined as Protestant instruments, and sing songs and tunes of Protestant supremacy. Generally, marches avoid Catholic areas, but in towns such as Portadown, violence flared in the 1990s when parades deliberately passed through Catholic areas. Catholics either turn their backs on the parades, set up barricades against them or throw stones and other objects at the marchers. Here there is no inversion of order, but a deliberate and dramatic invoking of the history, religion and tradition of Protestant settlers.

Wagner Festivals have been held in the Bavarian town of Bayreuth for more than a hundred years, but have been controversial because of the association between Wagner and Nazism (and with German nationalism in a broader sense). 'Wagner's works – and by extension himself – were embraced as the symbol of Aryan might by the Nazis, and even today there is great debate among music lovers about the 'correctness of supporting Wagnerian music and the Wagner Festival in Bayreuth' (Schulte-Peevers *et al.*, 2000: 513). In Cincinnati, racial tensions that followed the police shootings of a black youth in 2001 and the inability of the conservative mayor to resolve tensions resulted in a coalition of clergymen and prominent members of the African-American community that called for a boycott of the city by conventions and high-profile performers. Bill Cosby cancelled a concert, and the jazz festival, held annually for more than 40 years, was cancelled after its promoter declared it untenable. However, the May Festival – the oldest continuing choral festival in the United States, established in 1873 – offered a series of concerts entitled 'Beethoven, Bernstein and Brotherhood', each with black composers represented on the programme, while the Cincinnati Opera contributed to redevelopment in the nearby black depressed neighbourhood of Over-the Rhine where the disturbances had begun. Performances continued and the number of concert-goers remained at high levels (Paller, 2002). Just as Cincinnati sought to include black composers, so Israeli festivals in the 1990s emphasised local music and banned Wagner, in an era when 'it is no longer politically correct to fly the flag of traditional European high culture at full mast' (Waterman, 1998b: 262). Music and festivals cannot escape the wider political landscape.

Beyond 'Fun'?

Festival-goers, like other music tourists, rarely make long journeys, sometimes at considerable cost and for extended times, without the anticipation of pleasure. Tourists participate in festivals for many reasons, including the desire to escape their normal environment, for relaxation, self-discovery and social interaction (Raybould *et al.*, 1999: 201), all but the last probably being self-evident. Remarkably, explanations for festival participation rarely emphasise the opportunity to hear good live music and great musicians. At the Woodford Folk Festival in Queensland, the three most important reasons for participation were 'entertainment', 'experience of an authentic performing arts festival' and 'a break from normal routine or environment'. In a more detailed sense, there were five groups of reasons: learning, family, social stimulation, authenticity and uniqueness, and escape. Authenticity and uniqueness were most sought by return visitors (Raybould *et al.*, 1999). Festival participation may also be rather more than this. Even after a few hours of the Day of Dance, some participants were enthusiastic enough to recognise that it had been no mere workshop but 'a total revelation' (Macaskill, 1999: 20), much like the experience of drummers in West Africa. Festival tourism that may last several days often enables a greater decree of involvement than it does in theatres and concert halls.

Folk festivals tend to 'offer many avenues for visitors to actively seek their cultural roots', so supposedly differentiating themselves from those at 'high-art events', with individuals participating 'to connect with their authentic cultural heritage and to fulfil perceived needs' (Raybould *et al.*, 1999: 204; Cameron, 1995) beyond the simply musical, that are linked to 'alternative lifestyles' (Lewis & Dowsey-Magog, 1993). The Woodford Folk Festival has sought 'to create a village atmosphere where a community of strangers would come together into a community of friends' (Cameron, 1995: 205). At the other end of the scale are some participants at the Aspen Festival: 'A lot of chic people have come to Aspen and built enormous trophy homes. And some of them attend concerts to be seen' (Peters, 2002: 38). Similarly, at the Casals Festival in Puerto Rico, participants

> wear formal, elegant even sumptuous attire. Many look as if they'd spent many hours grooming themselves for the ceremonials. It does not have the air of a typical concert-going crowd; a great many people give the impression that they are here only because they feel it's important that they be seen attending the opening night of the Casals Festival. The prevailing attendance is middle-aged and right-eously middle class. One searches in vain for identifiably artistic types; they have either dressed the part or stayed away. (Lisker, 1993)

However, as at the Kfar Blum kibbutz (Israel), the travel of affluent elites to a chamber music festival made the kibbutz 'a place of cultural pilgrimage in the summer, with many of the characteristics of pilgrimage, such as release from mundane structure, homogenization of status, *communitas*, movement from a mundane centre to a sacred periphery and reflection of the meaning of cultural values' (Waterman, 1998b: 260). Pilgrimage might seem more evident at places like Glastonbury, through its history and the perceptions of participants, yet elements of pilgrimage – seasonality, ritual performance, attire, sense of release and commonality of purpose – may be ubiquitous. Medieval pilgrimages, with their musical accompaniments, might even have been the avatars of (music) tourism.

Festivals obviously provide places where fans of particular styles and performers can get together, meet and perhaps get to know each other, and purchase relevant merchandise. One American visitor who had witnessed English folk-song performer Richard Thompson's performance at the Cropredy Festival, stated on a website for fans that the festival provided 'an alternative universe of mud, mead and music'. Another observed:

> I met lots of RT listees, some for the first time, and several renewed acquaintances. The Dutch contingent were there in force . . . a top bunch of blokes. Australia was represented by Sarah Durant and also by Jon Penhallow. I chatted with the venerable Pam, met Bill and Irene Henry who were on the Festival Tour, and also spent a pleasant afternoon with Jesse Hochstadt from America. Of course there were plenty of UK listees. (www.rtlist.net/2leftfeet/index)

In this way festivals turn virtual communities briefly into real communities and are an 'alternative universe' for true fans, many of whom, like Phish fans, delight in recording how they heard unique versions of particular songs or new songs for the first time. Others, less enamoured of a sole performer, participate for the ambience and experience, or are simply absorbed in the music; as the *Sydney Morning Herald*'s music critic, Bruce Elder, has observed of WOMADelaide, the World Music Festival: 'Lying on the grass in Adelaide's beautiful Botanic Park, surrounded by huge and ancient fig trees and listening to great music is as close to heaven as we can hope for in this lifetime.'

At Cropredy the annual finale is the Fairport Convention classic 'Meet on the Ledge'. As one participant observed:

> After almost ten years of attending you'd think it would not affect me by now, but once again the site of 20,000 people linking arms and swaying while singing the traditional good-bye until meeting up in another twelve months brings a lump to my throat and a hint of a tear appears at the corner of my eye. It may have been cold mostly wet and dreary but once again Cropredy Festival waved its magic wand and made for a wonderful weekend, my last one as a single man. Cropredy has had a permanent affect [*sic*] on my life. This is where I met my future bride Laura three festivals ago. We marry next year and will return for our first Cropredy festival as a married couple. (www.faircrop.co.uk/crop2001)

Fans who develop their own websites, or are on particular fanbases, may be atypical, yet their experiences are widely shared, even more so when festivals seek to create a particular ambience (as do folk festivals).

Lesbian music festivals are part of this, evident in the statements from women at festivals in the 1980s and 1990s. One recalled: 'Like all women's gatherings, Rhythmfest is like an electrical charge for me, rejuvenates me so that I may again go out into the hetero world and remain sane.' For another: 'The opportunity to openly express my lesbian sexuality with other lesbians is so rare that I cherish every minute I spend in such an environment. The sense of belonging, the sense of being part of a much greater whole both touches and nourishes my spirit' (quoted in Morris 1999: 337–338). Most festival websites generate perceptions along the straightforward lines of one from Port Fairy: 'A fantastic weekend of great music, memories and the chance to chill and think about the important things in life.' Less obviously, the same festival was considered 'a magical time. The event came to a very sad end for me when I learned of the passing of my father, but I know he was happy I was there enjoying the joyful spirit of your festival' (www.portfairyfolkfestival.com/guestbook. cfm). Somewhat similarly, one participant at the Parkes Elvis Revival Festival said 'I wanted to come for years but my Dad, whose birthday was the same day as Elvis's, was ill for a number of years, so I did not come. But my Dad has passed on and is up with Elvis in heaven singing along. This is my first year and it's been fabulous'. Such testimonies indicate the manner in which festivals transcend daily life.

Critics might suggest that notions of community, cultural meaning and shared performance of identities at festivals are simply overblown and that, more materially, festivals are overtly commercial touristic events that consistently promise, but may often disappoint, to deliver a sense of community and identity. For one critic,

> Rock festivals are predicated on idyllic notions. They foster the idea that there is such a thing as a rock community, a 'we', a counter-culture, whose members periodically gather together in a field to show their strength in numbers. They represent a slight, ecologically friendly return to a halcyon age before the poisonous sprawl of the city stamped out the peasantry of Merrie England. ... The suggestion is that England was a happy land of tie-dye, lentil stews and jugglers before the horrors of the machine age. Bullshit. Rock festivals are actively the reverse of all this. Counterculture? A generation ago there was cynicism about that phrase. Today's hard-bitten adolescents are no more aware of the phrase counterculture than they are familiar with the details of the Profumo affair. 'We' has given way to 'I'. I wanna get stoned, pissed, shagged, up the front, out of the house for the weekend. Holding hands and forming a human daisy chain of peace, love and understanding is about as high on the list of priorities of today's fest-goer as remembering to pack a cummerbund. If this spirit of hippy brotherhood ever existed, it probably died after punk. (Stubbs, 1998: 12)

Such extreme appraisals, directed at events such as Glastonbury, are probably unfair to a good many festivals that might well enable performances of subaltern, subversive or inclusive identities, although this perspective demonstrates how culture, commerce, ideology and history are indelibly intertwined. The 'authenticity' and cultural meaning of festivals is always contested and negotiated. In the end the issue that Sampath has raised in Trinidad – 'the continuous question for Trinidadians is whether a "tourist carnival" evolves an escape from, or an immersion into, a localized culture' (1997: 168) – is universal. Equally important is the manner in which attendance goes beyond transitory pleasure.

All the World's a Stage

Festivals are the most common form of music tourism and encapsulate many of the themes discussed throughout this book, from the growing commercialism of music tourism to the interpretations of its economic dimensions, and the more subtle, problematic and contested politics of identity and performativity. Festivals have become pervasive, events where complex economic, cultural, social, political and environmental threads come together for a limited time. They emphasise how societies create spaces for expression, subversion and leisure, and how moral, regulatory and political tensions permeate social life. They may focus on shared symbols, invent traditions and, however temporarily, invert, challenge or emphasise the social and political order; they may merely be an excuse for recreation and money-making. They represent both community and commodity, and a space for the enjoyment of music. While festivals may have become mimetic of wider social relations, their capacity to change them is limited:

> Festivals, however much moral and practical opposition they engender, are a temporary indulgence, a few days recreation for the festival-goers, whereas the plight of the poor in the inner cities is an enduring condition, a way of life. Pop festivals will pass, even if they may return next summer; hence the costs of seeking to eliminate the nuisance they may cause, or be feared to cause, may outweigh the advantage. And so festivals continue. The price of remedy for the inner cities, however, is very high – their problems have been long recognized by governments, but the extent of reforms necessary to achieve real change was too great to be acceptable to governments. (Clarke, 1982: xi)

Festivals are much more than just the music or the local community; they are now deeply embedded in urban and regional tourism strategies. In some cases (as in Austria) they are central to national tourism campaigns; in many small towns they have become key components of local development, directly and through their impact on image, but they cannot succeed everywhere. And, paradoxically, festivals may create a powerful sense of place, but one that appeals to a global culture to attract both participants and audiences (Zukin, 1991). That paradox was evident in Brittany where the large regional Festival Interceltique was mainly ignored by local people who preferred French and American records, radio and television and felt that the festival was too remote from everyday life (Chapman, 1992). The paradox was also evident in the Hebridean islands of Scotland where Celtic music was marketed as part of 'mainstream' popular culture to appeal to local youth (Symon, 2002). Links between place, music and commerce are complex.

Like other forms of music tourism, festivals have changed over time. Some have been successful enough to have strengthened their 'purity' and creativity; others have embraced professionalism to ensure profitability, even at the loss of community ties. Most have evolved quickly through particular organisational life-cycles: origin, informal organisation, the emergence of leadership, formal organisation and professionalism. While such an evolution has often followed the desire for market access, it has invariably been challenged by regular festival-goers or local residents as a threat to the character, spontaneity and local ties of the festival (e.g. Raybould *et al.*, 1999: 211; Waterman, 1998b; Clark, 2000). Bluntly put in the context of national festivals in one part of the Pacific: 'How can the music industry help Papua New Guinea and still make money?' (Neuenfeldt, 1998: 334). Given the need for subsidy and sponsorship, such questions are frequently resolved in terms of the latter. Every festival changes over time, as at Tamworth, where there are now various Elvis impersonators, and 'regulars complain that the festival has become over-sophisticated and taken over by the "chardonnay set": yuppies from city centres' (Cox, 2003: 43). Changes invariably mean that some former or potential future participants will look elsewhere.

The continuity of festivals has also been threatened in part because of competition from growing numbers, but also because of unrealistic prices and wage demands. Festivals in Britain, such as the Phoenix Festival in Oxfordshire, have been cancelled through lack of support and 'excessive' demands from bands; fans have tended to go to those with reasonable prices and adequate facilities. Even so, Glastonbury was reported to have been the only British festival to have made a profit in 1999 (Wheat, 2000: 24). In Jamaica a second reggae festival brought the collapse of the first, as the market could only sustain one, despite attempts to diversify into hip-hop (Nurse, 2002: 138–141). In most places there are conflicts between the desire for place promotion and income gener-ation, and artistic independence and creativity, and even the nature of that creativity (Waterman, 1998a). Festivals, like other tourist attractions, evidence elements of a product life-cycle, rarely sustaining both commercial viability and critical acclaim. Proliferation and diversity have been a means to overcome this problem and, more importantly, to illustrate the extent to which music tourism has become an increasingly common and more eclectic dimension of both travel promotion and place identities. It is, despite its various political interpretations and interventions, a form of travel, escape, temporary transgression or hedonism. It reflects and embodies the contradictions of wider society and sometimes allows for a negotiation of these, but ultimately music festivals, like most forms of tourism, are about the temporary release from the everyday, from the mundane: degrees of both pleasure and fulfilment.

Chapter 8
Conclusion: Final Notes

Cultural tourism rapidly expanded in the last decades of the 20th century, as art, literature, food, wine and music gained greater significance in shaping the evolving structures of niche markets. Central to this development was the resurrection of heritage and the recourse to history as tourism took a retrospective turn. Cultural tours have emerged, from ornithology or football to art and wine appreciation, and shorter holidays have involved particular themes, even the 'enhancement travel' of acquiring new skills, from cooking to photography. Tourism researchers have examined heritage at length, as cities and regions have sought to profit from the past, museums have multiplied, and place marketing has taken on cultural and creative dimensions. Tourism nevertheless remains inherently concerned with recreation and entertainment. For all the enhancement and education that can be a part of cultural tourism, pleasure – sometimes exclusively so – is central to holidays. Some facets of cultural tourism, and notably musical tourism, have largely escaped attention, despite their growing significance. This book has sought to redress this, exploring the consequences and impacts of music tourism, whether economically or socially, the manner in which cultural expressions accompany most tourist experiences, and the role of personal and place identity.

Despite its genesis in the Grand Tour, music tourism is largely a contemporary phenomenon, the outcome of new affluence and leisure time in the West, and in part of the nostalgia that has accompanied such affluence. The transition from virtual to real tourism has been belated and remains incomplete. World music continues to offer virtual travel and clubs such as Hemmesphere (Sydney) continue to offer instant musical experiences that 'with the greatest and most unique music from around the globe, the tastiest cocktails on the planet, your journey will begin in Spain and we'll whisk you away to the summer of a lifetime' (www.petrolrecords.com). This book has attempted to provide a global overview of musical tourism, linking its cultural and economic dimensions, although there remain many lacunae in accounts of the relationship between music and tourism (especially outside the Anglophone world). Few detailed studies of its significance have sought to synthesise music tourism's diverse dimensions, from cultural symbolism to political economy. Where studies have been done, they have invariably focused on just one place, one dimension or one musical genre. Clearly, much remains to be done.

Music Tourism

In most contexts, music plays a role in tourism, if rarely a central one. With key exceptions, as when tourists hear the Ring Cycle in Bayreuth, travel Route 66, drum in Senegal, tour with the Grateful Dead or attend the Glastonbury Festival, music is simply an adjunct to tourism. Travellers will visit the Abbey Road crossing, Graceland, or Jim Morrison's and Edith Piaf's graves in Paris, or might expect to go to either a lavish show or an 'authentic' folk night in a pub during their holidays, but that will rarely be the key rationale for tourism. Rather, experience of musical sites will be part of a holiday which incorporates a diversity of themes.

Many destinations for music tourists stem from the past (or, as in the case of drumming, with intimations of a universal past). Tourist sites, such as those associated with Elvis Presley and Bob Marley, composers such as Mozart and Verdi, or even *The Sound of Music*, are linked to dead artists. That is unsurprising. Heritage has little to say about the living, but much to say about how the living relate to the dead, what they consider worth preserving and commemorating, and how they integrate past into present. Living artists tour themselves, and their status may rise or fall before their deaths. The dead usually only acquire status. Significantly some of the key music tourism sites – from the glitz of Graceland to the relative austerity of Morrison's grave – are those of performers who may be celebrated for their dramatic and untimely deaths (Cobain, Hendrix, Hutchence, Lennon and even Beethoven) as much as for their music.

Yet while nostalgia and memory may mark the music tourism of the baby-boom generation and the 'snowbirds', people who are now relatively wealthy and endowed with leisure time, music tourism is much more than the travels of 'golden oldies'. It is not only the baby-boomers who visit the Bob Marley Museum or cross Abbey Road. Equally, Mozart's music may be scarcely known to many Salzburg visitors, who tour for other reasons, but who take in classical music sites because they are there. Many such sites have acquired iconic status to become part of larger city-wide or national tours, rather than destinations only for those who were and are fans. Music tourism – as evident from Ibiza to the Phish Phans – is both part of contemporary youth culture, as well as an attraction for their elders, for whom sites and performances differ substantially.

At least for popular music, the decade that dominates music tourism is the 1960s, marked by the 'summer of love', the rise of the Beatles, Carnaby Street, the heyday of Elvis and the last years of the first country music boom. The 'swinging sixties' was also a period of rising affluence in the Western world, when leisure time expanded, consumption boomed and mobility increased, symbolised by the rise of 'car songs' and 'road songs' (Heining, 1998; Jarvis, 1985), and social controls were relaxed. Several decades after the 1960s, the music that accompanied those critical moments of adolescence became the memories that shaped tourism. The significance of adolescence may also explain why it is popular music that has played such a strong role in music tourism, rather than jazz or classical music, which are styles more likely to be appreciated in later life. (This might also partly explain why classical and jazz music tourists have greater spending power.) While books like *Rock 'n' Roll London* (Wooldridge, 2002) optimistically provide maps, such as that of Brixton that locates the former residences of Brian Ferry, David Bowie and Nick Cave, there is nothing to suggest that these have become regularly visited places. More recent stars such as the Spice Girls are barely mentioned, perhaps because they are seen as inauthentic, but certainly they have no sites linked to music tourism, or at least not yet. Whether popular music tourism proves to be primarily a phenomenon of a certain era remains to be seen.

Central to music tourism is a sense of place, even if (as in the *Sound of Music* tour or the Parkes Elvis Revival Festival) the nature of place is based on multiple fabrications: sites of creation, performance and death, where place had some apparent meaning for creative processes. Where performers are alive or too mobile, tourism is usually absent; there seems to be little market for a Rolling Stones tour in London, despite the Beatles walks. Conversely, where musicians appear to have been particularly inspired by place, as in the case of legendary guitarist Robert Johnson and the Delta Blues, there have been exhaustive attempts to trace his true place of origin and inspiration (Johnson, 1998). Only in part is this for commercial reasons, even though tiny towns like Wink (Texas), with a fading economy, have tried to maintain the significance of their link with Roy Orbison, through museums, statues or festivals.

Most tourist guidebooks now feature sections dedicated to various types of musical performances to be found in places and, increasingly, specialist guidebooks have been devoted to music tourism, although mostly exclusive to North America and the United Kingdom. A minority of these, notably Edward Lee's *Musical London* (1995), have focused exclusively on classical music; the vast majority of specialist guidebooks have covered contemporary popular music and few, if any, have discussed jazz or pre-war musical contexts. All of them, through their many maps, seek to attach a spatial authenticity to musical heritage and convey some loose sense of environmental determinism: how the place – its culture, scenery, economic conditions and performance spaces – had a direct influence on the music produced there.

Music tourists and the sites they visit are diverse; visitors to the great cities of Western Europe, where classical music was created and performed, are quite different from backpackers in places such as Goa and Byron Bay. While many tourists may be seeking some nostalgic experience, what this is varies substantially between elegant Austrian cities, 'back to nature' notions of purity that spawned West African drumming tours, or virtual travels to Ireland or Hawaii in an earlier age. Yet again, these are different from the evident hedonism of tourism in Ibiza.

No single definition of music tourist (let alone cultural tourist or simply tourist) is possible. Empirical studies of music tourism, few though there are, reveal a multiplicity of tourists at every site (as at both Abbey Road and the Bob Marley Museum, where tourists, from teenagers to retirees, come from all continents, and a diversity of rationales for the journey (in this case from mere pleasure or a way to pass a few spare moments, to a search for meaning bordering on a religious experience). Tourists see and experience particular sites differently and are both capable of challenging the intended order (as in the case of lesbian visitors to Dollywood or those who experience Graceland as kitsch rather than pilgrimage) and deriving very different forms of satisfaction (or lack of it) from the same experience.

Selling Place

Classical music tourism and festivals further demonstrate that music tourism is much more than mere memory and is becoming of greater economic significance. What were only recently simply the pleasures of a few, have become quickly commodified, as local and national authorities have identified music tourism as a ready means of stimulating income flows and revitalising moribund places. Houses are sold as the homes of musicians, and styles, past and present, and countries and regions are marketed – indeed invented – through the lyrics and symbols that music has created. The 'evocation strategies' of tourist promoters have thoroughly embraced the culture of music.

Festivals especially have eschewed associations between music and place to create new associations, such as that where Parkes created an Elvis Presley revival festival, or both the Seychelles and the North Yorkshire valley of Swaledale became temporary new homes for classical music. At festival and performance sites such as Cincinnati and New Orleans, just as at Graceland and Iweniar, music tourism has resulted in the contestation of the integrity of the site, its mode of representation and inclusiveness. The benefits are never evenly or equitably shared; nor can they be where local, regional and national interests conflict at and between every scale.

The extraordinary proliferation of festivals has demonstrated the lust for tourist income, but also the difficulty of sustaining festivals as competition mounts. There are limits to the potential for any form of tourism – and festivals – to support the economies of all those places that seek to benefit from them. Rivalry has become intense; Tupelo seeks to usurp Memphis as Branson and Bristol tried to depose Nashville. Moreover, only a few such iconic figures as Elvis Presley, Bob Marley or Mozart have engendered large-scale tourist industries. Most performers and composers have never created the same degree of enthusiasm or nostalgia, although the range of places where music and tourism converge, even at a small scale, is surprisingly long. While Parkes may have managed to succeed, against the odds, and Ayia Napa has challenged Ibiza, it may be the case that opportunities for new innovations are decreasing over time.

The Ring of Kerry Tourism Office may have convinced visitors that 'the remote and beautiful Ring of Kerry is an important destination for those wishing to hear Irish Traditional Music at its best' (www.ringof kerrytourism.com), but music tourists have still to reach Rochdale. Similarly, even careful efforts to link New Jersey and Bruce Springsteen in a 'Destination Asbury Park' campaign have borne little fruit. Some museums have closed and festivals have flopped, but the world of music and culture is one of whims and fashions, and rising costs. Despite perceptions that music may provide a panacea for industrial decline, only certain places have been able to gain in a substantial and sustained manner.

Musical Transformations

Tourism has transformed music wherever they have come together. Musical performances have been adapted to the limited gaze (and the limited ear) of tourists; many have been truncated, simplified and rendered less dissonant to alien ears. In various places what tourists watch and hear has minimal local significance, as when Australian Aborigines were encouraged to play and dance to 'touristic' Hawaiian music, rather than their own 'less harmonic and dramatic' forms of performance. Musical instruments, such as didjeridus in Bali and djembes in Australia, are now manufactured far beyond their cultural heartland. Yet while tourism has altered local musical traditions, it has just as often conserved them, where they might otherwise have disappeared. In other instances, as with Wagner's Ring Cycle, tourists demand a full, unaltered experience performed to a high standard, and with varying tolerance for experimentation.

The demand for entertainment and relaxation as much as nostalgia emphasised both the pace of change and stability in tourist destinations. Performances were adapted to the perceived needs of tourists, often by accommodating more 'lively' genres from elsewhere. Once that had been achieved, concerts and shows often took on fixed roles, impervious to the musical changes that affected performance away from the tourist gaze. As in New Orleans, Iweniar and Yunnan, the 'real' music and tourist performance evolved separately. Tourists do not always expect authenticity, nor do they recognise it; most are post-modern, post-tourists, in the sense that they are constantly aware that they are taking part in an entertaining performance rather than an intellectual inquiry or search for self-realisation. Music tourism therefore is so often one more form of 'invented tradition' or 'strategic inauthenticity' where what is presented to tourists is a partial, incomplete and distorted version of a past that never was.

Moreover, performers have easily and necessarily distinguished the superficiality of the performance from the realities of their lives, although often resenting the unequal commodification of their heritage, even where they have renegotiated their status and position with respect to a wider political economy. This is clearly so in New Orleans where 'second line' performers are well aware that tourists have no knowledge of their contemporary culture, despite its commodification as tourist spectacle and city image (Regis, 1999: 496). Museums may come closer to offering visions of authenticity. Graceland, the Magical Mystery Tour of Liverpool, Venetian opera and even the 'custom' performances at Iweniar, are all museums and even archives with tangential reference to the contemporary world. In many contexts, most obviously for overseas Chinese returning to their homeland, even one they may never have seen (Lau, 1998), that sense of history – and notions of continuity, however false – is exactly what they seek. Claims to authenticity are part of the tourism enterprise, however implausible they are. Yet such claims are just as often irrelevant. From tourists in New York attending Broadway shows to travellers in Argentina learning to tango, tourists seek music for the satisfaction of a 'good night out', to dance, to delight in the performance itself and the opportunity of hearing great musicians.

As in parts of Africa and the Caribbean, music tourism has created opportunities for musicians that otherwise might never have existed. In such obvious tourist centres as Las Vegas, Salzburg and Hawaii, significant numbers of jobs have been opened up by the demand for performance, whether they reflect local or foreign themes, in large or small venues, from more formal wage-earners to buskers. Musicians negotiate demands for their performances in different ways. Some perform predictable music, with little sense of satisfaction, in an effort to underwrite more credible projects that are not orientated towards tourists (and for which the monetary returns may not be as great). Others find opportunities in the tourist setting to innovate or forge links with cultural traditions. All large cities have developed musical diversions, some deliberately so, as tourism too has grown. Festivals have accentuated this trend and provided circuits of employment for musicians and others. Similarly, many marketing campaigns, advertising strategies and tourist guides – especially as these have sought to capture a more youthful market – have emphasised music and other ephemeral pleasures, rather than the austerity and order implicit in the red Baedeker's guides of earlier times.

Inside the Music

The diversity of music tourism and tourists is evident, from personal tours in search of sites associated with particular individuals (such as Robert Craft's tracing of Stravinsky's travels, residences and concert halls) to the simple hedonism of dance parties in the Mediterranean and on tropical islands. Yet in every context tourists derive meaning and pleasure from the experience; tourism is not usually intended to be an ordeal. Not only for ravers in Ibiza, but for most tourists, pleasure is an intended goal of tourism (and linking place, meaning and personal history may itself be intensely pleasurable), and part of the expression of a personal aesthetic.

For some tourists, travel is a rite of passage, the transition from youth to adulthood; for others it is akin to pilgrimage – the search for a greater depth of meaning and personal understanding – and may even be frequently repeated (in as diverse contexts as visitors to Elvis's grave, Phish fans on tour or participants in womyn's music festivals). This quest may follow predictable patterns, where tourists, as in the case of Graceland and Hawaii, validate their own preferences for a past and lost world of greater certainty (divorced from such challenges and threats as multiculturalism). Nostalgia is, however, rarely liberating, despite the notions of order and community that are a part. As MacCannell has suggested 'For moderns, reality and authenticity are thought to be elsewhere: in other historical periods and other cultures, in purer simpler lifestyles' (1976: 3). Many tourists thus collude in the evident staging and strategic inauthenticity of particular sites because it enables some recognition and understanding of a sought-after simplicity and order (or even, in the case of visitors to old festival sites such as Woodstock, the pleasures of disorder).

Tourism plays some part in enabling a wider comprehension of the world (however limited this may be) and the development of a sense of community, and some degree of intimacy, with other fans or with the world of which a particular performer was, or is, a part. At festivals participants and spectators are brought together to the extent that the performance as theatre 'evokes and solidifies a network of social and cognitive relationships existing in a triangular relationship between performer, spectator and the world at large' (Beeman, 1993: 386, in Cavicchi, 1998). Tourists and 'locals' are neither easily differentiated nor separated. Festivals enhance communities – that might previously have been virtual – while websites are contemporary means of creating community and fostering memory. Nevertheless, others may perceive that such relationships are threatened by commercial encroachment or predictability.

The Song (Rarely) Remains the Same

Although the longevity of many classical music sites and festivals as tourist destinations suggest otherwise, most forms of music tourism are recent inventions. The rapid expansion of cultural tourism in the last decades of the 20th century bore no suggestion of eventual decline. Yet little is more ephemeral than culture, and particularly popular culture. Icons such as Elvis and the Beatles may continue to stimulate visitors to Memphis and Liverpool, even as the baby-boom generation ages, but it is unclear that they will have successors from among more recent performers.

Other limitations, as with all kinds of tourism, are evident. Music tourism has its own business cycles, where once growing and innovative attractions may eventually become staid. In other ways, places may not be able to cope with large tourist influxes (as with festivals in small places) or desire its social impacts (as in Ibiza). Music tourism experiences limits to growth. Audiences have evolved and there has been concern that the 'opera generation' is aging, so that opera-going may become a thing of the past (Giles, 2000). This too explains new music tourism strategies, such as the staging of Opera in the Vines (in Australia's Hunter Valley wine district) or Opera in the Park (in major cities like New York and Sydney). Music is an industry dominated by fashion cycles; tourism linked to the popularity of certain artists, genres or eras will be ultimately reliant on them for sustained visitor numbers. Thus, their long-term viability is linked to the wider consumption of music more generally.

What is so important about sites such as Graceland, Liverpool, Salzburg, the Bob Marley Museum, but very few other musical sites, is that they are not merely musical sites. They are places associated with the formation and maintenance of national (or other) identity, even if perhaps only for some people and over what may eventually turn out to be a limited period. To a lesser extent, places such as Nashville and

Tamworth have laid claim to some part of national heritage. Such places function as museums, and even partial symbols of nationhood, in these cases through appeals to 'country', redefining rurality as the site of 'true' national cultures and ideologies (although these might also be seen as reinforcing 'whiteness'). At the New Salem Historic Site (the youthful home of Abraham Lincoln) tourists are broadly involved in five activities: learning about the past, enjoying encounters with other time frames, consuming nostalgia for a simpler bygone era, buying the idea of progress and advancement, and celebrating America (Bruner, 1994: 398; Pretes, 2003). In rather different ways, versions of such activities are present at most music tourist sites, and particularly at key locations, where nostalgia and nationalism are combined. In these sites, national identity, rather than musical popularity, may well ensure longevity.

At every tourist site there are tensions, whether of representation, as in Singapore where the 'local' is displaced by the 'global' in the quest for instant cultural heritage, or of distribution of costs and benefits, as in Manchester, where those who have gained most from tourism are not local people. Conflicts are greatest in places like Ibiza where there has been violence and environmental degradation, so that the 'rave scene' has moved on. San Antonio in Ibiza to some is a tawdry site, marked by drunkenness and debauchery. In Cuba, prostitution has been one beneficiary of music tourism. There are tensions where buskers and hawkers seem to overwhelm tourists. Such tensions and departures from even the most crude notions of authenticity make for frustration, and in developing world contexts initiate the collapse of once-thriving industries and sites. As the experience of Cleveland's and Sheffield's museums and centres has shown, most tourists travel relatively short distances – hence sites and experiences must constantly be changed or reinvented, unless new generations and more distant enthusiasts can be attracted. Similarly, Ibiza has begun to lose out as new house music destinations, such as Goa and Koh Phangan, have emerged, offering the thrill (and the relative cheapness) of the new. Many festivals struggled in the 21st century.

The marketing of music and musical sites entails standardisation and homogenisation in the search for a wider market. Places become commodities for tourists, as consumption challenges production in the reorientation of local economies. In the face of such trends, not only can places like Tjapukai and Iweniar capture tourists seeking the 'other', and sites like Graceland claim an iconic distinctiveness, but the construction of cultural homogeneity threatens the continuity of tourism. There is a constant tension between 'authenticity', 'creativity' and 'commercialism' at every tourist site, and at every festival, well described in the case of Kfar Blum (see Waterman, 1998b: 260–261), and such tensions may be annually revisited. Innovation and iconoclasm, often the rationale of festivals, can be overwhelmed by the desire to develop a place image, achieve success and ensure profitability. At the same time, commercialism can inspire creativity; receiving a reliable pay-cheque may improve the chances of innovation. New operatic works and full-scale productions require commissions to get off the ground. Tourism is an increasingly important means of income and a space of expression, for working musicians.

Music is intertwined with other creative and cultural activities and industries, and places have sought diversity in musical offerings. Just as Salzburg hosts everything from opera to the Sound of Music tour, so Liverpool hosts the Philharmonic Orchestra and the annual Creamfields Club music weekend. Music, too, has been linked to food, wine, landscapes and gardens; in Liverpool, football and music have been promoted together, and in the unusual case of the Seychelles International Festival, classical music has been integrated with big-game safaris in Africa. Conversely, food and wine festivals have taken on crucial musical elements. Through such cultural diversity, music tourism will continue, and will continue to grow, but perhaps in ways that diverge further from any notions of the authentic. Commercialism and commodification tend to emphasise conservatism and conservation, rather than creativity and challenge.

Music tourism is important because it illustrates how culture, commerce and identities are entangled. Notions of authenticity are problematic, if not false; nonetheless, they are often consumed with a sense of enjoyment and education. Music tourism implies the construction of diverse and fluid identities on the part of performers and audiences, and for places and even nations. Above all, music makes tourism enjoyable, framing and accompanying the travel experience. Sometimes music is the main attraction, at others merely the background to fun; music may take tourists inwards in search of themselves or outwards to new heights of exuberance. Whatever uncertainties are attached to the future of the travel industry, it is this enduring feature – music as social catalyst – that assures the future of music tourism.

References

Abbé-Decarroux, F. and Grin, F. (1992) Risk, risk aversion and the demand for performing arts. In R. Towse and A. Khakee (eds) *Cultural Economics* (pp. 121–140). Berlin: Springer-Verlag.

Abram, S. (1997) Performing for tourists in rural France. In S. Abram, J.D. Waldren and D.V.L. MacLeod (eds) *Tourists and Tourism: Identifying People with Place* (pp. 29–49). Oxford: Berg.

Adams, V. (1996) Karaoke as modern Lhasa, Tibet: western encounters with cultural politics. *Cultural Anthropology* 11, 510–546.

Aikenhead, D. (2001) *The Promised Land: Travels in Search of the Perfect E*. London: Fourth Estate.

Aksoy, A. (1992) Mapping the information economy: integration for flexibility. In K. Robins (ed.) *Understanding Information: Business, Technology and Geography* (pp. 43–60). London: Belhaven Press.

Albert, J. (2001) The secret festival. *The Australian* (31 August), 15.

Alderman, D.H. (2002) Writing on the Graceland wall: on the importance of authorship in pilgrimage landscapes. *Tourism Recreation Research* 27 (2), 27–33.

Aldskogius, H. (1993) Festivals and meets: the place of music in 'summer Sweden'. *Geografiska Annaler* 75B, 55–72.

Alford, R. (2002) Pilgrimage for Loretta. *Sun Herald* (15 December), 7.

Allen, M. (1988) *The Tamworth Country Music Festival*. Sydney: Horwitz Grahame.

Alvey, M. (1997) Wanderlust and wire wheels: the existential search for Route 66. In S. Cohan and I.R. Hark (eds) *The Road Movie Book* (pp. 143–165). London and New York: Routledge.

Americans for the Arts (2002) *Arts and Economic Prosperity*. Washington, DC: Americans for the Arts.

Amin, A., Cameron, A. and Hudson, R. (1999) Welfare as work? The potential of the UK social economy. *Environment and Planning A* 31, 2033–2051.

Andronicou, A. (1979) Tourism in Cyprus. In E. de Kadt (ed.) *Tourism: Passport to Development* (pp. 237–264). New York: Oxford University Press.

Anon. (1958) Liner notes, Stanley Black and His Orchestra, *Place Pigalle*.

Anon. (1959) Liner notes, Mantovani, *Continental Encores*.

Appadurai, A. (1990) Disjuncture and difference in the global cultural economy. *Public Culture* 2 (2), 1–24.

Ashworth, G.J. (1995) Managing the cultural tourist. In G. Ashworth and A. Dietworst (eds) *Tourism and Spatial Transformations* (pp. 265–283). Wallingford: CAB International.

Associated Press (2003) Hip-hop into history. *Sydney Morning Herald* (24 May), 27.

Atkinson, C.Z. (1996) 'Shakin' your butt for the tourist': music's role in the identification and selling of New Orleans'. In R.H. King and H. Taylor (eds) *Dixie Debates: Perspectives on Southern Cultures* (pp. 150–164). London: Pluto Press.

Atkinson, C.Z. (1997) Whose New Orleans? Music's place in the packaging of New Orleans for tourism. In S. Abram, J.D. Waldren and D.V.L. MacLeod (eds) *Tourists and Tourism: Identifying People with Place* (pp. 91–106). Oxford: Berg.

Attali, J. (1985) *Noise: The Political Economy of Music.* Manchester: Manchester University Press.

Australian Tourist Commission (ATC) (2001) *Tourism Industry Essentials.* www.atc.net.au/scontent.asp?art=722.

Bakhtin, M. (1984) *Rabelais and his World.* Bloomington: Indiana University Press.

Balkin, S. (2001) Keep the music alive. *Chicago Sun-Times* (29 April), 30A.

Ballantine, C. (1999) Looking to the USA: the politics of male close-harmony song style in South Africa during the 1940s and 1950s. *Popular Music* 18, 1–17.

Baumol, W. and Bowen, W. (1996) *Performing Arts – The Economic Dilemma.* New York: The Twentieth Century Found.

Bennett, A. (1913) *Paris Nights.* London: Doubleday.

Bennett, A. (2000) *Popular Music and Youth Culture Music: Identity and Place.* Basingstoke: Macmillan.

Bennett, T., Emmison, M. and Frow, J. (2001) Social class and cultural practice in contemporary Australia. In T. Bennett and D. Carter (eds) *Culture in Australia: Policies, Publics and Programs* (pp. 193–214). Melbourne: Cambridge University Press.

Bey, H. (1991) *T.A.Z.: The Temporary Autonomous Zone, Ontological Anarchy, Poetic Terrorism.* New York: Autonomedia.

Bianchi, A. and Gusoff, A. (1995) *Music Lover's Guide to Great Britain and Ireland,* Columbus: McGraw-Hill.

Black, J. (1992) *The British Abroad: The Grand Tour in the Eighteenth Century.* Stroud: Alan Sutton.

Blair, M.E. and Hyatt, E.M. (1992) Home is where the heart is: an analysis of meanings of the home in country music. *Popular Music and Society* 16, 69–82.

Bloomfield, T. (1993) Resisting songs: negative dialects in pop. *Popular Music* 12, 13–31.

Bohlman, P. (1986) Pilgrimage, politics and the musical remapping of the New Europe. *Ethnomusicology* 40, 375–412.

Boissevain, J. and Inglott, P.C. (1979) Tourism in Malta. In E. de Kadt (ed.) *Tourism. Passport to Development?* (pp. 265–284). New York: Oxford University Press.

Bonamy, M. (2001) *Aboriginal Cultural Tourism in Central Australia: Images and Perceptions of Aboriginality.* Unpublished B.A. Honours thesis, University of New South Wales, Sydney, Australia.

Bord Fáilte (Irish Tourism Board) (1996) *Investing in Strategic Marketing for Tourism.* Dublin: Bord Fáilte.

Borneman, J. and Senders, S. (2000) Politics without a head: is the 'Love Parade' a new form of political identification? *Cultural Anthropology* 15, 294–317.

Botsford, F. (2001) Clampdown on Ibiza nightlife. *BBC News* (12 July). www.news.bbc.co.uk/1/hi/world/eorope.

Bourdain, A. (2001) *A Cook's Tour: In Search of the Perfect Meal.* London: Bloomsbury.

Bourdieu, P. (1984) *Distinction: A Social Critique of the Judgement of Taste.* London: Routledge and Kegan Paul.

Bourdieu, P. (1993) *The Field of Cultural Production.* Cambridge: Polity Press.

Bowen, D. (1999) Lookin' for Margaritaville: place and imagination in Jimmy Buffett's Songs. *Journal of Cultural Geography* 16 (2), 99–108.

Brabazon, T. (1993) From Penny Lane to Dollar Drive: Liverpool tourism and Beatle-led recovery. *Public History Review* 2, 108–124.

Brabazon, T. (2000) *Tracking the Jack: A Retracing of the Antipodes*. Sydney: University of NSW Press.

Brennan, T. (2003) Global youth and local pleasure: Cuba and the right to popular music. In D. Fischlin and A. Heble (eds) *Rebel Musics: Human Rights, Resistant Sounds, and the Politics of Music Making* (pp. 209–231). New York: Black Rose Books.

Brennan-Horley, C., Gibson, C. and Connell, J. (2003) *Parkes Elvis Revival Festival: The Visitor Survey 2003*. Sydney: University of New South Wales.

British Broadcasting Corporation (BBC) (1999) Pop museum saved. www.news.bbc.co.uk.

British Broadcasting Corporation (BBC) (2001) 2 million pound relaunch for national pop centre. www.news.bbc.co.uk.

British Tourist Authority (1998) *Rock and Pop Music: One Nation Under a Groove*. London: British Tourist Authority.

Brown, A. (2002) Dance party. *Sydney Morning Herald* (21 September), 7.

Brown, M. (1993) *American Heartbeat: Travels from Woodstock to San Jose by Song Title*. London: Penguin.

Brown, M.D., Var, T. and Lee, S. (2002) Messina Hof Wine and Jazz Festival: an economic impact analysis. *Tourism Economics* 8, 23–279.

Bruner, E.M. (1994) Abraham Lincoln as authentic reproduction: a critique of postmodernism. *American Anthropologist* 96, 397–415.

Bruner, E.M. (1996) Tourism in the Balinese Borderzone. In S. Lavie and T. Swedenburg (eds) *Displacement, Diaspora and Geographies of Identity* (pp. 157–179). Durham: Duke University Press.

Bull, A. (1993) *Coast to Coast: A Rock Fan's U.S. Tour*. London: Black Swan.

Burchett, C. (1993) A Profile of Aboriginal and Torres Strait Islander Tourism: its history and future prospects. *Indigenous Australians and Tourism: A Focus on Northern Australia* (pp. 20–25). Darwin: Office of Northern Development.

Bureau of Tourism Research (2000) *International Visitors in Australia: Annual Results of the International Visitor Survey*. Canberra: Bureau of Tourism Research.

Bussmann, J. (1998) Glastonbury. *The Guardian Festival Guide* 16–17.

Butler, J. (1989) *Gender Trouble: Feminism and the Subversion of Identity*. London: Routledge.

Butler, R. (1980) The concept of a tourist area cycle of evolution: implications for the management of resources. *The Canadian Geographer* 24, 5–12.

Cameron, N. (1995) *Maleny Folk Festival: The Art of Celebration*. Maleny: Mimburi Press.

Cameron, C. and Gatewood, J. (2003) Seeking numinous experiences in the unremembered past. *Ethnology* 42, 55–71.

Carney, G.O. (1994) Branson: the new mecca of country music. *Journal of Cultural Geography* 14 (2), 17–32.

Carroll, J. and Connell, J. (2000) 'You gotta love this city': the Whitlams and inner Sydney. *Australian Geographer* 31, 41–154.

Cavicchi, D. (1998) *Tramps Like Us: Music and Meaning Amongst Springsteen Fans*. New York and Oxford: Oxford University Press.

Chapman (1992) *The Celts: The Construction of a Myth*. Basingstoke: Macmillan.

Charters, S. and Ali-Knight, J. (2002) Who is the wine tourist?. *Tourism Management* 23, 311–319.

Chase, J. and Healey, M. (1995) The spatial externality effects of football matches and rock concerts. *Applied Geography* 15, 18–34.

City of San Diego Commission for Arts and Culture (2002) *2001 Economic Impact Report*. San Diego: City of San Diego Commission for Arts and Culture.

Clark, A. (2000) Cherish your festival idea. *Opera Festival 2000* 11–18.

Clarke, D. (1995) *The Rise and Fall of Popular Music*. Harmondsworth: Penguin.

Clarke, M. (1982) *The Politics of Pop Festivals*. London: Junction Books.

Clune, F. (1954) *Roaming Around Europe*. Sydney: Angus & Robertson.

Cohen A. (1982) A polyethnic London carnival as a contested cultural performance. *Ethnic and Racial Studies* 5, 23–41.

Cohen, E. (1988) Authenticity and commoditization in tourism. *Annals of Tourism Research* 15, 371–386.

Cohen, S. (1991) Popular music and urban regeneration: the music industries of Merseyside. *Cultural Studies* 5, 332–346.

Cohen, S. (1997) More than the Beatles: popular music, tourism and urban regeneration. In S. Abram, J.D. Waldren and D.V.L. MacLeod (eds) *Tourists and Tourism: Identifying People with Place* (pp. 71–90). Oxford: Berg.

Collin, M. (1997) *Altered State*. London: Serpent's Tail.

Connell, J. (2003) Island dreaming: the contemplation of Polynesian paradise. *Journal of Historical Geography* 29 554–582.

Connell, J. and Gibson, C. (2003) *Sound Tracks: Popular Music, Identity and Place*. London and New York: Routledge.

Connell, J. and Gibson, C. (2004a) Vicarious journeys: travels in music. *Tourism Geographies* 6, 2–25.

Connell, J. and Gibson, C. (2004b) World music: ethnicity, commodification and global diversity. *Progress in Human Geography* 28, 342–361.

Connell, J. and Stanley-Niaah (2004) Remembering the fire: tourism at the Bob Marley Museum, Kingston, Jamaica. *Caribbean Geography* 15 (in press).

Cook, B. (1993) *The Town That Country Built: Welcome to Branson, Missouri*. New York: Avon Books.

Cooley, T.J. (1999) Folk festivals as modern ritual in the Polish Tatra Mountains. *The World of Music* 41 (3), 31–55.

Corry, T.C.S. (1866) *Ireland: Its Scenery, Music and Antiquities*. Dublin: Hodges Smith.

Cosgrove, S. (1988) Global style? *New Statesman and Society* (9 September), 50.

Cox, K. (2003) Hopes ride the high road in the heart of country. *The Sun Herald* (19 January), 43.

Craft, R. (2000) *Places: A Travel Companion for Music and Art Lovers*. London: Thames & Hudson.

Craik, J. (1997) The culture of tourism. In C. Rojek and J. Urry (eds) *Touring Cultures: Transformation of Travel and Theory* (pp. 113–136). London: Routledge.

Crang, P. (1997) Performing the tourist product. In C. Rojek and J. Urry (eds) *Touring Cultures: Transformations of Travel and Theory* (pp. 137–154). London and New York: Routledge.

Cummings, M.C. and Katz, R.S. (1987) *The Patron State: Government and the Arts in Europe, North America, and Japan*. New York: Oxford University Press.

Cusic, D. (1994) QWERTY, Nashville, and country music. *Popular Music and Society* 18 (4), 41–55.

Cvetkovich, A. and Wahng, S. (2001) Don't stop the music: roundtable discussion with workers from the Michigan Womyn's Music Festival. *GLQ* 7, 131–151.

Cwi, D. and Lydall, K. (1977) *Economic Impact of the Arts and Cultural Institutions: A Model for Assessment and a Case Study in Baltimore*. Washington, DC: Research Division, National Endowment for the Arts.

Czernin, F. (1937) *This Salzburg*. London: Peter Davies.

d'Andrea, A. (2003) Global nomads: techno and new age as transnational countercultures in Ibiza and Goa. In G. St John (ed.) *Rave Culture and Religion* (pp. 236–255). London: Routledge.

Daniel, Y.P. (1996) Tourism dance performances: authenticity and creativity. *Annals of Tourism Research* 23, 780–797.

Dann, G. (1994) Tourism: the nostalgia industry of the future. In W. Theobald (ed.) *Global Tourism: The Next Decade* (pp. 55–67). Oxford: Butterworth-Heinemann.

Dann, G. (1996) Images of destination people in travelogues. In R. Butler and T. Hinch (eds) *Tourism and Indigenous Peoples* (pp. 349–375). London: Thomson.

Delaney, B. (2003) Towns are alive with the sound of music. *Sydney Morning Herald* (11 February), 11.

Deleuze, G. and Guattari, F. (1987) *A Thousand Plateaus: Capitalism and Schizophrenia*. Minneapolis: University of Minnesota Press.

Denselow, R. (1989) *When The Music's Over: The Story of Political Pop*. London: Faber.

Derrett, R. (2001) Special interest tourism. In N. Douglas, N. Douglas and R. Derrett (eds) *Special Interest Tourism* (pp. 1–28). Brisbane: Wiley.

Derrett, R. (2003) Festivals and tourists in the Rainbow Region. In H. Wilson (ed.) *Belonging in the Rainbow Region: Cultural Perspectives on the NSW North Coast* (pp. 287–308). Lismore: Southern Cross University Press.

Desmond, J. (1999) *Staging Tourism: Bodies on Display from Waikiki to Seaworld*. Chicago: University of Chicago Press.

de Witt, M.F. (1999) Heritage, tradition and travel: Louisiana French culture placed on a California dance floor. *The World of Music* 41 (3), 57–83.

Dimanche, F. and Lepetic, A. (1999) New Orleans tourism and crime: a case study. *Journal of Travel Research* 38, 19–23.

DiMaggio, P.J. (1986) *Nonprofit Enterprise in the Arts*. New York: Oxford University Press.

DiNoto, M.J. and Merk, L.H. (1993) Small economy estimates on the impact of the arts. *Journal of Cultural Economics* 17, 41–53.

Dobbin, W. (1998) Fashionable to the end. *The Sun Herald*. 24 May, 72–78.

Doss, E. (1999) *Elvis Culture: Fans, Faith and Image*. Lawrence: University Press of Kansas.

Drabble, M. (1979) *A Writer's Britain: Landscape in Literature*. London: Thames & Hudson.

Dublin Tourism (n.d.) *Rock n Stroll: Pubs, Restaurants, Night Life and Music*. Dublin: Dublin Tourism Centre.

Duffy, M. (2000) Lines of drift: festival participation and performing a sense of place. *Popular Music* 19, 51–64.

Dunbar-Hall, P. (2001) Culture, tourism and culture tourism: boundaries and frontiers in performance of Balinese music and dance. *Journal of Intercultural Studies* 22, 173–188.

Dunbar-Hall, P. (2003) Tradisi and *turisme*: music, dance and cultural transformation at the Ubud palace, Bali, Indonesia. *Australian Geographical Studies* 41, 3–16.

Dunbar-Hall, P. and Gibson, C. (2004) *Deadly Sounds, Deadly Places: Contemporary Aboriginal Music in Australia*. Sydney: UNSW Press.

du Pont de Bie, N. (2004) *Ant Egg Soup: The Adventures of a Food Tourist in Laos.* London: Sceptre.

Dwyer, L., Agrusa, J. and Coats, W. (2001) Economic scale of a community event: the Lafayette Mardi Gras. *Pacific Tourism Review* 5, 167–179.

Dyer, P., Aberdeen, L. and Schuler, S. (2003) Tourism impacts on an Australian indigenous community: a Djabugay case study. *Tourism Management* 24, 83–95.

East, P. and Luger, K. (2001) Living in paradise: youth culture and tourism development in the mountains of Austria. In R. Voase (ed.) *Tourism in Western Europe: A Collection of Case Histories* (pp. 273–288). Wallingford: CABI Publishing.

Economic Development Edmonton (2003) *Edmonton's Arts Community.* www.info.ede.org.

Edensor, T. (2000) Staging tourism: tourists as performers. *Annals of Tourism Research* 27, 322–344.

Edensor, T. (2001) Performing tourism, staging tourism: (re)producing tourist space and practice. *Tourist Studies* 1, 59–81.

Elder, B. (2003a) The world on his strings. *Sydney Morning Herald* (22 February), 5.

Elder, B. (2003b) Around the world in three magical days. *Sydney Morning Herald* (26 February), 18.

Elsrud, T. (2001) Risk creation in traveling: backpacker adventure narration. *Annals of Tourism Research* 28, 597–617.

Erlmann, V. (1996) The aesthetics of the global imagination: reflections on world music in the 1990s. *Public Culture* 8, 467–487.

Esman, M.R. (1982) Festivals, change and unity: the celebration of ethnic identity among Louisiana Cajuns. *Anthropological Quarterly* 55, 199–210.

Esman, M.R. (1984) Tourism as ethnic preservation: the Cajuns of Louisiana. *Annals of Tourism Research* 11, 451–467.

Eyre, B. (2000) *In Griot Time: An American Guitarist in Mali.* Philadelphia: Temple University Press.

Fairburn, A.N. (1951) The Grand Tour. *Geographical Magazine* 24, 118–127.

Farren, M. (1996) *The Hitchhiker's Guide to Elvis: An A–Z of the Elvis Universe.* Burlington, Ontario: Collector's Guide Publishing.

Fawcett, C. and Cormack, P. (2001) Guarding authenticity at literary tourism sites. *Annals of Tourism Research* 28, 686–704.

Fein, A. (1998) *The LA Musical History Tour* (2nd edn). Los Angeles, 2.13.61.

Fitzgerald, J. and Hayward, P. (1999) Tropical cool: the Arthur Lyman sound. In P. Hayward (ed.) *Widening the Horizon. Exoticism in Post-War Popular Music* (pp. 94–113). Sydney: John Libbey.

Florida, R. (2002) *The Rise of the Creative Class.* New York: Basic Books.

Foley, M. (1996) Cultural Tourism in the United Kingdom. In G. Richards (ed.) *Cultural Tourism in Europe* (pp. 283–309). Wallingford: CAB International.

Formica, S. and Uysal, Y. (1996) A market segmentation of festival visitors: Umbria jazz festival in Italy. *Festival Management and Event Tourism* 3, 175–182.

Frame, P. (1999) *Rockin' Around Britain. Rock 'n' Roll Landmarks of the UK and Ireland.* London: Omnibus Press.

Frey, B. (1986) The Salzburg Festival: an economic point of view. *Journal of Cultural Economics* 10, 27–44

Frey, B. (1994) The economics of music festivals. *Journal of Cultural Economics* 18, 29–39.

Frey, B. and Pommerehne, W.W. (1989) *Muses and Markets: Explorations in the Economics of the Arts.* Cambridge: Basil Blackwell.

Frierson, J. (2000) Riverbend and beyond: the business of festivals. *On The Move* 1(3), 1–4.

Frith, S. (1989) Introduction. In S. Frith (ed.) *World Music, Politics and Social Change* (pp. 1–14). Manchester: Manchester University Press.

Fry, M. and Posner, J. (1993) *Cajun Country Guide*. Gretna, Louisiana: Pelican Publishing.

Fusco, C. (1994) The other history of intercultural performance. *The Drama Review* 38 (1), 143–167.

Garratt, S. (1998) *Adventures in Wonderland: A Decade of Club Culture*. London: Headline.

Gaylord Entertainment (2003) Property profiles. www.gaylordentertainment. com.

Gazel, R.C. and Schwer, R.K. (1997) Beyond rock and roll: the economic impact of The Grateful Dead on a local economy. *Journal of Cultural Economics* 21, 41–55.

Gebicki, M. (2003) Getting it together. *The Australian* (11 October), R24–25.

Gibson, C. (1998) 'We sing our home, we dance our land': indigenous self-determination and contemporary geopolitics in Australian popular music. *Environment and Planning D: Society and Space* 16, 163–184.

Gibson, C. (1999) Subversive sites: rave culture, spatial politics and the internet in Sydney, Australia. *Area* 31, 19–33.

Gibson, C. (2003) Cultures at work: why 'culture' matters in research on the 'cultural' industries. *Social and Cultural Geography* 4, 201–215.

Gibson, C. and Connell, J. (2003) 'Bongo Fury': tourism, music and cultural economy at Byron Bay, Australia. *Tijdschrift voor Economische en Sociale Geografie* 94, 164–187.

Gibson, C. and Davidson, D. (2004) Tamworth, Australia's 'country music capital': place marketing, rural narratives and resident reactions. *Journal of Rural Studies* 20(4), 387–404.

Gibson, C. and Homan, S. (2004) Urban redevelopment, live music and public space: cultural performance and the re-making of Marrickville. *International Journal of Cultural Policy* 10, 69–86.

Gibson, C., Murphy, P. and Freestone, R. (2002) Employment and socio-spatial relations in Australia's cultural economy. *Australian Geographer* 33, 173–189.

Gibson, C., Allen, K., Lee, V. and Mirow, K. (2004) Experiential learning in the field: measuring the economic impacts of a music festival in regional Australia. *Geography Bulletin* 36 (in press).

Gibson-Graham, J.K. (1996) *The End of Capitalism (As We Knew It): A Feminist Critique of Political Economy*. Oxford: Blackwell.

Gilbert, E.W. (1954) *Brighton: Old Ocean's Bauble*. London: Methuen.

Gilbert, J. (1997) Soundtrack to an uncivil society: rave culture, the Criminal Justice Act and the politics of modernity. *New Formations* 31, 5–22.

Gilbert, J. and Pearson, E. (1999) *Discographies*. London: Routledge.

Giles, P. (2000) Has Generation X lost its way to the opera? *Opera News* 64(8), 29–31.

Gillan, A. (2002) Spanish steps. *The Guardian* (19 January), 2–3.

Gilroy, P. (1993) *The Black Atlantic: Modernity and Double-Consciousness*. London: Verso.

Glinert, E. and Perry, T. (1997) *Rock & Roll Traveler Great Britain and Ireland: The Ultimate Guide to Famous Rock Hangouts Past and Present*. New York: Fodor's.

Gnuschke, J.E. (2002) Elvis is still big business in Memphis. *Business Perspectives* 14 (3), 2–7.

Goehr, L. (1992) *The Imaginary Museum of Musical Works: An Essay in the Philosophy of Music*. Oxford: Clarendon Press.

Goertzen, C. and Azzi, M.S. (1999) Globalization and the tango. *Yearbook for Traditional Music* 66, 67–76.

Goldfried, M. (1995) Ticket to ride. In A. Bianchi and A. Gusoff (eds) *Music Lovers' Guide to Great Britain and Ireland* (pp. 62–64). Columbus: McGrawHill.

Gordon, R. (1995) *It Came From Memphis: The Unturned Roots of Rock and Roll*. London: Secker & Warburg.

Gore, G. (1997) The beat goes on: trance, dance and tribalism in rave culture. In H. Thomas (ed.) *Dance in the City* (pp. 50–67). New York: St Martin's Press.

Gotham, K.F. (2002) Marketing Mardi Gras: commodification, spectacle and the political economy of tourism in New Orleans. *Urban Studies* 39, 1735–1756.

Gottdiener, M., Collins, C. and Dickens, D. (1999) *Las Vegas: The Social Production of an All-American City*. Oxford: Blackwell.

Gratton, C. and Taylor, P. (1995) Impacts of festival events: a case study of Edinburgh. In G. Ashworth and G. Dietvorst (eds) *Tourism and Spatial Transformation. Implications for Policy and Planning* (pp. 225–238).

Gratton, C. and Richards, G. (1996) The economic context of cultural tourism. In G. Richards (ed.) *Cultural Tourism in Europe* (pp. 71–86). Wallingford: CAB International.

Gray, M. and Osborne, R. (1996) *The Elvis Atlas: A Journey Through Elvis Presley's America*. New York: Henry Holt.

Gregory, D. (2002) Resort mayor tells tourists to keep out. *Sydney Morning Herald* (29 August), 47.

Green, G.L. (2002) Marketing the nation: Carnival and tourism in Trinidad and Tobago. *Critique of Anthropology* 22, 283–304.

Greenwood, D.J. (1977) Culture by the Pound: an anthropological perspective on tourism as cultural commoditization. In V. Smith (ed.) *Hosts and Guests: The Anthropology of Tourism* (pp. 129–138). Oxford: Blackwell.

Grimwade, J. (2003) Living is easy to the mariachi beat. *Sunday Telegraph* (24 August), 8–9.

Gritzner, C.F. (1978) Country music: a reflection of popular culture. *Journal of Popular Culture* 11, 857–864.

Grunewald, R. (2002) Tourism and cultural revival. *Annals of Tourism Research* 29, 1004–1021.

Guralnick, P. (1994) *Last Train to Memphis: The Rise of Elvis Presley*. Boston: Little Brown.

Halewood, C. and Hannam, K. (2001) Viking heritage tourism: authenticity and commodification. *Annals of Tourism Research* 28, 565–580.

Halfacree, K. and Kitchin, R. (1996) 'Madchester rave on': placing the fragments of popular music. *Area* 28, 47–55.

Halfacree, K. and Kitchin, R. (2000) 'Rock 'n' stroll': promoting the consumption of musical places. *The North West Geographer* 2, 4–14.

Hall, C.M. (1998) *Introduction to Tourism* (3rd edn). Melbourne: Longman Hall.

Hall, C.M., Sharples, L., Cambourne, B. and Macionis, N. (eds) (2000) *Wine Tourism Around the World: Development, Management and Markets*. Oxford: Butterworth-Heinemann.

Hall, P. (1998) *Cities and Civilization*. London: Weidenfeld & Nicolson.

Hall, T. and Hubbard, P. (1996) The entrepreneurial city: new urban politics, new urban geographies. *Progress in Human Geography* 20, 153–174.

Hannan, M. (2000) Musical practices and cultural identity in the village of Nimbin. In T. Mitchell, P. Doyle and B. Johnson (eds) *Changing Sounds: New*

Directions and Configurations in Popular Music (pp. 42–46). Sydney: University of Technology.

Hannan, M. (2003) From blockades to blue moon: musical cultures of Nimbin. In H. Wilson (ed.) *Belonging in the Rainbow Region: Cultural Perspectives on the NSW Far North Coast* (pp. 247–262). Lismore: Southern Cross University Press.

Hansmann, H. (1986) Nonprofit enterprise in the performing arts. In P.J. DiMaggio (ed.) *Nonprofit Enterprise in the Arts* (pp. 17–22). New York: Oxford University Press.

Harris, R. and Dawut, R. (2002) Mazar festivals of the Uyghurs: music, Islam and the Chinese State. *British Journal of Ethnomusicology* 11, 101–118.

Harrison-Pepper, S. (1990) *Drawing a Circle in the Square*. Jackson: University Press of Mississippi.

Harvey, D. (1989) Down towns. *Marxism Today* 33 (January), 21.

Haslam, D. (2000) *Manchester, England: the Story of the Pop Cult City*. London: Fourth Estate.

Hazen, C. and Freeman, M. (1997) *Memphis: Elvis Style*. Winston-Salem, NC: John F. Blair.

Hayward, P. (2001) *Tide Lines: Music, Tourism and Cultural Transition in the Whitsunday Islands*. Lismore: Music Archive for the Pacific Press.

Heathcote, G. (2001) Music in Mayfair. *The Sun-Herald* (25 November), 18.

Heining, D. (1998) Cars and girls – The car, masculinity and pop music. In D. Thorns, L. Holden and T. Claydon (eds) *The Motor Car and Popular Culture in the Twentieth Century* (pp. 96–119). Aldershot: Ashgate.

Henry, R. (2000) Dancing into being: the Tjapukai Aboriginal Cultural Park and the Laura Dance Festival. *The Australian Journal of Anthropology* 11 (3), 322–332.

Hill, M. (2000) Centennial spark. *The Sun-Herald* (1 September), 9.

Hinch, T. and Higham, J. (2001) Sport tourism: a framework for research. *International Journal of Tourism Research* 3, 45–58.

Hinton, B. (1995) *Message to Love: The Isle of Wight Festivals, 1968–1970*. Chessington: Castle Communications.

Hitchens, C. (2002) The ballad of Route 66. *Vanity Fair* 507 (November), 68–90.

Hjalager, A. and Richards, G. (2002) *Tourism and Gastronomy*. London: Routledge.

Hobsbawm, E. (1983) Introduction: inventing traditions. In E. Hobsbawm and T. Ranger (eds) *The Invention of Tradition* (pp. 1–14). Cambridge: Cambridge University Press.

Hoffman, L. (2000) Tourism and the revitalization of Harlem. *Research in Urban Sociology* 5, 207–223.

Hoffmann, L. (2003) The marketing of diversity in the inner city: tourism and regulation in Harlem. *International Journal of Urban and Regional Research* 27 (2), 286–299.

Hoffmann, R. (2001) 'Mozart and the image of Salzburg'. Paper presented at the *Satchmo Meets Amadeus* conference, 6 October, Salzburg.

Homan S. (1998) After the law: Sydney's Phoenician Club and the death of Anna Wood. *Perfect Beat* 4 (1), 56–83.

Homan, S. (2003) *The Mayor's a Square: Live Music and Law and Order in Sydney*. Sydney: Local Consumption Publications.

Hopkins, J. (2002) *Elvis in Hawai'i*, Honolulu: Bess Press.

Horowitz, H. (1985) The arts audiences/the arts public: two NEA studies. *Journal of Arts Management and Law* 15, 113–131.

Hosokawa, S. (1994) East of Honolulu: Hawaiian music in Japan from the 1920s to the 1940s. *Perfect Beat* 2 (1), 51–67.

Hosokawa, S. (1999a) Martin Denny and the development of musical exotica. In P. Hayward (ed.) *Widening the Horizon: Exoticism in Post-War Popular Music* (pp. 72–93). Sydney: John Libbey.

Hosokawa, S. (1999b) Strictly ballroom: the rumba in pre world war two Japan. *Perfect Beat* 4 (3), 3–23.

Hughes, G. (1995) Authenticity in tourism. *Annals of Tourism Research* 22, 781–803.

Hughes, H. (2000) *Arts, Entertainment and Tourism.* Oxford: Butterworth-Heinemann.

Hughes, H. and Benn, D. (1998) Holiday entertainment in a British seaside resort town. *Journal of Arts Management, Law and Society* 27, 295–307.

Hughes, R. (ed.) (1955) *A Mozart Pilgrimage: Being the Travel Diaries of Vincent and Mary Novello in the Year 1829.* London: Novello.

Hutnyk, J. (2000) *Critique of Exotica: Music, Politics and the Culture Industry.* London: Pluto.

Hutson, S. (2000) The rave: spiritual healing in modern western subcultures. *Anthropological Quarterly* 73, 35–49.

Ingham, J. (1999) Listening back from Blackburn: virtual sound worlds and the creation of temporary autonomy. In A. Blake (ed.) *Living Through Pop* (pp. 112–128). London: Routledge.

Ingham, J., Purvis, M. and Clarke, D. (1994) Hearing places, making spaces: sonorous geographies, ephemeral rhythms and the Blackburn warehouse parties. *Environment and Planning D: Society and Space* 17, 283–305.

Israel, J. (1999) U Can Come 2. *Sydney Morning Herald* (14 August), 92.

Jackson, P. (1988) Street life: the politics of carnival. *Environment and Planning D: Society and Space* 6, 213–227.

Jackson, P. (1992) The politics of the streets: a geography of Caribana. *Political Geography* 11, 130–151.

Jackson, P. (1993) Towards a cultural politics of consumption. In J. Bird, B. Curtis, T. Putnam, G. Robertson and L. Tickner (eds) *Mapping the Futures: Local Cultures, Global Change* (pp. 207–228). London: Routledge.

James, C. (1984) *Flying Visits.* London: Cape.

Jameson, J. (1995) Heartland of country. *The Daily Telegraph Mirror* (Sydney) (10 October), 45.

Jarvis, B. (1985) The truth is only known by guttersnipes. In J. Burgess and R. Gold (eds) *Geography, the Media and Popular Culture* (pp. 96–122). London: Croom Helm.

Jenkins, B. and Boucher, R. (1998) Senate passes Jenkins/Boucher Legislation designating Bristol as the 'birthplace of country music'. www.house.gov/boucher/docs/bristol2 (mimeo).

Jeong, S. and Sautos, C.A. (2004) Cultural politics and contested place identity. *Annals of Tourism Research* 31, 640–656.

Johnson, H. (2002) Balinese music, tourism and globalisation: inventing traditions within and across cultures. *New Zealand Journal of Asian Studies* 4 (2), 8–32.

Johnson, K.N. and Underiner, T. (2001) Command performances: staging Native Americans at Tillicum village. In C.J. Meyer and D. Royer (eds) *Selling the Indian: Commercializing and Appropriating American Indian Cultures* (pp. 44–61). Tucson: University of Arizona Press.

Johnson, R. (1998) Crossroad blues. *The Australian Magazine* (19 September), 32–35.

Jones, E.H. (1988) *Native Americans as Shown on the Stage, 1753–1916.* London: Methuen.

Jones, R. (1991) *The Beatles' Liverpool.* Wirral: Ron Jones.

Jones, R. (1998) What price the field of dreams?. *The Guardian* (30 May), 2.

Joyner, C. (1996) African and European roots of Southern culture: the 'central theme' revisited. In R.H. King and H. Taylor (eds) *Dixie Debates: Perspectives on Southern Cultures* (pp. 12–30). London: Pluto Press.

Judd, D.R. and Fainstein, S.S. (eds) (1999) *The Tourist City*. New Haven and London: Yale University Press.

Kaeppler, A. (1973) Polynesian dance as 'airplane art'. *Dance Research Journal 8*, 71–85.

Kaeppler, A. (1988) Pacific festivals and the promotion of identity, politics and tourism. In *Come Mek Me Hol' Yu Han': The Impact of Tourism on Traditional Music* (pp. 121–138). Kingston: Jamaica Memory Bank.

Keane, S. (1999) Elvis lives in blue Kauai. *The Sun-Herald* (31 October), 109.

Keen, I. (2001) Agency, history and tradition in the construction of 'classical' music: the debate over 'authentic performance'. In C. Pinney and N. Thomas (eds) *Beyond Aesthetics: Art and the Technologies of Enchantment* (pp. 31–56). Oxford: Berg.

Kell, C. (2003) Tango time in hardship city. *Sunday Telegraph* (2 November), 6–7.

Khan, F., Ditton, J., Elliott, L., Short, E., Morrison, A., Farrall, S. and Gruer, L. (2000) EscapeEs: what sort of ecstasy do package tour ravers seek?. In S. Clift and S. Carter (eds) *Tourism and Sex: Culture, Commerce and Coercion* (pp. 221–235). London: Pinter.

Kikau, R. (2003) The homecoming: islanders strengthen their roots in one day festival. *Fiji Times* (22 April), 21.

Kim, S. and Littrell, M.A. (2001) Souvenir buying intentions for self versus others. *Annals of Tourism Research 28*, 638–657.

King, C. (1994) His truth goes marching on: Elvis Presley and the pilgrimage to Graceland. In I. Reader and T. Walker (eds) *Pilgrimage in Popular Culture* (pp. 92–104). Macmillan: London.

King, J. and Nebesky, R. (1997) *Prague*. Melbourne: Lonely Planet.

Kirby, E. (1983) *From Africa to Beale Street*. Memphis: Lubin Press.

Kneafsey, M. (2001) Rural cultural economy: tourism and social relations. *Annals of Tourism Research 28*, 762–783.

Kneafsey, M. (2002) Sessions and gigs: tourism and traditional music in North Mayo, Ireland. *Cultural Geographies 9*, 354–358.

Kneafsey, M. (2003) 'If it wasn't for the tourists we wouldn't have an audience': the case of tourism and traditional music in North Mayo. In M. Cronin and B. O'Connor (eds) *Irish Tourism* (pp. 21–41). Clevedon: Channel View.

Kofsky, F. (1998) *Black Music, White Business: Illuminating the History and Political Economy of Jazz*. New York: Pathfinder Press.

Kong, L. (1995) Popular music in geographical analyses. *Progress in Human Geography 19* (2), 183–198.

Kong, L. (2000) Cultural policy in Singapore: negotiating economic and socio-cultural agendas. *Geoforum 31*, 409–424.

Kong, L. (2002) Cultural economy and cultural policy: refiguring urban change. In W.B. Kim and J.Y. Yoo (eds) *Culture, Economy and Place: Asia-Pacific Perspectives* (pp. 11–30). Seoul: Korea Research Institute for Human Settlements.

Krim, A. (1992) Route 66: auto river of the American West. In D. Janelle (ed.) *Geographical Snapshots of the American West* (pp. 30–33). New York: Guilford Press.

Krim, A. (1998) 'Get your kicks on Route 66!': a song map of post-war migration. *Journal of Cultural Geography 18*, 49–60.

Kruse, R. (2003) Imagining Strawberry Fields as a place of pilgrimage. *Area 35*, 154–162.

Kurabayashi, Y. and Ito, T. (1992) Socio-economic characteristics of audiences for western classical music in Japan: a statistical analysis. In R. Towse and A. Khakee (eds) *Cultural Economics* (pp. 257–287). Berlin: Springer-Verlag.

Kurosawa, S. (2000) Pump up the volume. *The Australian Magazine* (17 June), 47.

Kushner, R.J. and Brooks, A.C. (2000) The one-man band by the quick lunch stand: modeling audience response to street performance. *Journal of Cultural Economics* 24, 65–77.

Kwok, K.W. and Low, K.H. (2002) Cultural policy and the city-state: Singapore and the 'new Asian renaissance'. In D. Crane, N. Kawashima and K. Kawasaki (eds) *Global Culture: Media, Arts, Policy, and Globalization* (pp. 149–168). London and New York: Routledge.

Landry, C. (2000) *The Creative City*. London: Earthscan.

Lanza, J. (1994) *Elevator Music: A Surreal History of Muzak, Easy-listening and Other Moodsong*. London: Quartet Books.

Lau, F. (1998) Packaging identity though sound: tourist performances in contemporary China. *Journal of Musicological Research* 17, 113–134.

Lauret, M. (1996) 'I've got a right to sing the blues': Alice Walker's aesthetic. In R.H. King and H. Taylor (eds) *Dixie Debates: Perspectives on Southern Cultures* (pp. 51–66). London: Pluto Press.

Lee, E. (1995) *Musical London*. London: Omnibus Press.

Lee, S. (2002) The walled city. *Marie-Claire* 87 (November), 298–304.

Lee, T.S. (2002) Chinese street opera performance and the shaping of cultural aesthetics in contemporary Singapore. *Yearbook for Traditional Music* 34, 139–161.

Lefebvre, H. (1991) *The Production of Space*. Oxford: Blackwell.

Leiper, N. (1999) A conceptual analysis of tourism-supported employment which reduces the incidence of exaggerated, misleading statistics about jobs. *Tourism Management* 20, 605–613.

Lenthen, G. (2000) By the Bayou. *Sydney Morning Herald* (17 June), 4–5T.

Levenstein, H. (1998) *Seductive Journey: American Tourists in France from Jefferson to the Jazz Age*. Chicago: University of Chicago Press.

Levin, B. (1981) *Conducted Tour*. London: Jonathan Cape.

Lewin, S. (1997) Loft cause. In R. Benson (ed.) *Nightfever* (pp. 89–90). London: Boxtree.

Lewis, G. (1997) Lap dancer or hillbilly deluxe? The cultural constructions of modern country music. *Journal of Popular Culture* 25, 51–68.

Lewis, L. and Dowsey-Magog, P. (1993) The Maleny Fire Event: rehearsals towards neo-liminality. *Australian Journal of Anthropology* 4, 198–219.

Lewis, L. A. and Ross, M. (1995) The gay dance party culture in Sydney: a qualitative analysis. *Journal of Homosexuality* 29, 41–70.

Lewis, R. (1996) L'Acadie Retrouvée: the re-making of Cajun identity in Southwestern Louisiana, 1968–1994. In R.H. King and H. Taylor (eds) *Dixie Debates: Perspectives on Southern Cultures* (pp. 67–84). London: Pluto Press.

Leydon, R. (1999) Utopias of the tropics – the exotic music of Les Baxter and Yma Sumac. In P. Hayward (ed.) *Widening The Horizon: Exoticism in Post-War Popular Music* (pp. 45–71). Sydney: John Libbey.

Leyshon, A., Matless, D. and Revill, G. (eds) (1998) Introduction. In *The Place of Music* (pp. 1–30). New York: Guilford.

Leyshon, A., Matless, D. and Revill, G. (1995) The place of music. *Transactions of the Institute of British Geographers* 20, 423–433.

Linnekin, J. (1997) Consuming cultures: tourism and the commoditization of cultural identity in the Island Pacific. In R. Picard and R. Wood (eds) *Tourism,*

Ethnicity and the State in Asian and Pacific Societies (pp. 215–250). Honolulu: University of Hawaii Press.

Lisker, R. (1993) *Puerto Rico: Music, Tourism and Politics – The Casals Music Festival of 1982*. Middletown, Connecticut: Ferment Press.

Littrell, M.A., Anderson, L.F. and Brown, P.J. (1993) What makes a craft souvenir authentic?. *Annals of Tourism Research* 20 (11), 197–215.

Lloyd, D. (1998) *Battlefield Tourism*. Oxford: Berg.

Loftie, W.I. (1890) *Orient Line Guide*. London: Sampson Low.

Loftman, P. and Nevin, B. (1998) Pro-growth local economic development strategies: civil promotion and local needs in Britain's second city, 1981–1996. In T. Hall and P. Hubbard (eds) *The Entrepreneurial City: Geographies of Politics, Regime and Representation* (pp. 129–148). Chichester: Wiley.

Lohmann, M. and Mundt, J.W. (2001) Maturing markets for cultural tourism: Germany and the demand for the 'cultural' destination. In R. Voase (ed.) *Tourism in Western Europe: A Collection of Case Histories* (pp. 259–271). Wallingford: CABI Publishing.

Loker-Murphy, L. and Pearce, P.L. (1995) Young budget travelers: backpackers in Australia. *Annals of Tourism Research* 22, 819–843.

Lonely Planet (2003) www.lonelyplanet.com.

Long, L.M. (2004) *Culinary Tourism*. Lexington: University Press of Kentucky.

Luckman, S. (2001) What are they raving on about? Temporary autonomous zones and 'reclaim the streets'. *Perfect Beat* 5 (2), 49–68.

MacCannell, D. (1973) Staged authenticity: arrangements of social space in tourist settings. *American Journal of Sociology* 79, 589–603.

MacCannell, D. (1976) *The Tourist*. New York: Schocken.

McCray Pattacini, M. (2000) Deadheads yesterday and today: an audience study. *Popular Music and Society* 24 (1), 1–14.

McGillion, C. (2000) Uncle Sam, why won't you salsa?. *Sydney Morning Herald* (22 January), 5s.

MacGregor, A. (1949) *The Western Isles*. London: Hale.

McGregor, A. (2000) Dynamic texts and tourist gaze: death, bones and buffalo. *Annals of Tourism Research* 27, 27–50.

McGuirk, P., Winchester, H. and Dunn, K. (1998) On losing the local in responding to urban decline: the Honeysuckle redevelopment, New South Wales. In T. Hall and P. Hubbard (eds) *The Entrepreneurial City: Geographies of Politics, Regime and Representation* (pp. 107–128). Chichester: Wiley.

Macaskill, H. (1999) Dig out your dancing shoes for a stomping good cause. *The Independent* (10 April), 20.

McHone, W.W. and Rungeling, B. (2000) Practical issues in measuring the impact of a cultural tourist event in a. major tourist destination. *Journal of Travel Research* 38, 300–303.

McKay, G. (1996) *Senseless Acts of Beauty: Cultures of Resistance Since the Sixties*. London: Verso.

McKee, M. and Chisenhall, F. (1981) *Beale Black and Blue: Life and Music on Black America's Main Street*. Baton Rouge: Louisiana State University Press.

McLaughlin, N. and McLoone, M. (2000) Hybridity and national musics: the case of Irish rock music. *Popular Music* 19, 181–199.

McLean, D. (1997) *Lone Star Swing: On the Trail of Bob Wills and his Texas Playboys*. London: Random House.

McLeay, C.R. (1998) *The Circuit of Popular Music: Production, Consumption, Globalisation*. Unpublished PhD thesis, Macquarie University, Sydney.

McNutt, R. (2002) *Guitar Towns: A Journey to the Crossroads of Rock 'n' Roll*. Indiana University Press: Bloomington.

Maffesoli, M. (1995) *The Time of the Tribes* (trans.). London: Sage (original work published 1988).

Maiden, K. (2002) *Abbey Road Survey*. Brisbane (mimeo).

Malam, L. (2004) Embodiment and sexuality in cross-cultural research. *Australian Geographer* 53 (in press).

Malbon, B. (1999) *Clubbing: Dancing, Ecstasy, Vitality*. London: Routledge.

Man-Young, H. (1988) Folklore and tourism in Korea. In *Come Mek Me Hol' Yu Han'. The Impact of Tourism on Traditional Music* (pp. 67–74). Kingston: Jamaica Memory Bank.

Marcus, G. (1975) *Mystery Train: Images of America in Rock 'n' Roll Music*. New York: Dulton.

Marion, V. (1988) Kiribati adaptation of dance for the third South Pacific Arts Festival. In *Come Mek Me Hol' Yu Han'. The Impact of Tourism on Traditional Music* (pp. 139–144). Kingston: Jamaica Memory Bank.

Marling, K. (1996) *Graceland: Going Home With Elvis*. Cambridge: Harvard University Press.

Martin, G. (1998) Generational differences amongst new age travellers. *The Sociological Review* 46, 735–756.

Masters, R. (2000) The Cuban evolution. *Sydney Morning Herald* (5 February), 1–4T.

Masters, R. (2000b) Out of town. *Sydney Morning Herald* (18 March), 3T.

Mathias, P. (2000) *Burnt Barley*. Auckland: Vintage.

Max Ellis Marketing (1999) *How Tamworth Became Country Music Capital*. Tamworth: Max Ellis Marketing.

Meethan, K. (1996) Place, image and power: Brighton as a resort. In T. Selwyn (ed.) *The Tourist Image: Myths and Myth Making in Tourism* (pp. 179–195). Chichester: Wiley.

Memphis Convention and Visitors Bureau (2002) National tourism awareness week salutes the pros who provide hospitality. Press release, 8 May.

The Mersey Partnership (2001) *Tourism on Merseyside*. Liverpool (mimeo).

Middleton, N. (1999) *Ice Tea and Elvis*. London: Weidenfeld & Nicolson.

Miles, M. (1998) A game of appearance: public art and urban development – complicity of sustainability?. In T. Hall and P. Hubbard (eds) *The Entrepreneurial City: Geographies of Politics, Regime and Representation* (pp. 203–244). Chichester: Wiley.

Millington-Robertson, J. (1988) Traditional music: its place in Caribbean tourism. In *Come Mek Me Hol' Yu Han'. The Impact of Tourism on Traditional Music* (pp. 29–36). Kingston: Jamaica Memory Bank.

Milne, S. and Ateljevic, I. (2001) Tourism, economic development and the global-local nexus: theory embracing complexity. *Tourism Geographies* 3, 369–393.

Ministry for Information Technology and the Arts (MITA) (2000) *Renaissance City Report: Culture and the Arts in Renaissance Singapore*. Singapore: Ministry of Information and the Arts.

Mitchell, A. (1998) Tango tour de force. *The Sun-Herald* (20 December), 64–65.

Mitchell, C.J.A. (1993) Economic impact of the arts: theatre festivals in small Ontario communities. *Journal of Cultural Economics* 17, 55–67.

Mitchell, D. (2000) *Cultural Geography: A Critical Introduction*. Oxford: Blackwell.

Mitchell, R. (1999) 'I hated mondays': an investigation of the visitor experience at the Otago Settlers Museum. *Pacific Tourism Review* 3, 151–160.

Mordue, T. (1999) Heartbeat country: conflicting values, coinciding visions. *Environment and Planning A* 31, 629–646.

Morgan, C. (2003) Beethoven's rolling over in the tropics. *Sydney Morning Herald* (3 July), 15.

Morris, B.J. (1999) *Eden Built By Eves: The Culture of Women's Music Festivals*. Los Angeles: Alyson Books.

Morris, J. (2000) New Country Hall of Fame to provide definite economic boost, study says. *Nashville Business Journal* 6 (November).

Morris, S. (2000) Reality intrudes on fantasy island. *The Guardian* (29 July), 14.

Morrison, R. (2001) Notes from a small island. *The Times* (17 April), 16–17.

Mueller, A. (1998) Swamp thing. *The Guardian Festivals Guide* 11.

Mulcahy, K.V. (1986) The arts and their economic impact: the values of utility. *Journal of Arts Management and Law* 16, 33–48.

Murphy, L. (2001) Exploring social interactions of backpackers. *Annals of Tourism Research* 28, 50–67.

National Centre for Cultural and Recreation Statistics (NCCRS) (2001) *Cultural Tourism Statistics*. Adelaide: National Centre for Cultural and Recreation Statistics.

National Centre for Cultural and Recreation Statistics (NCCRS) (2002) *Multipliers for Culture-Related Industries*. Adelaide: National Centre for Cultural and Recreation Statistics.

National Centre for Popular Music (2003) 'National Centre for Popular Music could feature in regeneration plans'. Press release, www.ncpm.co.uk.

Negrier, E. (1993) Montpellier: international competition and community access. In F. Bianchini and M. Parkinson (eds) *Cultural Policy and Urban Regeneration: The West European Experience* (pp. 135–154). Manchester: Manchester University Press.

Negus, K. (1999) *Music Genres and Corporate Cultures*. London and New York: Routledge.

Neuenfeldt, K. (1997) The didjeridu in the desert: the social relations of an ethnographic object entangled in culture and commerce. In K. Neuenfeldt (ed.) *The Didjeridu: from Arnhem Land to Internet* (pp. 107–122). Sydney: John Libbey and Perfect Beat Publications.

Neuenfeldt, K. (1998) Grassroots, rock(s) and reggae: music and mayhem at the Port Moresby Show. *The Contemporary Pacific* 10, 317–334.

Newbery, B. (2004) The remotest festival on earth. *Geographical* 76(6), June, 53–59.

Newth, J.D. (1931) *Austria*. London: Black.

Noronha, F. (n.d.) Psychedelic Goa trance parties – how it all began. www.pwrgrrl.com/goatrance.

Nurse, K. (1999) Globalization and Trinidad carnival: diaspora, hybridity and identity in global culture. *Cultural Studies* 13, 661–690.

Nurse, K. (2002) Bringing culture into tourism: festival tourism and Reggae Sunsplash in Jamaica. *Social and Economic Studies* 51, 127–143.

O'Connor, J. (1998) Popular culture, cultural intermediaries and urban regeneration. In T. Hall and P. Hubbard (eds) *The Entrepreneurial City: Geographies of Politics, Regime and Representation* (pp. 225–239). Chichester: Wiley.

O'Donnchadha, G. and O'Connor, B. (1996) Cultural tourism in Ireland. In G. Richards (ed.) *Cultural Tourism in Europe* (pp. 197–214). CAB International: Wallingford.

O'Hagan, J. (1996) Access to and participation in the arts: the case of those with low incomes/educational attainment. *Journal of Cultural Economics* 20, 269–282.

O'Keeffe, M. (1996) It's much more than music for Phish heads. *Rocky Mountain News* (7 August).

Ottaway, M. (1999) Under the skin. *The Sunday Times* (13 March), 1–2.

Paller, R. (2002) Letter from Cincinnati. *Opera News* 67 (5) (November), 78–81.

Palmer, J. (2001) Karaoke and migrants threaten ancient land of Genghis Khan. *Asian Times* (11 April), 6.

Parkinson, M. and Bianchini, F. (1993) Liverpool: a tale of missed opportunities. In F. Bianchini and M. Parkinson (eds) *Cultural Policy and Urban Regeneration: The West European Experience* (pp. 155–177). Manchester: Manchester University Press.

Perrottet, T. (2003) Into limbo land. *Sunday Magazine (Sunday Telegraph)* (9 March), 20–22.

Perry, T. and Glinert, E. (1996) *Rock & Roll Traveler USA*. New York: Fodor's.

Peters, B. (2002) The Aspen Idea. *Opera News* 66 (12) (June), 36–39.

Picard, M. (1996) *Bali: Cultural Tourism and Touristic Culture*. Archipelago Press: Singapore.

Pini, M. (1997) Women and the early British rave scene. In A. McRobbie (ed.) *Back to Reality? Social experience and cultural studies* (pp. 152–169). Manchester: Manchester University Press.

Plantamura, C. (1997) *The Opera Lover's Guide to Europe*. London: Robson.

Popkin, J.M. (1986) *Musical Monuments*. London and Munich: K.G. Saur.

Potts, D. (2003) The seven hills of . . . Lisbon. *The Sun-Herald* (2 November), 9.

Prentice, R. and Anderson, V. (2000) Evoking Ireland: modeling tourist propensity. *Annals of Tourism Research* 27, 490–516.

Prentice, R. and Anderson, V. (2003) Festival as creative destination. *Annals of Tourism Research* 30, 7–30.

Pretes, M. (2003) Tourism and nationalism. *Annals of Tourism Research* 30, 125–142.

Priestley, G.K. (1995) Sports tourism: the case of golf. In G. Ashworth and A. Dietvorst (eds) *Tourism and Spatial Transformations* (pp. 205–223). Wallingford: CAB International.

Prieto-Rodríguez, J. and Fernández-Blanco, V. (2000) Are popular and classical music listeners the same people?. *Journal of Cultural Economics* 24, 147–164.

Pritchard, S. (1999) Musical heirs. *The Observer* (23 May), 8.

Quinn, B. (1996) The sounds of tourism: exploring music as a tourist resource with particular reference to music festivals. In M. Robinson, N. Evans and P. Callaghan (eds) *Tourism and Culture Towards the 21st Century* (pp. 383–396). Centre for Travel and Tourism and Business Education Publishers, Sunderland.

Ravenscroft, N. and Matteuci, X. (2003) The festival as carnivalesque: social governance and control in Pamplona's San Fermin Fiesta. *Tourism, Culture and Communication* 1, 1–15.

Raybould, M., Digance, J. and McCullough, C. (1999) Fire and festival: authenticity and visitor motivation at an Australian folk festival. *Pacific Tourism Review* 3, 201–212.

Rees, H. (1998) 'Authenticity' and the foreign audience for traditional music in Southwest China. *Journal of Musicological Research* 17, 135–159.

Regis, H. (1999) Second lines, minstrelsy and the contested landscapes of New Orleans Afro-Creole festivals. *Cultural Anthropology* 14, 472–504.

Regis, H. (2001) Blackness and the politics of memory in the New Orleans Second Line. *American Ethnologist* 28, 752–777.

Reist, N. (1997) Counting stars by candlelight: an analysis of the mythic appeal of The Grateful Dead. *Journal of Popular Culture* 30, 183–209.

Richard, B. and Kruger, H. (1998) Ravers' paradise?: German youth cultures in the 1990s. In T. Skelton and G. Valentine (eds) *Cool Places* (pp. 161–174). London: Routledge.

Riches, D. (2003) Counter-cultural egalitarianism: a comparative analysis of New Age and other 'alternative' communities. *Culture and Religion* 4, 121–139.

Richards, G. (1996) Introduction. In G. Richards (ed.) *Cultural Tourism in Europe* (pp. 1–18). Wallingford: CAB International.

Riemer, A. (1993) *The Habsburg Café*. Sydney: Angus and Robertson.

Riley, R., Baker, D. and Van Doren, C. (1998) Movie Induced Tourism. *Annals of Tourism Research* 25, 919–935.

Rochdale Metropolitan Borough Council (2001) *Rochdale Preview*. Rochdale (mimeo).

Roberts, E. (1999) Blasts from the past. *Yorkshire Post* (4 January), 8.

Roberts, J. (2003) Flushed with peace and love. *The Australian* (6 August), 17.

Robertson, J. (1998) *Takarazuka. Sexual Politics and Popular Culture in Modern Japan*. Berkeley: University of California Press.

Robinson, H. (1976) *A Geography of Tourism*. London: Macdonald & Evans.

Rodman, G.B. (1996) *Elvis After Elvis: The Posthumous Career of a Living Legend*. London: Routledge.

Rodriguez, P. (2000) Changes in New Orleans. *The Sun-Herald* (15 October), 100.

Rojek, C. (1993) *Ways of Escape: Modern Transformations in Leisure and Travel*. London: Routledge.

Rojek, C. (1995) *Decentring Leisure*. Sage: London.

Rollins, A. (2004) On the road. *Sydney Morning Herald*, 26 June, 13.

Roth, P. and Langemeyer, A. (1996) Cultural tourism in Germany. In G. Richards (ed.) *Cultural Tourism in Europe* (pp. 165–181). Wallingford: CAB International.

Rolston, B. (2001) 'This is not a rebel song': the Irish conflict and popular music. *Race and Class* 42 (3), 49–67.

Root, D. (1996) *Cannibal Culture: Art, Appropriation, and the Commodification of Difference*. Boulder: Westview Press.

Rossi, N. (1995) *Opera in Italy Today: A Guide*. Portland: Amadeus Press.

Rotenstein, D.S. (1992) The Helena Blues: cultural tourism and African–Americans folk music. *Southern Folklore* 49, 133–146.

Rothwell, N. (2002) The stringybark kids. *The Australian* (5 October), R4–6.

Routledge, D. (2000) Consuming Goa: tourist site as dispensable space. *Economic and Political Weekly* 35 (30) (22 July), 2647–2656.

Routledge, D. (2001) Selling the rain, resisting the sale: resistant identities and the conflict over tourism in Goa. *Social and Cultural Geography* 2, 221–240.

Rundle, M.L. (2001) Tourism, social change and *Jineterismo* in contemporary Cuba. In S. Courtman (ed.) *The Society for Caribbean Studies Annual Conference Papers* (Vol. 2). www.scsonline.freeserve.co.uk/olvol2.html.

Russell, D. (1997) *Popular Music in England 1840–1914*. Manchester: Manchester University Press.

Ryburn-Lamonte, T. (1998) Route 66: still kickin' for students and international visitors. In C.T.Williams (ed.) *Travel Culture. Essays On What makes Us Go* (pp. 121–132). Westport: Praeger.

Ryle, G. (2000) It takes two. *Sydney Morning Herald* (30 December), 3T.

Sadler, D. (1997) The global music business as an information industry: reinterpreting economies of culture. *Environment and Planning A* 29, 1919–1236.

Sage, A. (2002) Sound tracks. *The Australian Magazine* (2 November), 13.

Saldanha, A. (1999) Goa trance in Goa: globalization, musical practice and the politics of place. Unpublished paper, 10th Annual IASPM International Conference, Sydney.

Saldanha, A. (2002) Music tourism and factions of bodies in Goa. *Tourist Studies* 2, 43–62.

Saldanha, A. (2003a) Identity, spatiality and post-colonial resistance. *Current Issues in Tourism* (in press).

Saldanha, A. (2003b) Goa trance and trance in Goa: smooth striations. In G. St John (ed.) *Rave Culture and Religion* (pp. 273–286). London: Routledge (in press).

Saleh, F. and Ryan, C. (1993) Jazz and knitwear: factors that attract tourists to festivals. *Tourism Management* 14, 289–297.

Sampath, N. (1997) 'Mas' identity: tourism and global and local aspects of Trinidad carnival. In S. Abram, J.D. Waldren and D.V.L. MacLeod (eds) *Tourists and Tourism: Identifying People with Place* (pp. 149–171). Oxford: Berg.

Samuels, D. (1999) Rock is dead: sex, drugs and raw sewage at Woodstock 99. *Harper's Magazine* 299 (1794) (November), 69–82.

Sanger, A. (1988) Blessing or blight? The effects of touristic dance-drama on village life in Singapadu, Bali. In *Come Mek Me Hol' Yu Han'. The Impacts of Tourism on Traditional Music* (pp. 89–104). Kingston: Jamaica Memory Bank.

Sanjek, D. (1998) Popular music and the synergy of corporate culture. In T. Swiss, J. Sloop and A. Herman (eds) *Mapping the Beat: Popular Music and Contemporary Theory* (pp. 171–186). Oxford: Blackwell.

Sardiello, R. (1994) Secular rituals in popular culture: a case for Grateful Dead concerts and Dead Head identity. In J.S. Epstein (ed.) *Adolescents and their Music* (pp. 115–139). New York: Garland.

Sarkissian, M. (1995) 'Sinhalese Girl' meets 'Aunty Annie': competing expressions of ethnic identity in the Portuguese settlement, Melaka, Malaysia. *Asian Music* 27, 37–62.

Scanlon, A. (1997) *Those Tourists Are Money: The Rock n Roll Guide to Camden.* London: Tristia.

Schofield, L. (1996) Opera *al fresco. Sydney Morning Herald* (22 February), 1.

Schulte-Peevers, A., Gray, J., Haywood, A., Fallon, S. and Selby, N. (2000) *Germany.* Melbourne: Lonely Planet.

Scott, A.J. (2000) *The Cultural Economy of Cities.* Sage: London.

Seaton, A.V. (1999) Book towns as tourism developments in peripheral areas. *International Journal of Tourism Research* 1, 389–399.

Selanniemi, T. (2001) Pale skin on playa del anywhere: Finnish tourists in the Liminoid South. In V. Smith and M. Brent (eds) *Hosts and Guests Revisited: Tourism Issues of the 21st Century* (pp. 80–92). New York: Cognizant Communication Corporation.

Sellars, A. (1998) The influence of dance music on the UK youth tourism market. *Tourism Management* 19, 611–615.

Sellars, A. and Wilson-Youlden, L. (1996) Visual arts UK: lost opportunities for tourism. In M. Robinson, N. Evans and P. Callaghan (eds) *Tourism and Culture Towards the 21st Century* (pp. 93–112). Sunderland: Centre for Travel and Tourism and Business Education Publishers.

Shepherd, R. (2002) Commodification, culture and tourism. *Tourist Studies* 2, 183–201.

Shohat, E. and Stam, R. (1994) *Unthinking Eurocentrism: Multiculturalism and the Media.* London: Routledge.

Shrik (2002) Ibizan nights. www.mouthshut.com/readreview/27581-1.
Shrimpton, J. (2003) Spectacle is the best bet. *Sun-Herald* (19 January), 24.
Shukman, H. (1993) *Travels with my Trombone: A Caribbean Journey.* London: Flamingo.
Sibley, D. (1989) Survey 13: purification of space. *Environment and Planning D: Society and Space* 6, 409–421.
Sibley, D. (1994) The sin of transgression. *Area* 26, 300–303.
Simeone, N. (2000) *Paris. A musical gazetteer.* Yale University Press: New Haven.
Skřivánková, N. (2001) Bohemian rhapsody. *Sydney Morning Herald* (7 July), 26.
Slattery, L. (1999) Livin' la vida loca. *The Australian* (16 October), 7–8.
Smith, C. (2002) Backpackers Inc. *Sydney Morning Herald* (8 June), 1, 4.
Smith, G. and Brett, J. (1998) Nation, authenticity and social difference in Australian popular music: folk, country, multicultural. *Journal of Australian Studies* 1, 3–17.
Smith, J. (1995) *Holidays in Retirement.* London: Foulsham.
Smith, S.J. (1994) Soundscape. *Area* 26, 232–240.
Smith, S.J. (1997) Beyond geography's visible worlds: a cultural politics of music. *Progress in Human Geography* 21, 502–529.
Sorrenti, V. (2000) Ibiza discovered. *The Australian* (16 December), 20–21.
Squire, S.J. (1988) Wordsworth and Lake District tourism: romantic reshapings of landscape. *Canadian Geographer* 32, 237–247.
Squire, S.J. (1993) Valuing countryside: reflections on Beatrix Potter tourism. *Area* 25, 5–10.
Stanard, A. (2004) Buenos Aires. Where passion and politics mix. *The Sun Herald*, 4 January, 8–9.
Standeven, J. and de Knop, P. (1999) *Sport Tourism.* Champaign: Human Kinetics.
Stebbins, R.A. (1996) Cultural tourism as serious leisure. *Annals of Tourism Research* 23, 945–950.
Steinberg, M.P. (1990) *The Meaning of the Salzburg Festival.* Ithaca: Cornell University Press.
Sternberg, R. (1998) Fantasy, geography, Wagner and opera. *Geographical Review* 88, 327–348.
Steketee, M. (2001) Hope for healing springs at festival. *The Australian* (8 September), 5.
Stillman, A.K. (1988) Images and realities: visitors' responses to Tahitian music and dance. In *Come Mek Me Hol' Yu Han'. The Impacts of Tourism on Traditional Music* (pp. 145–166). Kingston: Jamaica Memory Bank.
Stocks, J. (1996) Heritage and tourism in the Irish Republic: towards a giant theme park. In M. Robinson, N. Evans and P. Callaghan (eds) *Tourism and Culture: Image, Identity and Marketing* (pp. 251–260). Sunderland: Centre for Travel and Tourism.
Stokes, M. (1999) Music, travel and tourism: an afterword. *The World of Music* 41 (3), 141–155.
Stubbs, D. (1998) Home and dry. *The Guardian Festivals Guide*, 12–13.
Suppan, W. (1988) Folkmusic and tourism in Austria. In *Come Mek me Hol' Yu Han'. The Impact of Tourism on Traditional Music* (pp. 167–174). Kingston: Jamaica Memory Bank.
Sydney Morning Herald (2002) Singsings with no G-strings attached. *Sydney Morning Herald* (20 September), 1.
Symon, P. (2002) From *Blas* to *Bothy* culture: the musical re-making of Celtic culture in a Hebridean festival. In D. Harvey, R. Jones, N. McInroy and C. Milligan (eds) *Celtic Geographies* (pp. 192–207). London: Routledge.

Tanenbaum, S.J. (1995) *Underground Harmonies: Music and Politics in the Subways of New York*. Ithaca: Cornell University Press.

Tatar, E. (1987) *Strains of Change: The Impact of Tourism on Hawaiian Music*. Honolulu: Bishop Museum.

Taylor, T. (1997) *Global Pop: World Music, World Markets*. London: Routledge.

Thornton, S. (1995) *Club Cultures: Music, Media and Subcultural Capital*. Cambridge: Polity Press.

Thrane, C. (2002) Music quality, satisfaction and behavioral intentions within a jazz festival context. *Event Management* 7, 143–150.

Throsby, D. and Withers, G. (1979) *The Economics of Performing Arts*. Melbourne: Edward Arnold.

Tiber, E. (1994) *Knock on Woodstock*. New York: Festival Books.

Tichi, C. (1994) *High Lonesome: The American Culture of Country Music*. Chapel Hill: University of North Carolina Press.

Tighe, A.J. (1985) Cultural tourism in the USA. *Tourism Management* 6, 234–251.

Tooke, N. and Baker, M. (1996) Seeing is believing: the effect of film on visitor numbers in screened locations. *Tourism Management* 17, 87–94.

Toop, D. (1995) *Ocean of Sound: Aether Talk, Ambient Sound and Imaginary Worlds*. London and New York: Serpent's Tail.

Toop, D. (1999) *Exotica: Fabricated Soundscapes in a Real World*. London: Serpent's Tail.

Tourism New South Wales (1997) Understanding the backpacker market. *Tourism Business Information Paper* 5 (1), Sydney: Tourism New South Wales.

Tran, M. (2003) If the music's like the food – no thanks, love. *Guardian Unlimited Travel* (9 January). www.travel.guardian.co.uk/countries/story.

Trépanier, C. (1991) The Cajunization of French Louisiana: forging a regional identity. *The Geographical Journal* 157, 167–171.

Trimillos, R.D. (1988) Aesthetic change in Philippine performing arts. In *Come Mek Me Hol' Yu Han': The Impact of Tourism on Traditional Music* (pp. 105–120). Kingston: Jamaica Memory Bank.

Trinh, Minh-ha T. (1989) *Woman, Native, Other: Writing Postcoloniality and Feminism*. Bloomington: Indiana University Press.

Turner, V. (1983) Carnival in Rio: Dionysian drama in an industrialising society. In F.E. Manning (ed.) *The Celebration of Society* (pp. 103–124). Bowling Green Ohio: Bowling Green University Popular Press.

Tyler, R. (2002) New Orleans and that old jazz magic. *Evening Standard* (12 January), 12–15.

Ulack, R. (1993) The impact of tourism in Fiji. *Focus* 38 (Summer), 1–7.

Urry, J. (1991) The sociology of tourism. In C.P. Cooper (ed.) *Tourism, Recreation, and Hospitality Management*. London: Belhaven.

Urry, J. (1990) *The Tourist Gaze: Leisure and Travel in Contemporary Society*. London: Sage.

Urry, J. (1994) Europe, tourism and the nation-state. In C. Cooper and A. Lockwood (eds) *Progress in Tourism, Recreation and Hospitality Management* (pp. 89–98). Chichester: Wiley.

van den Berghe, P. and Keyes, C. (1984) Introduction: tourism and re-created ethnicity. *Annals of Tourism Research* 11, 343–352.

Vaughan, A. (1999) *Danny Boy: A Life of Daniel O'Donnell*. London: Chameleon.

Verhagen, S., van Wel, F., ter Bogt, T. and Hibbel, B. (2000) Fast on 200 beats per minute: the youth culture of gabbers in the Netherlands. *Youth and Society* 32, 147–164.

von Uthman, J. (2002) The duelists. *Opera News* 67 (1), 26–32.
Wade, L. (1994) New Orleans' Bourbon Street: the evolution of an entertainment district. In R.B. Browne and M.T. Marsden (eds) *The Cultures of Celebrations* (pp. 181–201). Bowling Green, OH: Bowling Green State University Popular Press.
Wagnleitner, R. (2001) 'Satchmo meets Amadeus'. Paper presented at the *Satchmo Meets Amadeus* conference, 6 October, Salzburg.
Waller, J. and Lea, S.E.G. (1998) Seeking the real Spain? Authenticity in motivation. *Annals of Tourism Research* 25, 110–128.
Walton, J.K. (2000) *The British Seaside: Holidays and Resorts in the Twentieth Century*. Manchester: Manchester University Press.
Wang, N. (1999) Rethinking authenticity in tourism experience. *Annals of Tourism Research* 26, 349–370.
Wark, M. (1994) *Virtual Geography: Living with Global Media Events*. Bloomington: Indiana University Press.
Waterman, S. (1998a) Carnivals for élites? The cultural politics of arts festivals. *Progress in Human Geography* 22, 54–74.
Waterman, S. (1998b) Place, culture and identity: summer music in Upper Galilee. *Transactions of the Institute of British Geographers* 23, 253–267.
Weber, T. (1999) Raving in Toronto: peace, love, unity and respect in transition. *Journal of Youth Studies* 2, 317–336.
Webster, J. (2002) *Duende: A Journey in Search of Flamenco*. London: Doubleday.
Werner, C. (1998) *A Change is Gonna Come: Music, Race and the Soul of America*. Edinburgh: Payback Press.
Westerhausen, K. (2002) *Beyond the Beach: An Ethnography of Modern Travelers in Asia*. Bangkok: White Lotus Press.
Wheat, S. (2000) Where there's muck there's brass. *Geographical* 72 (7) (June), 23–25.
Wheeller, B. (1996) No particular place to go: travel, tourism and popular music, a mid-life crisis perspective. In M. Robinson, N. Evans and P. Callaghan (eds) *Tourism and Culture Towards the 21st Century* (pp. 333–340). Sunderland: Centre for Travel and Tourism and Business Education Publishers.
Whitt, J.A. (1987) Mozart in the metropolis: the arts coalition and the urban growth machine. *Urban Affairs Quarterly* 23, 15–36.
Wilder, G. (2002) Global warming. *Sydney Morning Herald* (28 December), 4.
Williams, S. (1988) Yellow Bird – Ai Zuzuwah: stagnation or growth. In *Come Mek Me Hol' Yu Han': The Impact of Tourism on Traditional Music* (pp. 17–28). Kingston: Jamaica Memory Bank.
Williams, S. (1998) *Tourism Geography*. London and New York: Routledge.
Williams, S. (2001) Bayreuth: summer pilgrimage. *Opera News* 65 (11) (May), 22–33.
Williams, S. (2002) Country hits. *Australian Financial Review* (30 November–1 December), 43–44.
Wilson, D. (1979) The early effects of tourism in the Seychelles. In E. de Kadt (ed.) *Tourism. Passport to Development?* (pp. 205–236). Oxford: Oxford University Press.
Wilson, D. (1997) Strategies for sustainability: lessons from Goa and the Seychelles. In M. Stabler (ed.) *Tourism and Sustainability* (pp. 173–197). Wallingford: CAB International.
Winegardner, M. (1987) *Elvis Presley Boulevard. From Sea to Shining Sea, Almost*. New York: Atlantic Monthly Press.
Wockner, C. (2001) Where Creole jazz meets the civil war. *The Sunday Telegraph* (25 February), 12.

Wood, R. (1998) Tourist ethnicity: a brief itinerary. *Ethnic and Racial Studies* 21, 218–241.

Woods, A. (2003) Hooray for Dollywood. *Gay Australia Guide* (8 August), 14–15.

Woods, L. and Gritzner, C. (1990) A million miles to the city: country music's sacred and profane images of place. In L. Zonn (ed.) *Place Images in Media* (pp. 231–254). Savage, MD: Rowman & Littlefield.

Wooldridge, M. (2002) *Rock 'n' Roll London*. London: St Martin's Press.

Worley, W.S. (1998) *Beale Street: Crossroads of America's Music*. Lenexa, Kansas: Addax Publishing.

Wright M.A. (1993) *The Rave Scene in Britain: A Metaphor for Metanoia*. Unpublished dissertation, Centre for Human Ecology, University of Edinburgh.

Xie, P.F. (2003) The bamboo-beating dance in Hainan, China: authenticity and commodification. *Journal of Sustainable Tourism* 11, 5–16.

Young, K. (1968) *Music's Great Days in the Spas and Watering-Places*. London: Macmillan.

Zebrowski, J. (2000) Selling EMP to tourists will be next big project. *The Seattle Times* (11 June), 1–5.

Zeppel, H. (1998) Selling the dreamtime: Aboriginal culture in Australian tourism. In D. Rowe and G. Lawrence (eds) *Tourism, Leisure, Sport: Critical Perspectives* (pp. 23–38). Sydney: Hodder.

Zukin, S. (1991) *Landscapes of Power: From Detroit to DisneyWorld*. Berkeley: University of California Press.

Index